ATS-130   ADMISSION TEST SERIES

This is your
PASSBOOK for...

Test of Adult Basic Education (TABE)

Test Preparation Study Guide
Questions & Answers

NATIONAL LEARNING CORPORATION®

COPYRIGHT NOTICE

This book is SOLELY intended for, is sold ONLY to, and its use is RESTRICTED to individual, bona fide applicants or candidates who qualify by virtue of having seriously filed applications for appropriate license, certificate, professional and/or promotional advancement, higher school matriculation, scholarship, or other legitimate requirements of education and/or governmental authorities.

This book is NOT intended for use, class instruction, tutoring, training, duplication, copying, reprinting, excerption, or adaptation, etc., by:

1) Other publishers
2) Proprietors and/or Instructors of "Coaching" and/or Preparatory Courses
3) Personnel and/or Training Divisions of commercial, industrial, and governmental organizations
4) Schools, colleges, or universities and/or their departments and staffs, including teachers and other personnel
5) Testing Agencies or Bureaus
6) Study groups which seek by the purchase of a single volume to copy and/or duplicate and/or adapt this material for use by the group as a whole without having purchased individual volumes for each of the members of the group
7) Et al.

Such persons would be in violation of appropriate Federal and State statutes.

PROVISION OF LICENSING AGREEMENTS – Recognized educational, commercial, industrial, and governmental institutions and organizations, and others legitimately engaged in educational pursuits, including training, testing, and measurement activities, may address request for a licensing agreement to the copyright owners, who will determine whether, and under what conditions, including fees and charges, the materials in this book may be used them. In other words, a licensing facility exists for the legitimate use of the material in this book on other than an individual basis. However, it is asseverated and affirmed here that the material in this book CANNOT be used without the receipt of the express permission of such a licensing agreement from the Publishers. Inquiries re licensing should be addressed to the company, attention rights and permissions department.

All rights reserved, including the right of reproduction in whole or in part, in any form or by any means, electronic or mechanical, including photocopying, recording, or by any information storage and retrieval system, without permission in writing from the Publisher.

Copyright © 2025 by
National Learning Corporation

212 Michael Drive, Syosset, NY 11791
(516) 921-8888 • www.passbooks.com
E-mail: info@passbooks.com

PASSBOOK® SERIES

THE *PASSBOOK® SERIES* has been created to prepare applicants and candidates for the ultimate academic battlefield – the examination room.

At some time in our lives, each and every one of us may be required to take an examination – for validation, matriculation, admission, qualification, registration, certification, or licensure.

Based on the assumption that every applicant or candidate has met the basic formal educational standards, has taken the required number of courses, and read the necessary texts, the *PASSBOOK® SERIES* furnishes the one special preparation which may assure passing with confidence, instead of failing with insecurity. Examination questions – together with answers – are furnished as the basic vehicle for study so that the mysteries of the examination and its compounding difficulties may be eliminated or diminished by a sure method.

This book is meant to help you pass your examination provided that you qualify and are serious in your objective.

The entire field is reviewed through the huge store of content information which is succinctly presented through a provocative and challenging approach – the question-and-answer method.

A climate of success is established by furnishing the correct answers at the end of each test.

You soon learn to recognize types of questions, forms of questions, and patterns of questioning. You may even begin to anticipate expected outcomes.

You perceive that many questions are repeated or adapted so that you can gain acute insights, which may enable you to score many sure points.

You learn how to confront new questions, or types of questions, and to attack them confidently and work out the correct answers.

You note objectives and emphases, and recognize pitfalls and dangers, so that you may make positive educational adjustments.

Moreover, you are kept fully informed in relation to new concepts, methods, practices, and directions in the field.

You discover that you are actually taking the examination all the time: you are preparing for the examination by "taking" an examination, not by reading extraneous and/or supererogatory textbooks.

In short, this PASSBOOK®, used directedly, should be an important factor in helping you to pass your test.

TESTS OF ADULT BASIC EDUCATION (TABE)

OVERVIEW

The Tests of Adult Basic Education (TABE) help adult educators effectively plan group and individual instruction using content and language appropriate for adults. TABE assesses basic reading, mathematics and language skills. The assessments yield objective-mastery information for skills usually learned in grades 1-12, and provide percentiles and scale scores. Grade equivalent scores are also provided by TABE.

TEST CONTENT

Test items focus on a variety of cultures and life skills, and all items and passages are free as possible from ethnic, age and gender bias.

Reading

This subtest measures basic reading skills in a variety of life-skill and academic contexts. It assesses even beginning reading skills in a manner appropriate for adults. It includes items that measure both prose and document literacy, such as the ability to read diagrams, maps, charts, tables, forms and consumer labels.

Because reading is a complex, interactive process, the test measures vocabulary skills as part of the reading process. This integrated assessment supports holistic teaching. It also reduces testing time because the test reports vocabulary as competency rather than as a separate subtest.

Mathematics

The Mathematics Computation and Applied Mathematics subtests measure mathematical skills and concepts useful for adult life and work. For example, test contexts include household measuring and cooking, budgeting, comparison shopping and interpreting data. Like the Reading subtest, Applied Mathematics also uses real-life documents, such as tax forms, to enhance the context and make the test more relevant to daily life. A wide range of difficulty addresses the needs of all skill levels.

Language

The Language subtest helps adults build the communication skills necessary to function effectively on the job and in daily life. It supports and reinforces adult writing instruction for programs at all levels. It integrates skill assessment in usage, mechanics, sentence formation and paragraph development. Most items focus directly on problem areas typically encountered when adults write business letters, resumés, job-related reports, or essays for the GED.

Spelling

Since spelling is often an area of particular difficulty involving a wide range of interrelated language traits – listening, speaking, reading and writing – it receives an isolated focus in TABE. Item format de-emphasizes reading and vocabulary skills and focuses directly on spelling skills.

HOW TO TAKE A TEST

I. YOU MUST PASS AN EXAMINATION

A. *WHAT EVERY CANDIDATE SHOULD KNOW*

Examination applicants often ask us for help in preparing for the written test. What can I study in advance? What kinds of questions will be asked? How will the test be given? How will the papers be graded?

As an applicant for a civil service examination, you may be wondering about some of these things. Our purpose here is to suggest effective methods of advance study and to describe civil service examinations.

Your chances for success on this examination can be increased if you know how to prepare. Those "pre-examination jitters" can be reduced if you know what to expect. You can even experience an adventure in good citizenship if you know why civil service exams are given.

B. *WHY ARE CIVIL SERVICE EXAMINATIONS GIVEN?*

Civil service examinations are important to you in two ways. As a citizen, you want public jobs filled by employees who know how to do their work. As a job seeker, you want a fair chance to compete for that job on an equal footing with other candidates. The best-known means of accomplishing this two-fold goal is the competitive examination.

Exams are widely publicized throughout the nation. They may be administered for jobs in federal, state, city, municipal, town or village governments or agencies.

Any citizen may apply, with some limitations, such as the age or residence of applicants. Your experience and education may be reviewed to see whether you meet the requirements for the particular examination. When these requirements exist, they are reasonable and applied consistently to all applicants. Thus, a competitive examination may cause you some uneasiness now, but it is your privilege and safeguard.

C. *HOW ARE CIVIL SERVICE EXAMS DEVELOPED?*

Examinations are carefully written by trained technicians who are specialists in the field known as "psychological measurement," in consultation with recognized authorities in the field of work that the test will cover. These experts recommend the subject matter areas or skills to be tested; only those knowledges or skills important to your success on the job are included. The most reliable books and source materials available are used as references. Together, the experts and technicians judge the difficulty level of the questions.

Test technicians know how to phrase questions so that the problem is clearly stated. Their ethics do not permit "trick" or "catch" questions. Questions may have been tried out on sample groups, or subjected to statistical analysis, to determine their usefulness.

Written tests are often used in combination with performance tests, ratings of training and experience, and oral interviews. All of these measures combine to form the best-known means of finding the right person for the right job.

II. HOW TO PASS THE WRITTEN TEST

A. NATURE OF THE EXAMINATION

To prepare intelligently for civil service examinations, you should know how they differ from school examinations you have taken. In school you were assigned certain definite pages to read or subjects to cover. The examination questions were quite detailed and usually emphasized memory. Civil service exams, on the other hand, try to discover your present ability to perform the duties of a position, plus your potentiality to learn these duties. In other words, a civil service exam attempts to predict how successful you will be. Questions cover such a broad area that they cannot be as minute and detailed as school exam questions.

In the public service similar kinds of work, or positions, are grouped together in one "class." This process is known as *position-classification*. All the positions in a class are paid according to the salary range for that class. One class title covers all of these positions, and they are all tested by the same examination.

B. FOUR BASIC STEPS

1) Study the announcement

How, then, can you know what subjects to study? Our best answer is: "Learn as much as possible about the class of positions for which you've applied." The exam will test the knowledge, skills and abilities needed to do the work.

Your most valuable source of information about the position you want is the official exam announcement. This announcement lists the training and experience qualifications. Check these standards and apply only if you come reasonably close to meeting them.

The brief description of the position in the examination announcement offers some clues to the subjects which will be tested. Think about the job itself. Review the duties in your mind. Can you perform them, or are there some in which you are rusty? Fill in the blank spots in your preparation.

Many jurisdictions preview the written test in the exam announcement by including a section called "Knowledge and Abilities Required," "Scope of the Examination," or some similar heading. Here you will find out specifically what fields will be tested.

2) Review your own background

Once you learn in general what the position is all about, and what you need to know to do the work, ask yourself which subjects you already know fairly well and which need improvement. You may wonder whether to concentrate on improving your strong areas or on building some background in your fields of weakness. When the announcement has specified "some knowledge" or "considerable knowledge," or has used adjectives like "beginning principles of…" or "advanced … methods," you can get a clue as to the number and difficulty of questions to be asked in any given field. More questions, and hence broader coverage, would be included for those subjects which are more important in the work. Now weigh your strengths and weaknesses against the job requirements and prepare accordingly.

3) Determine the level of the position

Another way to tell how intensively you should prepare is to understand the level of the job for which you are applying. Is it the entering level? In other words, is this the position in which beginners in a field of work are hired? Or is it an intermediate or advanced level? Sometimes this is indicated by such words as "Junior" or "Senior" in the class title. Other jurisdictions use Roman numerals to designate the level – Clerk I, Clerk II, for example. The word "Supervisor" sometimes appears in the title. If the level is not indicated by the title, check the description of duties. Will you be working under very close supervision, or will you have responsibility for independent decisions in this work?

4) Choose appropriate study materials

Now that you know the subjects to be examined and the relative amount of each subject to be covered, you can choose suitable study materials. For beginning level jobs, or even advanced ones, if you have a pronounced weakness in some aspect of your training, read a modern, standard textbook in that field. Be sure it is up to date and has general coverage. Such books are normally available at your library, and the librarian will be glad to help you locate one. For entry-level positions, questions of appropriate difficulty are chosen – neither highly advanced questions, nor those too simple. Such questions require careful thought but not advanced training.

If the position for which you are applying is technical or advanced, you will read more advanced, specialized material. If you are already familiar with the basic principles of your field, elementary textbooks would waste your time. Concentrate on advanced textbooks and technical periodicals. Think through the concepts and review difficult problems in your field.

These are all general sources. You can get more ideas on your own initiative, following these leads. For example, training manuals and publications of the government agency which employs workers in your field can be useful, particularly for technical and professional positions. A letter or visit to the government department involved may result in more specific study suggestions, and certainly will provide you with a more definite idea of the exact nature of the position you are seeking.

III. KINDS OF TESTS

Tests are used for purposes other than measuring knowledge and ability to perform specified duties. For some positions, it is equally important to test ability to make adjustments to new situations or to profit from training. In others, basic mental abilities not dependent on information are essential. Questions which test these things may not appear as pertinent to the duties of the position as those which test for knowledge and information. Yet they are often highly important parts of a fair examination. For very general questions, it is almost impossible to help you direct your study efforts. What we can do is to point out some of the more common of these general abilities needed in public service positions and describe some typical questions.

1) General information

Broad, general information has been found useful for predicting job success in some kinds of work. This is tested in a variety of ways, from vocabulary lists to questions about current events. Basic background in some field of work, such as sociology or economics, may be sampled in a group of questions. Often these are principles which have become familiar to most persons through exposure rather than through formal training. It is difficult to advise you how to study for these questions; being alert to the world around you is our best suggestion.

2) Verbal ability

An example of an ability needed in many positions is verbal or language ability. Verbal ability is, in brief, the ability to use and understand words. Vocabulary and grammar tests are typical measures of this ability. Reading comprehension or paragraph interpretation questions are common in many kinds of civil service tests. You are given a paragraph of written material and asked to find its central meaning.

3) Numerical ability

Number skills can be tested by the familiar arithmetic problem, by checking paired lists of numbers to see which are alike and which are different, or by interpreting charts and graphs. In the latter test, a graph may be printed in the test booklet which you are asked to use as the basis for answering questions.

4) Observation

A popular test for law-enforcement positions is the observation test. A picture is shown to you for several minutes, then taken away. Questions about the picture test your ability to observe both details and larger elements.

5) Following directions

In many positions in the public service, the employee must be able to carry out written instructions dependably and accurately. You may be given a chart with several columns, each column listing a variety of information. The questions require you to carry out directions involving the information given in the chart.

6) Skills and aptitudes

Performance tests effectively measure some manual skills and aptitudes. When the skill is one in which you are trained, such as typing or shorthand, you can practice. These tests are often very much like those given in business school or high school courses. For many of the other skills and aptitudes, however, no short-time preparation can be made. Skills and abilities natural to you or that you have developed throughout your lifetime are being tested.

Many of the general questions just described provide all the data needed to answer the questions and ask you to use your reasoning ability to find the answers. Your best preparation for these tests, as well as for tests of facts and ideas, is to be at your physical and mental best. You, no doubt, have your own methods of getting into an exam-taking mood and keeping "in shape." The next section lists some ideas on this subject.

IV. KINDS OF QUESTIONS

Only rarely is the "essay" question, which you answer in narrative form, used in civil service tests. Civil service tests are usually of the short-answer type. Full instructions for answering these questions will be given to you at the examination. But in case this is your first experience with short-answer questions and separate answer sheets, here is what you need to know:

1) Multiple-choice Questions

Most popular of the short-answer questions is the "multiple choice" or "best answer" question. It can be used, for example, to test for factual knowledge, ability to solve problems or judgment in meeting situations found at work.

A multiple-choice question is normally one of three types—
- It can begin with an incomplete statement followed by several possible endings. You are to find the one ending which *best* completes the statement, although some of the others may not be entirely wrong.
- It can also be a complete statement in the form of a question which is answered by choosing one of the statements listed.

- It can be in the form of a problem – again you select the best answer.

Here is an example of a multiple-choice question with a discussion which should give you some clues as to the method for choosing the right answer:

When an employee has a complaint about his assignment, the action which will *best* help him overcome his difficulty is to
- A. discuss his difficulty with his coworkers
- B. take the problem to the head of the organization
- C. take the problem to the person who gave him the assignment
- D. say nothing to anyone about his complaint

In answering this question, you should study each of the choices to find which is best. Consider choice "A" – Certainly an employee may discuss his complaint with fellow employees, but no change or improvement can result, and the complaint remains unresolved. Choice "B" is a poor choice since the head of the organization probably does not know what assignment you have been given, and taking your problem to him is known as "going over the head" of the supervisor. The supervisor, or person who made the assignment, is the person who can clarify it or correct any injustice. Choice "C" is, therefore, correct. To say nothing, as in choice "D," is unwise. Supervisors have and interest in knowing the problems employees are facing, and the employee is seeking a solution to his problem.

2) True/False Questions

The "true/false" or "right/wrong" form of question is sometimes used. Here a complete statement is given. Your job is to decide whether the statement is right or wrong.

SAMPLE: A roaming cell-phone call to a nearby city costs less than a non-roaming call to a distant city.

This statement is wrong, or false, since roaming calls are more expensive.

This is not a complete list of all possible question forms, although most of the others are variations of these common types. You will always get complete directions for answering questions. Be sure you understand *how* to mark your answers – ask questions until you do.

V. RECORDING YOUR ANSWERS

Computer terminals are used more and more today for many different kinds of exams.

For an examination with very few applicants, you may be told to record your answers in the test booklet itself. Separate answer sheets are much more common. If this separate answer sheet is to be scored by machine – and this is often the case – it is highly important that you mark your answers correctly in order to get credit.

An electronic scoring machine is often used in civil service offices because of the speed with which papers can be scored. Machine-scored answer sheets must be marked with a pencil, which will be given to you. This pencil has a high graphite content which responds to the electronic scoring machine. As a matter of fact, stray dots may register as answers, so do not let your pencil rest on the answer sheet while you are pondering the correct answer. Also, if your pencil lead breaks or is otherwise defective, ask for another.

Since the answer sheet will be dropped in a slot in the scoring machine, be careful not to bend the corners or get the paper crumpled.

The answer sheet normally has five vertical columns of numbers, with 30 numbers to a column. These numbers correspond to the question numbers in your test booklet. After each number, going across the page are four or five pairs of dotted lines. These short dotted lines have small letters or numbers above them. The first two pairs may also have a "T" or "F" above the letters. This indicates that the first two pairs only are to be used if the questions are of the true-false type. If the questions are multiple choice, disregard the "T" and "F" and pay attention only to the small letters or numbers.

Answer your questions in the manner of the sample that follows:

32. The largest city in the United States is
    A. Washington, D.C.
    B. New York City
    C. Chicago
    D. Detroit
    E. San Francisco

1) Choose the answer you think is best. (New York City is the largest, so "B" is correct.)
2) Find the row of dotted lines numbered the same as the question you are answering. (Find row number 32)
3) Find the pair of dotted lines corresponding to the answer. (Find the pair of lines under the mark "B.")
4) Make a solid black mark between the dotted lines.

VI. BEFORE THE TEST

Common sense will help you find procedures to follow to get ready for an examination. Too many of us, however, overlook these sensible measures. Indeed, nervousness and fatigue have been found to be the most serious reasons why applicants fail to do their best on civil service tests. Here is a list of reminders:

- Begin your preparation early – Don't wait until the last minute to go scurrying around for books and materials or to find out what the position is all about.
- Prepare continuously – An hour a night for a week is better than an all-night cram session. This has been definitely established. What is more, a night a week for a month will return better dividends than crowding your study into a shorter period of time.
- Locate the place of the exam – You have been sent a notice telling you when and where to report for the examination. If the location is in a different town or otherwise unfamiliar to you, it would be well to inquire the best route and learn something about the building.
- Relax the night before the test – Allow your mind to rest. Do not study at all that night. Plan some mild recreation or diversion; then go to bed early and get a good night's sleep.
- Get up early enough to make a leisurely trip to the place for the test – This way unforeseen events, traffic snarls, unfamiliar buildings, etc. will not upset you.
- Dress comfortably – A written test is not a fashion show. You will be known by number and not by name, so wear something comfortable.

- Leave excess paraphernalia at home – Shopping bags and odd bundles will get in your way. You need bring only the items mentioned in the official notice you received; usually everything you need is provided. Do not bring reference books to the exam. They will only confuse those last minutes and be taken away from you when in the test room.
- Arrive somewhat ahead of time – If because of transportation schedules you must get there very early, bring a newspaper or magazine to take your mind off yourself while waiting.
- Locate the examination room – When you have found the proper room, you will be directed to the seat or part of the room where you will sit. Sometimes you are given a sheet of instructions to read while you are waiting. Do not fill out any forms until you are told to do so; just read them and be prepared.
- Relax and prepare to listen to the instructions
- If you have any physical problem that may keep you from doing your best, be sure to tell the test administrator. If you are sick or in poor health, you really cannot do your best on the exam. You can come back and take the test some other time.

VII. AT THE TEST

The day of the test is here and you have the test booklet in your hand. The temptation to get going is very strong. Caution! There is more to success than knowing the right answers. You must know how to identify your papers and understand variations in the type of short-answer question used in this particular examination. Follow these suggestions for maximum results from your efforts:

1) Cooperate with the monitor

The test administrator has a duty to create a situation in which you can be as much at ease as possible. He will give instructions, tell you when to begin, check to see that you are marking your answer sheet correctly, and so on. He is not there to guard you, although he will see that your competitors do not take unfair advantage. He wants to help you do your best.

2) Listen to all instructions

Don't jump the gun! Wait until you understand all directions. In most civil service tests you get more time than you need to answer the questions. So don't be in a hurry. Read each word of instructions until you clearly understand the meaning. Study the examples, listen to all announcements and follow directions. Ask questions if you do not understand what to do.

3) Identify your papers

Civil service exams are usually identified by number only. You will be assigned a number; you must not put your name on your test papers. Be sure to copy your number correctly. Since more than one exam may be given, copy your exact examination title.

4) Plan your time

Unless you are told that a test is a "speed" or "rate of work" test, speed itself is usually not important. Time enough to answer all the questions will be provided, but this does not mean that you have all day. An overall time limit has been set. Divide the total time (in minutes) by the number of questions to determine the approximate time you have for each question.

5) Do not linger over difficult questions

If you come across a difficult question, mark it with a paper clip (useful to have along) and come back to it when you have been through the booklet. One caution if you do this – be sure to skip a number on your answer sheet as well. Check often to be sure that you have not lost your place and that you are marking in the row numbered the same as the question you are answering.

6) Read the questions

Be sure you know what the question asks! Many capable people are unsuccessful because they failed to *read* the questions correctly.

7) Answer all questions

Unless you have been instructed that a penalty will be deducted for incorrect answers, it is better to guess than to omit a question.

8) Speed tests

It is often better NOT to guess on speed tests. It has been found that on timed tests people are tempted to spend the last few seconds before time is called in marking answers at random – without even reading them – in the hope of picking up a few extra points. To discourage this practice, the instructions may warn you that your score will be "corrected" for guessing. That is, a penalty will be applied. The incorrect answers will be deducted from the correct ones, or some other penalty formula will be used.

9) Review your answers

If you finish before time is called, go back to the questions you guessed or omitted to give them further thought. Review other answers if you have time.

10) Return your test materials

If you are ready to leave before others have finished or time is called, take ALL your materials to the monitor and leave quietly. Never take any test material with you. The monitor can discover whose papers are not complete, and taking a test booklet may be grounds for disqualification.

VIII. EXAMINATION TECHNIQUES

1) Read the general instructions carefully. These are usually printed on the first page of the exam booklet. As a rule, these instructions refer to the timing of the examination; the fact that you should not start work until the signal and must stop work at a signal, etc. If there are any *special* instructions, such as a choice of questions to be answered, make sure that you note this instruction carefully.

2) When you are ready to start work on the examination, that is as soon as the signal has been given, read the instructions to each question booklet, underline any key words or phrases, such as *least, best, outline, describe* and the like. In this way you will tend to answer as requested rather than discover on reviewing your paper that you *listed without describing*, that you selected the *worst* choice rather than the *best* choice, etc.

3) If the examination is of the objective or multiple-choice type – that is, each question will also give a series of possible answers: A, B, C or D, and you are called upon to select the best answer and write the letter next to that answer on your answer paper – it is advisable to start answering each question in turn. There may be anywhere from 50 to 100 such questions in the three or four hours allotted and you can see how much time would be taken if you read through all the questions before beginning to answer any. Furthermore, if you come across a question or group of questions which you know would be difficult to answer, it would undoubtedly affect your handling of all the other questions.

4) If the examination is of the essay type and contains but a few questions, it is a moot point as to whether you should read all the questions before starting to answer any one. Of course, if you are given a choice – say five out of seven and the like – then it is essential to read all the questions so you can eliminate the two that are most difficult. If, however, you are asked to answer all the questions, there may be danger in trying to answer the easiest one first because you may find that you will spend too much time on it. The best technique is to answer the first question, then proceed to the second, etc.

5) Time your answers. Before the exam begins, write down the time it started, then add the time allowed for the examination and write down the time it must be completed, then divide the time available somewhat as follows:
    - If 3-1/2 hours are allowed, that would be 210 minutes. If you have 80 objective-type questions, that would be an average of 2-1/2 minutes per question. Allow yourself no more than 2 minutes per question, or a total of 160 minutes, which will permit about 50 minutes to review.
    - If for the time allotment of 210 minutes there are 7 essay questions to answer, that would average about 30 minutes a question. Give yourself only 25 minutes per question so that you have about 35 minutes to review.

6) The most important instruction is to *read each question* and make sure you know what is wanted. The second most important instruction is to *time yourself properly* so that you answer every question. The third most important instruction is to *answer every question*. Guess if you have to but include something for each question. Remember that you will receive no credit for a blank and will probably receive some credit if you write something in answer to an essay question. If you guess a letter – say "B" for a multiple-choice question – you may have guessed right. If you leave a blank as an answer to a multiple-choice question, the examiners may respect your feelings but it will not add a point to your score. Some exams may penalize you for wrong answers, so in such cases *only*, you may not want to guess unless you have some basis for your answer.

7) Suggestions
    a. Objective-type questions
        1. Examine the question booklet for proper sequence of pages and questions
        2. Read all instructions carefully
        3. Skip any question which seems too difficult; return to it after all other questions have been answered
        4. Apportion your time properly; do not spend too much time on any single question or group of questions

5. Note and underline key words – *all, most, fewest, least, best, worst, same, opposite*, etc.
6. Pay particular attention to negatives
7. Note unusual option, e.g., unduly long, short, complex, different or similar in content to the body of the question
8. Observe the use of "hedging" words – *probably, may, most likely*, etc.
9. Make sure that your answer is put next to the same number as the question
10. Do not second-guess unless you have good reason to believe the second answer is definitely more correct
11. Cross out original answer if you decide another answer is more accurate; do not erase until you are ready to hand your paper in
12. Answer all questions; guess unless instructed otherwise
13. Leave time for review

  b. Essay questions
1. Read each question carefully
2. Determine exactly what is wanted. Underline key words or phrases.
3. Decide on outline or paragraph answer
4. Include many different points and elements unless asked to develop any one or two points or elements
5. Show impartiality by giving pros and cons unless directed to select one side only
6. Make and write down any assumptions you find necessary to answer the questions
7. Watch your English, grammar, punctuation and choice of words
8. Time your answers; don't crowd material

8) Answering the essay question

Most essay questions can be answered by framing the specific response around several key words or ideas. Here are a few such key words or ideas:

M's: manpower, materials, methods, money, management
P's: purpose, program, policy, plan, procedure, practice, problems, pitfalls, personnel, public relations

  a. Six basic steps in handling problems:
1. Preliminary plan and background development
2. Collect information, data and facts
3. Analyze and interpret information, data and facts
4. Analyze and develop solutions as well as make recommendations
5. Prepare report and sell recommendations
6. Install recommendations and follow up effectiveness

  b. Pitfalls to avoid
1. *Taking things for granted* – A statement of the situation does not necessarily imply that each of the elements is necessarily true; for example, a complaint may be invalid and biased so that all that can be taken for granted is that a complaint has been registered

2. *Considering only one side of a situation* – Wherever possible, indicate several alternatives and then point out the reasons you selected the best one
3. *Failing to indicate follow up* – Whenever your answer indicates action on your part, make certain that you will take proper follow-up action to see how successful your recommendations, procedures or actions turn out to be
4. *Taking too long in answering any single question* – Remember to time your answers properly

IX. AFTER THE TEST

Scoring procedures differ in detail among civil service jurisdictions although the general principles are the same. Whether the papers are hand-scored or graded by machine we have described, they are nearly always graded by number. That is, the person who marks the paper knows only the number – never the name – of the applicant. Not until all the papers have been graded will they be matched with names. If other tests, such as training and experience or oral interview ratings have been given, scores will be combined. Different parts of the examination usually have different weights. For example, the written test might count 60 percent of the final grade, and a rating of training and experience 40 percent. In many jurisdictions, veterans will have a certain number of points added to their grades.

After the final grade has been determined, the names are placed in grade order and an eligible list is established. There are various methods for resolving ties between those who get the same final grade – probably the most common is to place first the name of the person whose application was received first. Job offers are made from the eligible list in the order the names appear on it. You will be notified of your grade and your rank as soon as all these computations have been made. This will be done as rapidly as possible.

People who are found to meet the requirements in the announcement are called "eligibles." Their names are put on a list of eligible candidates. An eligible's chances of getting a job depend on how high he stands on this list and how fast agencies are filling jobs from the list.

When a job is to be filled from a list of eligibles, the agency asks for the names of people on the list of eligibles for that job. When the civil service commission receives this request, it sends to the agency the names of the three people highest on this list. Or, if the job to be filled has specialized requirements, the office sends the agency the names of the top three persons who meet these requirements from the general list.

The appointing officer makes a choice from among the three people whose names were sent to him. If the selected person accepts the appointment, the names of the others are put back on the list to be considered for future openings.

That is the rule in hiring from all kinds of eligible lists, whether they are for typist, carpenter, chemist, or something else. For every vacancy, the appointing officer has his choice of any one of the top three eligibles on the list. This explains why the person whose name is on top of the list sometimes does not get an appointment when some of the persons lower on the list do. If the appointing officer chooses the second or third eligible, the No. 1 eligible does not get a job at once, but stays on the list until he is appointed or the list is terminated.

X. HOW TO PASS THE INTERVIEW TEST

The examination for which you applied requires an oral interview test. You have already taken the written test and you are now being called for the interview test – the final part of the formal examination.

You may think that it is not possible to prepare for an interview test and that there are no procedures to follow during an interview. Our purpose is to point out some things you can do in advance that will help you and some good rules to follow and pitfalls to avoid while you are being interviewed.

What is an interview supposed to test?

The written examination is designed to test the technical knowledge and competence of the candidate; the oral is designed to evaluate intangible qualities, not readily measured otherwise, and to establish a list showing the relative fitness of each candidate – as measured against his competitors – for the position sought. Scoring is not on the basis of "right" and "wrong," but on a sliding scale of values ranging from "not passable" to "outstanding." As a matter of fact, it is possible to achieve a relatively low score without a single "incorrect" answer because of evident weakness in the qualities being measured.

Occasionally, an examination may consist entirely of an oral test – either an individual or a group oral. In such cases, information is sought concerning the technical knowledges and abilities of the candidate, since there has been no written examination for this purpose. More commonly, however, an oral test is used to supplement a written examination.

Who conducts interviews?

The composition of oral boards varies among different jurisdictions. In nearly all, a representative of the personnel department serves as chairman. One of the members of the board may be a representative of the department in which the candidate would work. In some cases, "outside experts" are used, and, frequently, a businessman or some other representative of the general public is asked to serve. Labor and management or other special groups may be represented. The aim is to secure the services of experts in the appropriate field.

However the board is composed, it is a good idea (and not at all improper or unethical) to ascertain in advance of the interview who the members are and what groups they represent. When you are introduced to them, you will have some idea of their backgrounds and interests, and at least you will not stutter and stammer over their names.

What should be done before the interview?

While knowledge about the board members is useful and takes some of the surprise element out of the interview, there is other preparation which is more substantive. It *is* possible to prepare for an oral interview – in several ways:

1) Keep a copy of your application and review it carefully before the interview

This may be the only document before the oral board, and the starting point of the interview. Know what education and experience you have listed there, and the sequence and dates of all of it. Sometimes the board will ask you to review the highlights of your experience for them; you should not have to hem and haw doing it.

2) Study the class specification and the examination announcement

Usually, the oral board has one or both of these to guide them. The qualities, characteristics or knowledges required by the position sought are stated in these documents. They offer valuable clues as to the nature of the oral interview. For example, if the job involves supervisory responsibilities, the announcement will usually indicate that knowledge of modern supervisory methods and the qualifications of the candidate as a supervisor will be tested. If so, you can expect such questions, frequently in the form of a hypothetical situation which you are expected to solve. NEVER go into an oral without knowledge of the duties and responsibilities of the job you seek.

3) Think through each qualification required

Try to visualize the kind of questions you would ask if you were a board member. How well could you answer them? Try especially to appraise your own knowledge and background in each area, *measured against the job sought*, and identify any areas in which you are weak. Be critical and realistic – do not flatter yourself.

4) Do some general reading in areas in which you feel you may be weak

For example, if the job involves supervision and your past experience has NOT, some general reading in supervisory methods and practices, particularly in the field of human relations, might be useful. Do NOT study agency procedures or detailed manuals. The oral board will be testing your understanding and capacity, not your memory.

5) Get a good night's sleep and watch your general health and mental attitude

You will want a clear head at the interview. Take care of a cold or any other minor ailment, and of course, no hangovers.

What should be done on the day of the interview?

Now comes the day of the interview itself. Give yourself plenty of time to get there. Plan to arrive somewhat ahead of the scheduled time, particularly if your appointment is in the fore part of the day. If a previous candidate fails to appear, the board might be ready for you a bit early. By early afternoon an oral board is almost invariably behind schedule if there are many candidates, and you may have to wait. Take along a book or magazine to read, or your application to review, but leave any extraneous material in the waiting room when you go in for your interview. In any event, relax and compose yourself.

The matter of dress is important. The board is forming impressions about you – from your experience, your manners, your attitude, and your appearance. Give your personal appearance careful attention. Dress your best, but not your flashiest. Choose conservative, appropriate clothing, and be sure it is immaculate. This is a business interview, and your appearance should indicate that you regard it as such. Besides, being well groomed and properly dressed will help boost your confidence.

Sooner or later, someone will call your name and escort you into the interview room. *This is it.* From here on you are on your own. It is too late for any more preparation. But remember, you asked for this opportunity to prove your fitness, and you are here because your request was granted.

What happens when you go in?

The usual sequence of events will be as follows: The clerk (who is often the board stenographer) will introduce you to the chairman of the oral board, who will introduce you to the other members of the board. Acknowledge the introductions before you sit down. Do not be surprised if you find a microphone facing you or a stenotypist sitting by. Oral interviews are usually recorded in the event of an appeal or other review.

Usually the chairman of the board will open the interview by reviewing the highlights of your education and work experience from your application – primarily for the benefit of the other members of the board, as well as to get the material into the record. Do not interrupt or comment unless there is an error or significant misinterpretation; if that is the case, do not hesitate. But do not quibble about insignificant matters. Also, he will usually ask you some question about your education, experience or your present job – partly to get you to start talking and to establish the interviewing "rapport." He may start the actual questioning, or turn it over to one of the other members. Frequently, each member undertakes the questioning on a particular area, one in which he is perhaps most competent, so you can expect each member to participate in the examination. Because time is limited, you may also expect some rather abrupt switches in the direction the questioning takes, so do not be upset by it. Normally, a board member will not pursue a single line of questioning unless he discovers a particular strength or weakness.

After each member has participated, the chairman will usually ask whether any member has any further questions, then will ask you if you have anything you wish to add. Unless you are expecting this question, it may floor you. Worse, it may start you off on an extended, extemporaneous speech. The board is not usually seeking more information. The question is principally to offer you a last opportunity to present further qualifications or to indicate that you have nothing to add. So, if you feel that a significant qualification or characteristic has been overlooked, it is proper to point it out in a sentence or so. Do not compliment the board on the thoroughness of their examination – they have been sketchy, and you know it. If you wish, merely say, "No thank you, I have nothing further to add." This is a point where you can "talk yourself out" of a good impression or fail to present an important bit of information. Remember, *you close the interview yourself*.

The chairman will then say, "That is all, Mr. _____, thank you." Do not be startled; the interview is over, and quicker than you think. Thank him, gather your belongings and take your leave. Save your sigh of relief for the other side of the door.

How to put your best foot forward

Throughout this entire process, you may feel that the board individually and collectively is trying to pierce your defenses, seek out your hidden weaknesses and embarrass and confuse you. Actually, this is not true. They are obliged to make an appraisal of your qualifications for the job you are seeking, and they want to see you in your best light. Remember, they must interview all candidates and a non-cooperative candidate may become a failure in spite of their best efforts to bring out his qualifications. Here are 15 suggestions that will help you:

1) Be natural – Keep your attitude confident, not cocky

If you are not confident that you can do the job, do not expect the board to be. Do not apologize for your weaknesses, try to bring out your strong points. The board is interested in a positive, not negative, presentation. Cockiness will antagonize any board member and make him wonder if you are covering up a weakness by a false show of strength.

2) Get comfortable, but don't lounge or sprawl

Sit erectly but not stiffly. A careless posture may lead the board to conclude that you are careless in other things, or at least that you are not impressed by the importance of the occasion. Either conclusion is natural, even if incorrect. Do not fuss with your clothing, a pencil or an ashtray. Your hands may occasionally be useful to emphasize a point; do not let them become a point of distraction.

3) Do not wisecrack or make small talk

This is a serious situation, and your attitude should show that you consider it as such. Further, the time of the board is limited – they do not want to waste it, and neither should you.

4) Do not exaggerate your experience or abilities

In the first place, from information in the application or other interviews and sources, the board may know more about you than you think. Secondly, you probably will not get away with it. An experienced board is rather adept at spotting such a situation, so do not take the chance.

5) If you know a board member, do not make a point of it, yet do not hide it

Certainly you are not fooling him, and probably not the other members of the board. Do not try to take advantage of your acquaintanceship – it will probably do you little good.

6) Do not dominate the interview

Let the board do that. They will give you the clues – do not assume that you have to do all the talking. Realize that the board has a number of questions to ask you, and do not try to take up all the interview time by showing off your extensive knowledge of the answer to the first one.

7) Be attentive

You only have 20 minutes or so, and you should keep your attention at its sharpest throughout. When a member is addressing a problem or question to you, give him your undivided attention. Address your reply principally to him, but do not exclude the other board members.

8) Do not interrupt

A board member may be stating a problem for you to analyze. He will ask you a question when the time comes. Let him state the problem, and wait for the question.

9) Make sure you understand the question

Do not try to answer until you are sure what the question is. If it is not clear, restate it in your own words or ask the board member to clarify it for you. However, do not haggle about minor elements.

10) Reply promptly but not hastily

A common entry on oral board rating sheets is "candidate responded readily," or "candidate hesitated in replies." Respond as promptly and quickly as you can, but do not jump to a hasty, ill-considered answer.

11) Do not be peremptory in your answers

A brief answer is proper – but do not fire your answer back. That is a losing game from your point of view. The board member can probably ask questions much faster than you can answer them.

12) Do not try to create the answer you think the board member wants

He is interested in what kind of mind you have and how it works – not in playing games. Furthermore, he can usually spot this practice and will actually grade you down on it.

13) Do not switch sides in your reply merely to agree with a board member

Frequently, a member will take a contrary position merely to draw you out and to see if you are willing and able to defend your point of view. Do not start a debate, yet do not surrender a good position. If a position is worth taking, it is worth defending.

14) Do not be afraid to admit an error in judgment if you are shown to be wrong

The board knows that you are forced to reply without any opportunity for careful consideration. Your answer may be demonstrably wrong. If so, admit it and get on with the interview.

15) Do not dwell at length on your present job

The opening question may relate to your present assignment. Answer the question but do not go into an extended discussion. You are being examined for a *new* job, not your present one. As a matter of fact, try to phrase ALL your answers in terms of the job for which you are being examined.

Basis of Rating

Probably you will forget most of these "do's" and "don'ts" when you walk into the oral interview room. Even remembering them all will not ensure you a passing grade. Perhaps you did not have the qualifications in the first place. But remembering them will help you to put your best foot forward, without treading on the toes of the board members.

Rumor and popular opinion to the contrary notwithstanding, an oral board wants you to make the best appearance possible. They know you are under pressure – but they also want to see how you respond to it as a guide to what your reaction would be under the pressures of the job you seek. They will be influenced by the degree of poise you display, the personal traits you show and the manner in which you respond.

ABOUT THIS BOOK

This book contains tests divided into Examination Sections. Go through each test, answering every question in the margin. We have also attached a sample answer sheet at the back of the book that can be removed and used. At the end of each test look at the answer key and check your answers. On the ones you got wrong, look at the right answer choice and learn. Do not fill in the answers first. Do not memorize the questions and answers, but understand the answer and principles involved. On your test, the questions will likely be different from the samples. Questions are changed and new ones added. If you understand these past questions you should have success with any changes that arise. Tests may consist of several types of questions. We have additional books on each subject should more study be advisable or necessary for you. Finally, the more you study, the better prepared you will be. This book is intended to be the last thing you study before you walk into the examination room. Prior study of relevant texts is also recommended. NLC publishes some of these in our Fundamental Series. Knowledge and good sense are important factors in passing your exam. Good luck also helps. So now study this Passbook, absorb the material contained within and take that knowledge into the examination. Then do your best to pass that exam.

EXAMINATION SECTION

MATHEMATICS
EXAMINATION SECTION
TEST 1

DIRECTIONS: Each question or incomplete statement is followed by several suggested answers or completions. Select the one that BEST answers the question or completes the statement. *PRINT THE LETTER OF THE CORRECT ANSWER IN THE SPACE AT THE RIGHT.*

Questions 1-60.

DIRECTIONS: For problems 1 through 22, compute an answer for each. For problems 23 through 60, select an answer from among the four choices given.

1. Add: 215
         86
         193   1._____

2. From 761, subtract 257.   2._____

3. Multiply: 206
              ×57   3._____

4. Divide: 25)4175   4._____

5. Divide: 408 ÷ 4   5._____

6. Multiply: 1/2 × 3/4   6._____

7. Add: 3.4 and 1.16   7._____

8. Find the product of 3.4 and 7.8.   8._____

9. If 12.36 is divided by 6, what is the quotient?   9._____

10. What is 2/3 of 300?   10._____

11. Subtract: 9.67
               4.85   11._____

12. Divide: 8 ÷ 1/3   12._____

13. If John spends $6.45, how much change should he receive from a $10 bill?   13._____

14. What is the average (mean) of 81, 72, and 78?   14._____

15. How many cubic centimeters are in the volume of a rectangular box 6 cm long, 4 cm wide, and 4 cm high? 15._____

16. What is the perimeter of a rectangle with length 6 and width 2? 16._____

17. A number of test scores are arranged as follows: 58, 65, 65, 75, 85, 85, 99. What is the median score? 17._____

18. Solve for x: 4x + 1 = 17. 18._____

19. Solve for x: $\frac{6}{10} = \frac{x}{30}$ 19._____

20. A team lost 40% of its games. If the team played 30 games, how many games were lost? 20._____

21. On a map, 1 centimeter represents 12 kilometers. How many kilometers does 2 ½ centimeters on the map represent? 21._____

22. What is the area of a square with each side of length 5? 22._____

23. ☐ - 186 = 54 23._____
    Which number makes this open sentence TRUE?
    A. 132   B. 238   C. 240   D. 250

24. The sum of 3/5 and 2/3 is 24._____
    A. 5/8   B. 5/15   C. 19/15   D. 6/8

25. What is he LEAST common denominator of the fractions 1/2, 2/3, and 5/6? 25._____
    A. 36   B. 18   C. 12   D. 6

26. Which of the following has the same value as 17/5? 26._____
    A. 12   B. 2 2/5   C. 3 2/5   D. 5 2/3

27. When written as a percent, the fraction 3/4 is 27._____
    A. 25%   B. 66 2/3%   C. 75%   D. 86 1/2%

28. If 45,534 people were at a football game, what would be the total attendance reported to the nearest thousand? 28._____
    A. 40,000   B. 46,000   C. 47,000   D. 50,000

29. Which number represents seventy thousand eight hundred? 29._____
    A. 7,080   B. 70,080   C. 70,800   D. 78,000

30. When listed in order from smallest to largest, which fraction would be the FIRST? 30._____
    A. 1/5   B. 1/2   C. 1/3   D. 1/4

31. The cost of a telephone call was listed as:
    $1.00 for the first 3 minutes
    $0.30 for each additional minute
    What would be the total cost of a telephone call that was 6 minutes long?
    A. $1.80   B. $1.90   C. $2.00   D. $2.80

32. If A and B are points on the circle, then AB is a(n)
    AB is a(n)
    A. arc
    B. chord
    C. diameter
    D. radius

33. In the triangle ABC, what is the ratio of AB to BC?
    A. 5:6
    B. 5:7
    C. 7:5
    D. 6:5

34. Which number has the GREATEST value?
    A. .0824   B. .1032   C. .125   D. .091

35. Mr. White had a balance of $325.15 in his checking account. If he made a deposit of $75, what would be the amount of the new balance in his checking account?
    A. $250.15   B. $324.40   C. $325.90   D. $400.15

36. The sum of -11 and -8 is
    A. -19   B. -3   C. 3   D. 19

37. One day in March the highest temperature was 8 degrees C and the lowest was -3 degrees C.
    What was the total number of degree difference between the highest and lowest temperatures that day?
    A. 8   B. 11   C. 3   D. 5

38. The expression 10^3 is equal to
    A. -0   B. 300   C. 1,000   D. 10,000

39. On the accompanying graph, point A has coordinates
    A. (0,3)
    B. (1,3)
    C. (3,0)
    D. (3,1)

40. The circle graph to the right shows how each tax dollar is spent in Salt Lake City.
    What is the LARGEST part of the tax dollar spent for?
    A. Repairs
    B. Salaries
    C. Education
    D. Parks

    40.____

41. The graph to the right shows the number of people attending each game of the World Series one year.
    On which day did the FEWEST number of people attend a World Series game?
    A. Friday
    B. Monday
    C. Tuesday
    D. Thursday

    41.____

42. The graph to the right represents the relationship between distance traveled and flying time for a certain airplane.
    How many hours of flying time did the airplane require to travel 450 miles?
    A. 2 1/2
    B. 2
    C. 3
    D. 3 1/2

    42.____

43. Which is the prime number?
    A. 21   B. 99   C. 101   D. 125

    43.____

44. Mr. Ford bought a t-shirt for $15.00 and had to pay a 7% sales tax.
    If he gave the clerk $20, what should his change be?
    A. $1.05   B. $3.95   C. $4.95   D. $16.05

    44.____

45. Of carpeting costs $9.50 a square meter, what is the total cost of carpeting an entire room floor which is 3 meters by 4 meters?
    A. $133   B. $114   C. $85.50   D. $66.50

    45.____

46. Ruby buys a television set with a $25 downpayment and 6 installment payments of $20.
    The total cost of the television set is
    A. $95   B. $120   C. $145   D. $150

    46.____

47. Carver High School has an enrollment of 50 freshmen, 40 sophomores, 60 juniors, and 30 seniors.
    What is the ratio of the number of jurors to the total enrollment?
       A. 1:6   B. 1:4   C. 2:3   D. 1:3

47.____

48. The area pf a circle with a radius of 5 centimeters is
       A. 10π cm²   B. 20π cm²   C. 25π cm²   D. 100π cm²

48.____

49. The circumference of a circle with a radius of 4 is
       A. 2π B. 4π C. 8π D. 16π

49.____

50. Which of the following is a picture of a cylinder?

50.____

51. A nail is placed against a ruler as shown in the above drawing.
    How many centimeters long is the nail?
       A. 7.0   B. 6.5   C. 6.0   D. 5.5

51.____

52. Each race began at 11:00 A.M. The winner ran the course in 2 hours and 19 minutes.
    At what time did the winner cross the finish line?
       A. 8:41 A.M.   B. 12:19 P.M.   C. 1:19 P.M.   D. 2:19 P.M.

52.____

53. Each house above represents 10,000 homes.
    What is the total number of homes represented by the figures?
       A. 40,500   B. 45,000   C. 405,000   D. 450,000

53.____

54. A radio is sold in a store for $54.50. The same radio can be ordered through the mail for $24.50 plus $1.50 for postage.
    How much would be saved by buying the radio through the mail?
       A. $28.50   B. $30.00   C. $30.50   D. $53.00

54.____

55. A stereo which usually sells for $450 is on sale for 1/3 off. 55._____
What is the sale price?

56. Mary has a board 12 1/2 inches long. 56._____
If she cuts 1 1/4 inches off the board, how long will the board be?
    A. 10 1/4 inches   B. 11 inches   C. 11 1/4 inches   D. 11 1/2 inches

57. If 3 cases of canned fruit cost $27, then 1 of these cases would cost 57._____
    A. $81   B. $18   C. $3   D. $9

58. Carlo earns $18 per hour at a part-time job. 58._____
How much does he earn in a day when he works 5 1/2 hours?
    A. $90   B. $99   C. $108   D. $112.50

59. How many kilometers are there in the 10,000 meter run? 59._____
    A. 1   B. 2   C. 10   D. 100

60. What is the probability of obtaining a head when a coin is tossed? 60._____
    A. 1   B. 1/2   C. 1/3   D. 1/4

KEY (CORRECT ANSWERS)

1. 494	11. 4.82	21. 30	31. B	41. C	51. B
2. 504	12. 24	22. 25	32. B	42. C	52. C
3. 11,742	13. $3.55	23. C	33. B	43. C	53. B
4. 167	14. 77	24. C	34. C	44. B	54. A
5. 102	15. 96	25. D	35. D	45. B	55. C
6. 3/8	16. 16	26. C	36. A	46. C	56. C
7. 4.56	17. 75	27. C	37. B	47. D	57. D
8. 26.52	18. 4	28. C	38. C	48. C	58. B
9. 2.06	19. 18	29. C	39. B	49. C	59. C
10. 20	20. 12	30. A	40. C	50. A	60. B

SOLUTIONS TO PROBLEMS

1. 215 + 86 + 193 = 494

2. 761 − 257 = 504

3. (206)(57) = 11,742

4. 4175 ÷ 25 = 167

5. 408 ÷ 4 = 102

6. $(\frac{1}{2})(\frac{3}{4}) = \frac{3}{8}$

7. 3.40 + 1.16 = 4.56

8. (3.4)(7.8) = 26.52

9. 12.36 ÷ 6 = 2.06

10. $\frac{2}{3}(30) = 20$

11. 9.67 − 4.85 = 4.82

12. $8 \div \frac{1}{3} = (8)(\frac{3}{1}) = 24$

13. $10 - $6.45 = $3.55

14. (81+72+78) ÷ 3 = 77

15. Volume = (6)(4)(4) = 96 cubic cen.

16. Perimeter = (2)(6+2) = 16

17. Median = (7+1)/2 = 4th score = 75

18. If 4x + 1 = 17, then 4x = 16. Solving, x = 4

19. If $\frac{6}{10} = \frac{x}{30}$, then 10x = 180. Solving, x = 18

20. (.40)(30) = 12 games lost

21. $(2\frac{1}{2})(12) = 30$ kilometers

22. Area = 5^2 = 25

8 (#1)

23. Missing number = 54 + 186 = 240

24. $\frac{3}{5} + \frac{2}{3} = \frac{9}{15} + \frac{10}{15} = \frac{19}{15}$

25. Least common denominator of $\frac{1}{2}, \frac{2}{3},$ and $\frac{5}{6}$ is 6.

26. $\frac{17}{5} = 3\frac{2}{5}$

27. $\frac{3}{4} = (\frac{3}{4})(100)\% = 75\%$

28. 46,534 is 47,000 to the nearest thousand

29. Seventy thousand eight hundred = 70,800

30. $\frac{1}{5}$ is smaller than $\frac{1}{2}, \frac{1}{3},$ and $\frac{1}{4}$

31. Total cost = $1.00 + (3)(.30) = $1.90

32. AB is a chord since it joins 2 points on the circle but does not pass through the center.

33. AB:BC = 5:7

34. .125 is larger than .0824, .1032, and .091

35. New balance = $325.15 + $75 = $400.15

36. (-11) + (-8) = -19

37. 8 – (-3) = 11 degrees difference

38. $10^3 = (10)(10)(10) = 1000$

39. Point A has coordinates (1,3)

40. Education represents the largest section.

41. On Tuesday, about 30,000 people attended the World Series. This was the lowest attendance figure in the chart.

42. On the graph, 450 miles corresponds to 3 hours.

43. 101 is prime since it can only be divided evenly by itself and 1.

44. $15 + (.07)($15) = $16.05. Then, $20 - $16.05 = $3.95

45. Total cost = ($9.50)(3)(4) = $114.00

46. Total cost = $25 + (6)($20) = $145

47. Juniors: total enrollment = 60:180 = $\frac{1}{3}$

48. Area = $(\pi)(5cm)^2 = 25\pi$ cm^2

49. Circumference = $(2\pi)(4) = 8\pi$

50. Selection A represents a cylinder. (The other 3 selections are cube, cone, triangular prism.)

51. Length of nail = 6.5 cm

52. 11:00 A.M. + 2 hrs. 19 min. = 1:19 P.M.

53. (10,000)(4.5) = 45,000

54. Amount saved = $54.50 - $24.50 - $1.50 = $28.50

55. Sale price = $450 – $(\frac{1}{3})$($450) = $300

56. $12\frac{1}{2}"$ - $1\frac{1}{4}"$ = $11\frac{1}{4}$ inches

57. 1 case costs $27 ÷ 3 = $9

58. ($18)(5 ½) = $99

59. Since 1 km = 1000m, 10 kilometers = 10,000 meters

60. In tossing a coin, the probability of getting a head = $\frac{1}{2}$

MATHEMATICS
EXAMINATION SECTION
TEST 1

DIRECTIONS: Each question or incomplete statement is followed by several suggested answers or completions. Select the one that *BEST* answers the question or completes the statement. *PRINT THE LETTER OF THE CORRECT ANSWER IN THE SPACE AT THE RIGHT.*

[Ability No. 1. *Determine the time between two events.*(Questions 1-4)]

1. School starts at 7:45 a.m. The last period ends at 2:10 p.m. How long is the school day?

    A. 5 hours 35 minutes
    B. 6 hours 25 minutes
    C. 6 hours 35 minutes
    D. 535 minutes

    1._____

2. You get to the bus station in Orlando at 8:30 a.m. How long do you have to wait for the next bus to Tallahassee? (See Schedule below)

    A. 1 hour 10 minutes
    B. 3 hours 15 minutes
    C. 4 hours 50 minutes
    D. 7 hours 10 minutes

    2._____

THE GRAYFOX BUS LINES, Orlando, Florida			
From Arrivals	Time	To Departures	Time
Tampa	5:30 a.m.	Miami	7:45 a.m.
Jacksonvl	6:50 a.m.	Melbourne	9:30 a.m.
Melbourne	8:30 a.m.	Tampa	12:00 p.m.
Tallahassee	11:45 a.m.	Tallahassee	1:20 p.m.

3. Mr. Arnold parks his car at the airport to catch a plane. Entering the parking lot, he picks up a ticket which reads: 13 Nov 3:20 p.m. He checks his car out on November 15 at 8:30 a.m.
   How long was his car in the parking lot?

    A. 1 day, 5 hours, 10 minutes
    B. 1 day, 17 hours, 10 minutes
    C. 2 days, 4 hours, 50 minutes
    D. 2 days, 5 hours, 10 minutes

    3._____

4. The Army had a special 30-month recruitment program. Pete joined the Army on October 1, 2010.
   When will Pete be discharged?

    A. May 1, 2012
    B. March 1, 2013
    C. April 1, 2013
    D. May 1, 2013

    4._____

[Ability No. *2. Determine equivalent amounts of money.* (Questions 5-8)]

5. Look at the picture at the top of the next page. How much money do you have?

    A. $28.97
    B. $29.27
    C. $29.52
    D. $29.77

    5._____

11

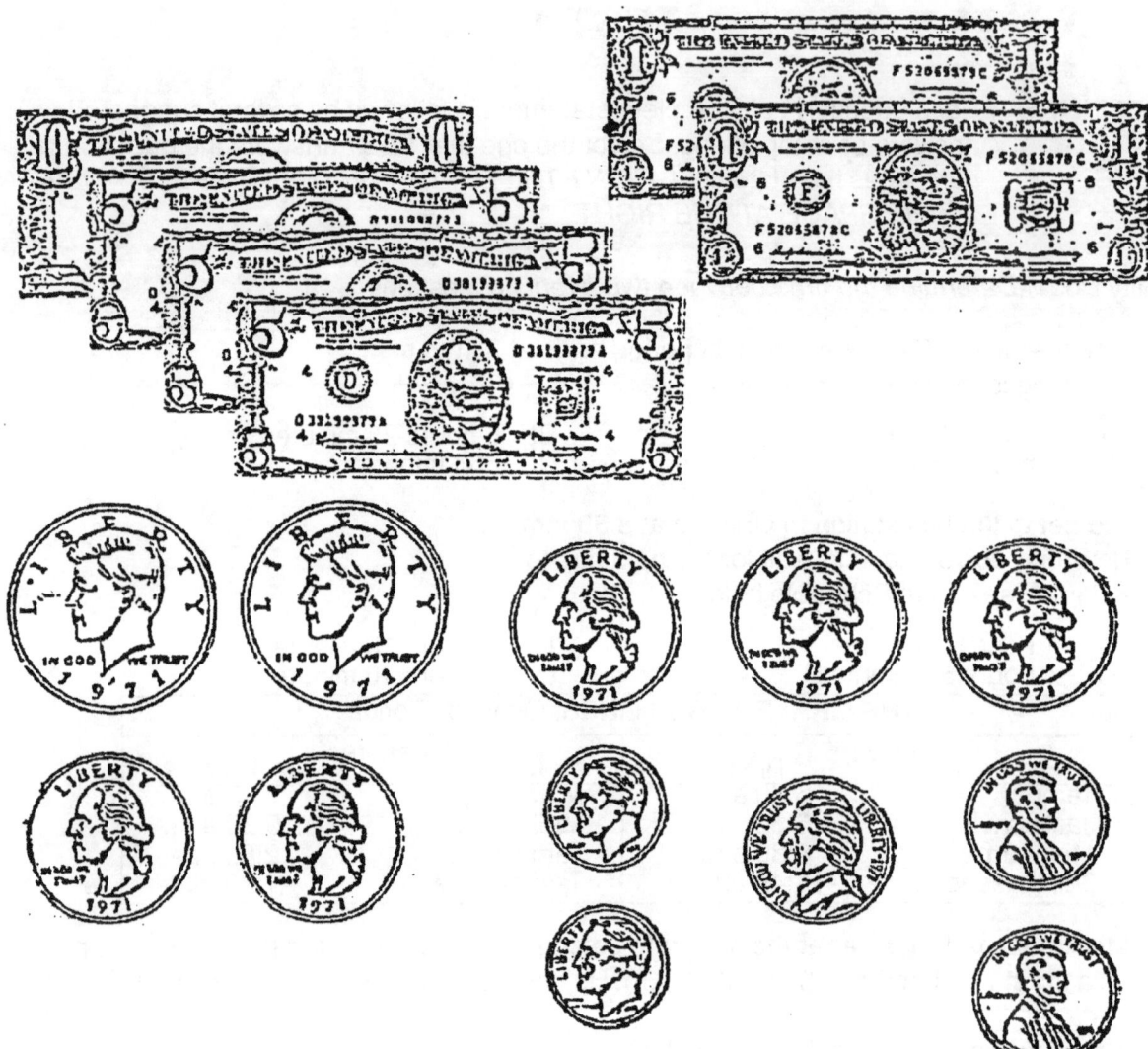

6. You are a cashier in a cafeteria. A customer's bill comes to $3.48, with tax. He gives you a $10 bill. Which of the following would be his change?

    A. Seven dollars - four dimes - one nickel - three pennies
    B. Seven dollars - two quarters - two pennies
    C. Six dollars - two quarters - two pennies
    D. Six dollars - four dimes - one nickel - three pennies

6.____

7. A book costs $7.58. You pay for the book with a $20 bill. The cashier counts your change as follows: "60 cents, 65 cents, 75 cents, 8 dollars, 9 dollars, 10 dollars, 15 dollars, 20 dollars."
Which of the following shows the coins and bills you *most likely* received?

    A. 2 pennies, 1 nickel, 1 dime, 1 quarter, 3 dollar bills, 1 five-dollar bill
    B. 2 pennies, 1 nickel, 1 dime, 1 quarter, 3 dollar bills, 2 five-dollar bills
    C. 2 pennies, 1 nickel, 1 dime, 1 quarter, 2 dollar bills, 2 five-dollar bills
    D. 3 pennies, 1 nickel, 1 dime, 1 quarter, 2 dollar bills, 2 five-dollar bills

7.____

8. You are a clerk in a store. A customer's purchases come to $28.73. He gives you two twenty-dollar bills.
   Which of the following would be the *correct* change?

8.____

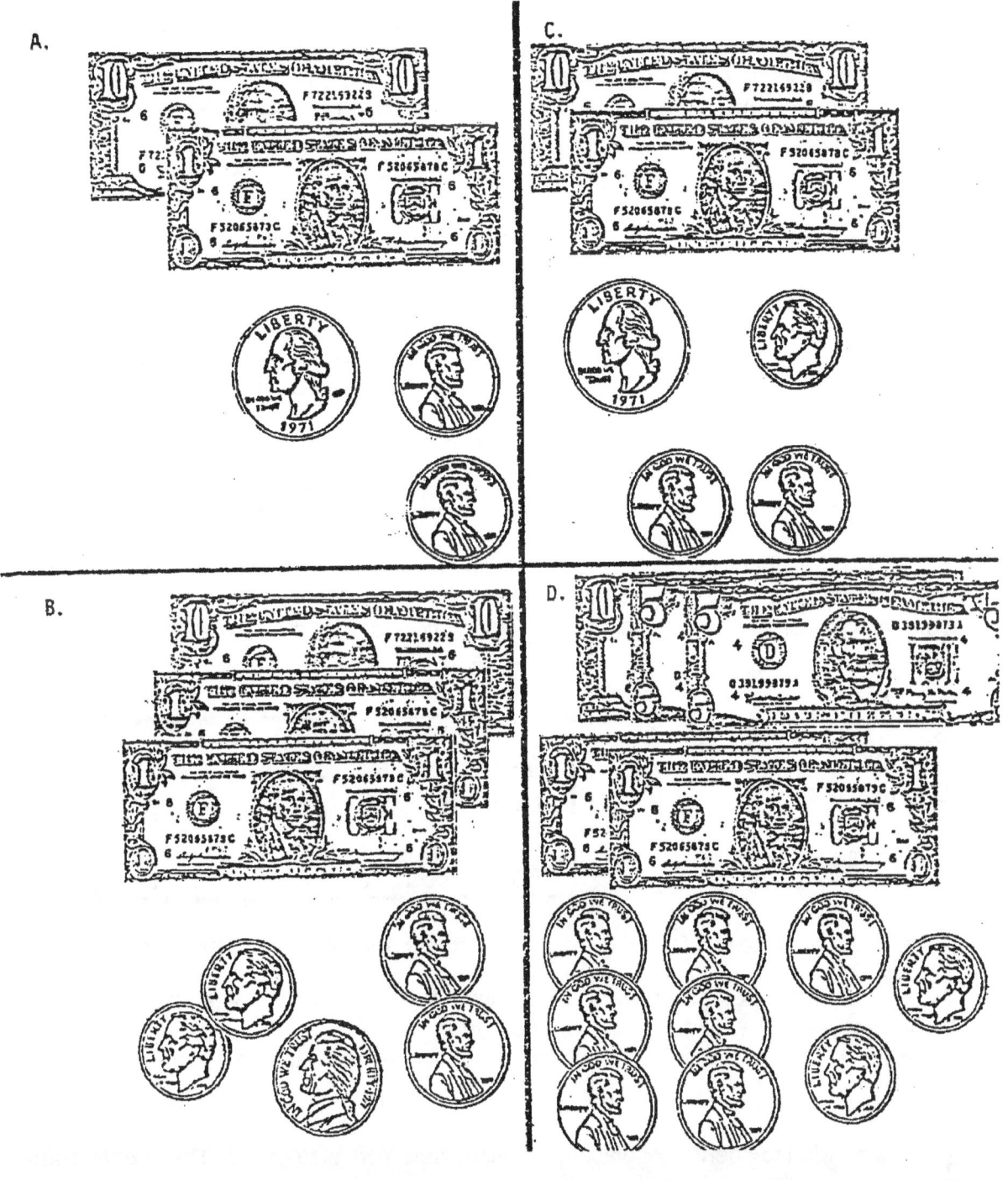

[Ability No. 3. *Solve problems involving whole numbers.* (Questions 9-13)]

9. Mr. Johnson maps out a route from Miami to Pensacola, The distance is 685 miles. If Mr. Johnson drives this distance in about 14 hours, his *average* driving speed was about how many miles per hour?

9.____

   A. 40   B. 45   C. 50   D. 55

10. The High and Mighty High School is a two-story building. There are 16 classrooms on each floor. One period there were exactly 25 students in each room.
How many students were in class that period?

    A. 224   B. 400   C. 790   D. 800

11. A swimming pool holds 30,000 gallons of water.
If water is pumped out of the pool at the rate of 50 gallons per minute, how long will it take to drain the pool?

    A. 6 hours   B. 10 hours   C. 60 hours   D. 600 hours

12. Chuck is in charge of buying the chicken for the class picnic. He buys 3 buckets, 5 barrels, and 1 tub.
How many pieces of chicken did he get? (See Menu at right)

    A. 84
    B. 111
    C. 186
    D. 198

    Menu

Size	No. Pieces
Box	5
Bucket	15
Barrel	21
Tub	48

13. The High and Mighty High. School Booster Club rented 1 van, 2 coaches, and 1 bus to take students to an out-of-town football game.
In order for the project to be a sell-out, how many tickets must the club sell? (See table below)

    A. 97
    B. 117
    C. 127
    D. 187

    ```
    Seating Capacity
    Van . . . . . . . . . 12
    Coach . . . . . . . . 30
    Bus . . . . . . . . . 55
    Cruiser . . . . . . . 90
    ```

[Ability No. 4. *Solve problems involving decimal numbers and percents.* (Questions 14-17)]

14. A car dealer urged potential buyers to take advantage of his end-of-year sale, because the price of his cars would increase 8% next year.
For example, a car costing $6200 this year would cost how much next year?

    A. $496   B. $4960   C. $6208   D. $6696

15. A family decided to spend their vacation visiting New York state parks. They drove 1436 miles and used 62.4 gallons of gasoline.
On this trip, they got how many miles per gallon?

    A. 23.0   B. 23.1   C. 23.8   D. 89,606

16. The Simpson family was planning a big reunion. Mrs. Simpson bought two turkeys, one weighing 14.5 pounds and one weighing 23.0 pounds.
    How much did she pay for the turkeys?

    A. $13.57
    B. $22.13
    C. $23.58
    D. $221.25

    ```
    Turkey Sale
    Weight           Cost/lb.
    8-11 lbs.          79¢
    12-18 lbs.         69¢
    19-25 lbs.         59¢
    ```

17. A label on a pair of pants warns that 8% shrinkage may be expected after washing. If the length of the new pants is 30 inches, after washing the length may be only

    A. 24 inches
    B. 27.6 inches
    C. 29.76 inches
    D. 32.4 inches

    [Ability No. 5. *Solve problems involving comparison shopping.* (Questions 18-22)]

18. The ad says that you can buy an air gun for $29.90 cash plus $1.87 for postage and handling. Or, you may make 6 equal payments of $5.41.
    How much do you save by paying for the gun in a *SINGLE* payment?

    A. $0.00   B. $0.60   C. $0.87   D. $1.87

19. Super-Gen radial tires are on sale. Four stores advertise their terms for the sale of the same tire. If you are buying four tires, which store offers the *BEST* price?

    A. Big-Eight Tire Store — Regular price $40. Buy one at regular price -- second tire half price.

    B. Tire Pile — Regular price $40. Prices reduced ¼.

    C. Rex's Auto Center — Regular price $40. Buy 3 at regular price - get one FREE.

    D. Car Care Headquarters — Regular price $40. Sale $29.50.

20. You receive the following advertisement for a satellite radio in the mail.
    How much more do you pay if you decide to pay for the radio in six installments?

    A. nothing
    B. $0.01
    C. $1.98
    D. $40.01

    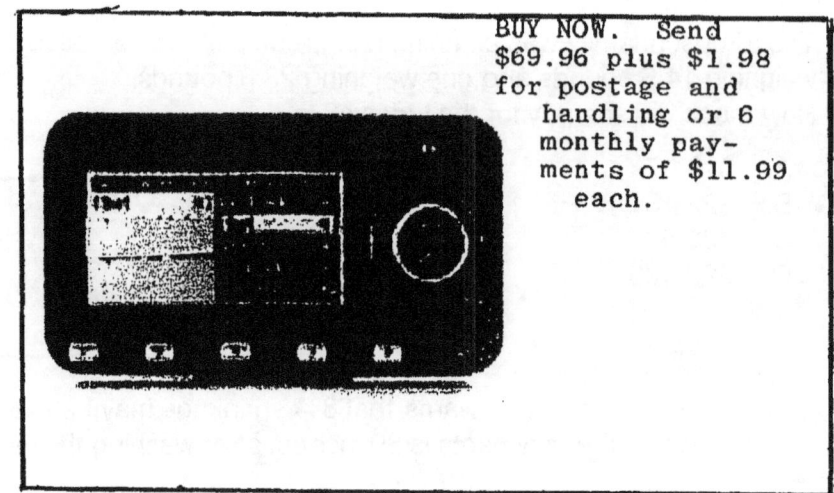

    BUY NOW. Send $69.96 plus $1.98 for postage and handling or 6 monthly payments of $11.99 each.

21. Spotless Miracle detergent is packaged in boxes of four different sizes: regular, large, giant, commercial.
    Which size of container is the BEST buy per ounce?

    A. Regular
    B. Large
    C. Giant
    D. Commercial

    Regular 12 oz. 40¢   Large 20 oz. 60¢   Giant 30 oz. 95¢   Commercial 60 oz. $1.95

22. A package of 8 hamburger buns costs 65¢. A package of 12 buns costs 95¢. You need to buy 4 dozen buns.
    What would you *save* if you bought packages of 12 instead of packages of 8?

    A. $0.10
    B. $0.30
    C. Nothing. The cost is the same.
    D. Nothing. You would lose money.

[Ability No. 6. *Solve problems involving a rate of interest.* (Questions 23-27)]

23. A savings bank runs the following ad (see figure) of a new savings plan.
    If you invest $800, how much money will you have in the account at the end of one year?

    A. $40
    B. $64
    C. $840
    D. $864

    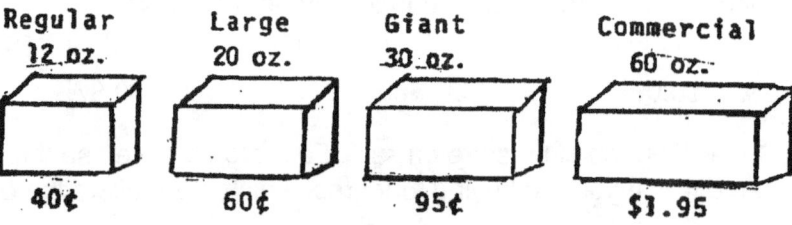

    A NEW IDEA in savings.
    A savings plan paying
    8% per annum.
    Minimum investment: $500

24. A college loan fund provides money for educational expenses. The terms of loan are as follows: No interest is charged on money borrowed while the student is in school. After the student leaves school, interest at the rate of 5% per year is charged on the total amount borrowed.
    If a student had borrowed $3800 from the fund, how much interest will he owe one year after graduation?

    A. $150   B. $190   C. $3950   D. $3990

25. A bank's interest rate on regular passbook savings accounts is 6% per annum payable quarterly.
    If you open an account with $200, how much interest will you earn the first 3 months?

    A. $1.00   B. $3.00   C. $12.00   D. $30.00

26. You buy a car for $3000 - $500 down, balance in 36 equal payments. The finance charge is 10% per year on the original unpaid balance for 3 years.
    What is the amount of interest you pay?

    A. $250   B. $300   C. $500   D. $750

27. Barbara earned $1300 as a lifeguard at a summer resort. She spent $400 and put the remainder in a savings account. The savings plan paid interest semi-annually at the rate of 6% per annum.
    At the end of six months, how much was in Barbara's savings account?

    A. $54   B. $78   C. $927   D. $954

[Ability No. 7. *Solve purchase problems involving sales tax,* (Questions 28-32)]

Questions 28-32.

DIRECTIONS: Information on how to figure the State Sales Tax is provided in the table below. Refer to this table as you do Questions 28-32.

STATE SALES TAX	
Amount of Purchase	Tax
10¢-25¢	1¢
26¢-50¢	2¢
51¢-75¢	3¢
76¢-$1.00	4¢
$1.01-$1.25	5¢
The tax is 4¢ on each whole dollar above $1. The tax on part of a dollar can be found from the scale above.	

28. The menu price of the Fisherman's Net is $6.50. What is the cost of the dinner after adding the sales tax?

    A. 24¢   B. 26¢   C. $6.74   D. $6.76

29. The State Sales Tax is applied to motel and hotel room charges. Some cities also assess a 1% Resort Tax on room charges.
    If a room rents for $40 per day, what is the TOTAL weekly charge for this room, including the sales and resort taxes?

    A. $2.00   B. $42.00   C. $294.00   D. $294.11

30. You buy a power drill on sale (see ad). How much do you pay for it, including the sales tax?
   A. $3.12
   B. $10.28
   C. $13.51
   D. $13.52

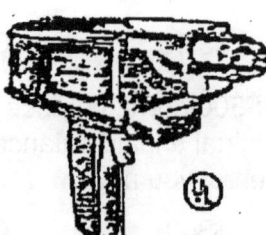

31. The State sales tax on new cars is 4%. the sticker price of a car including extras, title, transportation, and dealer preparation is $35,000. What is the TOTAL cost of the car, including sales tax?
   A. $1,400   B. $35,140   C. $36,200   D. $36,400

32. A new van costs $28,500. Trader Vic is offering a $4,500 end-of-year discount on this van. If you buy the van on sale, you will also have a savings on the sales tax you pay. How much is the TOTAL savings, discount plus savings on sales tax?
   A. $180   B. $960   C. $4,680   D. $5,460

Ability No. 8. *Solve purchase problems involving discounts* (Questions 33-36)]

33. Jeans are on sale. How much would you save on 2 pairs?
   A. $5
   B. $10
   C. $20
   D. $30

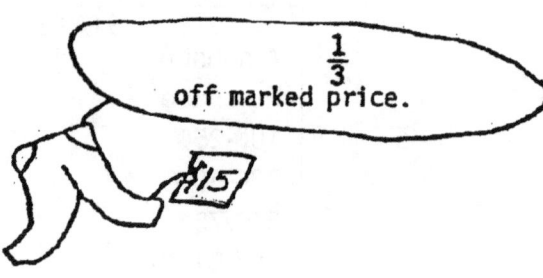

34. A sporting goods store is giving a 20% discount on all tennis equipment. What would be the total bill, before tax, on the following items?
   A. $5.80
   B. $31.20
   C. $33.20
   D. $39.00

   Tennis racket $25
   Can tennis balls. . . $ 4
   Football. $10

35. A store is having an Anniversary Sale. For details, refer to the table below. What would be the sale price of a sofa which regularly sells for $258?
   A. $77.40
   B. $180.60
   C. $206.40
   D. $258.00

STOREWIDE DISCOUNTS		
10% discount on purchases from $10-$100	20% discount on purchases from $101-$200	30% discount on purchases over $200

36. The following ad was run for a going-out-of-business sale. Altogether, how much would you have to pay for a shirt, a pair of jeans, and a sweater?

LAST CHANCE BARGAINS		
Shirts	– reg. $10	1/4 off
Jeans	– reg. $15	1/3 off
Hats	– reg. $6	1/2 off
Sweaters	– reg. $24	1/3 off
Belts	– reg. $7.50	1/4 off

   A. $15.50
   B. $29.50
   C. $33.50
   D. $49.00

36.____

[Ability No, 9. *Solve problems involving measurement.* (Questions 37-40)]

Questions 37-38.

DIRECTIONS: Use this table with Problems 37 and 38.

```
12 inches = 1 foot
3 feet = 1 yard
1760 yards = 1 mile
5280 feet = 1 mile
```

37. Agnes plans to make new curtains for her living room. She estimates that it will take 55 inches of material for each curtain panel. About how many yards of material should she buy to make 8 of the panels?

   A. 1 1/2 yards   B. 13 yards   C. 14 yards   D. 37 yards

37.____

38. Ten (10) laps around the school track is one mile. What is the distance around the track?

   A. 176 yards
   B. 528 yards
   C. 17,600 yards
   D. 52,800 yards

38.____

Questions 39-40.

DIRECTIONS: Use this table with Problems 39 and 40.

```
1 centimeter = 10 millimeters
1 meter = 100 centimeters
1 kilometer = 1000 meters
```

39. About how much shelf space is needed to store 4 boxes with widths of 30.4 cm?

   A. 11 meters
   B. 21 meters
   C. .30 meter
   D. 121.60 meters

39.____

40. Seventy-five (75) sections of pipe are laid to connect the Haningers' house to the nearest water main. If the distance between the Haningers' house and the water main is 2.28 kilometers, how long is each section of pipe?

   A. 3.04 meters   B. 30.4 meters   C. 34 meters   D. 684 meters

40.____

[Ability No. 9. *Solve problems involving the area of a rectangle* (Questions 41-44)]

41. A carpet-cleaning company figures the cost of cleaning carpets on a sliding scale (see table). A school has 40 yards of carpeted hallways. The halls are 3-1/3 yards wide. How much per square yard will the company charge the school to clean the hallways?

CHARGES FOR CLEANING CARPET	
Number Sq. Yards	Cost/Sq. Yard
5-50	$3.25
51-100	$3.10
101-150	$2.85
over 150	$2.50

    A. $3.25
    B. $3.10
    C. $2.85
    D. $2.50

    41.____

42. A company has a 2.5-meter-high wire fence around its equipment storage area. The area measures 30 meters by 50 meters. The company plans to add extra security to the area by stringing 3 strands of barbed wire along the top of the fence.
    How many meters of barbed wire does the company need for this job?

    A. 160 meters   B. 240 meters   C. 480 meters   D. 960 meters

    42.____

43. One liter of paint will cover about 50 square meters. How many liters of paint should you buy to cover a rectangular area which measures 20.1 meters by 28.9 meters?

    A. 1 liter   B. 11 liters   C. 12 liters   D. 581 liters

    43.____

44. You are going to bake cookies in a 9-inch by 12-inch pan. How many cookies will you have if you cut them into 3-inch squares?

    A. 9   B. 12   C. 27   D. 36

    44.____

[Ability No. 10. *Solve problems involving capacity* (Questions 45-48)]

Questions 45-46.

DIRECTIONS: Use the following table with Problems 45 and 46.

| 3 teaspoons = 1 tablespoon |
| 16 tablespoons = 1 cup |
| 2 cups = 1 pint |
| 2 pints = 1 quart |
| 4 quarts = 1 gallon |

45. Adam buys a new 15-gallon aquarium. The directions say to put no more than 13.5 gallons of water in the tank. This allows an air space at the top and room for decorations and equipment. Adam doesn't have a gallon container, but he does have a quart jar. How many quarts are needed to fill the tank to the specified level?

    A. 3.375   B. 3.75   C. 54   D. 60

    45.____

46. Bret is preparing an insecticide solution to spray on his fruit trees. The directions are to mix 3 tablespoons of the insecticide concentrate with each gallon of water, Bret should add how much insecticide concentrate to 20 gallons of water?

    A. 1 1/4 cups   B. 3 3/4 cups   C. 5 1/3 cups   D. 6 2/3 cups

    46.____

Questions 47-48.

DIRECTIONS: Use the following table with Problems 47 and 48.

```
250 milliliters = 1 metric cup
  4 metric cups = 1 liter
1000 milliliters = 1 liter
```

47. The ratio for mixing oil and gas for a certain motor is 200 ml of outboard motor oil to 3 liters of gasoline. Using this ratio, one liter of motor oil should be mixed with what quantity of gasoline? 47.____

    A. 5 liters   B. 15 liters   C. 66 liters   D. 600 liters

48. A big economy bottle of Cheer-Up contains 2.5 liters. About *how many* 150-ml servings are there in one bottle? 48.____

    A. 6   B. 17   C. 60   D. 167

[Ability No. 11. *Solve problems involving weight* (Questions 49-52)]

Questions 49-50.

DIRECTIONS: Use the following table with Problems 49 and 50.

```
  16 ounces = 1 pound
2000 pounds = 1 ton
```

49. A farmer has a grove of 1000 fruit trees. If he plans to use 5 pounds of fertilizer per tree, *how many* tons of fertilizer should he buy? 49.____

    A. 200 pounds   B. 2.5 tons
    C. 5 tons   D. 10,000 pounds

50. Hamburger patties for Mac's King are made by a machine. The machine is set to make 100 patties out of 20 pounds of hamburger. Patties at this setting of the machine weigh how much? 50.____

    A. Exactly 3 ozs.
    B. A little more than 3 ozs.
    C. A little less than 5 ozs.
    D. Exactly 5 ozs.

Questions 51-52.

DIRECTIONS: Use the following table with Problems 51 and 52.

```
1000 miligrams  = 1 gram
1000 grams      = 1 kilogram
1000 kilograms  = 1 metric ton
```

51. A shipping label contains the following information (see figure). What is the TOTAL weight of just the boat, motor, and trailer?

    A. 1.25 metric tons
    B. 2.4 metric tons
    C. 2.5 metric tons
    D. 2.7 metric tons

Item	Weight
Boat	1350 kilograms
Motor	425 kilograms
Trailer	725 kilograms
Packing	200 kilograms

    51.____

52. Chet has a 3-metric-ton truck. That is, his truck can carry a load of 3 metric tons. Chet has a freight order to carry 60 surfboards weighing 40 kilograms each.
    The weight of this load is how much below the load capacity of his truck?

    A. 600 kilograms
    B. 1400 kilograms
    C. 1600 kilograms
    D. 2400 kilograms

    52.____

[Ability No. 12. *Find the information in graphs and tables* (Questions 53-59)]

53. This is an advertisement for a tire sale (see figure). How much does a H78-15 sized tire cost on sale?

    A. $39.60
    B. $40.80
    C. $46.41
    D. $75.21

TUBELESS WHITEWALL SIZE	REGULAR PRICE EACH	SALE PRICE EACH	PLUS F.E.T. EACH
A78-13	$46	27.60	2.06
C78-14	$55	33.00	2.33
E78-14	$59	35.40	2.55
F78-14	$63	37.80	2.82
G78-14	$66	39.60	2.97
H78-14	$68	40.80	3.24
G78-15	$68	40.80	3.03
H78-15	$72	43.20	3.21
J78-15†	$77	46.20	3.32
L78-15†	$80	48.00	3.46

    NO TRADE-IN NEEDED. *† pol yester cord plies.*

    53.____

54. Each day the National Weather Service reports the low and high temperatures and the precipitation for selected cities.
    In this report, the maximum temperature in the state was reported in which city? (See chart)

    A. Tallahassee
    B. Jacksonville
    C. Miami
    D. Orlando

    Florida Cities

City	High	Low	Precip
Apalachicola	87	73	.31
Crestview	91	69	...
Daytona Bch	87	71	...
Ft Lauderdale	88	77	...
Ft Myers	90	74	...
Gainesville	90	66	...
Homestead	91	68	...
Jacksonville	84	63	.33
Key West	89	79	...
Lakeland	93	73	...

    54.____

Miami	89	75	...
Orlando	94	74	...
Pensacola	88	80	...
Sarasota	89	69	...
Tallahassee	83	69	1.23
Tampa	91	75	...
Vero Beach	90	71	...
Wst Plm Bch	90	71	...

55. A bank prepared a graph to help its customers plan their budgets (see figure). Following the bank's recommendations. if you earn $80 weekly, about how much should you spend on a car?

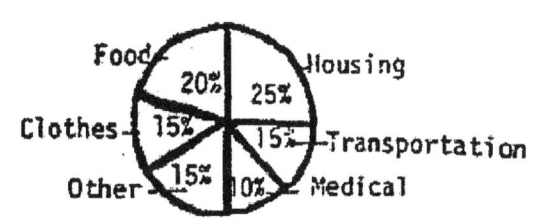

A. $8
B. $12
C. $15
D. $120

55.____

56. A consumers' group prepares reports on changes in the cost of selected items. This report shows the changes in the cost of coffee during a one-year period. According to this report, the cost of a pound of coffee rose how much from April 1 to July 1?

A. $0.50
B. $1.00
C. $1.50
D. $2.50

56.____

57. A certain type of cereal provides the following vitamins and minerals. If you ate 2 ounces of the cereal, you would have what percent of your daily need of iron?

A. 4%
B. 15%
C. 30%
D. 166%

PERCENTAGE OF U.S. RECOM- MENDED DAILY ALLOWANCES (U.S.R.D.A.)	
	1 oz.
Protein	4
Vitamin C	45
Vitamin B	45
Niacin	45
Calcium	2
Iron	15
Zinc	10

57.____

58. The graph below provides a breakdown of retail sales for 2007. Based on this data, at least, what percent of the total retail sales are spent on items related to cars?

   A. 7.3%
   B. 16.6%
   C. 19.3%
   D. 26.6%

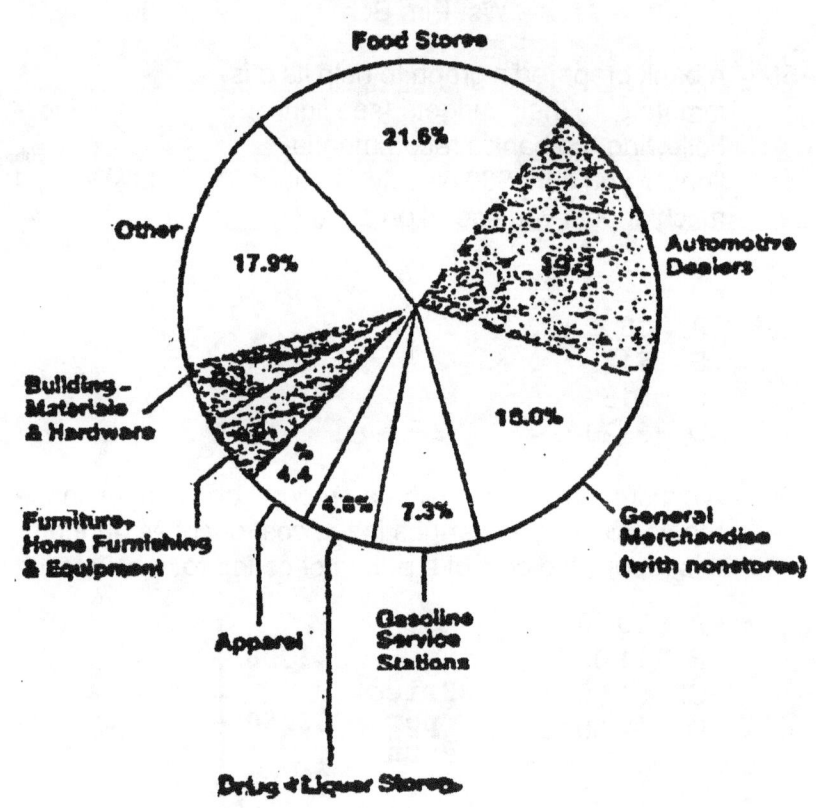

58.____

59. Riverview High School prepared a monthly report on absences. During which week was there the *GREATEST* increase in the number of students absent from school?

   A. First
   B. Second
   C. Third
   D. Fourth

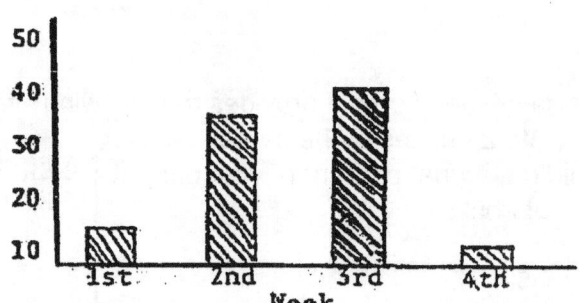

59.____

EDUCATION LEVEL ATTAINED BY HIGH SCHOOL STUDENTS ENTERING HIGH SCHOOL IN 2010 AND 2011

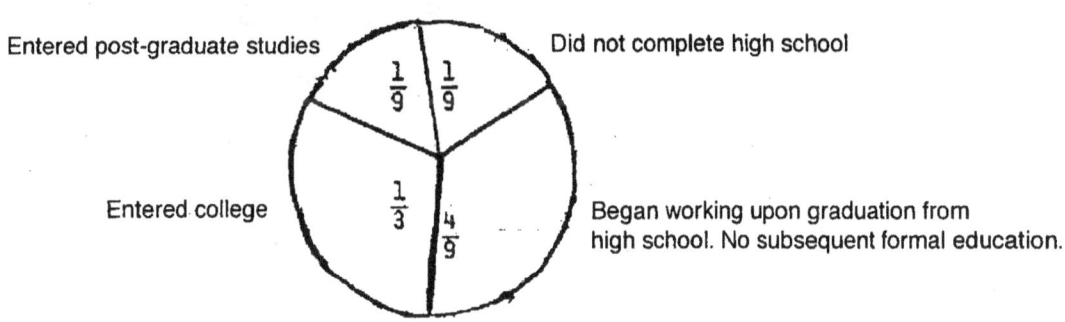

ENTERING CLASS OF 2010 – TOTAL OF 117

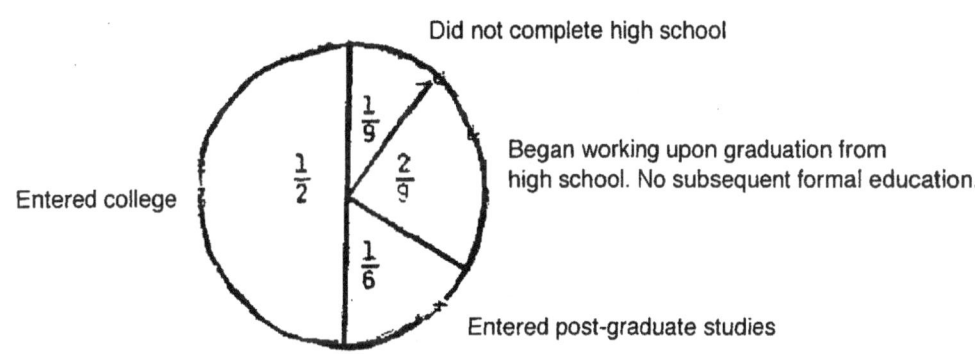

ENTERING CLASS OF 2011 – TOTAL OF 180

60. The total number of students from both classes who went to work immediately after high school graduation was   60._____

    A. 33   B. 40   C. 92   D. 129

KEY (CORRECT ANSWERS)

1.	B	16.	C	31.	D	46.	B
2.	C	17.	B	32.	C	47.	B
3.	B	18.	B	33.	B	48.	B
4.	C	19.	D	34.	C	49.	B
5.	C	20.	A	35.	B	50.	B
6.	C	21.	B	36.	C	51.	C
7.	C	22.	A	37.	B	52.	A
8.	A	23.	D	38.	A	53.	C
9.	C	24.	B	39.	B	54.	D
10.	D	25.	B	40.	B	55.	B
11.	B	26.	D	41.	C	56.	B
12.	D	27.	C	42.	C	57.	C
13.	C	28.	D	43.	C	58.	D
14.	D	29.	C	44.	B	59.	B
15.	A	30.	B	45.	C	60.	C

MATHEMATICS
SOLUTIONS TO PROBLEMS

1. Answer: B. 6 hours, 25 minutes

    ### SOLUTION
    1. 7:45 A.M. to 8:00 A.M.   =   15 min.
    2. 8:00 A.M. to 2:00 P.M.   =   6 hours
    3. 2:00 P.M. to 2:10 P.M.   =   10 min.
    4. (Adding)   6 hours, 25 min

2. Answer: C. 4 hours, 50 minutes

    ### SOLUTION
    1. Look under the heading, Departures. The next bus to Tallahassee is scheduled to leave at 1:20 P.M.
    2. 8:30 A.M. to 1:20 P.M. = 4 hours, 50 minutes

3. Answer: B. 1 day 17 hours 10 minutes

    ### SOLUTION
    1. 3:20 P.M., 13 Nov to 3:20 P.M., 15 Nov = 2 days = 48 hrs
    2. 8:30 A.M. to 3:20 P.M. = 6 hours, 50 minutes
    3. 48 hours - 6 hours, 50 minutes = 41 hours, 10 minutes
    4. 41 hours, 10 minutes = 1 day, 17 hours, 10 minutes

4. Answer: C. April 1, 2013   4.____

    ### SOLUTION
    1. 30 months = 2 years, 6 months
    2. 10/1/10 + 2 years = 10/1/12
    3. 10/1 + 6 months = 4/1/13
    4. That is, 4/1/13

5. Answer: C. $29.52   5.____

    ### SOLUTION
    $25.00   (1 ten, 3 five-dollar bills)
     2.00   (2 one-dollar bills)
     1.00   (2 50-cent pieces)
     1.25   (5 quarters)
      .20   (2 dimes)
      .05   (1 nickel)
      .02   (2 pennies)
    $29.52

6. Answer: C. Six dollars - two quarters - two pennies   6.____

    ### SOLUTION
    1. $10.00 - $3.48 = $6.52
    2. $ 6.52 = six dollars, two quarters - two pennies

27

7. Answer: C. 2 pennies, 1 nickel, 1 dime, 1 quarter, 2 dollar bills, 2 five-dollar bills

SOLUTION
1. $20.00 - $7.58 = $12.42
2. $12.42 = 2 pennies, 1 nickel, 1 dime, 1 quarter, two dollar bills, 2 five-dollar bills

8. Answer: A.

SOLUTION
A. $40.00 - $28.73 = $11.27
B. $11.27 = one ten-dollar bill, one dollar, 1 quarter, 2 pennies (Answer A)

9. Answer: C. 50

SOLUTION
1. Divide 685 by 14, thus:

2.
$$14 \overline{)\begin{array}{r} 48 \\ 685 \\ \underline{56} \\ 125 \\ \underline{112} \\ 13 \end{array}}$$

3. 48 13/14 is nearest to 50

10. Answer: D. 800

SOLUTION
1. 16 X 2 (2 stories) = 32 classrooms
2. Multiply 32 X 25, thus:

3.
$$\begin{array}{r} 32 \\ \times 25 \\ \hline 160 \\ 64 \\ \hline 800 \end{array}$$

11. Answer: B. 10 hours

SOLUTION
1. Divide 30,000 by 50 = 600 (minutes)
2. 600 (minutes) divided by 60 (60 minutes to an hour) = 10 hours

12. Answer: D. 198

SOLUTION
1. 3 buckets = 45
2. 5 barrels = 105
3. 1 tub = 48/198

13. Answer: C. 127

SOLUTION

1. Add: 12 - 1 Van
    60 - 2 Coaches
    55 - 1 Bus
    ―――
    127

14. Answer: D. $6696   14.____

<u>SOLUTION</u>

1. $6200 X .08 = $496.00
2. $6200 + $496 = $6696

15. Answer: A. 23.0   15.____

<u>SOLUTION</u>

1. Divide 1436 by 62.4, thus:

2. $$62.4\overline{)1436.0}$$
    $$\,\,23.0$$
    1248
    ――――
    1880
    1872
    ――――
    8

16. Answer: C. $23.58   16.____

<u>SOLUTION</u>

1. 14.5 X .69 = $10.01
2. 23.0 X .59 = 13.57
3. (Adding) $23.58
   WORK:

1.   14.5   2.   23
     X   .69   X .59
        ――――   ――――
        1305   207
        870   115
        ――――――   ――――――
        10.005 = $10.01 $13.57

17. Answer: B. 27.6 inches   17.____

<u>SOLUTION</u>

1. 30 X .08 = 2.4
2. 30 - 2.4 = 27.6 (Answer B)

18. Answer: B. $0.69   18.____

<u>SOLUTION</u>

1. $29.90 + $1.87 = $31.77
2. $5.41 X 6 = $32.46
3. $32.46 - 31.77 = $ .69

19. Answer: D. Car Care Center - Regular price $40. Sale $29.50.   19.____

    A. $40 (1st tire)　　　　　　　SOLUTION
         $20 (2nd tire)　　　　　　B.　$40 X 1/4 = $10
         $40 (3rd tire)　　　　　　　　$40 - $10 = $30
         $20 (4th tire)　　　　　　　　$30 X 4 = $120
         $120

    C. $40 X 3 = 120　　　　　　D.　　　$29.50
        4th tire =　 0　　　　　　　　　　X 4
                $120　　　　　　　　　　　　$118.00

20. Answer: A. nothing

                         SOLUTION
   1.　　$69.96　　　　　　　　2.　　$11.99
      +　 1.98　　　　　　　　　　　x　6
      　$71.94　　　　　　　　　　　$71.94

21. Answer: B. Large

                         SOLUTION

   1.　$.40 ÷ 12 = .03 1/3
   2.　.60 ÷ 20 = .03
   3.　.95 ÷ 30 = .03 1/4
   4.　.95 ÷ 60 = .03 1/4

22. Answer: A. $ .10

                         SOLUTION

   1.　4 dozens = 48
   2.　48 = 6 x .65 = $3.90
   3.　48 = 4 X .95 = $3.80
   4.　$3.90 - $3.80 = $0.10 (saving)

23. Answer: D. $864

                         SOLUTION

   1.　$800 X .08 = $ 64
   2.　$800 + $64 = $864

24. Answer: B. $190

                         SOLUTION

   1.　$3800 X .05 = $190

25. Answer: B. $3.00

                         SOLUTION

   A.　12 months / 3 months = 1/4
   B.　1/4 X .06 = .015
   C.　$200 X .015 = $3.00

26. Answer: D. $750

SOLUTION
1. $3000 - $500 = $2500 (unpaid balance)
2. $2500 X .10 X 3 = $750

27. Answer: C. $927

SOLUTION
1. $1300 - $400 = $900
2. 6% per annum = 3% for six months
3. $900 X .03 = $27
4. $900 + $27 = $927

28. Answer: D. $6.76

SOLUTION
1. Tax on first dollar   = $.04
2. Tax on five whole dollars =   .20
3. Tax on .50   =   .02
4. Total tax   =   .26
5. Cost of dinner   = $6.76

29. Answer: C. $ 294.00

SOLUTION
1. Daily sales tax = 40 X .04 = $1.60
2. Daily resort tax = 40 X .01 = $ .40
3. $40 + $1.60 + $.40 = $42.00/day. Then, (42)(7) = $294.00/week

30. Answer: B. $10.28

SOLUTION
1. Sales Tax: On $9   = $ .36
             On $.88 = $ .04
                       $ .40
2. $9.88 + $.40 = $10.28

31. Answer: D. $36,400

SOLUTION
1. $35,000 X .04 = $1,400
2. $35,000 + $1,400 = $36,400

32. Answer: C. $4,680

SOLUTION
1. $4,500 savings   = $4,500
2. +4,500 x .04   = $180
3. $4,500 + $180   = $4,680 (total savings)

33. Answers B. $10

   SOLUTION
   1. $15. X 1/3 = $5
   2. 2 X $5 = $10

34. Answer: B. $31.20

   SOLUTION
   1. $25 X .80 = $20.00
   2. $4 X .80 = 3.20
   3. $10 .80 = 10.00 (no "discount; not tenolsr equipment)
      $33.20

35. Answer: B. $180.60

   SOLUTION
   1. $258 X .70 = $180.60

36. Answer: C. $33.50

   SOLUTION
   1. Shirt: $10 X .75 = $ 7.50
   2. Jeans: $15 X 2/3 = $10.00
   3. Sweater: $24 X 2/3 = $16.00
                          $33.50

37. Answer: B. 13 yards

   SOLUTION
   1. 8 X 55 = 440 inches
   2. 440 ÷ 36 = 12 8/36 = 12 2/9 yards

38. Answer: A. 176 yards

   SOLUTION
   1. 1760 yards 10 = 176 yards

39. Answer: B. 1.21 meters

   SOLUTION
   1. 4 X 30.4 cm = 121.6 cm
   2. 121.6 cm = 1.216 meters

40. Answer: B. 30.4 meters

   SOLUTION
   1. 2.28 kilometers = 2280 meters
   2. 2280 ÷ 75 = 30.4 meters

WORK:
$$75 \overline{)\begin{array}{r} 30.4 \\ 2280.0 \\ \underline{225} \\ 300 \\ \underline{300} \end{array}}$$

41. Answer: C. $2.85   41.____

SOLUTION
1. Area of rectangle = 1 X W
2. 40 X 3 1/3 = 40 X 10/3 = 400/3 = 133,33 square yards

42. Answer: C. 480 meters   42.____

SOLUTION

A.
```
         50
    ┌─────────┐
 30 │    .    │ 30
    └─────────┘
         50
```
Equipment Storage Area

B. 30 + 50 + 30 + 50 = 160 meters/strands
Then, (160)(3) = 480 meters for 3 strands.

43. Answer: C. 12 liters   43.____

SOLUTION
1. 20.1 X 28.9 = 580.89 square meters
2. 580.89 ÷ 50 = 11.61 liters or 12 liters

WORK:
$$\begin{array}{r} 20.0 \\ 28.9 \\ \hline 1809 \\ 1608 \\ 402 \\ \hline 580.89 \end{array}$$

$$50 \overline{)\begin{array}{r} 11.61 \\ 580.89 \\ \underline{50} \\ 80 \\ \underline{50} \\ 308 \\ \underline{300} \\ 89 \\ \underline{50} \\ 39 \end{array}}$$

44. Answer: B. 12   44.____

SOLUTION
1. 3 in.sq.= 9 sq.in.
2. 9 X 12 = 108
3. 108 9 = 12

45. Answer: C. 54   45.____

SOLUTION
1. 13.5 X 4 = 54.0

46. Answer: B. 3 3/4 cups   46.____

SOLUTION
1. 3 tablespoons ÷ 16 = 3/16 cup

2. $\cancel{20}^{\,5} \times \dfrac{3}{\cancel{16}_{\,4}} = 15/4 = 3\ 3/4$ cups

47. Answer: B. 15 liters   47.____

SOLUTION

1. 200 ml = 1/5 liter
2. 1/5 liter motor oil is required for 3 liters of gasoline
3. Therefore, 1 liter will require 5X3 liters of gasoline or 15 liters

48. Answer: B. 17   48.____

SOLUTION

1. 2.5 liters = 2,500 ml
2. 2500 ÷ 150 = 16.60

49. Answer: B. 2.5 tons   49.____

SOLUTION

1. 1000 X 5 = 5000
2. 5000 ÷ 2000. = 2.5 tons

50. Answer: B. a little more tnan 3 ozs.   50.____

SOLUTION

1. 20 X 16 = 320 ozs.
2. 320 ÷ 100 = 3.2

51. Answer: C. 2.5 metric tons   51.____

SOLUTION

A. Boat: 1350 kg
B. Motor: 425 kg
C. Trailer: <u>725 kg</u>
          2500 kg
D. 2500 kg = 2.5 metric tons

52. Answer: A. 600 kilograms   52.____

SOLUTION

1. 60 X 40 = 2400 kg
2. 3 X 1000 = 3000 kg
3. 3000 kg - 240.0 kg = 600 kg

53. Answer: C. $46.41   53.____

SOLUTION

1. $43.20 + $3.21 = $46.41

54. Answer: D. Orlando

SOLUTION

1. Orlando - 94° (by inspection)

55. Answer: B. $12

SOLUTION

1. Transportation - 15%
2. $80 X .15 = $12

56. Answer: B. $1.00

SOLUTION

1. April 1 - $1.50
2. July 1 - $2.50
3. $2.50 - $1.50 = $1.00

57. Answer: C. 30%

SOLUTION

1. 15% X 2 = 30%

58. Answer: D. 26.6%

SOLUTION

1. Automotive dealers - 19.3%
2. Gasoline service stations - 7.3%/26.6%

59. Answer: B. Second

SOLUTION

1. Second (by inspection)

60. Answer: C. 92

SOLUTION

1. $\dfrac{4}{9} \times \overset{13}{\cancel{117}} = 52$ (2010)

2. $\dfrac{2}{9} \times \overset{20}{\cancel{180}} = 40$ (2011)

3. 52+40 = 92

BASIC MATHEMATICS
EXAMINATION SECTION
TEST 1

DIRECTIONS: Each question or incomplete statement is followed by several suggested answers or completions. Select the one that BEST answers the question or completes the statement. *PRINT THE LETTER OF THE CORRECT ANSWER IN THE SPACE AT THE RIGHT.*

1. Add: 5,796 + 6 + 243 + 24

   A. 6,069   B. 6,079   C. 6,169   D. 6,179

2. Subtract: 8,007 - 6,898

   A. 1,109   B. 1,119   C. 1,209   D. 2,109

3. Multiply: 3,876 x 904

   A. 364,344   B. 3,493,904
   C. 3,494,904   D. 3,503,904

4. Divide: $76\sqrt{58,976}$

   A. 775   B. 776   C. 786   D. 876

5. Combine: (+4) + (-3) - (-7)

   A. -6   B. +6   C. +8   D. +14

6. Simplify: [(-8) x (-6)] ÷ (-3)

   A. -16   B. -14   C. +14   D. +16

7. Add: 1 3/5 + 3 7/8

   A. 4 10/40   B. 4 10/13   C. 4 19/40   D. 5 19/40

8. Subtract: 4 3/8 - 2 2/3

   A. 1 17/24   B. 2 1/24   C. 2 1/5   D. 2 17/24

9. Multiply: 3 2/3 x 5 1/2

   A. 15 1/3   B. 16 1/3   C. 20 1/6   D. 21 1/6

10. Divide: $7\frac{1}{2} \div 2\frac{1}{4}$

    A. 3/10   B. 3 1/3   C. 3 1/2   D. 16 7/8

11. Add: 434.7 + .04 + 7.107

    A. .441847   B. .442207   C. 441.847   D. 442.207

12. Subtract: 986.4 - 34.87

    A. 6.377 B. 63.77 C. 951.53 D. 9,515.3

13. Multiply: 5.96
              x87.4

    A. 51.0904 B. 52.0904 C. 510.904 D. 520.904

14. Divide: $.034\overline{)6.698}$

    A. 19.2 B. 19.7 C. 192 D. 197

15. Add: $.7 + \frac{1}{2}$

    A. .12 B. 1.2 C. 7/2 D. 15/2

16. What is 5.5% of 75?

    A. 4.125 B. 13.65 C. 41.25 D. 412.5

17. 12 is what percent of 6?

    A. $\frac{1}{2}$% B. 5% C. 50% D. 200%

18. 14 is 28% of _____.

    A. 2 B. 5 C. 50 D. 500

19. A record player sells for $92.00. It is discounted 15% for a special sale. What is the sale price?

    A. $13.80 B. $68.20 C. $77.00 D. $78.20

20. Table A - Acme Mortgage Company
    $320 Loan - 3/4 of 1% Interest

Month	Payment	Principal Paid/Month	Interest Paid/Month
1	$ 27.98	$ 25.58	$ 2.40
2	27.98	25.77	2.21
3	27.98	25.96	2.02
4	27.98	26.15	1.83
5	27.98	26.35	1.63
6	27.98	26.55	1.43
7	27.98	26.75	1.23
8	27.98	26.95	1.03
9	27.98	27.15	.83
10	27.98	27.35	.63
11	27.98	27.56	.42
12	27.93	27.77	.16
Total	$335.82	$ 320.00	$ 15.82

Acme Mortgage Company charges 3/4 of 1% (.0075) on the unpaid balance per month. Bowman Mortgage Company charges 9% per year on the total loan. Which company charges the LEAST amount of interest on a $320 loan held for one year?

- A. Acme charges the least amount.
- B. Bowman charges the least amount.
- C. Acme and Bowman charge the same.
- D. Insufficient information to determine.

21. Percent of Auto Insurance Discounts for High School Students with Certain Grade Point Averages

Policy Coverage	Grade Point Averages Percent of Discount		
	A	B	C
Liability	33 1/3%	33 1/3%	10%
Comprehensive	20%	10%	-
Collision	25%	20%	-

Frank Verna has a B average. The regular 6-month amounts to be paid for insurance before discount follow:

Liability	$18.00
Comprehensive	$20.00
Collision	$60.00
Total	$98.00

How much does Frank pay for insurance for 6 months?

- A. $20.00
- B. $58.00
- C. $78.00
- D. $156.00

22. Mr. Martinez had a fire in his home. Repairing the damage will cost about $900. His home is valued at $14,000 and is insured for $12,000. Mr. Martinez had paid $32.00 a year for ten years for his insurance. The insurance company has agreed to pay the full amount of the claim ($900).
Which of the following statements are TRUE?
- I. The amount of the claim is more than what has been paid to the company.
- II. The insurance company should pay $14,000 for this claim.
- III. If the house had been completely burned, the insurance company would pay $14,000.
- IV. The maximum claim Mr. Martinez could collect is $12,000

The CORRECT answer is:

- A. I, II
- B. I, III
- C. II, III
- D. I, IV

23. When two coins are tossed, what is the chance that both will be heads? 1 in
- A. 1
- B. 2
- C. 3
- D. 4

24. If 4 teams are in a football league, how many games are necessary to allow each team to play every team one time? _____ games.
- A. 6
- B. 9
- C. 12
- D. 16

25. Five people donated money to the Red Cross. The donations were: $52.00, $76.00, $18.00, $94.00, and $120.00.
    What was the AVERAGE donation?

    A. $70   B. $72   C. $76   D. $360

26. From the following statements, determine the CORRECT conclusion.
    I. If Lauraine is a red-head, then Lauraine is hot-tempered.
    II. Lauraine is not hot-tempered.
    The CORRECT answer is:

    A. Lauraine is a red-head.
    B. Lauraine is not a red-head.
    C. Lauraine could be a red-head.
    D. All red-heads are hot-tempered.

27. The graph represents the way the Jones family spends its money (budget). What is the monthly income if they are spending $4080 per year for food?
    A. $1,020
    B. $1,360
    C. $4,080
    D. $16,320

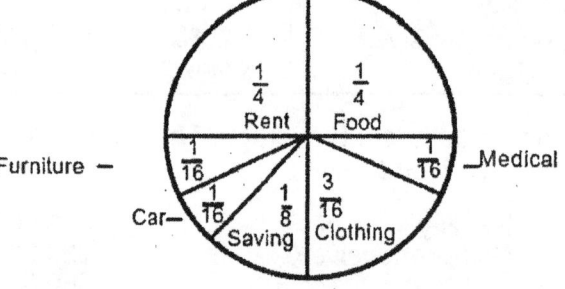

28.

	S	M	T	W	T	F	S
Charlie Simms	?	8	8	8	8	8	3
Jim Chow	2	9	8	8	9	9	4

Time and one-half is paid on Saturdays and for hours worked beyond 8 hours each day. Double-time is paid for Sunday work.
Mr. Simms would have to work how many hours on Sunday to earn as much as Mr. Chow?

    Regular time - $2.00/hour
    Time and one-half - $3.00/hour
    Double time - $4.00/hour

_____ hours.

    A. 2   B. 5   C. 6   D. 20

29. Jane Gunther wrote checks for these items:
    $16.95 for a hair dryer
    $125.50 for a car payment
    $33.68 for television repair
    $21.59 for a dress
    Jane had a beginning check balance (before she wrote the checks) of $351.76. She also deposited $41.50 into her account.
    After the checks were written and the deposit made, what was her new balance?

    A. $154.04   B. $195.54   C. $196.54   D. $239.22

30. Given the formula I = PRT:
If I = 24, R = .05, T = 3, find P.

    A. .00625   B. 1.6   C. 3.6   D. 160.0

31. Fencing is needed to enclose a piece of land 26 meters on a side.
How much fencing is needed?
_____ meters.
    A. 52
    B. 98
    C. 104
    D. 676

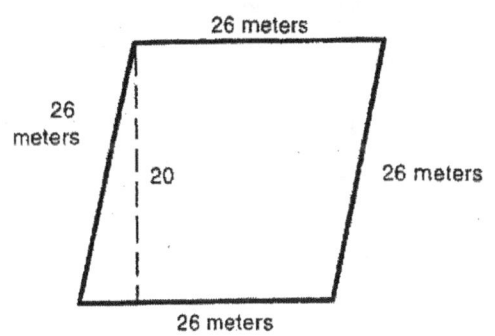

32. The area of figure A is 12 square units, and the area of B is 18 square units.
What is the area of figure C?
_____ square units.
    A. 16
    B. 16 1/2
    C. 17
    D. 17 1/2

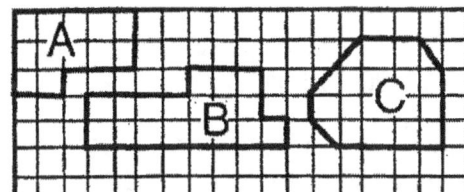

33. Using a 3 gallon spray can with a mixture rate of 1 teaspoon of insecticide per quart of water and an application rate of 1 gallon of mixture per 100 square feet, how much water and how much insecticide will be needed to spray an 85 feet by 10 feet lawn?
_____ teaspoons of insecticide and _____ gallons of water.

    A. 34; 8 1/2   B. 34; 11   C. 17; 8 1/2   D. 24; 6

34. Bill Mata will carpet his living room which has the following dimensions. If Bill pays $6.00 per square yard for the carpet, how much will it cost to carpet his living room?
(9 square feet = 1 square yard)
    A. $192
    B. $216
    C. $1,728
    D. $1,944

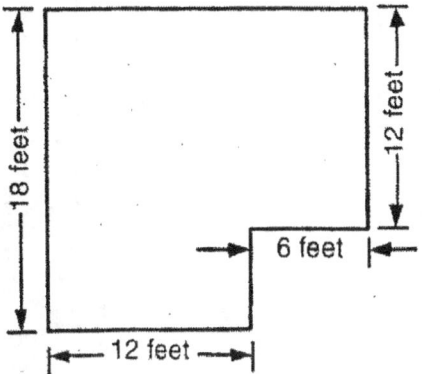

35. A cube is painted red and then divided into 27 smaller cubes. How many of the smaller cubes are painted on one side only?
    A. 4
    B. 6
    C. 8
    D. 10

36. John and Frank wish to pour a cement walk 108 feet long, 4 feet wide, and 3 inches deep.
    If ready-mix concrete can be delivered on weekdays for $19.50 a cubic yard and on weekends for $22.50 a cubic yard, how much would they save on the complete job if they decide on Thursday rather than on the weekend? (1 cubic yard = 27 cubic feet)

    A. $3.00   B. $12.00   C. $36.00   D. $78.00

37. Antifreeze may be purchased in different size containers for different prices:
    8 oz. can - 43¢
    10 oz. can - 51¢
    12 oz. can - 62¢
    If exactly 15 pints of antifreeze are needed, how many cans of each size are needed for the cost to be minimum? (16 oz. = 1 pint)

    A. 12 - 10 oz. cans and 10 - 12 oz. cans
    B. 24 - 10 oz. cans
    C. 18 - 12 oz. cans and 3-8 oz. cans
    D. 20 - 12 oz. cans

38. From the graph, assuming the growth rate in the senior class is constant, how many students will be seniors in 2006?

    A. 225
    B. 250
    C. 300
    D. 375

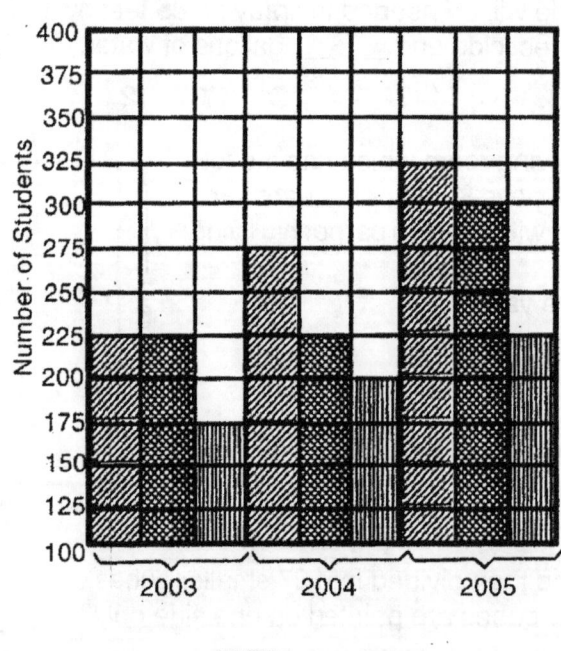

39.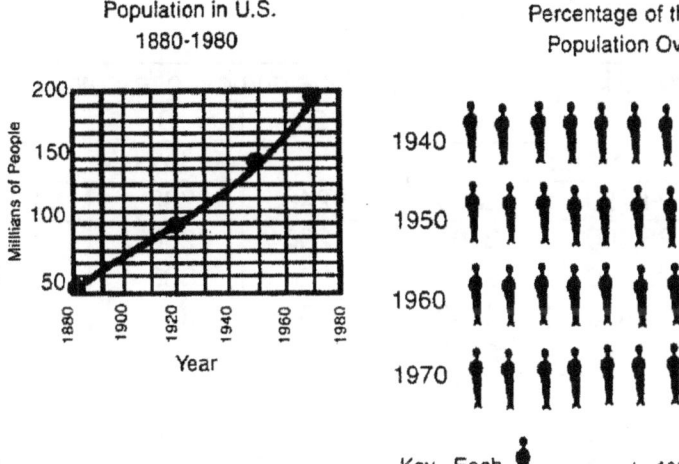

In looking at the two graphs, which of the following conclusions are TRUE?
  I. Both graphs show population growth.
  II. Both graphs cover exactly the same time period.
  III. The percentage of *over 65* population remains the same over the 1940 to 1970 period.
  IV. If you were in the retail business, you might expect greater sales to the *over 65* population in 1970 than in 1940.
  V. In the general population of about 200 million people in 1970, 24 million were over 65.
  VI. In 1920, there were only about 7 million people *over 65* out of about 100 million people.

The CORRECT answer is:

A. I, III, IV
C. II, III, VI
B. II, IV, V
D. I, IV, V

40. Jerry Martin owns a home with a market value of $180,000. Its assessed value is 25% of the market value. The tax rate is $5.00 per $100 of assessed value.
What is the amount of his tax?

A. $225.00
B. $2,250.00
C. $4,500.00
D. $6,750.00

41. You are governor of the state and you need an additional 500 million dollars in tax money. To raise the money, an increase in sales tax is required.
What information would be MOST helpful in determining the new tax rate?
  I. Average income per person in the state
  II. Number of people out of work
  III. Population of the state over 18 years of age
  IV. Birth rate in the state
  V. Percent of income spent on taxable goods
  VI. Percent of income spent on non-taxable goods
  VII. Number of people filing income tax returns

The CORRECT answer is:

A. I, IV, VI
C. V, VI
B. II, III, VII
D. I, V

42. Income Tax Table

If adjusted gross income is-		And the number of exemptions is -					
		1	2	3	4	5	6
At least	But less than	Your tax is -					
$24,500	$24,750	$2360	$1240	$230	$0	$0	$0
24,750	25,000	2400	1280	260	0	0	0
25,000	25,250	2440	1320	300	0	0	0
25,250	25,500	2480	1360	330	0	0	0
25,500	25,750	2530	1390	370	0	0	0
25,750	26,000	2570	1430	400	0	0	0
26,000	26,250	2610	1470	440	0	0	0
26,250	26,500	2650	1510	470	0	0	0
26,500	26,750	2700	1550	510	0	0	0
26,750	27,000	2740	1590	540	0	0	0
27,000	27,250	2780	1630	580	0	0	0
27,250	27,500	2820	1670	610	0	0	0
27,500	27,750	2870	1710	650	0	0	0
27,750	28,000	2910	1750	680	0	0	0
28,000	28,250	2950	1790	720	0	0	0
28,250	28,500	2990	1830	760	0	0	0
28,500	28,750	3040	1870	790	0	0	0

Jerry Ladd earned $28,390.00 during the year. To find his adjusted gross income, he must reduce the amount earned by the standard 10% deduction. He had only one exemption, himself.
How much tax did Jerry pay?

A. $1390 B. $1830 C. $2530 D. $2990

43.

Weight in Ounces	2 oz.	4 oz.	12 oz.	21 oz.
Price	5¢	7¢	15¢	24¢

Using the above table, predict the price if the weight is 32 ounces.

A. 27¢ B. 28¢ C. 29¢ D. 35¢

44. Given [(0,2), (1,4), (2,6),...(5,y)].
What is the value of y?

A. 8 B. 10 C. 12 D. 14

45. If the larger of two numbers is two and one-half times the smaller number, what fraction is the smaller of the larger?

A. 3/4 B. 4/5 C. 5/8 D. 2/5

46. John can save 75¢ a week. He has $3.75 in the bank now. How many weeks will it take him to have a total deposit of $12?

A. 16 B. 9 C. 11 D. 17

47. Using the approximation of 3.14 for pi, find the area of a circle whose diameter is 20 inches.
   _____ square inches.
   A. 31.4   B. 314   C. 628   D. 1256

47.____

48. Express .045 as a percent.
   A. 45%   B. 4.5%   C. .45%   D. .045%

48.____

49. Twenty is what percent of 50?
   A. 40   B. 60   C. 25   D. 16 2/3

49.____

50. Two hundred twenty-five percent of 160 is
   A. 80   B. 350   C. 360   D. 440

50.____

KEY (CORRECT ANSWERS)

1. A	11. C	21. C	31. C	41. C
2. A	12. C	22. D	32. C	42. C
3. D	13. D	23. D	33. A	43. D
4. B	14. D	24. A	34. A	44. C
5. C	15. B	25. B	35. B	45. D
6. A	16. A	26. B	36. B	46. C
7. D	17. D	27. D	37. B	47. B
8. A	18. C	28. B	38. B	48. B
9. C	19. D	29. B	39. D	49. A
10. B	20. A	30. D	40. B	50. C

SOLUTIONS TO PROBLEMS

1. $5796 + 6 + 243 + 24 = 6069$

2. $8007 - 6898 = 1109$

3. $(3876)(904) = 3,503,904$

4. $58,976 \div 76 = 776$

5. $(+4) + (-3) - (-7) = 4 - 3 + 7 = +8$

6. $[(-8)(-6)] \div -3 = 48 \div -3 = -16$

7. $1\frac{3}{5} + 3\frac{7}{8} = 1\frac{24}{40} + 3\frac{35}{40} = 4\frac{59}{40} = 5\frac{19}{40}$

8. $4\frac{3}{8} - 2\frac{2}{3} = 4\frac{9}{24} - 2\frac{16}{24} = 3\frac{33}{24} - 2\frac{16}{24} = 1\frac{17}{24}$

9. $(3\frac{2}{3})(5\frac{1}{2}) = (\frac{11}{3})(\frac{11}{2}) = \frac{121}{6} = 20\frac{1}{6}$

10. $7\frac{1}{2} \div 2\frac{1}{4} = \frac{15}{2} \div \frac{9}{4} = (\frac{15}{2})(\frac{4}{9}) = \frac{60}{18} = 3\frac{1}{3}$

11. $434.7 + .04 + 7.107 = 441.847$

12. $986.4 - 34.87 = 951.53$

13. $(5.96)(87.4) = 520.904$

14. $6.698 \div .034 = 197$

15. $.7 + \frac{1}{2} = .7 + .5 = 1.2$

16. $(.055)(75) = 4.125$

17. $\frac{12}{6} = 2 = 200\%$

18. $14 \div .28 = 50$

19. $\$92 - (.15)(\$92) = \$78.20$

20. Acme's interest charge = $15.82, whereas Bowman's interest charge = $(.09)(\$320) = \$28.80$. Thus, Acme charges less.

11 (#1)

21. ($18.00)(66$\frac{2}{3}$%) + ($20.00)(90%) + ($60.00)(80%) = $78.00

22. Statements I and IV are correct. For 10 years, he has paid $320, but collected $900 on his claim. Also, since the insured value of the home is $12,000, he could not collect more than that amount on any claim.

23. Probability of 2 heads = (1/2) (1/2) = 1/4, which means 1 in 4.

24. The number of required games = (4)(3) ÷ 2 = 6

25. Average donation = ($52.00 + $76.00 + $18.00 + $94.00 + $120.00) ÷ 5 = $72

26. The correct conclusion is B: Lauraine is not a redhead. Let p = Lauraine is a redhead, q = Lauraine is hot-tempered. The given statement says: *If p, then q.* The contrapositive, which is also true, says, *If not q, then not p.* This corresponds to statement B.

27. Let x = monthly income. Then, $4080 = Solving, x = $16,320.

28. Mr. Chow's earnings = (2)($4) + (40)($2) + (7)($3) = $109.
    For Monday through Saturday, Mr. Simms' earnings =
    (40)($2) + (3)($3) = $89. Thus, Mr. Simms would need to earn
    109 - 89 = $20 on Sunday. This means Sunday's time =
    $20 ÷ $4 = 5 hours.

29. New balance = $351.76 + $41.50 - $16.95 - $125.50 - $33.68 - $21.59 = $195.54.

30. 24 = (P)(.05)(3), 24 = .15P, so P = 160

31. Fencing: (26)(4) = 104 meters.

32. Area of C = (4)(5) - ($\frac{1}{2}$)(1)(1) - ($\frac{1}{2}$)(2)(2) - ($\frac{1}{2}$)(1)(1) = 17

33. (85)(10) = 850 sq.ft. = 8.5 gallons of water. Now, 8.5 gallons = 34 quarts, so 34 teaspoons of insecticide are needed.

34. Area = (12)(6) + (12)(18) = 288 sq.ft. = 32 sq.yds. Total cost = (32)($6) = $192

35. There are 6 cubes painted red on only one side. They are found in the center of each face of the original cube.

36. (108)(4)($\frac{1}{4}$) = 108 cu.ft. = 4 cu.yds. Savings would be ($22.50)(4) - ($19.50)(4) = $12.00

37. 15 pints = 240 oz. The costs for each selection are:
    For A: (12)(.51) + (10)(.62) = $12.32; for B: (24)(.51) = $12.24; for
        C: (18)(.62) + (3)(.43) = $12.45; for D: (20)(.62) = $12.40.
    So, selection B is the minimum cost.

38. The number of seniors in 2003, 2004, 2005 are 175, 200, and 225, respectively. If growth is constant, the number of seniors in 2006 is 250.

39. Statements I, IV, V are correct. Statement II is wrong because the 1st graph covers 1800-1970, whereas the 2nd graph covers 1940-1970. Statement III is wrong because the *over 65* population increases in percent from 7% in 1940 to 12% in 1970.

40. (25%)($180,000) = $45,000 assessed value. Amount of tax = ($5.00)($45,000 ÷ $100) = $2,250

41. For increasing sales tax, it would be helpful in knowing the respective percent of incor spent on taxable vs. non-taxable goods.

42. Adjusted gross income = ($28390)(.90) = $25551.00. On the tax chart, this figure lies between $25500 and $25750. Using the column for 1 exemption, the tax is $2530.

43. Using 2 oz. = .05, note that each additional oz. = 1 cent more. So, 32 oz. = .05 + .30 = .35.

44. (5,y) represents the sixth point in this sequence. Thus, the corresponding y value = (2)(6) = 12

45. Let x = smaller number, 2.5x = larger number.
Then, $\dfrac{x}{2.5x} = \dfrac{1}{2.5} = \dfrac{10}{25} = \dfrac{2}{5}$

46. $12 - $3.75 = $8.25. Then, $8.25 ÷ .75 = 11 weeks

47. Radius = 10 in. Area = (3.14)(10^2) = 314 sq.in.

48. .045 = 4.5%

49. $\dfrac{20}{50} = 40\%$

50. (225%) (160) = (2.25) (160) = 360

BASIC MATHEMATICS
EXAMINATION SECTION
TEST 1

DIRECTIONS: Each question or incomplete statement is followed by several suggested answers or completions. Select the one that BEST answers the question or completes the statement. *PRINT THE LETTER OF THE CORRECT ANSWER IN THE SPACE AT THE RIGHT.*

1.   534
      18
  +1291

    A. 1733   B. 1743   C. 1833   D. 1843   E. 1853

1.____

2. (17×23) − 16 + 20 =
    A. 459   B. 427   C. 411   D. 395   E. 355

2.____

3. 3/7 + 5/11 =
    A. 33/35   B. 4/9   C. 8/18   D. 68/77   E. 15/77

3.____

4. 4832 ÷ 6 =
    A. 905 1/3   B. 805 1/3   C. 95 1/3   D. 95   E. 85 1/3

4.____

5. 62.3 − 4.9 =
    A. 5.74   B. 7.4   C. 57.4   D. 58.4   E. 67.4

5.____

6. 3/5 × 4/9 =
    A. 4/15   B. 7/45   C. 27/20   D. 12/14   E. 15/4

6.____

7. 14/16 − 5/16 =
    A. 8/16   B. 9/16   C. 11/16   D. 8   E. 9

7.____

8. 5.03 + 2.7 + 40 =
    A. .570   B. 4.773   C. 5.70   D. 11.73   E. 47.73

8.____

9. 5.37 × 21.4 =
    A. 11491.8   B. 1149.18   C. 114.918
    D. 11,4918   E. 1.14918

9.____

10. 5 1/4 + 2 7/8 =
    A. 8 1/4   B. 8 1/8   C. 7 2/3   D. 7 1/4   E. 7 1/8

10.____

11. −14 + 5 =
    A. −19   B. −9   C. 9   D. 19   E. 70

11.____

12. 2/7 of 28 =
    A. 98   B. 16   C. 14   D. 8   E. 4

13. 2/5 =
    A. .10   B. .20   C. .25   D. .40   E. .52

14. 20% of _____ is 38.
    A. 7.6   B. 19   C. 76   D. 190   E. 760

15. $\frac{8.4}{400}$ =
    A. .0021   B. .021   C. .21   D. 2.1   E. 21

16. $\frac{4}{5} = \frac{?}{60}$
    A. 240   B. 48   C. 20   D. 15   E. 12

17. What is the area of the rectangle shown at the right?
    A. 47 mm²
    B. 94 mm²
    C. 240 mm²
    D. 480 mm²
    E. 960 mm²

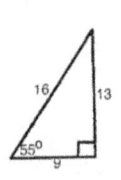

18. What number does ☐ represent in the following equation: 25 - ☐ ☐ ☐ ☐ = 13?
    A. 13   B. 12   C. 7   D. 4   E. 3

19. Approximate lengths are given in the right triangles shown at the right.
    What does length x equal?
    A. 48
    B. 39
    C. 37
    D. 35
    E. 32

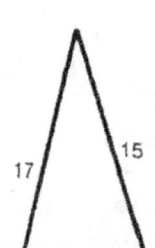

20. What is the perimeter of the triangle shown at the right?
    A. 10 × 15 × 17
    B. 10 + 15 + 17
    C. 1/2 × 10 × 15
    D. 1/2 × 10 × 17
    E. 1/2(10+15+17)

21. Which of the following expressions will give the same answer as 45 × 9?
    A. 5 × 3³   B. (4×9)+(5×9)   C. (40+9) × 5
    D. (45×3) + (45×3)   E. (45×10) − (45×1)

22. Find the average of 19, 21, 21, 22, and 27.
    A. 23 B. 22 C. 21 D. 20 E. 19

23. In the triangle at the right, how many degrees is <T?
    A. 75°
    B. 85°
    C. 95°
    D. 114°
    E. 180°

24. About how long is the paper clip?
    A. 5 cm B. 4 cm C. 3 cm D. 2 cm E. 1 cm

25. Five stores sell the same size cans of tomato soup. Their prices are listed below.
    Which sells the soup for the LOWEST price per can? _____ cans for _____.
    A. 6; 99¢ B. 6; 90¢ C. 5; 93¢ D. 3; 56¢ E. 3; 50¢

26. Rock star Peter Giles receives $1.97 royalty on each of his albums that is sold. 14,127 albums are sold.
    Estimate how much Peter Giles will receive.
    A. $7,000 B. $14,000 C. $20,000 D. $26,000 E. $28,000

27. An amplifier is advertised for 20% off the list price of $430.
    What is the sale price?
    A. $516 B. $454 C. $354 D. $344 E. $215

28. If 9 dozen eggs cost $3.60, what do 25 dozen eggs cost?
    A. $90.00 B. $10.00 C. $9.00 D. $2.54 E. $40

29. The distance between New York State and San Antonio is 1,860 miles. If a jet averages 465 miles per hour, how many hours will it take to travel the distance?
    A. 9 B. 5 C. 4 D. 3 E. 2

30. In a high school homeroom of 32 students, 24 are girls.
    What percent are girls?
    A. 3/4% B. 24% C. 25% D. 75% E. 80%

31. Which problem could give the answer shown on the calculator?
    A. 2 + .3
    B. 2 × 3/10
    C. 2 × 1/3
    D. 33333 + .2
    E. 7 ÷ 3

32. **Cost of Eating at Home**
    (One Week)

Age	Male	Female
6-11 yrs.	$14	$14
12-19 yrs.	$19	$15
20-54 yrs.	$20	$16
55 and Up	$14	$14

    According to the above table, how much will it cost in a typical week for the 3 members of the Wright family to eat at home? Mr. Wright is 56 years old; Mrs. Wright, 52; and their son, Harry, 17.
    A. $125   B. $52   C. $49   D. $42   E. $40

33. According to the above table shown in Question 32, how much does it cost in a typical four-week month to feed a 12-year-old girl?
    A. $4   B. $16   C. $48   D. $64   E. $78

34. Reverend Whilhite jogs for 1½ hours each day, 6 days a week. If he burns 800 calories per hour of jogging, how many calories does he burn in a week?
    A. 4800   B. 5600   C. 7200   D. 8400   E. 9000

35. Ground meat costs 90¢ per pound. How much does the meat on the scale cost?
    A. $1.80
    B. $1.60
    C. $1.54
    D. $1.44
    E. $.90

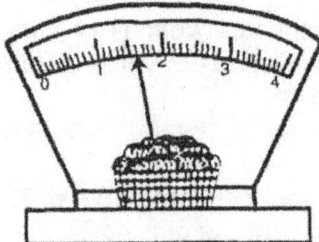

36. According to the graph at the right, about when did the weekly wages for a minimum wage worker go over $100?
    A. 2005
    B. 2010
    C. 2014
    D. 2019
    E. 2020

36.____

37. According to the bar graph at the right, what is the approximate height of the Crystal Beach Comet?
    A. 40 ft.
    B. 90 ft.
    C. 92 ft.
    D. 94 ft.
    E. 98 ft.

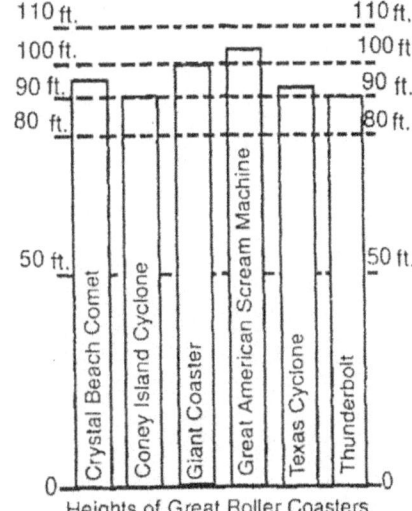

37.____

38. According to the bar graph shown in Question 37, what is the difference in height between the tallest and shortest roller coasters? _____ feet.
    A. 5   B. 10   C. 15   D. 20   E. 50

38.____

39. How much change will you receive from a $10 bill when you buy 4 grapefruits at 90¢ each and 3 apples at 40¢ each?
    A. $6.20   B. $5.20   C. $4.80   D. $4.20   E. $4.00

39.____

40. A medical supplier packages medicine in boxes. The cost of packaging is computed with the flow chart at the right.
What is the cost of packaging medicine in a box that is 30 cm long, 20 cm wide, and 20 cm high?
   A. $.20
   B. $.24
   C. $2.00
   D. $2.40
   E. $3.00

40.____

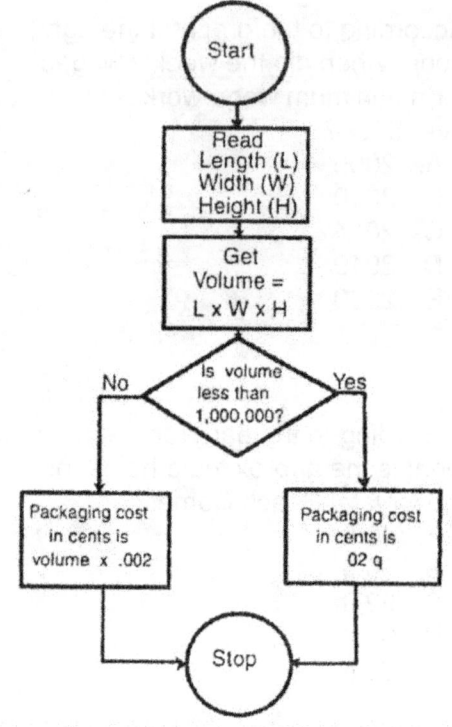

KEY (CORRECT ANSWERS)

1.	D	11.	B	21.	E	31.	E
2.	D	12.	D	22.	B	32.	C
3.	D	13.	D	23.	B	33.	D
4.	B	14.	D	24.	C	34.	C
5.	C	15.	B	25.	B	35.	D
6.	A	16.	B	26.	E	36.	C
7.	B	17.	D	27.	D	37.	D
8.	E	18.	E	28.	B	38.	C
9.	C	19.	A	29.	C	39.	B
10.	B	20.	B	30.	D	40.	A

SOLUTIONS TO PROBLEMS

1. 534 + 18 + 1291 = 1843

2. (17×23) − 16 + 20 = 391 − 16 + 20 = 395

3. $\frac{3}{7} + \frac{5}{11} = \frac{33}{77} + \frac{35}{77} = \frac{68}{77}$

4. 4832 ÷ 6 = 805$\frac{1}{3}$

5. 62.3 − 4.9 = 57.4

6. $\frac{3}{5} \times \frac{4}{9} = \frac{12}{45} = \frac{4}{15}$

7. $\frac{14}{16} \cdot \frac{5}{16} = \frac{9}{16}$

8. 5.03 + 2.7 + 40 = 47.73

9. 5.37 × 21.4 = 114.918

10. $5\frac{1}{4} + 2\frac{7}{8} = 7\frac{9}{8} = 8\frac{1}{8}$

11. -14 + 5 = -9

12. $\frac{2}{7}$ of 28 = $\left(\frac{2}{7}\right)\left(\frac{28}{1}\right) = 8$

13. $\frac{2}{5}$ = .40 as a decimal

14. Let x = missing number. Then, .20x = 38. Solving, x = 190

15. $\frac{84}{400}$ = .021

16. Let x = missing number. Then, $\frac{4}{5} = \frac{x}{60}$. 5x = 240, so x = 48

17. Area = (15)(32) = 480mm^2

18. Let x = □. Then, 25 − 4x = 13. So, -4x = -12. Solving, x = 3.

19. $\frac{9}{27} = \frac{16}{x}$. Then, 9x = 432. Solving, x = 48.

20. Perimeter = 17 + 10 + 15 = 42

21. 45 × 9 = 405 = (45×10)-(45×1)

8 (#1)

22. 19 + 21 + 21 + 22 + 27 = 110. Then, 110 ÷ 5 = 22

23. ∠T = 180° - 50° - 45° = 85°

24. The paper clip's length is about 5 – 2 = 3 cm.

25. For A: price per can = $\frac{.99}{6}$ = .165
    For B: price per can = $\frac{.90}{6}$ = .15
    For C: price per can = $\frac{.93}{5}$ = 186
    For D: price per can = $\frac{.56}{3}$ = .18$\overline{6}$
    For E: price per can = $\frac{.50}{3}$ = .1$\overline{6}$

    Lowest price is for B.

26. $1.97 = $2.00. Then, ($2.00)(14,127) = $28,254 = $28,000

27. Sale price = ($430)(.80) = $344

28. Let x = cost. Then, 9x = $90, so x = $10.00

29. $\frac{1860}{465}$ = 4 hours

30. $\frac{24}{32}$ = 75%

31. $\frac{7}{3}$ = 2.$\overline{3}$ = 2.33333 on the calculator shown

32. Total cost = $14 + $16 + $19 = $49

33. Cost = ($16)(4) = $64

34. (800)(1$\frac{1}{2}$)(6) = 7200 calories

35. (.90)(1.6) = $1.44

36. Around 2015, the minimum weekly wages exceeded $100.

37. The Crystal Beach Comet's height is about 94 ft.

38. Tallest = 105 ft. and the shortest = 90 ft. Difference = 15 ft.

39. $10 – (3)(.90) – (3)(.40) = $5.20 change.

40. (30)(20)(20) = 12,000 cm³. Since 12,000 < 1,000,000, the price is 20 cents.

EXAMINATION SECTION
TEST 1

DIRECTIONS: Each question or incomplete statement is followed by several suggested answers or completions. Select the one that BEST answers the question or completes the statement. *PRINT THE LETTER OF THE CORRECT ANSWER IN THE SPACE AT THE RIGHT.*

Questions 1-15.

DIRECTIONS: In Questions 1 through 15, choose the answer which shows the set of numbers CORRECTLY ordered from least to greatest. Write the letter of the CORRECT answer in the space at the right.

1. A. 2111, 1120, 1010, 863
    B. 1121, 1211, 1387, 1864
    C. 1111, 1222, 1010, 1783
    D. 2345, 6789, 1112, 1314

2. A. -110, -179, -203, -600
    B. -63, -14, 0.2, -0.9
    C. -107, -90, -51, -14
    D. -16, -32, -27, -49

3. A. 9.1, 2.3, 5.6, 18.4
    B. 6.8, 12.1, 14.5, 107.2
    C. 1.4, 1.3, 1.09, 83.9
    D. 134, 15, 11.2, 4.6

4. A. -73.5, -42.6, -30.2, -17.1
    B. -5.8, -10.2, -60.3, -91.8
    C. -6, -23, -14.7, -0.76
    D. 17.3, -4.6, -5.5, -82.1

5. A. -14, -34, -40, -54
    B. -43, -42, -24, -4
    C. 104, 74, 46, 24
    D. 13, 88, 47, 14

6. A. 19.07, 16.3, 8.9, 3.22
    B. 21.9, 8.4, 17.1, 6.46
    C. 2.21, 7.18, 12.16, 17.08
    D. 52.8, 22.5, 31.4, 48.7

7. A. 0, 1.5, 2.4, 3.3
    B. 6.4, 4.6, 5.1, 3.6
    C. 3.5, 2.6, 5.6, 1.7
    D. 4.2, 0, -3.9, -6.8

1.____

2.____

3.____

4.____

5.____

6.____

7.____

8. A. 196.78, 48.06, 527.39, 274.31
    B. 273.14, 368.12, 451.07, 621.1
    C. 413.72, 218.63, 107.54, 96.16
    D. 931.47, 941.36, 618.54, 428.26

9. A. 0.5, 0.3, 0.16, 0.04
    B. 0.3, 0.06, 0.9, 0.09
    C. 0.076, 0.102, 0.25, 0.4
    D. 0.02, 0.002, 2, 20

10. A. 24, 18.3, 14, 12.2
    B. 1.6, 22, 37.4, 49
    C. 57.3, 14, 68.73, 5.02
    D. 1.5, 9.8, 62, 12

11. A. 6, -7, 52, -66
    B. -286, -83, -4, 5
    C. -23, -168, -2, -207
    D. 7, 6, -8, -9

12. A. 1024, 512, 256, 128
    B. 84, 98, 12, 106
    C. 48, 64, 128, 256
    D. 614, 290, 103, 175

13. A. -18.2, -10.4, 0.6, 9
    B. -9.3, -12.4, -14.7, -8.5
    C. 8, 7, -0.2, -6.5
    D. 1.7, -4, 2.4, -8.9

14. A. 21.03, 21.032, 21.30, 21.04
    B. 7.37, 7.382, 7.38, 7.384
    C. 25.10, 25.12, 25.119, 25.30
    D. 10.07, 10.072, 10.073, 10.080

15. A. 0.003, 0.006, 0.013, 0.0135
    B. 0.00251, 0.0025, 0.0027, 0.0023
    C. 0.872, 0.8719, 0.900, 0.9001
    D. -8.735, -8.739, -7.993, -6.568

16. Which answer choice shows 27 rounded to the nearest tens?

    A. 20   B. 30   C. 27.5   D. 40

17. Which answer choice shows 188.65 rounded to the nearest hundreds?

    A. 200   B. 180   C. 100   D. 188.7

18. Which answer choice shows 4718 rounded to the nearest thousands?

    A. 4000   B. 4700   C. 4710   D. 5000

19. Which answer choice shows 13.18 rounded to the nearest tenths?

    A. 13.1   B. 13   C. 13.2   D. 14

20. Which answer choice shows 7.2 rounded to the nearest whole number? 20.____
    A. 2   B. 5.7   C. 7   D. 72

21. Which answer choice shows 0.3465 rounded to the nearest hundredths? 21.____
    A. 0.3   B. 0.35   C. 0.34   D. 0.4

22. Which answer choice shows 1.9931 rounded to the nearest thousandths? 22.____
    A. 2   B. 1.993   C. 1.99   D. 1.9

23. Which answer choice shows 1.9 rounded to the nearest whole number? 23.____
    A. 3   B. 10   C. 1   D. 2

24. Which answer choice shows 92 rounded to the nearest tens? 24.____
    A. 92   B. 90.2   C. 100   D. 90

25. Which answer choice shows 134.06 rounded to the nearest hundreds? 25.____
    A. 200   B. 100   C. 134   D. 134.1

26. Which answer choice shows 2250 rounded to the nearest thousands? 26.____
    A. 3000   B. 2200   C. 2000   D. 2250

27. Which answer choice shows 0.1416 rounded to the nearest thousandths? 27.____
    A. 0.14   B. 0.142   C. 0.1   D. 0.2

28. Which answer choice shows 322.4 rounded to the nearest hundreds? 28.____
    A. 320   B. 322.5   C. 323   D. 300

29. Which answer choice shows 8.76 rounded to the nearest tenth? 29.____
    A. 8.7   B. 8.8   C. 8.4   D. 8.10

30. Which of the following answer choices shows 76.4 rounded to the nearest whole number? 30.____
    A. 77   B. 80   C. 76   D. 100

31. Choose the answer that shows 1/4 as a decimal. 31.____
    A. 0.4   B. 0.25   C. 0.2   D. 2.5

32. Choose the answer that shows 3/5 as a percentage. 32.____
    A. 60%   B. 0.6%   C. 1.6%   D. 80%

33. Choose the answer that shows 0.45 as a fraction. 33.____
    A. 11/20   B. 9/20   C. 4/5   D. 2 2/9

34. Choose the answer that shows 30% as a fraction. 34.____
    A. 33/100   B. 10/3   C. 3/10   D. 1/3

35. Choose the answer that shows .67 as a percentage.
    A. 670%   B. 7.6%   C. 6.7%   D. 67%

36. Choose the answer that shows 84.5% as a decimal.
    A. 0.8   B. 84.5   C. 0.845   D. 8.45

37. Choose the answer that shows 5/8 as a decimal.
    A. 0.625   B. 0.062   C. 0.16   D. 1.6

38. Choose the answer that shows 3/4 as a percentage.
    A. .75%   B. 7.5%   C. 50%   D. 75%

39. Choose the answer that shows 0.36 as a fraction.
    A. 3/10   B. 25/9   C. 9/50   D. 9/25

40. Choose the answer that shows 0.718 as a percentage.
    A. 71.8%   B. 7.81%   C. 1.4%   D. 7.8%

41. Choose the answer that shows 12.5% as a fraction.
    A. 1/8   B. 1/25   C. 1/80   D. 8/1

42. Choose the answer that shows 94.52% as a decimal.
    A. 9.452   B. 0.95   C. 0.94   D. 0.9452

43. Choose the answer that shows 2/5 as a decimal.
    A. 0.2   B. 0.4   C. 0.7   D. 2.5

44. Choose the answer that shows 1/8 as a decimal.
    A. 0.120   B. 0.125   C. 1.250   D. 0.1205

45. Choose the answer that shows 28% as a fraction.
    A. 1/8   B. 1/4   C. 8/37   D. 7/25

46. Which answer choice is equal to 4^3?
    A. 12   B. 7   C. 64   D. 16

47. Which answer choice is equal to 7^2?
    A. 49   B. 14   C. 9   D. 36

48. Which answer choice is equal to 9^2?
    A. 18   B. 11   C. 49   D. 81

49. Which answer choice is equal to 3^3?
    A. 6   B. 9   C. 27   D. 81

50. Which answer choice is equal to 3^4?   50.____
    A. 7   B. 27   C. 81   D. 90

51. Which answer choice is equal to 8^4?   51.____
    A. 12   B. 496   C. 4096   D. 32

52. Which answer choice is equal to 5^3?   52.____
    A. 125   B. 15   C. 8   D. 102

53. Which answer choice is equal to 6^2?   53.____
    A. 12   B. 36   C. 8   D. 35

54. Which answer choice is equal to 6^3?   54.____
    A. 9   B. 216   C. 18   D. 186

55. Which answer choice is equal to 5^2?   55.____
    A. 36   B. 32   C. 25   D. 7

56. Which answer choice is equal to 9^3?   56.____
    A. 12   B. 27   C. 81   D. 729

57. Which answer choice is equal to 2^3?   57.____
    A. 16   B. 8   C. 6   D. 5

58. Which answer choice is equal to 4^2?   58.____
    A. 8   B. 6   C. 64   D. 16

59. Which answer choice is equal to 3^5?   59.____
    A. 729   B. 81   C. 243   D. 6561

60. Which answer choice is equal to 12^3?   60.____
    A. 144   B. 1728   C. 20736   D. 36

KEY (CORRECT ANSWERS)

1.	B	16.	B	31.	B	46.	C
2.	C	17.	A	32.	A	47.	A
3.	B	18.	D	33.	B	48.	D
4.	A	19.	C	34.	C	49.	C
5.	B	20.	C	35.	D	50.	C
6.	C	21.	B	36.	C	51.	C
7.	A	22.	B	37.	A	52.	A
8.	B	23.	D	38.	D	53.	B
9.	C	24.	D	39.	D	54.	B
10.	B	25.	B	40.	A	55.	C
11.	B	26.	C	41.	A	56.	D
12.	C	27.	B	42.	D	57.	B
13.	A	28.	D	43.	B	58.	D
14.	D	29.	B	44.	B	59.	C
15.	A	30.	C	45.	D	60.	B

SOLUTIONS TO PROBLEMS

1. 1121, 1211, 1387, 1864 is in correct increasing order.

2. -107, -90, -51, -14 is in correct increasing order.

3. 6.8, 12.1, 14.5, 107.2 is in correct increasing order.

4. -73.5, -42.6, -30.2, -17.1 is in correct increasing order.

5. -43, -42, -24, -4 is in correct increasing order.

6. 2.21, 7.18, 12.16, 17.08 is in correct increasing order.

7. 0, 1.5, 2.4, 3.3 is in correct increasing order.

8. 273.14, 386.12, 451.07, 621.1 is in correct increasing order.

9. .076, .102, .25, .4 is in correct increasing order.

10. 1.6, 22, 37.4, 49 is in correct increasing order.

11. -286, -83, -4, 5 is in correct increasing order.

12. 48, 64, 128, 256 is in correct increasing order.

13. -18.2, -10.4, .6, 9 is in correct increasing order.

14. 10.07, 10.072, 10.073, 10.080 is in correct increasing order.

15. .003, .006, .013, .0135 is in correct increasing order.

16. 27 rounds off to 30 in nearest tens.

17. 188.65 rounds off to 200 in nearest hundredths.

18. 4718 rounds off to 5000 in nearest thousands.

19. 13.18 rounds off to 13.2 in nearest tenths.

20. 7.2 rounds off to 7 in nearest whole number.

21. .3465 rounds off to .35 in nearest hundredths.

22. 1.9931 rounds off to 1.993 in nearest thousandths.

23. 1.9 rounds off to 2 in nearest whole numbers.

24. 92 rounds off to 90 in nearest tens.

25. 134.06 rounds off to 100 in nearest hundredths.

26. 2250 rounds off to 2000 in nearest thousandths.

8 (#1)

27. .1416 rounds off to .142 in nearest thousandths.

28. 322.4 rounds off to 300 in nearest hundredths.

29. 8.76 rounds off to 8.8 in nearest tenths.

30. 76.4 rounds off to 76 in nearest whole number.

31. 1/4 = .25

32. 3/5 = .60 = 60%

33. .45 = 45/100 = 9/20

34. 30% = 30/100 = 3/10

35. .67 = 67%

36. 84.5% = .845

37. 5/8 = .625

38. 3/4 = .75 = 75%

39. .36 = 36/100 = 9/25

40. .718 = 71.8%

41. 12.5% = 12.5/100 = 125/1000 = 1/8

42. 94.52% = .9452

43. 2/5 = .4

44. 1/8 = .125

45. 28% = .28 = 28/100 = 7/25

46. 4^3 = (4)(4)(4) = 64

47. 7^2 = (7)(7) = 49

48. 9^2 = (9)(9) = 81

49. 3^3 - (3)(3)(3) = 27

50. 3^4 = (3)(3)(3)(3) = 81

51. 8^4 = (8)(8)(8)(8) = 4096

52. 5^3 = (5)(5)(5) - 125

53. 6^2 = (6)(6) = 36

54. $6^3 = (6)(6)(6) = 216$

55. $5^2 = (5)(5) = 25$

56. $9^3 = (9)(9)(9) = 729$

57. $2^3 = (2)(2)(2) = 8$

58. $4^2 = (4)(4) = 16$

59. $3^5 = (3)(3)(3)(3)(3) = 243$

60. $12^3 = (12)(12)(12) = 1728$

TEST 2

DIRECTIONS: Each question or incomplete statement is followed by several suggested answers or completions. Select the one that BEST answers the question or completes the statement. *PRINT THE LETTER OF THE CORRECT ANSWER IN THE SPACE AT THE RIGHT.*

1. $5 + 2/7 =$
   A. 5 2/7   B. 4 5/7   C. 1 3/7   D. 5 3/7

2. $2/5 \times 2/7 =$
   A. 24/35   B. 4/35   C. 4/25   D. 10/14

3. $2/3 + 1/4 =$
   A. 5/12   B. 1/6   C. 11/12   D. 5/11

4. $2 + 4\frac{5}{6} + 8\frac{5}{18} =$
   A. 14 1/9   B. 14 1/8   C. 15 1/8   D. 15 1/9

5. $\frac{5}{11} + \frac{1}{3}$
   A. 1 1/11   B. 4/33   C. 26/33   D. 26/36

6. $2 - 5/6 =$
   A. 2 5/6   B. 1/6   C. 1 1/3   D. 1 1/6

7. $3\frac{1}{2} - 1\frac{5}{11}$
   A. 2 1/2   B. 5 1/22   C. 2 1/22   D. 1 1/22

8. $1/6 \times 4 =$
   A. 3 5/6   B. 1/2   C. 4 1/6   D. 2/3

9. $2\frac{2}{3} \times 8\frac{5}{8}$
   A. 21   B. 16 5/12   C. 23   D. 11 7/24

2 (#2)

10. 3 3/5 + 7 1/3 =   10.____
    A. 10 2/3   B. 9 7/15   C. 10 14/15   D. 11 2/15

11. 74.27
    +85.76   11.____
    A. 160.93   B. 160.03   C. 6369.3952   D. 828.46

12. 8)0.8264   12.____
    A. 0.1033   B. 10.33   C. 0.1233   D. 0.133

13. 4.8
    ×5.7   13.____
    A. 10.5   B. 27.36   C. 2.736   D. 20.56

14. 54.76 - 19.89 =   14.____
    A. 3.487   B. 34.87   C. 44.87   D. 1089.1764

15. 32 - 8.5 =   15.____
    A. 2.35   B. 23.5   C. 24.5   D. 2.45

16. 263.4
    18.75
    + 1.982   16.____
    A. 28.4122   B. 28.4132   C. 284.122   D. 284.132

17. 2.2)19.36   17.____
    A. 0.1136   B. 8.8   C. 11.36   D. .088

18. 48.7 + 76.29 =   18.____
    A. 1249.9   B. 124.99   C. 3715.323   D. 811.6

19. 42.19
    - 21.88   19.____
    A. 20.31   B. 21.31   C. 20.21   D. 923.11

20. 56 x .859 =   20.____
    A. 48.04   B. 48.104   C. 55.141   D. 56.859

21. 748.1 ÷ 2.5 =   21.____
    A. 382.98   B. 299.24   C. 29.924   D. 745.6

22. 75
    -68.742

    A. 68.733   B. 143.742   C. 13.742   D. 6.258

23. 23.87
    +18.21

    A. 42.08   B. 434.672   C. 5.66   D. 32.08

24. 649.801 ÷ 35.735 =

    A. 20.01774   B. 16.7981   C. 18.1839   D. 18.0479

25. 8.0016(6.0137) =

    A. 48.1192.   B. 48.1093   C. 46.0996   D. 48.1182

26. 17 + (-6) =

    A. -23   B. 10   C. 11   D. 23

27. (-4) + 16 + (-2) =

    A. 18   B. 10   C. -22   D. 22

28. 3 + (-18) + (-9) =

    A. -23   B. -24   C. 12   D. -30

29. 16 + (-4) + 27 + (-15) =

    A. 32   B. 38   C. 24   D. 54

30. (-5) + 8 =

    A. 13   B. 2   C. -3   D. 3

31. (-8) + (-12) + (-9) + 23 =

    A. 6   B. -6   C. 11   D. -52

32. (-6) + 7 =

    A. -13   B. 1   C. 13   D. -1

33. (-16) + 35 + (-19) + 73 =

    A. 132   B. 3   C. 73   D. -3

34. 9 + 12 + 6 + (-27) =

    A. 54   B. 0   C. 6   D. -54

35. (-64) + (-43) + (-21) + 96 =

    A. 32   B. -128   C. -32   D. 138

36. 9 + 2 + (-15) =

    A. -4   B. -26   C. 26   D. -22

37. 10 + (-20) + (-30) + (-40) =

    A. -100   B. 100   C. -80   D. 80

38. (-21) + 32 + (-45) + 56 =

    A. 2   B. -2   C. 0   D. 22

39. 18 +(-3) -4+6=

    A. 15   B. 17   C. 21   D. -17

40. -12 - 8 + (-1) =

    A. -19   B. -21   C. 19   D. -17

41. There are 1200 students in Foothills High School. One-third of the students are involved in sports and one-fourth of the athletes are on the honor roll.
    How many athletes are on the honor roll?

    A. 400   B. 300   C. 100   D. 200

42. Each of the walls in a room is 12 feet long and 8 feet high. It takes 5 minutes to paint 16 square feet of wall and 10 minutes to paint the same amount of ceiling.
    How long will it take to paint all four walls?

    A. 30 minutes   B. 1 hour 20 minutes
    C. 2 hours   D. 1 hour 36 minutes

43. TWX International Airline has 14 planes, each of which can hold 210 passengers and a crew of 7. They normally fly two-thirds full.
    If all of the planes were in service, how many passengers would TWX be carrying on a typical day?

    A. 2060   B. 140   C. 2025   D. 1960

44. The temperature in a room is 62.5°. It takes $7.42 worth of energy to raise the temperature 0.5 of a degree.
    How much would it cost to bring the room to 65°?

    A. $18.55   B. $37.10   C. $482.30   D. $48.23

45. When Grant runs, he uses up about 6 calories per minute. If he runs 5 days a week for one-quarter of an hour each day, how many calories will he burn up in a week?

    A. 30   B. 450   C. 90   D. 120

46. A 13 ft. x 8 ft. greenhouse costs $8950.00. Installation costs are $10.25 per square foot, and it usually takes four days to install.
    How much would it cost to buy a greenhouse and have it installed?

    A. $10,016.00   B. $1066.00
    C. $1001.60   D. $8950.00

47. A housing development covers 4950 acres. There is one house for each 2.5 acres in the development.
    If each household pays an annual maintenance fee of $82.00, how much is paid by the entire development each year for maintenance?

    A. $1980.00 B. $162,360.00
    C. $205.00   D. $12,375.00

48. Cassette tapes are on sale through a mail-order house for $7.95 each plus $1.25 shipping and handling.
    How much would it cost to buy 5 cassette tapes and have them shipped? You already own 14 cassette tapes.

    A. $39.75   B. $46.00   C. $6.75   D. $103.20

49. Last year, a total of 103.2 inches of rain fell in Midville. This year, 116.4 inches fell. On the average, how much more rain fell each month this year than last year?
    _____ inches.

    A. 9.7   B. 1.1   C. 8.6   D. 13.2

50. Tracy had $378.60 in her savings account. She earned $8.90 in interest and made a deposit of $50.00 that she had received for her birthday.
    How much more must she deposit to reach her goal of $500.00?

    A. $447.50   B. $121.40   C. $53.50   D. $62.50

KEY (CORRECT ANSWERS)

1. A	11. B	21. B	31. B	41. C
2. B	12. A	22. D	32. B	42. C
3. C	13. B	23. A	33. C	43. D
4. D	14. B	24. C	34. B	44. B
5. C	15. B	25. A	35. C	45. B
6. D	16. D	26. C	36. A	46. A
7. C	17. B	27. B	37. C	47. B
8. D	18. B	28. B	38. D	48. B
9. C	19. A	29. C	39. B	49. B
10. C	20. B	30. D	40. B	50. D

6 (#2)

SOLUTIONS TO PROBLEMS

1. 5 + 2/7 = 5 2/7

2. 2/5 x 2/7 = 4/35

3. 2/3+1/4=8/12+3/12=11/12

4. 2 + 4 5/6 + 8 5/18 = 2 + 4 15/18 + 8 5/18 = 14 20/18 = 15 1/9

5. 5/11 + 1/3 = 15/33 + 11/33 = 26/33

6. 2 - 5/6 = 1 6/6 - 5/6 = 1 1/6

7. 3 1/2 - 1 5/11 = 3 11/32 - 1 10/22 = 2 1/22

8. 1/6 x 4 = 4/6 = 2/3

9. (2 2/3)(8 5/8) = (8/3)(69/3) = 552/24 = 23

10. 3 3/5 + 7 1/3 = 3 9/15 + 7 5/15 = 10 14/15

11. 74.27 + 85.76 = 160.03

12. .8264 8 = .1033

13. 4.8 x 5.7 = 27.36

14. 54.76 - 19.89 = 34.87

15. 32 - 8.5 = 23.5

16. 263.4 + 18.75 + 1.982 = 284.132

17. 19.36 ÷ 2.2 = 8.8

18. 48.7 + 76.29 = 124.99

19. 42.19 - 21.88 = 20.31

20. 56 x .859 = 48.104

21. 748.1 ÷ 2.5 = 299.24

22. 75 - 68.742 = 6.258

23. 23.87 + 18.21 = 42.08

24. 649.801 ÷ 35.735 = 18.1839

25. (8.0016)(6.0137) ≈ 48.1192

26. 17 + (-6) = 11

7 (#2)

27. (-4) + 16 + (-2) = 10

28. 3 + (-18) + (-9) = -24

29. 16 + (-4) + 27 + (-15) = 24

30. (-5) +8=3

31. (-8) + (-12) + (-9) + 23 = -6

32. (-6) +7=1

33. (-16) + 35 + (-19) + 73 = 73

34. 9 + 12 + 6 + (-27) = 0

35. (-64) + (-43) + (-21) + 96 = -32

36. 9 + 2 + (-15) = -4

37. 10 + (-20) + (-30) + (-40) = -80

38. (-21) + 32 + (-45) + 56 = 22

39. 18 + (-3) - 4 + 6 = 17

40. - 12 - 8 + (-1) = -21

41. (1/3)(1/4)(1200) = 100 students

42. Total wall area = (4)(12)(8) = 384 sq.ft. Let x = number of minutes to paint these walls. Then, 5/16 = x/384 . Solving, x = 120 min. = 2 hours

43. (14)(210)(2/3) = 1960 passengers

44. 65° - 62.5° = 2.5°. Then, 2.5 ÷ .5 = 5. Finally, (5)($7.42) = $37.10

45. (5)(15)(6) = 450 calories

46. ($10.25)(13)(8) + $8950 = $10,016

47. 4950 ÷ 2.5 = 1980 houses. Then, (1980)($82) = $162,360

48. ($7.95 + $1.25)(5) = $46.00

49. (116.4 - 103.2) ÷ 12 = 1.1

50. $500.00 - ($378.60 + $8.90 + $50.00) = $62.50

TEST 3

DIRECTIONS: Each question or incomplete statement is followed by several suggested answers or completions. Select the one that BEST answers the question or completes the statement. *PRINT THE LETTER OF THE CORRECT ANSWER IN THE SPACE AT THE RIGHT.*

1. $H = \sqrt{a^2 + b^2}$

   Where H = hypotenuse or diagonal
   a = altitude or height
   b = base

   Use the above formula to find the diagonal of the triangle shown at the right.

   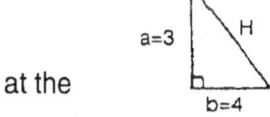

   A. 3.5   B. 5   C. 7   D. 25

   1.____

2. Mark discovered that he could predict the noontime temperature from the morning temperature using the following formula: N = 1.25 m + 3.6

   Where N = noontime temperature
   m = morning temperature

   What would the noontime temperature be if the morning temperature was 11.6° Celsius?

   _____ ° Celsius.

   A. 31.5   B. 27   C. 23.45   D. 18.1

   2.____

3. Sarah wants to know how much she will have in the bank at the end of a year. She has $400 in her account now. Use this formula to find how much she will have if the interest rate is 6%: T = a(1.00 + r)

   Where T = total in the account
   a = amount of savings now
   r = interest rate

   A. $24   B. $424   C. $64   D. $422

   3.____

4. The cost of heating a house for a day can be estimated using the following formula:
   C = (a x .0034) + (1/t x 60)

   Where C = cost per day
   a = area in square feet
   t = average outside temperature

   How much would it cost to heat a house of 1800 square feet if the average outside temperature was 30° F?

   A. $6.30   B. $3.15   C. $12.60   D. $8.12

   4.____

5. A store manager prices his merchandise using the following formula:
   P = (c x 3 1/3) + (s x 1 4/5)

   Where P = price
   c = cost of the shoe
   s = shipping charge

   What would the price of a pair of shoes be if his cost was $9.00 and shipping was $.45 per pair?

   A. $12.00   B. $30.81   C. $9.72   D. $30.00

   5.____

6. The air travel time between two cities can be calculated using the following formula:

$$T = \frac{(.1 \times d) + (s \times 27)}{60}$$

   Where T = travel time in hours
          d = distance between cities
          s = number of stops

   How long would it take to fly between two cities that are 2160 miles apart when there are two intermediate stops on the trip?
   _____ hours.

   A. 3   B. 3.5   C. 4   D. 4.5

7. The depth of a stream is determined by the amount of rain that falls in the area. Use the formula below to find the depth of a stream after a rainfall of .86 inches. The normal depth of the stream is 2.8 feet.

   $D = (r \times 4.5) + n$

   Where D = depth in feet after a storm
          r = amount of rainfall
          n = normal depth

    inches.

   A. 6.67   B. 6.87   C. 10.836   D. 13.46

8. Find the area of the shaded part of the circle shown at the right.
   Use the formula:

   $A = \pi R^2 / 4$

   $\pi = 3.14$

   _____ square feet.

   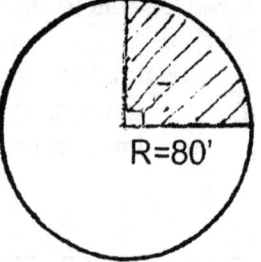

   A. 1600
   B. 20096
   C. 5024
   D. 15072

9. Using the formula below, find the area of a triangular plot of land.
   $A = 1/2\ bh$

   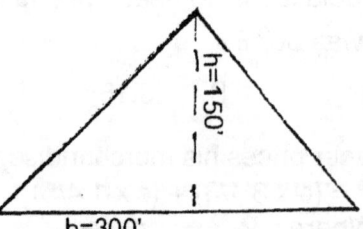

   A. 22,500 square feet
   B. 45,000 square feet
   C. 27,000 square feet
   D. 2,250 square feet

10. Using the formula below, calculate the net asset value per share of XYZ Corp.   10.____

    $$NAV = \frac{A-L}{S}$$ Where A = $180,000
                                    L = $70,000
                                    S = 8500

    A. $29.41   B. $129.40   C. $6.47   D. $12.94

11. A can of 3 tennis balls costs $2.50.   11.____
    How much will it cost to buy 36 tennis balls for the local tournament?

    A. $38.50   B. $90.00   C. $12.00   D. $30.00

12. The standard house in the Dove Creek development has 6 rooms and 12 windows.   12.____
    How many windows would be in the deluxe model with 9 rooms?

    A. 18   B. 15   C. 12   D. 27

13. An office staffed by 5 people uses $427.00 worth of energy a day.   13.____
    How much energy would be used if the staff doubled in size?

    A. $10.00   B. $844.00   C. $854.00   D. $432.00

14. An airline company with a fleet of 6 planes carries 120 passengers a day.   14.____
    How many passengers could the airline carry if the fleet was increased to 8 planes?

    A. 960   B. 128   C. 80   D. 160

15. A baseball team of 9 players uses 63 rolls of wrapping tape in a season.   15.____
    How many rolls of tape would a basketball team of 5 players need for a season of the same length?

    A. 72   B. 35   C. 36   D. 45

16. A hotel is installing 4 overhead lights for each 64 square yards of floor space.   16.____
    How many lights will they need for the lobby which is 256 square yards?

    A. 68   B. 256   C. 16   D. 32

17. In an airport there must be 3 security guards for every 15 flights. An average of 45 flights   17.____
    take off every day. How many security guards must work during a day?

    A. 18   B. 48   C. 60   D. 9

18. A librarian found that 4 shelves were needed to hold 50 books. A shipment of 750 books   18.____
    just arrived.
    How many shelves will the books fill?

    A. 72   B. 60   C. 200   D. 15

19. A roller-rink manager keeps a half-dozen spare wheels for every 30 pairs of rental   19.____
    skates. There are 95 pairs of rental skates at the rink.
    How many spare wheels does he have?

    A. 20   B. 36   C. 17   D. 19

20. For a salesperson to make her quota, she must close 8 sales for every 24 customers she visits. Last month, she visited 360 customers and made her quota.
How many sales did she make?

   A. 43   B. 90   C. 120   D. 16

21. A ski slope employs 28 instructors, 14 maintenance people, and 8 lift operators.
What percentage of the employees are instructors?

   A. 28%   B. 5.6%   C. 2.8%   D. 56%

22. There are 1850 square miles of timberland in Sierra National Forest. Grizzly bears are found in 60% of the timberland.
How much of Sierra National Forest supports a grizzly bear population?
_____ square miles.

   A. 111   B. 1110   C. 740   D. 610

23. A city cleanup crew can sweep 12 miles of streets in a day. There are 60 miles of streets in the city.
What percentage of the city streets can the crew sweep in a day?

   A. 12%   B. 60%   C. 5%   D. 20%

24. Coach Martin has won 65% of the games his team has played. In 1993 the team played 74 games, in 1994 they played 61 games, and in 1995 they played 65 games.
How many games did the team win during these three years?

   A. 200   B. 130   C. 124   D. 120

25. Senator Harrison's bill was supported by 48% of the members of the Education Committee. There are 25 senators on the committee.
How many votes did the bill receive?

   A. 48   B. 25   C. 16   D. 12

26. An auto factory produces 500 cars per day. The quality control team rejects 2% of the cars.
How many cars are rejected in a day?

   A. 100   B. 1   C. 10   D. 12

27. A librarian kept track of the most popular books and posted the chart shown below.

FAVORITE FIVE LIBRARY BOOKS

TITLE	NUMBER OF STUDENTS
Texas	473
Grant and Lee	218
The Right Stuff	182
Washington, D.C.	119
Tale of Two Cities	108

What percentage of the students read Texas?

   A. 47.3%   B. 46%   C. 1100%   D. 43%

28. A museum has 46 pictures on the first floor, 134 on the second floor, and 45 in the west wing.
    What percentage of the museum's pictures are in the west wing?

    A. 25%   B. 18%   C. 20%   D. 2%

29. A dentist sees an average of 30 patients each day. Of these patients, 30% are teenagers.
    How many teenage patients does the dentist see in a typical day?

    A. 90   B. 27   C. 9   D. 33

30. A farmer plants 110 acres with soybeans, 95 acres with corn, and 909 acres with cotton. A summer drought killed off 40% of the crops.
    How many acres survived the drought?

    A. 445.6   B. 668.4   C. 1114   D. 444

Questions 31-40.

DIRECTIONS: Questions 31 through 40 are to be answered on the basis of the information provided in the Conversion Table below.

CONVERSION TABLE

1 foot = 12 inches
1 yard = 3 feet
1 mile = 1760 yards
1 meter = 100 centimeters
1 kilometer = 1000 meters
1 square yard = 9 square feet
1 square centimeter = 100 square millimeters
1 pound = 16 ounces
1 gallon = 8 pints
1 liter = 1000 milliliters

31. A chef is preparing dinner for 50 people. He plans to serve 7 ounces of fish to each guest.
    How much fish will he need for dinner?

    A. 350 pounds   B. 21 pounds 14 ounces
    C. 20 pounds 12 ounces   D. 35 pounds

32. In a 10 kilometer race, Sue plans to sprint the last 400 meters. The rest of the race, she'll run at her regular pace.
    How far, in kilometers, will she run at her normal pace?

    A. 400   B. 9.4   C. 10   D. 9.6

33. A recipe for punch calls for 2 liters of club soda, 500 milliliters of orange juice, and 400 milliliters of cranberry juice.
    How much punch, in liters, will this recipe make?

    A. 2.9   B. 2900   C. 290   D. 0.9

34. How many square yards of carpet will be needed for a room that is 12 feet wide and 18 feet long?   34._____

    A. 216   B. 24   C. 72   D. 3.3

35. The Mid-State Canal is 15 yards across, and there is a 5 yard maintenance path on each side of the canal. How many feet of wire are necessary to cross the canal and both maintenance paths?   35._____

    A. 25   B. 20   C. 60   D. 75

36. The Prairie Limited takes 2 hours and 18 minutes to go from Springdale to Cactus Junction. It takes 35 minutes to load passengers and freight at Cactus Junction. The run from Cactus Junction to Valley View takes an additional hour and 24 minutes.
    How long does it take to go by train from Springdale to Valley View?   36._____

    A. 3 hours 17 minutes   B. 3 hours 42 minutes
    C. 4 hours 17 minutes   D. 4 hours 7 minutes

37. The Circle M ranch is shaped like a triangle. The sides are 6 miles, 1 1/2 miles, and 4 1/4 miles long.
    How many yards of barbed wire will be needed to fence the ranch?   37._____

    A. 154,000   B. 20,680   C. 15,400   D. 11.75

38. Nick spends an average of 15 hours a week on homework. The school year is 32 weeks long.
    The time he spends on homework each year is equal to how many days?   38._____

    A. 480   B. 365   C. 20   D. 40

39. Ralph is building the steps for a 3-meter board. There are 12 steps between the ground and the board.
    How many centimeters high will each step be?   39._____

    A. 25   B. 24   C. 2.4   D. 250

40. When Heidi's arms are stretched over her head, her reach is 7 feet 6 inches.
    How high will she have to jump to touch a 10-foot high basketball rim?   40._____

    A. 2 feet 4 inches   B. 3 feet 6 inches
    C. 2 feet 1 inch   D. 2 feet 6 inches

41. The height of the starting players on the Coast High School basketball team is: 41._____

    | Pancho Martinez | 2.02 meters |
    | Tim Riordan | 1.82 meters |
    | Marc Gold | 2.02 meters |
    | Biff Marshall | 2.10 meters |
    | Harrison | 2.04 meters |

    What is the mean average height of the players, in meters?

    A. 1.58   B. 1.975   C. 2   D. 2.25

42. The temperature on the first day of five consecutive months is:

July	74.25° F
August	75.54° F
September	71.02° F
October	70.22° F
November	68.57° F

    What is the mean (average) temperature during the time period shown?

    A. 89.9° F B. 70.05° F C. 71.92° F D. 72.145° F

43. Jill keeps track of the distance she runs each day.

Monday	3.2 miles
Tuesday	4.3 miles
Wednesday	0 miles
Thursday	4.8 miles
Friday	5.5 miles

    What is her mean (average) daily run, in miles?

    A. 2.245 B. 3.56 C. 4.45 D. 17.8

44. Starting salaries for jobs at International Semiconductor are:

POSITION	WEEKLY SALARY
Utility Worker	$200.00
Assembler	$225.00
Shift Supervisor	$260.00
Assistant Foreman	$300.00
Foreman	$350.00

    What is the mean (average) weekly salary?

    A. $167.20 B. $333.75 C. $1335.00 D. $267.00

45. Jack's diet calls for a breakfast of 350 calories, a lunch of 450 calories, and a dinner of 700 calories. What is the mean (average) number of calories per meal on his diet?

    A. 400 B. 375 C. 500 D. 1500

46. The room sizes in an apartment are:

Living room	193 square feet
Kitchen	115 square feet
Dining room	174 square feet
Bedroom	186 square feet

    What is the mean (average) size of the rooms, in square feet?

    A. 208.75 B. 167 C. 165 D. 16.5

47. Hazel caught and released 5 fish on Friday, 6 on Saturday, and 9 on Sunday. Even though she caught nothing on Monday, she won the fishing tournament. What was her mean (average) daily catch?

    A. 4 B. 5 C. 20 D. 8

48. The prices of automobile tires are:

TIRE STYLE	PRICE
Standard	$48.00
Radial	$63.00
Wide Profile	$76.00
Snow	$55.00

What is the mean (average) price of the tires?

   A. $242.00   B. $240.00   C. $60.50   D. $60.00

49. The price of a typical meal in five restaurants is:

Applejack	$7.50
Juanita's	$6.25
The Greenery	$10.20
Rick's	$14.75
House of Chu	$9.50

What is the mean (average) price of a meal in the restaurants?

   A. $11.57   B. $48.20   C. $12.05   D. $9.64

50. The closing price of a share of NSI, Corp. over a 5-day trading period ran as follows:

Monday	15 1/8
Tuesday	14 3/4
Wednesday	17
Thursday	16 1/2
Friday	16 3/8

For this trading week, what was the average price per share of NSI, Corp.?

   A. $15.95   B. 15 5/8   C. 15 3/8   D. $14.87

KEY (CORRECT ANSWERS)

1. B	11. D	21. D	31. B	41. C
2. D	12. A	22. B	32. D	42. C
3. B	13. C	23. D	33. A	43. B
4. D	14. D	24. B	34. B	44. D
5. B	15. B	25. D	35. D	45. C
6. D	16. C	26. C	36. C	46. B
7. A	17. D	27. D	37. B	47. B
8. C	18. B	28. C	38. C	48. C
9. A	19. D	29. C	39. A	49. D
10. D	20. C	30. B	40. D	50. A

SOLUTIONS TO PROBLEMS

1. $H = \sqrt{3^2 + 4^2} = \sqrt{25} = 5$

2. $N = (1.25)(11.6°) + 3.6 = 18.1°$

3. $T = (\$400)(1.06) = \$424$

4. $C = (1800)(.0034) + (1/30)(60) = \$6.12 + \$2 = \$8.12$

5. $P = (\$9)(3\ 1/3) + (.45)(1\ 4/5) = \$30 + .81 = \$30.81$

6. $T = \dfrac{(.1)(2160) + (2)(27)}{60} = \dfrac{270}{60} = 4.5\ \text{hours}$

7. $D = (.86)(4.5) + 2.8 = 6.67$ in.

8. $A = (\pi)(80^2)/4\ (3.14)(6400)/4 = 5024$ sq.ft.

9. $A = (1/2)(300)(150) = 22{,}500$ sq.ft.

10. NAV = ($180,000 - $70,000)/8500 ~ $12.94

11. Let x = cost. Then, $\dfrac{3}{\$2.50} = \dfrac{36}{x}$, 3x = 90, x = $30.00

12. Let x = number of windows. Then, 6/12 = 9/x, 6x = 108, x = 18

13. Let x = energy use. Then, $\dfrac{5}{\$427} = \dfrac{10}{x}$, 5x = 4270, x = $854.00

14. Let x = number of passengers. Then, 6/120 = 8/x , 6x = 960, x = 160

15. Let x = number of rolls. Then, 9/63 = 5/x, 9x = 315, x = 35

16. Let x = number of lights. Then, 4/64 = x/256 , 64x = 1024, x = 16

17. Let x = number of guards. Then, 3/15 = x/45 , 15x = 135, x = 9

18. Let x = number of shelves. Then, 4/50 = x/750, 50x = 3000, x = 60

19. Let x = number of spares. Then, 6/30 = x/95 = 570, x = 19

20. Let x = number of sales. Then, 8/24 = x/360, 24x = 2880, x = 120

21. 28/(28 + 14 + 8) = 28/50 = 56%

22. (.60)(1850) = 1110 sq.mi.

23. 12/60 = 1/5 = 20%

11 (#3)

24. (74 + 61 + 65)(.65) = (200)(.65) = 130 games won

25. (.48)(25) = 12 votes

26. (.02)(500) = 10 rejections

27. 473 ÷ (473 + 218 + 182 + 119 + 108) = 473/1100 = 43%

28. 45 ÷ (46 + 134 + 45) = 45/225 = 20%

29. (30)(.30) = 9 teenage patients

30. (.60)(110 + 95 + 909) = (.60)(1114) = 668.4 acres

31. (7)(50) = 350 oz., 350/16 = 21 lbs. 14 oz.

32. 400 m. = .4 km. Then, 10 - .4 = 9.6 km.

33. 2 + 500/1000 + 400/1000 = 2.9 liters

34. (12/3)(18/3) = (4)(6) = 24 sq.yds.

35. 15 + 5 + 5 = 25 yds. Then, (25)(3) = 75 ft.

36. 2 hrs. 18 min. + 35 min. + 1 hr. 24 min. = 3 hrs. 77 min. = 4 hrs. 17 min.

37. 6 + 1 1/2 + 4 1/4 = 11 3/4 mi. Then, (11 3/4)(1760) = 20,680 yds.

38. (15)(32) = 480 hrs. Then, 480/24 = 20 days.

39. 3 ÷ 12 = .25 m. Then, (.25)(100) = 25 cm.

40. 10 ft. - 7 ft. 6 in. = 2 ft. 6 in.

41. (2.02 + 1.82 + 2.02 + 2.10 + 2.04)/5 = 10/5 = 2 meters

42. (74.25° + 75.54° + 71.02° + 70.22° + 68.57°)/5 = $\frac{359.6°}{5}$ = 71.92F

43. (3.2 + 4.3 + 0 + 4.8 + 5.5)/5 = 17.8/5 = 3.56 mi.

44. ($200 + $225 + $260 + $300 + $350)/5 = 1335/5 = $267.00

45. (350 + 450 + 700)/3 = 1500/3 = 500 calories

46. (193 + 115 + 174 + 186)/4 = 668/4 = 167 sq.ft.

47. (5 + 6 + 9 + 0)/4 = 20/4 = 5

48. ($48 + $63 + $76 + $55)/4 = 242/4 = $60.5

49. ($7.50 + $6.25 + $10.20 + $14.75 + $9.50)/5 = 48.20/5 = $9.64

50. (15 1/8 + 14 3/4 + 17 + 16 1/2 + 16 3/8)/5 = $\frac{79\frac{3}{4}}{5}$ = $15.95

TEST 4

DIRECTIONS: Each question or incomplete statement is followed by several suggested answers or completions. Select the one that BEST answers the question or completes the statement. *PRINT THE LETTER OF THE CORRECT ANSWER IN THE SPACE AT THE RIGHT.*

1. An inspector chooses at random 4 tires from every 900 being manufactured. What is the probability that any one tire will be selected?

    A. 25/1   B. 1/250   C. 1/225   D. 1/150

    1.___

2. A bus holds 40 passengers. Two of them will be chosen at random to receive free tickets to a play.
What is the probability of any one passenger getting a free ticket to a play?

    A. 1/40   B. 1/2   C. 1/20   D. 20/1

    2.___

3. There are 24 students in a class. Two of them will be chosen at random to attend a state-wide meeting.
If you were in the class, what are the chances that you would be chosen?

    A. 12/1   B. 1/12   C. 1/24   D. 24/1

    3.___

4. A team of 800 students is searching for a pair of rare birds. The birds are known to be in the area in which the team is searching.
What is the probability of any one student being the first to spot one of the birds?

    A. 1/800   B. 1/2   C. 1/400   D. 2/1

    4.___

5. Each day an average of 6 lightbulbs burn out in a hotel. There are 850 lightbulbs in the hotel.
What is the probability that any given bulb will burn out in a day?

    A. 3/425   B. 3/415   C. 1/140   D. 1/6

    5.___

6. The Internal Revenue Service checks one out of every 900 tax returns.
If there are 2 taxpayers in your family, what is the probability that someone in the family will be audited?

    A. 1/900   B. 1/450   C. 450/1   D. 1/45

    6.___

7. A total of 28 major meteors have hit the planet Paxtar in the last 600 years.
What is the probability that a major meteor will hit the planet during the year you are visiting there?

    A. 7/150   B. 1/20   C. 150/1   D. 1/28

    7.___

8. An exploration team drilled 800 wells and hit oil only 18 times.
Given this history, what are the chances that they will strike oil on their next drilling attempt?

    A. 1/18   B. 6/400   C. 1/400   D. 9/400

    8.___

9. At the pre-season tryout for the football team, 455 players showed up. There are 25 openings on the team. What is the probability that any one player will make the team?

    A. 5/18   B. 1/25   C. 1/455   D. 5/91

    9.___

84

10. A slot machine in a Las Vegas casino will be played by 750 people in one day. Of the 750, 65 will win 3rd prize, 20 will win 2nd prize, and 5 will win a 1st prize. What is the probability of somebody winning any prize?

   A. 13/150   B. 3/25   C. 2/75   D. 7/75

11. Connie bought 100 shares of Texas Cattle Company in 2000 and sold it in 2003. How much money did she make?

   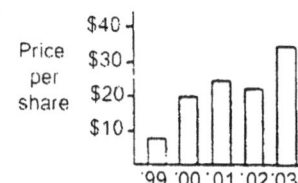

   A. $3500
   B. $1500
   C. $1000
   D. $15,000

12. Five students spent their weekends cleaning up roadside litter. They gathered a total of 1278 pounds of aluminum for the recycling center. How much of the aluminum was picked up by Tom, Laura, and Jane all together?

   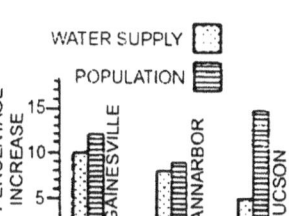

   A. 41 pounds
   B. 523.98 pounds
   C. 357.84 pounds
   D. 542.98 pounds

13.

	RATE PER MINUTE	
TIME	IN STATE	OUT OF STATE
8:00 A.M. - 4:00 P.M.	$.06	$.19
4:00 P.M. - 1:00 A.M.	$.04	$.12
1:00 A.M. - 8:00 A.M.	$.02	$.08

   The above chart shows the cost of using a new telephone service.
   What would it cost to make an out-of-state call from 10:00 P.M. to 10:23 P.M.?

   A. $.12   B. $.92   C. $2.75   D. $2.76

14. Lester's exercise program includes rowing, running, and swimming. The chart shows how each type of exercise increases his heart rate.
   How long will he have to run before his pulse rate is the same as if he had rowed for 3 minutes?

   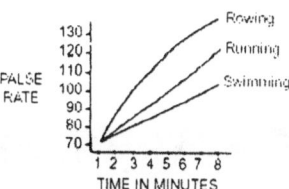

   A. 3 minutes   B. 4 minutes   C. 5 minutes   D. 6 minutes

15. This chart shows the cost of printing 1,000 brochures on different kinds of paper. How much would it cost to print 5,000 two-color brochures on paper with a linen finish? The brochures are 8 pages long.

NUMBER OF PAGES	COLORS	PAPER FINISH BOND	LINEN	GLOSS
4	ONE	$600	$700	$775
	TWO	$840	$980	$1085
8	ONE	$1150	$1350	$1410
	TWO	$1610	$1890	$1974
16	ONE	$2175	$2460	$2660
	TWO	$3045	$3444	$3724

A. $1890
B. $9450
C. $17,220
D. $6750

15.____

16. The *thirst gap* is the difference between the growth of the water supply and the population of a city. The chart compares the thirst gap of three medium-sized cities.
What is the difference in the thirst gap between Tucson and Gainesville?

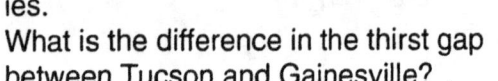

A. 10%
B. 5%
C. 8%
D. 15%

16.____

17. The houses in Smallville are heated by five different energy sources. This chart shows the percentage of homes that are heated by each energy source. Next year, the percentage of homes heated by wood is expected to double because people will be converting from oil to wood.

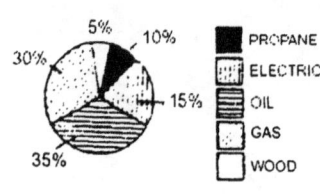

What percentage of homes will be heated by oil next year?

A. 30%
B. 35%
C. 40%
D. 25%

17.____

Questions 18-20.

DIRECTIONS: Questions 18 through 20 are to be answered using the information provided in the bar graph shown below.

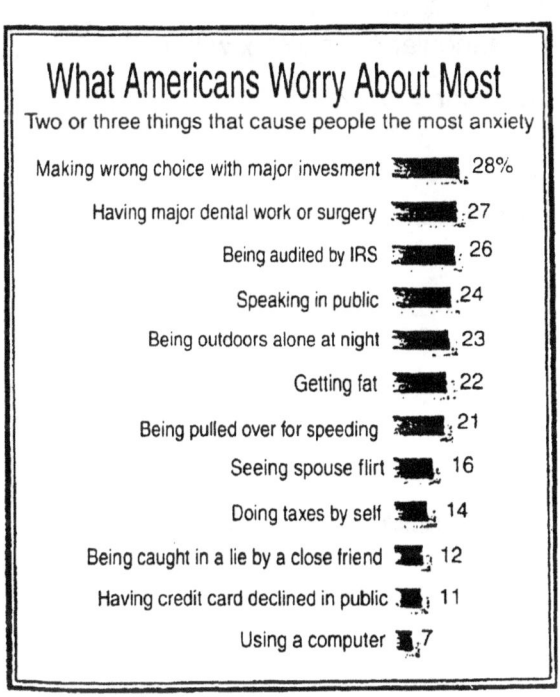

18. Assuming 500 people were surveyed, how many Americans are MOST concerned about doing their own taxes?

    A. 80   B. 115   C. 70   D. 73

19. Increasing the survey to 800 Americans, how many MORE people are concerned with being audited by the IRS as opposed to having a credit card declined in public?

    A. 112   B. 120   C. 168   D. 24

20. How many more people worry about speaking in public than using a computer?

    A. 17
    B. 12
    C. 5
    D. it cannot be determined from the information given

Questions 21-30.

DIRECTIONS: Questions 21 through 30 are to be answered on the basis of the information provided in the table shown below.

5 (#4)

TABLE OF FORMULAS

Area of a circle = πr^2

Circumference of a circle = πd

Volume of a rectangular prism = l x w x h

Volume of a cylinder = πr^2 x h

$\pi = 3.14$

21. Find the perimeter of the rectangle shown at the right.

    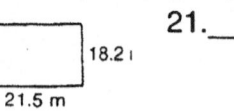

    21.____

    A. 391.3m
    B. 79.4m
    C. 794m
    D. 89m

22. Find the volume of the rectangular prism shown at the right.

    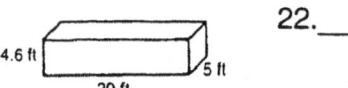

    22.____

    A. 29.6 ft.³
    B. 460 ft.³
    C. 46 ft.³
    D. 115 ft.³

23. Find the area of the circle shown at the right.

    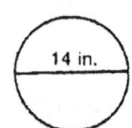

    23.____

    A. 7 π or 21.98 in.²
    B. 14 π or 43.96 in.²
    C. 49 π or 153.86 in.²
    D. 48 π or 150.72 in.²

24. Find the perimeter of the hexagon shown at the right.

    24.____

    A. 33 yd.
    B. 48.5 yd.
    C. 49.5 yd.
    D. 495 yd.

25. Find the volume of the cylinder shown at the right.

    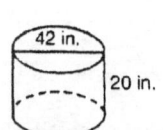

    25.____

    A. 8820 π or 27,694.8 in.³
    B. 882 π or 2769.48 in.³
    C. 840 π or 2640 in.³
    D. 441 π or 1384.74 in.³

26. The inside of the Smith's freezer is 3 feet long by 1.5 feet wide by 1.8 feet high. How many cubic feet of storage space is in the freezer?

   A. 3 ft.^{3}
   B. 4.5 ft.^{3}
   C. 5.4 ft.^{3}
   D. 8.1 ft.^{3}

26.____

27. Find the area of the triangle shown at the right.

   A. 19.21 km^2
   B. 268.4 km^2
   C. 368.4 km^2
   D. 184.2 km^2

27.____

28. The Mesa Air Base has a circular radar center that is .55 miles across. A sentry drives around the center every hour.
   How far must the sentry drive to encircle the radar center?

   A. .55 π or 1.627 miles
   B. .55 π or 1.727 miles
   C. .08 π or .25 miles
   D. .275 π or .88 miles

28.____

29. Find the perimeter of the irregular shape shown at the right.

   A. 31.5 m
   B. 11.3 m
   C. 22.6 m
   D. 23.25 m

29.____

30. Find the area, in square feet, of the irregular shape shown at the right

   A. 5,625
   B. 6,250
   C. 3,125
   D. 6,525

30.____

31. What is the length of side C?

   A. 3.4 m
   B. 3.5 m
   C. 5 m
   D. 7 m

31.____

32. How many degrees are there in angle B? 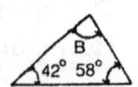 32._____

   A. 90°
   B. 280°
   C. 16°
   D. 80°

33. How many degrees are there in angle A? 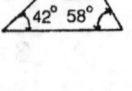 33._____

   A. 45°
   B. 55°
   C. 135°
   D. 145°

34. How many degrees are there in angle C? 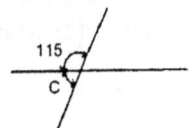 34._____

   A. 25°
   B. 65°
   C. 245°
   D. 55°

35. What is the length of side A? 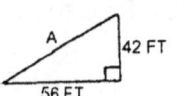 35._____

   A. 14 ft.
   B. 49 ft.
   C. 70 ft.
   D. 700 ft.

36. What is the length of side X? 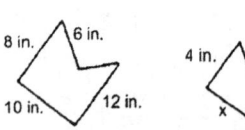 36._____

   A. 10 in.
   B. 5 in.
   C. 2 in.
   D. 6 in.

37. How many degrees are there in angle B? 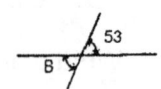 37._____

   A. 53°
   B. 37°
   C. 137°
   D. 123°

38. Lauren's yard is 75 feet wide and 100 feet long. She wants to bury a telephone wire diagonally across the yard. 38._____
   How many feet of cable will she need to cross the yard?

   A. 125   B. 100   C. 75   D. 87.5

39. How many degrees are there in angle A?   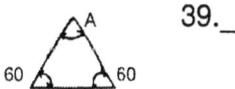   39.____

   A. 90°
   B. 45°
   C. 120°
   D. 60°

40. What is the length of side B?      40.____

   A. 18 ft.
   B. 14.5 ft.
   C. 16 ft.
   D. 19 ft.

41. Solve for the value of x: 3x = 42   41.____
   A. 45   B. 14   C. 15   D. 39

42. Solve for the value of n: 1/5 n = 25   42.____
   A. 5   B. 125   C. 50   D. 20

43. Solve for the value of a: 12a - 14 = 130   43.____
   A. 144   B. 11   C. 2   D. 12

44. Solve for the value of b: b/6 + 8 = 12   44.____
   A. 2/3   B. 120   C. 4   D. 24

45. Solve for the value of n: 45 = 4n - 3   45.____
   A. 1/12   B. 11   C. 12   D. 41

46. Solve for the value of m: 15.5 = 9m - 7   46.____
   A. 22.5   B. 9/22   C. 22/9   D. 2.5

47. Solve for the value of z: 36 = 1/4 z + 4   47.____
   A. 8   B. 144   C. 128   D. 32

48. Solve for the value of a: 4a = 17   48.____
   A. 4   B. 21/4   C. 17/4   D. 4/17

49. Solve for the value of m: m + 6 = 59   49.____
   A. 54   B. 65   C. 53   D. 59/6

50. Solve for the value of b: 1/7 b = 56   50.____
   A. 8   B. 392   C. 352   D. 1/8

KEY (CORRECT ANSWERS)

1. C	11. B	21. B	31. C	41. B
2. C	12. B	22. B	32. D	42. B
3. B	13. D	23. C	33. C	43. D
4. C	14. C	24. C	34. B	44. D
5. A	15. B	25. A	35. C	45. C
6. B	16. C	26. D	36. B	46. D
7. A	17. A	27. D	37. A	47. C
8. D	18. C	28. B	38. A	48. C
9. D	19. B	29. C	39. D	49. C
10. B	20. D	30. A	40. C	50. B

10 (#4)

SOLUTIONS TO PROBLEMS

1. 4/900 = 1/225

2. 2/40 = 1/20

3. 2/24 = 1/12

4. To spot 1 of the 2 birds is 2/1 x 1/800 = 1/400

5. 6/850 = 3/425

6. 2/900 = 1/450

7. 28/600 = 7/150

8. 18/800 = 9/400

9. 25/455 = 5/91

10. $\dfrac{65+20+5}{750} = \dfrac{90}{750} = \dfrac{9}{75} = \dfrac{3}{25}$

11. ($35)(100) - ($20)(100) = $1500 profit

12. (.08 + .20 + .13)(1278) = (.41)(1278) = 523.98 lbs.

13. (.12)(23) = $2.76

14. Rowing for 3 min. = pulse rate of 100 = running for 5 min.

15. Cost = (5)($1890) = $9450

16. (15% - 5%) - (12% - 10%) = 10% - 2% = 8%

17. Wood becomes 10%, an increase of 5%. Oil becomes 35% - 5% = 30%

18. (.14)(500) = 70 people

19. (.26)(800) - (.11)(800) = 208 - 88 = 120 people

20. .24 - .07 = .17 or 17%. However, we cannot determine the actual number of people.

21. Perimeter = (2)(18.2 + 21.5) = 79.4 m.

22. Volume = (4.6)(20)(5) = 460 cu.ft.

23. Area = $(\pi)(7^2)$ = 49 π ≈ = 153.86 sq.in.

24. (6)(8.25) - 49.5 yds.

25. Volume = $(21^2)(20)$ = 8820 π ≈ 27,694.8 cu.in.

26. (3)(1.5)(1.8) = 8.1 cu.ft.

27. Area = (1/2)(18.42)(20) = 184.2 sq.km.

28. Circumference = .55 π 1.727 mi.

29. Perimeter = 3 + 5 + 6.3 + 2.5 + 3.3 + 2.5 = 22.6 m.

30. Total area = area of I + area of II = (100X50) + (1/2)(25)(50) = 5000 + 625 = 5625 sq.ft.

31. Side C = $\sqrt{3^2 + 4^2} = \sqrt{25}$ = 5m

32. ∠B = 180° - 42° - 58° = 80°

33. ∠A = 180° - 45° = 135°

34. ∠C = = 180° - 115° = 65°

35. Side A = $\sqrt{56^2 + 42^2} = \sqrt{4900}$ = 70ft.

36. The 2 figures are proportional, so x = (1/2)(10) = 5 in.

37. ∠B = 53°, since it is opposite (vertical) to 53°.

38. $\sqrt{75^2 + 100^2} = \sqrt{15,625}$ = 125 ft. of wire

39. ∠A = 180° - 60° - 60° = 60°

40. Side B = $\sqrt{20^2 - 12^2} = \sqrt{256}$ = 16 ft

41. If 3x = 42, x = 42/3 = 14

42. If 1/5 n = 25, n = 25 ÷ 1/5 = 125

43. If 12a - 14 = 130, then 12a = 144, so a = 144/12 = 12

44. If b/6 + 8 = 12, then b/6 = 4, so b = (6)(4) = 24

45. If 45 = 4n - 3, then 48 = 4n, so n = 12

46. If 15.5 = 9m - 7, then 22.5 = 9m, so m = 22.5/9 = 2.5

47. If 36 = 1/4 z + 4, then 32 = 1/4 z, so z = 32 ÷ 1/4 = 128

48. If 4a = 17, then a = 17/4

49. If m + 6 = 59, then m = 59 - 6 = 53

50. If 1/7 b = 56, b = 56 ÷ 1/7 = 392

COMMUNICATION EXAMINATION SECTION

DIRECTIONS: Each question or incomplete statement is followed by several suggested answers or completions. Select the one that *BEST* answers the question or completes the statement. *PRINT THE LETTER OF THE CORRECT ANSWER IN THE SPACE AT THE RIGHT.*

Ability No. 1. *Infer the main idea of a passage.* (Questions 1-6)]

DIRECTIONS: Read each passage and answer the questions which follow.

Al and Bob were to organize the company picnic which usually occurred in the spring. Although it was several months ahead of time, they decided to start organizing immediately.

First, they made a list of the jobs that would have to be done. Some of the tasks listed were fund raising, food, decorations, and recreational activities. When they had completed the list, they realized they would need assistance.

They decided to organize committees to handle each of the major jobs. They advertised in the company newsletter and on the bulletin boards for volunteers. When they had 15 people, they held a meeting. At that time, committees were formed, coordinators were selected, and tasks for each committee were listed.

1. Which sentence tells the *main* idea *BEST*?

    A. Al and Bob were chosen to organize the company picnic.
    B. There were many tasks which had to be accomplished before the picnic could take place.
    C. Al and Bob advertised well ahead of time so that they could form committees.
    D. Al and Bob set up a well-organized plan for the company picnic.

The Martin family wanted to eat out. There were five members in the family and they had $30.00 they could spend. They went to the Pride Restaurant and looked at the menu posted at the door. They saw that the cheapest dinner was $8.95. They headed back for their car.

At the next restaurant, the cheapest dinner on the menu was $2.95. They went inside and were seated in a comfortable booth by the window.

2. Which sentence tells the *main* idea *BEST*?

    A. The five members of the Martin family decided to eat out at a restaurant.
    B. By looking at menus ahead of time, the Martins were able to decide whether they could afford to eat at certain restaurants.
    C. The Martins chose the second restaurant because they could be seated comfortably in a booth by the window.
    D. One restaurant had a menu that was less expensive than the other restaurant.

My cousin and her family wanted to vacation near the ocean. In order to plan for the trip, they went to a travel agency and picked up brochures which described several cities on the Atlantic coast. They decided they wanted to go to Pompano Beach and that they would drive rather than fly.

They checked a map to determine how far away Pompano Beach was and figured out the approximate number of hours it would take them to get there. Then they made a list of the types of clothes and other items they wanted to take with them. They also got a list of the hotels and motels near the beach and checked their daily rates. Based on the amount of money they had, they decided to stay at a hotel with moderate rates for a period of four days.

3. Which sentence below tells the *main* idea *BEST*?

    A. My cousin's family was going to stay in Pompano Beach for four days.
    B. They decided to drive rather than fly because it was not so expensive.
    C. They gathered information before deciding where they would go and for how long.
    D. The family made a list of the items they would need for their trip.

Classified ads are one place to look when you want to find a job. Most of the time, people writing these ads try to keep them short but factual. It is important when reading these ads to think carefully about the information given to you.

Other sources for employment are public and private employment agencies. Public agencies do not charge you a fee when helping you find a job. These agencies receive their money from taxes. Private agencies charge you a fee but are able to give more help since they do not serve so large a number of people.

However you find a job, you should be sure it fits your skills, pays the amount of money you need, and has opportunities for promotion.

4. Which sentence below tells the *main* idea *BEST*?

    A. There are several sources available to help you in finding the right job.
    B. Public employment agencies are the best source for finding a job.
    C. Classified ads are not always clearly written, but are short and give you the facts.
    D. Your job should pay enough and should fit the skills you have.

Marie was very nervous. She was on her way to the department store for a job interview. It was the first one she had ever had. She had sent an application together with a resume. The personnel director had called her and scheduled an appointment.

In preparing for the interview, Marie decided to wear a tailored suit. She also decided against using too much make-up. During the interview she was careful to be polite, to listen carefully, and to answer the personnel manager's questions as completely and honestly as she could. A week later the store called her and asked her to report to work the following Monday at 8:00 A.M.

5. Which sentence below tells the *main* idea *BEST*?

    A. The personnel manager hired Marie because he was impressed with her application and the way she conducted herself during the interview.
    B. Applying for a job can make you nervous.
    C. In applying for a job, you should fill out an application and also make up a resume which tells about you and your skills.
    D. It usually takes a week after the interview for an employer to let you know whether or not you have the job.

There are many places to look if you want to purchase a used car. You can look in the classified ads and find a private owner who wishes to sell his car directly. In this situation, you will probably have to pay cash, and you should make sure the car is in good running condition.

Another place to look for a used car is at a new-car dealer. These dealers usually keep the best of the cars that are traded in. For this reason, a used car might be more expensive than if you bought from someplace else.

A third place is a used-car lot. The prices of the cars are usually less, but used-car dealers generally get their cars from auctions or from new-car dealers. A good car can be bought, but it is wise to check it out for mechanical difficulties.

6. Which sentence below tells the *main* idea *BEST*?

    A. Most of the used cars at a new-car dealer are expensive, but not in good shape.
    B. There are advantages and disadvantages to purchasing a used car, no matter where you get it.
    C. The safest place to buy a used car is through a private owner.
    D. The best price on a used car will probably be found at a used-car lot because these dealers generally get their cars from auctions.

[Ability No. 2. *Find specific information in a passage.* (Questions 7-11)]

Questions 7-9.

DIRECTIONS: Use the prescription label below to answer Questions 7-9.

```
Salem Drugstore
1978 Cain
Miami, Florida    33133
(305) 328-6671

                 2/17/
Dr. T. E. Mortmain
#134522
Sally Bellyache
Take 1 tsp. after each meal.
Store in refrigerator.
              Not refillable
```

7. How much medicine should Sally take after dinner? One

    A. tablespoon   B. tablet   C. teaspoon   D. mouthful

8. Where should this medicine be kept?

    A. In the medicine chest   B. In a cool place
    C. In a dark place   D. Close to Sally

9. How many times may this prescription be purchased?   9.____

   A. Once   B. Twice
   C. Three times   D. As often as one wishes

Questions 10-11.

DIRECTIONS: Use the recipe below to answer Questions 10 and 11.

```
                    CHOCOLATE CHIP COOKIES
 1C brown sugar              2¼C flour
 1C white sugar              1 tsp. salt
 1C shortening               1 tsp. vanilla
 2  eggs                     1 pkg. chocolate chips
 1 tsp. baking soda
 Add sugar to shortening and cream.  Add vanilla.  Add both
 eggs.  Combine flour, salt, and baking soda.  Add a little
 at a time to mixture.  Add 1 large package of chocolate
 chips.  Drop by teaspoon on cookie sheet.  Bake at 350°-
 375° for 12 minutes.
```

10. What should be combined with the baking soda?   10.____

    A. Flour and salt   B. Flour and eggs
    C. Salt and chocolate chips   D. Eggs and white sugar

11. What is the LAST thing to be added?   11.____

    A. Eggs   B. Chocolate chips   C. Butter   D. Flour

[Ability No. 3. *Infer the cause or effect of an action.* (Questions 12-16)]

Jim found a color television set in the department store for $489. He had read in Consumer's Guide that this particular model was one of the best. He was talking to his neighbor, Artie, about buying the sat. Jim was a little concerned because of the expense of the set.

Artie suggested that they check the papers for sales. They looked through the advertisements and found the same model for $389 at a different store. Jim decided to take advantage of the sale.

12. Which sentence below BEST tells the cause and effect of the main action in the story?   12.____

    A. Because Jim did some comparison shopping, he was able to save money.
    B. Artie told Jim to buy the more expensive set because it was of better quality.
    C. Because Jim was concerned about the price, he checked Consumer's Guide to see whether the set was of good quality.
    D. Because Jim had enough money, he decided to buy the set in the store where he usually shopped.

Judy worked as a secretary for a big electrical power company. She was always fifteen minutes to half an hour late to work. Other secretaries had to leave their desks to answer her phone and her supervisor missed several important phone calls. Her supervisor called her into the office and explained how important it was to him for her to be on time, particularly because of answering the phone. He explained that he was getting complaints from his supervisors and that he was in a very uncomfortable position. Judy tried to be on time, but something always seemed to prevent her from getting there. A month later she was looking for another job.

13. Which sentence below BEST tells the cause and effect of the main action? 13._____

    A. Because other secretaries answered her phone, Judy did not have to be at work on time.
    B. Because her excuses for being late were reasonable, Judy's supervisor allowed her to continue to be a few minutes late.
    C. Since Judy continued to arrive at work late, she lost her job.
    D. Judy's supervisor had a long talk with her; therefore, Judy began arriving at work on time.

Helen was very disappointed. She had bought a pair of blue jeans on sale for $9.98 at Marcy's Department Store. They had a label that stated "washing in hot water may cause discoloration." She had seen a pair of blue jeans on sale for $11.50 at Gumble's Department Store, but didn't buy them. There was no such label in these jeans. After washing the jeans she had bought, Helen was horrified because they turned purple.

14. Which sentence below BEST tells the cause and effect of the main action? 14._____

    A. Because she didn't pay attention to the label, Helen washed the jeans in hot water; therefore, they turned color.
    B. Since Helen bought the cheaper pair of jeans, they did not last well.
    C. Since the jeans from Marcy's changed color, it can be concluded that Gumble's is a better department store.
    D. Because the $11.50 jeans had no label, they would not have changed color.

Enrico and Jose took their dates out to dinner. They selected a nice restaurant with a pleasant atmosphere and facilities for dancing. After they were seated, they had to wait a long time before the waitress brought them their water and place settings. Although they were ready to order, the waitress said, "I'll be right back." They waited another 10 minutes. Finally she came to take their order. They had to wait another 15 minutes before they were served. By this time, they were getting impatient because they wanted to be on time to a movie afterwards. When they finally got their check, they decided to leave a ten-cent tip.

15. Which sentence below BEST tells the cause and effect of the main action? 15._____

    A. Since the restaurant had a pleasant atmosphere, Enrico and Jose decided they would go there again.
    B. Enrico and Jose left a small tip because the service was not good.
    C. Since they had to go to a movie, Enrico and Jose decided to leave.
    D. Because the waitress took such a long time to serve them, Enrico and Jose were late to the movie.

Nancy heard a knock on the door. When she opened it, there was a young man selling cookware. He was nice looking, and she decided to listen to what he had to say. She really became impressed with the advantages of the cookware and decided she wanted to buy it. At first the price of $499 made her hesitate, but the salesman insisted that the monthly payments were so small she would easily be able to afford it. Later that evening, she figured out that she would be paying almost 20% interest by making time payments. The real cost of the cook-ware would be close to $600. She really wished she had not signed the contract. Then she re-read the contract and found a buyer's right to cancel. It said that if she cancelled any time prior to midnight of the third business day, she would not have to stick to the contract. The next morning she called the salesman's office.

16. Which sentence below *BEST* tells the cause and effect of the main action?

    A. Nancy decided she had to purchase the cookware anyway because she had signed a contract.
    B. Nancy cancelled the contract because she was angry with the salesman.
    C. Since the contract contained a buyer's right to cancel, Nancy was able to request that her order be stopped,
    D. Because $600 for the full set of cookware seemed reasonable, Nancy told the salesman she would keep it.

[Ability No. 4. *Identify facts and opinions.* (Questions 17-20)]

DIRECTIONS: Read the following articles. Select the best answers. Questions 17-18.

SATURDAY ACCIDENT LEAVES TWO HOSPITALIZED

Two tourists to the Miami area, Tom Lord and Vincent Hanes of Connecticut, suffered serious injury when their Dodge van, driven by Tom Lord, collided with the Buick driven by Miami resident Alma Marter. The accident occurred at 11 a.m. Saturday at the intersection of West Dixie Highway and 29th Street.

The cause of the accident is under investigation and neither driver has been charged as of this report. Witnesses have stated that the van was out of control. At least one witness believes the driver of the van was "on something," Mechanical failure is another possibility,

Tom Lord is listed in critical condition at Jackson. Vincent Hanes is listed as serious, but stable. Alma Marter was treated for injuries and released late last night. The investigation will continue.

17. Which of the following sentences is *FACT*?

    A. Tom Lord was charged with reckless driving.
    B. Mechanical failure caused the accident.
    C. The investigation has been completed.
    D. Three people were injured.

18. Which of the following sentences is *OPINION*?

    A. Tom Lord and Vincent Hanes are visitors.
    B. The accident happened in the morning.
    C. The driver of the van was "on something."
    D. There are witnesses to the accident.

Questions 19-20.

FIRE LEVELS HOUSE

Bill and Ann Gurney and their 10-year-old son are homeless after a fire Thursday night. The house, located at 35431 N.W. 3rd Avenue, suffered extensive fire and smoke damage.

The blaze started at approximately 8 p.m. Thursday in the son's bedroom. After attempting to put the fire out, the son notified neighbors who in turn called the fire department. Mr. and Mrs. Gurney were not home at the time of the fire.

The cause of the fire has not yet been determined. Fire department officials stated "arson or faulty wiring may be the cause." At least one neighbor believes the son set the fire. The official investigation into the cause will continue.

19. Which of the following sentences is FACT? 19.____

    A. The fire was caused by faulty wiring.
    B. The house was badly damaged,
    C. Mr, and Mrs, Gurney tried to put the fire out.
    D. The investigation has been completed.

20. Which of the following sentences is OPINION? 20.____

    A. The Gurney family is homeless.
    B. The fire was Thursday night.
    C. Bill and Anne Gurney were out when the fire started.
    D. The son started the fire.

[Ability No. 5, *Identify an unstated opinion.* (Questions 21-25)]

DIRECTIONS: Read the paragraphs below and choose the statements which *BEST* express each writer's opinion.

It's time this state had a governor who wasn't owned by the big-city bosses and the crooked machines. Our present governor has been taking orders from big-time gamblers and racketeers for the last four years. That's why I support John Smith to replace the present governor.

21. The writer believes that: 21.____

    A. One of the big-city bosses is the governor
    B. Gamblers control John Smith
    C. The present governor deserves support
    D. John Smith is an honest man

Billie Sunday is certainly an unusual person. Despite drastically changed conditions, runaway inflation, and ecological problems, she clings stubbornly to the "tried and true" ways of the past. I urge you to consider this fact as you cast your ballot.

22. The writer believes that: 22.____

    A. People should vote for Billie Sunday because she is an unusual person
    B. Billie Sunday's strength lies in her understanding of changed conditions
    C. People should not vote for Billie Sunday
    D. The ways of the past are the best ways

The healthfood craze is sweeping the country. Despite high prices, unverified claims, and dubious standards of cleanliness, people continue to buy so-called organic food instead of foods processed under modern, sanitary conditions.

23. The writer believes that:

    A. Organic foods are worth their high prices
    B. Organic foods are not so good for people as processed foods
    C. Organic foods are healthier than processed foods
    D. Processing food destroys its health benefits

23.____

The President, in his energy address to the nation, stressed the energy crisis as the major problem confronting the nation. Yet, almost unbelievably, many reports are being written stating that there is really no critical shortage of oil now. Some of these reports even say that the oil companies are pretending there is a shortage so that they can reap huge profits. This fact or fiction of an oil shortage must be resolved so that severe conservation measures will be accepted by the people.

24. The writer of this article believes:

    A. There really is a severe energy crisis
    B. The President is unaware of the critical shortage of oil
    C. Oil companies are correct in believing there is no energy crisis
    D. People are prepared to accept severe conservation measures

24.____

Human beings have traveled a great road. They have evolved from a primitive, tribal state to the sophisticated, expansive human beings of today. Because they have consumed a large portion of the world's natural resources, they shall again in the future, as in the past, be compelled to live in closer contact with fellow human beings.

25. The writer

    A. is extremely critical of today's people
    B. is certain that man will be more sophisticated in the future
    C. believes that tribal human beings were better than modern human beings
    D. feels that the evolution of human beings is a cycle

25.____

[Ability No. 6. *Identify source to obtain information on a topic.* (Questions 26-30)]

26. If you want to find out what the word *satisfy* means, you should look in the

    A. yellow pages   B. newspaper
    C. dictionary   D. encyclopedia

26.____

27. You need a job. The place to look is in the

    A. telephone directory   B. encyclopedia
    C. want ads   D. almanac

27.____

28. If you wanted to order something, you would use a(n)

    A. catalog   B. encyclopedia   C. atlas   D. dictionary

28.____

29. You are going to travel to Tallahassee. You want to know whether to take a warm coat.   29.____
    You should consult a(n)

    A. newspaper   B. atlas   C. telephone directory   D. catalog

30. You want to plan a trip from Miami to New Orleans. In order to find the *BEST* route, you   30.____
    would use a(n)

    A. telephone directory   B. atlas   C. newspaper   D. encyclopedia

[Ability No. 7. *Use index cross-references to find information.* (Questions 31-35)]

DIRECTIONS: Use the sample catalog index on the following page to answer Questions 31-35.

31. On which of the following pages would you find cases for pillows?   31.____

    A. 39   B. 57   C. 83   D. 204

32. How many different pages are there which show shirts for women?   32.____

    A. 2   B. 3   C. 4   D. None

33. Where would you look to find a heater for your car?   33.____

    A. 34, 47   B. 40-46   C. 78   D. 1, 20-24, 28

34. Where would you look to find a machine to strengthen your muscles?   34.____

    A. 24   B. 147, 150, 151   C. 47-49   D. 167

CATALOG INDEX

A

Abrasives, Sanding..28
Acetylene Welders...16
Adhesives, Pipe....58
Agricultural Equipment
........35-39
Air Brushes.........29
- Cleaners, Electronic
........9
- Compressors......29
- Impact Tools.....28
- Pumps, Auto.....42
- Tools............28
Airless Sprayers...29
Alarm Clocks..57, 208
Alarms, Fire........8
Alarms, Freezer....75
All-in-One Corsetry
..147, 150, 151, 153
Amplifiers, Sound
Systems, Auto....40
Analyzers, Auto....41
Anchors, Rug......175
Antennas, Radio....76
Anti-skid Rug Backing
........175
Aprons, Men's...2, 17
Arc Welders.......16
Athletic Shirts, Men's
........102
Attache Cases.....83
Augers, Drain.....19
Auto Repair Tools
........1, 20-24, 28
Auto Supplies...40-46

B

Baby Goods
........104, 105, 108
Backrests....206, 207
Bags,
Shredder-Bagger..35
Bags, Trash........47
Bags, Vacuum
Cleaner...........56
Band Saws and
Supplies......12, 15
Bandanas, Men's...88
Bar Sinks.........59
Barkcloth Fabrics.122
Bars, Towel.......50
Base Cabinets..58, 60
Baskets, Waste
........200, 201, 203
Bath Mats........203
Bath Towels......203
Bathroom Cabinets
........50, 51
- Carpeting..200, 201
- Curtains........202
- Ensembles..200-203
- Fixtures..34, 50, 51
- Furniture......203
- Heaters.....34, 47
- Rugs..176, 177,
........200, 201
- Scales.........203
- Shelves........203
- Sinks.......50, 51
- Ventilators....34
- Window Shades..202
Baths, Steam....187
Bathtub Doors....51
Bathtub Enclosures..49
Bathtubs......50, 51
Batteries, Tractor..37
Battery Chargers..42
Batts, Bedding...211
Bed Blankets
..204, 205, 218,
..219, 223, 224
- Bolsters...222, 223
- Comforters
..204, 205,
........222, 223
- Frames.........184
- Headboards
........183, 184
- Mattresses
..169, 182, 184
- Pads......170, 171
- Pillowcases
..204, 205,
........211-217
- Pillows........172
- Quilts.........222
- Ruffles..204, 205,
........222, 223
- Sheets..204, 205,
........211-217
- Spring Covers
........169, 214
Bedding
..169-172, 182, 184,
..204, 205, 211-219,
........222-224

Bedroom Draperies
..204, 205, 223
- Ensembles
..197, 204-211,
..220, 221, 223
- Furniture
..169, 182-184
- Heaters.........47
- Rugs......175-177
- Slippers, Women's
........142
Beds....182, 184, 185
Bedspreads
..197, 206-211,
..220, 221
Belts, Men's..95-97
Belts, Women's
........134, 140
Bench Grinders and
Accessories...16, 28
Bench Saws, Blades
........10, 11
Bench Vises.....1, 17
Benches, Organ....71
Benches, Vanity..183
Benches, Work..4, 14
Beverage Glasses..191
Beverage Sets....191
Bifold Doors..48, 49
Bikes, Exercise..166
Bits, Drill..1, 6, 25
Bits, Molding Cutter..14
Bits, Router......1
Blades, Dozer..36, 37
Blades, Saw
........10, 12, 15, 25
Blanket Chests...183
Blankets, Automatic
........224
Blankets, Bed
..204, 205, 218,
..219, 223, 224
Blazers, Misses',
Women's...126, 127
Blouses, Misses',
Women's...128-129
Boards, Exercise..167
Body and Fender
Tools............24
Body Briefers
..147, 150, 151
Body Building
Equipment.......167
Body Suits......141
Bolsters....222, 223
Boots, Men's..121, 168
Boots, Women's
........115-118, 168

BOXES

Fire.............158
Miter.............2
Security........166
Sewing............58
Storage.........165
Tool.........2, 4
Brackets, Saw Horse
........17
Bras, Women's
........146-153
Breakfast Room
Furniture..186, 187
Brick Wallcoverings,
Decorator........48

BRIEFS

Boys'...........113
Children's......105
Men's...........102
Misses', Women's
........146
Misses', Women's
Support..127, 150,
........151, 154
Teen Males'.....113
Broadcloth Fabrics.122
Brushes, Air
Compressor.......29
Brushes, Wire....17
Buffets.........187
Buffing Compounds..28

BUILDING MATERIAL 47-49

Buildings........35
Bulldozer Blades
........36, 37
Bunk Beds.......182
Buntings, Baby..108
Business Cases...83
Business Equipment
........155-163

C

CB Radios and Supplies
........76
Cabinet Shelves...3
Cabinet Tops...60, 61
Cabinet Valances..60

CABINETS

Base..........59, 60
Bathroom....50, 51
Built-in Oven....60
Corner...59, 60, 186
Dish.......186, 187
File........156-158
Kitchen.....59, 60
Office.....155-157
Sewing Machine...57
Shop........3, 4, 26
Storage........155
Tool..............3
Wall........59, 60
Cafe Doors.......49
Calculators and
Supplies, Electronic
........159
Calipers.........18
Camper Tires.....43
Canopy Covers, Bed
..206, 207, 210, 211
Canopy Curtains, Bed
........206, 207
Cardboard Tables.189
Carpenters' Clothes
........98, 99
Carpet Cleaning
Supplies..56, 58, 175
Carpet Sweepers..52

CARPETS AND RUGS
175-177, 200, 201,
206, 207

Carriers, Garbage Can
........47
Cartridges, Water
Filter...........31
Carts, Dump......37
Carts, Microwave
Oven.............64
Cases, Chain Saw..39
Cases, Sewing
Machine..........57
Cases, Travel....83
Cassette
Playing-Recording
Equipment........69
Ceiling Ventilators,
Bathroom.........34
Chain Hoists.....24
Chain Lamps..190, 191
Chain Saws and
Accessories..38, 39
Chains, Implement
Tire.............37
Chair Covers....179
Chairs..183, 186, 187
........183-187
Chalk and Plumb
Lines............17
Charge Accounts...79
Chargers, Battery..42
Check Files.....158

CHESTS

Bedroom.........183
Medicine.....50, 51
Storage........183
Tableware.......53
Tool.............3
Utility, Pick-up
Truck............42
China Cabinets..187
Chisels...17, 24, 25
Circular Saws and
Supplies.......5, 10
Cleaners, Air,
Electronic.......9
Cleaners, Vacuum
........56, 58
Cleaners, Vacuum,
Shop.............11
Clippers, Pet....30
Clock Radios.....70
Clocks.......57, 208
Closet Doors,
Mirrored.........49
Clothes Dryers..54, 55
Clothes Hampers..203
Clothes Steamers..58
Clothes Washers
........54, 55

COATS

Girls'..........107
Half Sizes
..126, 130, 133
Juniors'........135
Little Girls'...107
Men's Leisure...88
Men's Outerwear
........90-92, 95
Men's Ski.......165
Misses'..95, 130-133
Misses' Ski....165
Cocktail Tables
........184, 185
Comforters, Bed
..204, 205, 222, 223

35. Which of the following items is NOT listed in the sample catalog?   35._____

    A. Quilts
    B. Tool chests
    C. Automobiles
    D. Sewing machine cabinets

[Ability No. 8. *Use highway and city maps.* (Questions 36-41)]

MAP OF NORTHEAST HIGHLAND

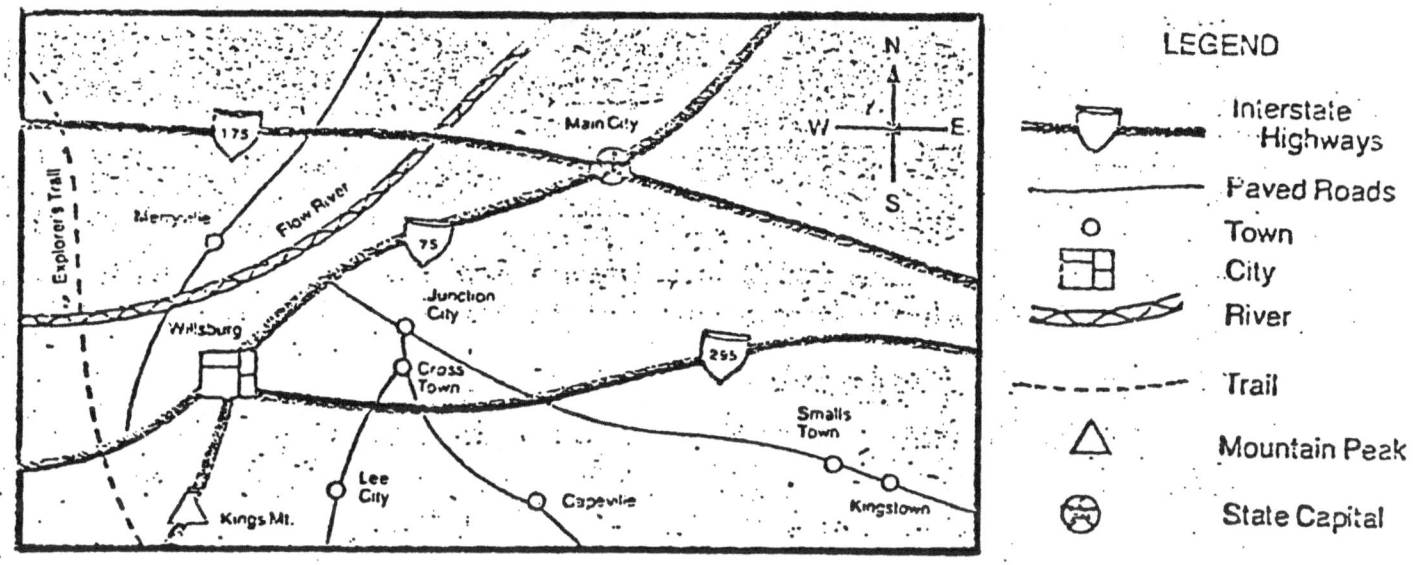

36. There are two cities between Interstate Highways 75 and 295. *What* are their names?   36._____

    A. Merryville and Junction City
    B. Main City and Cross Town
    C. Cross Town and Lee City
    D. Junction City and Cross Town

37. What is the name of the trail?   37._____

    A. Merryville's Trail
    B. Explorer's Trail
    C. Willsburg's Trail
    D. Kingstown's Trail

38. What is the name of the river north of Willsburg?   38._____

    A. Junction River
    B. Cross River
    C. Flow River
    D. Explorer's River

39. What is the name of the mountain peak?   39._____

    A. Kingstown's Peak
    B. Capeville's Peak
    C. King's Mountain
    D. Lee City's Mountain

40. What is the name of the state capital?   40._____

    A. Willsburg
    B. Main City
    C. Junction City
    D. Merryville

41. Which city is west of Capeville?   41._____

    A. Lee City   B. Kingstown   C. Smalls Town   D. Main City

[Ability No. 9. *Include necessary information in letters.* (Questions 42-48)]

42. Choose the letter which includes ALL of the *specific* information.   42._____
Write to the Continental Moving Company giving them directions to your summer cabin. Tell them to turn off Highway 75 at Route 234 and go east 10 miles to Brook Lane. Cabin #31 is at the top of the hill. Have them place the furniture in the living room.

   A. Dear Sir:
Our summer cabin, #31, can be reached from Highway 75.
It is at the top of the hill.

   B. Dear Sir:
Deliver the furniture to our cabin, #31, and place it in the living room. The cabin can be reached by turning off Highway 75 and going east on Route 234 for 10 miles. The cabin is at the top of the hill on Brook Lane.

   C. Dear Sir:
The furniture is to be brought to our cabin and left in the living room. If you go down Highway 75 to Route 234, you will have no trouble finding the cabin. It is at the top of the hill.

   D. Dear Sir:
Deliver the furniture to our cabin, #31. The cabin can be reached by turning off Highway 75 and going east on Route 234 for 10 miles. The cabin is at the top of the hill on Brook Lane.

43. Read the information below that is to be included in a letter. After reading the letters that   43._____
follow, choose the letter that has ONLY the correct, necessary information. Merv, the calculator is not working correctly, and our entire department is being slowed down. Write to the Arkansas Calculator Company and ask where we should send the calculator to be repaired. Also, ask how long it will take and if we are covered by a guarantee. Phone the Burrows Business Corporation to arrange for a rental calculator.

   A. Dear Sir:
Our entire department is being slowed down because our calculator is broken. We would like to know where to have it fixed and how long it will take.

   B. Dear Sir:
Our calculator is broken. Where should we send it? How long will it take? Are we covered by a guarantee? We would also like to rent a calculator to use in the meantime.

   C. Dear Sir:
Our calculator is broken, and we would like to know where to have it fixed and how long it will take. Also, could you tell us how much it will cost?

   D. Dear Sir:
Our calculator is broken. We would like to know where to send it and how long the repairs will take. Also, are we covered by a guarantee?

44. Read the information below that is to be included in a letter. After reading the letters that   44._____
follow, choose the letter that has ONLY the correct, necessary information.
George, send a letter to Stingee's U-Rent One, reserving a car for the week of September 3rd. Ask for a compact. The last car we rented was too big. It guzzled gas and almost broke me. Tell them to send the contract and insurance forms right away.

- A. Dear Sir:
  I would like to reserve a small car for the week of September 3rd. The large car I rented last time was too expensive to run. Send the contract and insurance forms right away.
- B. Dear Sir:
  Please reserve a compact car for the week of September 3. Also send the necessary forms as soon as possible.
- C. Dear Sir:
  Please reserve a car for me for the week of September 3rd. I would like the contract and insurance forms sent to me right away.
- D. Dear Sir:
  I want to reserve a compact car for the week of September 3rd. Send the contract and insurance forms as soon as possible.

45. Choose the letter which includes ALL of the *specific* information.   45._____
Write to the Climax TV Company, telling them where their delivery man can find the TV he is to pick up for repair. It is covered with a blanket and placed in the garage behind the storage cabinet.

- A. Gentlemen:
  The TV set to be picked up for repair is covered and is in the garage near the storage cabinet.
- B. Gentlemen:
  The TV set to be repaired is in the garage close to the storage cabinet.
- C. Gentlemen:
  The TV set to be picked up for repair is covered with a blanket and is standing behind the storage cabinet.
- D. Gentlemen:
  The TV set to be picked up for repair is in my garage behind the storage cabinet. It is covered with a blanket.

46. Read the information below that is to be included in a letter. After reading the letters that   46._____
follow, choose the one that has ONLY the correct, necessary information. Write to the Westbury Bowl and ask them to send you six tickets at $4.00 each for the Big Band Concert on December 21. The same concert was given last month in Nashville and was a great success. Tell them that you are enclosing a check for the necessary amount.

- A. Gentlemen:
  I heard about the Big Band Concert and want four tickets. Enclosed is a check to cover all costs.
- B. Gentlemen:
  The Big Band Concert sounds great. I would like to reserve tickets for it. Enclosed is a check. Please send the tickets as soon as possible.
- C. Gentlemen:
  Please send me six tickets for the Big Band Concert on December 21. Enclosed is a check for $24.00.
- D. Gentlemen:
  Please reserve four tickets for me for the Big Band Concert on December 21 ($16). Many thanks.

47. Choose the letter that includes *ALL* of the information. Write to the Complete Leather Company and order the wallet advertised in Sunday's newspaper. It is item #A3131. Order it in black pigskin. Ask for a catalog of other mail-order items.

   A. Gentlemen:
   Please send me the black pigskin wallet, item #A3131, advertised in Sunday's paper. Also send a catalog of your mail-order products.
   B. Gentlemen:
   I would like the wallet advertised in Sunday's newspaper. It is item #A3131, and I would like it in black leather. Please send an order form for other mait-order items.
   C. Gentlemen:
   Please send me a catalog of your mail-order products as well as the leather wallet advertised in Sunday's newspaper.
   D. Gentlemen:
   Send me item #A3131 and a mail-order catalog so that I can order any other leather items I need.

47.___

48. Choose the letter that includes ALL of the information. Write to the Chief of Police, Captain Strongman, inviting him to speak to the social studies classes in honor of Law Day. Ask him to speak on Thursday, March 17, at 1:45 P.M., and ask him to give you the title or topic of his speech so that you can print a program. Have him write to you at school or call you at home after 7:00 P.M., at 527-2004.

   A. Dear Captain Strongman:
   We are celebrating Law Day in our social studies classes and would like you to be our speaker. Please try to set aside Thursday, March 17. Let me know if you can come that day. You may write to me at school or call me at home after 7:00 P.M., at 527-2004.
   B. Dear Captain Strongman:
   Our social studies classes would like you to speak to us on Thursday, March 17, at 1:45 P.M. We are honoring Law Day and would appreciate your choosing any topic you consider appropriate. Please let us know if you can come and what your exact topic will be. You can write to me at school or call me at home after 7:00 P.M., at 527-2004.
   C. Dear Captain Strongman:
   Law Day is an important day which we celebrate at our school. We would like you to discuss the topic of law with our social studies classes. Please contact me personally to let me know if you can come. You can write to me at the above address or call me at home after 7:00P.M., at 527-2004.
   D. Dear Captain Strongman:
   Our social studies classes would like you to share Law Day with us on March 17, at 1:45 P.M. The topic of the day can be decided later. Please contact me by writing to me at school or calling me at home after 7:00 P.M., at 527-2004.

48.___

[Ability No. 10. *Complete a check and its stub.* (Questions 49-53)]

Questions 49-51.

DIRECTIONS: Read the following and answer each question about the check.

Joan Biondi bought two cook books on July 9, from Good Book Company. The total cost was $11.38.

```
┌─────────────────────────────────────────────────────────────┐
│    THIRD MIAMI BANK              No. 101      10-101        │
│                                                  670        │
│                              (1)         20___              │
│  Pay to the                                                 │
│  Order of _____(2)_____  $____(3)____     │
│                                                             │
│  _____(4)_____  DOLLARS      │
│                                                             │
│  Memo_____(5)_____    ____(6)____               │
│                                                             │
│     :067   /0101/:                                          │
└─────────────────────────────────────────────────────────────┘
```

Circle the correct letter.

49. Which of the following would be written in the space marked 4 on the check?   49._____

    A. 11 38/100   B. Joan Biondi
    C. July 9   D. Eleven and 38/100

50. Which of the following would be written in the space marked 2   50._____

    A. Joan Biondi   B. Good Book Company
    C. Cook books   D. Eleven and 38/100

51. Which of the following would be written in the space marked 3 on the check?   51._____

    A. July 9   B. Cook books
    C. 11 38/100   D. Books

Questions 52-53.

DIRECTIONS: Now look at Joan Biondi's check stub to the right and answer questions 52 and 53.

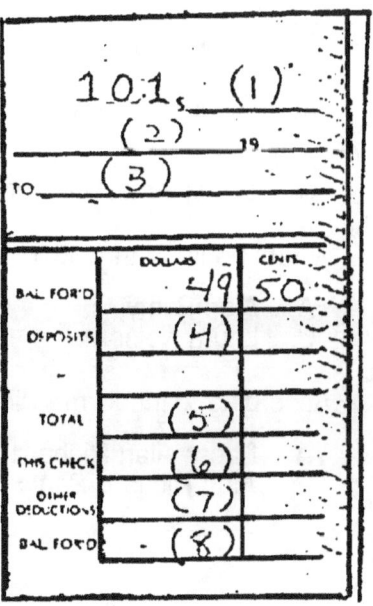

16 (#1)

52. Which of the following would be written in the space marked *6* on the check stub?   52.___

   A. 11.38   B. Good Book Co.   C. 1Q1   D. Cook books

53. Which of the following would be written in the space marked *8* on the check stub?   53.___

   A. 49.50   B. 11.38   C. 60.88   D. 38.12

[Ability No. 11. *Complete accurately common application forms.* (Questions 54-58).]

DIRECTIONS: Read the following information about a person who is filling out a job application form. Then answer Questions 54-58.

Alan Richard Panty is a seventeen-year-old student who is applying for a job as a cashier in Bloomdale's department store. He has never done this kind of work before. He is not a high school graduate but feels that he can learn how to do this job. He will use his math teacher at Miami High, Mrs. Laura Nelson, as a reference.

```
                          APPLICATION
   Name _____(1)_____
            Last           First              M.I.
   Address _____
   Education
     Last School Attended _____(2)_____
     Graduated:      Yes (3)      No (4)
   Position Desired _____(5)_____
   Experience _____(6)_____
   Personal Reference: Name _____(7)_____
                       Occupation _____(8)_____
```

54. What should Alan write on the line marked 5?   54.___

   A. Yes   B. Cashier
   C. Department store D. Math teacher

55. What should Alan write on the line marked 8?   55.___

   A. Cashier   B. Student
   C. Math teacher   D. Applying

56. Where should Alan write *NONE*?   56.___

   A. Line 4   B. Line 2
   C. The line marked Address   D. Line 6

57. What should Alan write on line 7?   57.___

   A. Alan Panty   B. Bloomdale's
   C. Laura Nelson   D. Miami High

58. According to the form's directions, how should Alan write his name?   58.___

   A. Panty, Alan Richard   B. Panty, Alan R.
   C. Alan Richard Panty   D. Alan R. Panty

59. What should Alan write on the line marked 2?

    A. Ulmer Elementary School
    B. Biscayne Junior High
    C. Ulmer Intermediate School
    D. None of the above

60. What should Alan write on the line marked 8?

    A. High school student
    B. No experience
    C. Some knowledge
    D. Want to be an accountant

KEY (CORRECT ANSWERS)

1. D	16. C	31. D	46. C
2. D	17. D	32. C	47. A
3. C	18. C	33. B	48. B
4. A	19. B	34. D	49. D
5. A	20. D	35. C	50. B
6. B	21. B	36. D	51. C
7. C	22. D	37. B	52. A
8. B	23. B	38. D	53. D
9. A	24. D	39. C	54. B
10. A	25. D	40. B	55. B
11. B	26. C	41. A	56. D
12. A	27. C	42. B	57. C
13. C	28. A	43. B	58. B
14. A	29. A	44. D	59. D
15. B	30. B	45. D	60. A

112

READING COMPREHENSION
UNDERSTANDING AND INTERPRETING WRITTEN MATERIAL

STRATEGIES

SURVEYING PASSAGES, SENTENCES AS CUES

While individual readers develop unique reading styles and skills, there are some known strategies which can assist any reader in improving his or her reading comprehension and performance on the reading subtest. These strategies include understanding how single paragraphs and entire passages are structured, how the ideas in them are ordered, and how the author of the passage has connected these ideas in a logical and sequential way for the reader.

The section that follows highlights the importance of reading a passage through once for meaning, and provides instruction on careful reading for context cues within the sentences before and after the missing word.

SURVEY THE ENTIRE PASSAGE

To get a sense of the topic and the organization of ideas in a passage, it is important to survey each passage initially in its entirety and to identify the main idea. (The first sentence of a paragraph usually states the main idea.) Do not try to fill in the blanks initially. The purpose or surveying a passage is to prepare for the more careful reading which will follow. You need a sense of the big picture before you start to fill in the details; for example, a quick survey of the passage on page 11 indicate that the topic is the early history of universities. The paragraphs are organized to provide information on the origin of the first universities, the associations formed by teachers and students, the early curriculum, and graduation requirements.

READ PRECEDING SENTENCES CAREFULLY

The missing words in a passage cannot be determined by reading and understanding only the sentences in which the deletions occur. Information from the sentences which precede or follow can provide important cues to determine the correct choice. For example, if you read the first sentence from the passage about universities which contains a blank, you will notice that all the alternatives make sense if this one sentence is read in isolation:

Nobody actually _____ them.
   A. started   B. guarded   C. blamed
   D. compared   E. remembered

The only way that you can make the correct word choice is to read the preceding sentences. In the excerpt below, notice that the first sentence tells the reader what the passage will be about: how universities developed. A key word in the first sentence is *emerged*, which is closely related in meaning to one of the five choices for the first blank. The second sentence explains the key word *emerged*, by pointing out that we have no historical record of a decree or a date indicating when the first university was established. Understanding the ideas in the first two sentences makes it possible to select the correct word for the blank. Look at the sentence with the deleted word in the context of the preceding sentences and think about why you are now able to make the correct choice.

> The first universities emerged at the end of the 11th century and beginning of the 12th. These institutions were not founded on any particular date or created by any formal action. Nobody actually _____ them.
> A. started B. guarded C. blamed
> D. compared E. remembered

Started is the best choice because it fits the main idea of the passage and is closely related to the key word *emerged*.

READ THE SENTENCE WHICH FOLLOWS TO VERIFY YOUR CHOICE

The sentences which follow the one from which a word has been deleted may also provide cues to the correct choice. For example, look at an excerpt from the passage about universities again, and consider how the sentence which follows the one with the blank helps to reinforce the choice of the word *started*.

> The first universities emerged at the end of the 11th century and the beginning of the 12th. These institutions were not founded on any particular date or created by any formal action. Nobody actually _____ them. Instead, they developed gradually in places like Paris, Oxford, and Bologna, where scholars had long been teaching students.
> A. started B. guarded C. blamed
> D. compared E. remembered

The words *developed gradually* mean the same as the key word *emerged*. The signal word *instead* helps to distinguish the difference between starting on a specific date as a result of some particular act or event and emerging over a period of time as a result of various factors.

Here is another example of how the sentence which follows the one from which a word is deleted might help you decide which of two good alternatives is the correct choice. This excerpt is from the practice passage about bridges (page 10).

> Bridges are built to allow a continuous flow of highway and railway traffic across water lying in their paths. But engineers cannot forget that river traffic, too, is essential to our economy. The role of _____ is important. To keep these vessels moving freely, bridges are built big enough, when possible, to let them pass underneath.
> A. wind B. boats C. weight
> D. wires E. experience

After the first two sentences, the reader may be uncertain about the direction the writer intended to take in the rest of the paragraph. If the writer intended to continue the paragraph with information concerning how engineers make choices about the relative importance and requirements of land traffic and rive traffic, *experience* might be the appropriate choice for the missing word. However, the sentence following the one in which the deletion occurs makes it clear that *boats* is the correct choice. It provides the synonym *vessels*, which in the noun phrase *these vessels* must refer back to the previous sentence or sentences. The phrase *to let them pass underneath* also helps make it clear that *boats* is the appropriate choice. *Them* refers back to *these vessels* which, in turn, refers back to *boats* when the word *boats* is placed in the previous sentence. Thus, the reader may use these cohesive ties (the pronoun referents) to verify the final choice.

Even when the text following a sentence with a deletion is not necessary to choose the best alternative, it may be helpful in other ways. Specifically, complete sentences provide important transitions into a related topic which is developed in the rest of the paragraph or in the next paragraph of the same passage. For example, the first paragraph in the passage about universities ends with a sentence which introduces the term *guilds*: *But, over time, they joined together to form guilds.* Prior to this sentence, information about the slow emergence of universities and about how independently scholars had acted was introduced. The next paragraph begins with two sentences about guilds in general. Someone who had not read the last sentence in the first paragraph might have missed the link between guilds and scholars and universities and, thus, might have been unnecessarily confused.

COHESIVE TIES AS CUES

Sentences in a paragraph may be linked together by several devices called cohesive ties. Attention to these ties may provide further cues about missing words. This section will describe the different types of cohesive ties and show how attention to them can help you to select the correct word.

PERSONAL PRONOUNS

Personal pronouns (e.g., he, she, they, it, its) are often used in adjoining sentences to refer back to an already mentioned person, place, thing, or idea. The word to which the pronoun refers is called the antecedent.

Tools used in farm work changed very slowly from ancient times to the eighteenth century, and the changes were minor. Since the eighteenth century *they* have changed quickly and dramatically.

The word *they* refers back to *tools* in the example above.

In the examination reading subtest, a deleted word sometimes occurs in a sentence in which the sentence subject is a pronoun that refers back to a previously mentioned noun. You must correctly identify the referent for the particular pronoun in order to interpret the sentence and select the correct answer. Here is an example from the passage about bridges.

An ingenious engineer designed the bridge so that it did not have to be raised above traffic. Instead it was _____.
  A. burned   B. emptied   C. secured
  D. shared   E. lowered

Q. What is the antecedent of *it* in both cases in the example?
A. The antecedent, of course, is *bridge*.

DEMONSTRATIVE PRONOUNS

Demonstrative pronouns (e.g., this, that, these) are also used to refer to a specific, previously mentioned noun. They may occur alone as noun replacements, or they may accompany and modify nouns.

I like jogging, swimming, and tennis. *These* are the only sports I enjoy.

In the sentence above, the word *these* is a replacement noun. However, demonstrative pronouns may also occur as adjectives modifying nouns.

I like jogging, swimming, and tennis. *These* sports are the only ones I enjoy.

The word *these* in the example above is an adjective modifier. The word *these* in each of the two previous examples refers to *jogging, swimming,* and *tennis.*

Here is an example from the passage about universities on page 11.

Undergraduates took classes in Greek philosophy, Latin grammar, arithmetic, music, and astronomy. These were the only _____ available.
  A. rooms   B. subjects   C. clothes
  D. pens   E. company

Q. Which word is a noun replacement?
A. The word *these* is the replacement for *Greek philosophy, Latin grammar, arithmetic, music,* and *astronomy.*

Here is another example from the same passage.

The concept of a fixed program of study leading to a degree first evolved in Medieval Europe. This _____ had not appeared before.
  A. idea   B. desk   C. library   D. capital

Q. What is the antecedent of *this*?
A. The antecedent is *the concept of a fixed program of study leading to a degree.*

COMPARATIVE ADJECTIVES AND ADVERBS

When comparative adjectives and adverbs (e.g., so, such, better, more) occur, they refer to something else in the passage, otherwise a comparison could not be made.

The hotels in the city were all full; so were the motels and boarding houses.

Q. To what in the first sentence does the word *so* refer?
A. *So* tells us to compare the *motels* and *boarding houses* to the *hotels in the city.*

Q. In what way are the *hotels, motels,* and *boarding houses* similar to each other?
A. The *hotels, motels,* and *boarding houses* are similar in that they were all *full*.

Look at an example from the passage about universities.

Guilds were groups of tradespeople, somewhat akin to modern trade unions. In the Middle Ages, all the crafts had such
  A. taxes   B. secrets   C. products
  D. problems   E. organizations

Q. To what in the first sentence does the word *such* refer?
A. *Such* refers to *groups of tradespeople*.

SUBSTITUTIONS

Substitution is another form of cohesive tie. A substitution occurs when one linguistic item (e.g., a noun) is replaced by another. Sometimes the substitution provides new or contrasting information. The substitution is not identical to the original, or antecedent, idea. A frequently occurring substitution involves the use of *one*. A noun substitution may involve another member of the same class as the original one.

My car is falling apart. I need a new one.

Q. What in the first sentence is replaced in the second sentence with *one*?
A. *One* is a substitute for the specific car mentioned in the first sentence. The contrast comes from the fact that the *new one* isn't the writer's current car.

The substitution may also pinpoint a specific member of a general class.

1. There are many unusual courses available at the university this summer. The *one* I am taking is called *Death and Dying*.
2. There are many unusual courses available at the university this summer. *Some* have never been offered before.

Q. In these examples, what is the general class in the first sentence that is replaced by *one* and by *some*?
A. In both cases the words *one* and *some* replace *many unusual* courses.

SYNONYMS

Synonyms are words that have similar meaning. In the examination reading subtest, a synonym of a deleted word is sometimes found in one of the sentences before and/or after the sentence with the deletion. Examine the following excerpt from the passage about bridges again.

But engineers cannot forget that river traffic, too, is essential to our economy. The role of _____ is important. To keep these vessels moving freely, bridges are built high enough, when possible, to let them pass underneath.
  A. wind   B. boats   C. weight
  D. wires   E. experience

Q. Can you identify synonyms in the sentences, before and after the sentence containing the deletion, which are cues to the correct deleted word?
A. If you identified the correct words, you probably noticed that *river traffic* is not exactly a synonym since it is a slightly more general term than the word *boats* (the correct choice). But the word *vessels* is a direct synonym. Demonstrative pronouns (this, that, these, those) are sometimes used as modifiers for synonymous nouns in sentences which follow those containing deletions. The word *these* in *these vessels* is the demonstrative pronoun (modifier) for the synonymous noun *vessels*.

ANTONYMS

Antonyms are words of opposite meaning. In the examination reading subtest passages, antonyms may be cues for missing words. A contrasting relationship, which calls for the use of an antonym, is often signaled by the connective words *instead*, *however*, *but*, etc. Look at an excerpt from the passage about bridges.

An ingenious engineer designed the bridges so that it did not have to be raised above traffic. Instead it was
  A. burned   B. emptied   C. secured
  D. shared   E. lowered

Q: Can you identify an antonym in the first sentence for one of the five alternatives?
A. The word *raised* is an antonym for the word *lowered*.

SUBORDINATE-SUBORDINATE WORDS

In the examination reading subtest, a passage sometimes contains a general term which provides a cue that a more specific term is the appropriate alternative. At other times, the passage may contain a specific term which provides cues that a general term is the appropriate alternative for a particular deletion. The general and more specific words are said to have superordinate-subordinate relationships.

Look at Example 1 below. The more specific word *boy* in the first sentence serves as the antecedent for the more general word *child* in the second sentence. In Example 2, the relationship is reversed. In both examples, the words *child* and *boy* reflect a superordinate-subordinate relationship.

1. The *boy* climbed the tree. Then the *child* fell.
2. The *child* climbed the tree. Then the *boy* fell.

In the practice passage about bridges on Page 11, the phrase *river traffic* is a general term that is superordinate to the alternative *boats* (Item 1). Later in the passage about bridges the following sentences also contain superordinate-subordinate words:

A lift bridge was desired, but there were wartime shortages of steel and machinery needed for the towers. It was hard to find enough _____.
  A. work   B. material   C. time
  D. power   E. space

Q. Can you identify two words in the first sentence that are specific examples for the correct response in the second sentence?
A. Of course, the words *steel* and *machinery* are the specific examples for the more general term *material*.

WORDS ASSOCIATED BY ENTAILMENT

Sometimes the concept described by one word within the context of the passage entails, or implies, the concept described by another word. For example, consider again Item 7 in the practice passage about bridges. Notice how the follow-up sentence to Item 7 provides a cue to the correct response.

An ingenious engineer designed the bridge so that it did not have to be raised above traffic. Instead it was _____. It could be submerged seven meters below the surface of the river.
  A. burned   B. emptied   C. secured
  D. shared   E. lowered

Q. What word in the sentence after the blank implies the concept of an alternative?
A. *Submerged* implies *lowered*. The concept of submerging something implies the idea of lowering the object beneath the surface of the water.

WORDS ASSOCIATED BY PART-WHOLE RELATIONSHIPS

Words may be related because they involve part of a whole and the whole itself; for example, *nose* and *face*. Words may also be related because they involve two parts of the same whole; for example, *radiator* and *muffler* both refer to parts of a car.

The captain of the ship was nervous. The storm was becoming worse and worse. The hardened man paced the _____.
  A. floor   B. hall   C. deck   D. court

Q. Which choice has a part-whole relationship with a word in the sentences above?
A. A *deck* is a part of a *ship*. Therefore, *deck* has a part-whole relationship with *ship*.

CONJUNCTIVE AND CONNECTIVE WORDS AND PHRASES

Conjunctions or connectives are words or phrases that connect parts of sentences or parts of a passage to each other. Their purpose is to help the reader understand the logical and conceptual relationships between ideas and events within a passage. Examples of these words and phrases include coordinate conjunctions (e.g., and, but, yet), subordinate conjunctions (e.g., because, although, since, after), and other connective words and phrases (e.g., too, also, on the other hand, as a result).

Listed below are types of logical relationships expressed by conjunctive, or connective words. Also listed are examples of words used to cue relationships to the reader.

Additive and comparative words and phrases: and, in addition to, too, also, furthermore, similarly.

Adversative and contrastive words and phrases: yet, though, only, but, however, instead, rather, on the other hand, conversely.

Causal words or phrases: so, therefore, because, as a result, if…then, unless, except, in that case, under the circumstances.

Temporal words and phrases: before, after, when, while, initially, lastly, finally, until.

<u>Examples</u>

1. I enjoy fast-paced sports like tennis and volleyball, but my brother prefers _____ sports.
   A. running   B. slower   C. team   D. active

   Q. What is the connective word that tells you to look for a contrast relationship between the two parts of the sentence?
   A. The connective word *but* signals that a contrast relationship exists between the two parts of the sentence.

   Q. Of the four options, what is the best choice for the blank?
   A. The word *slower* is the best response here.

2. The child stepped to close to the edge of the brook. As a result, he _____ in.
   A. fell   B. waded   C. ran   D. jumped

   Q. What is the connective phrase that links the two sentences?
   A. The connective phrase *as a result* links the two sentences.

   Q. Of the four relationships of words and phrases listed previously, what kind of relationship between the two sentences does the connective phrase in the example signal to the reader?
   A. The phrase *as a result* signals that a cause and effect relationship exists between the two sentences.

   Q. Identify the correct response which makes the second sentence reflect and cause and effect relationship.
   A. The correct response is *fell*.

Understanding connectives is very important to success on the examination reading subtest. Sentences with deletions are often very closely related to adjacent sentences in meaning, and the relationships often signaled by connective words or phrases. Here is an example from the practice passage about universities.

At first, these tutors had not been associated with one another. Rather, they had been _____. But, over time, they joined together to form guilds.
A. curious   B. poor   C. religious
D. ready   E. independent

Q. Identify the connective and contrastive words and phrases in the example.
A. *At first* and *over time* are connective phrases that set up temporal progression. *Rather* and *but* are contrastive items. The use of *rather* in the sentence with the deletion tells the reader that the missing word has to convey a meaning in contrast to *associated with one another*. (Notice also that *rather* occurs after a negative statement.) The use of *but* in the sentence after the one with the deletion indicates that the deleted word in the previous sentence has to reflect a meaning that contrasts with *joined together*. Thus, the reader is given two substantial cues to the meaning of the missing word. *Independent* is the only choice that meets the requirement for contrastive meaning.

10

SAMPLE QUESTIOINS

DIRECTIONS: There are two passages on the following pages. In each passage some words are missing. Wherever a word is missing, there is a blank line with a number on it. Below the passage you will find the same number and five words. Choose the word that makes the best sense in the blank. You may not be sure of the answer to a question until you read the sentences that come after the blank, so be sure to read enough to answer the questions. As you work on these passages, you will find that the second passage is harder to read than the first. Answer as many questions as you can.

    Bridges are built to allow a continuous flow of highway and railway traffic across water lying in their paths. But engineers cannot forget that river traffic, too, is essential to our economy. The role of __1__ is important. To keep these vessels moving freely, bridges are built high enough, when possible, to let them pass underneath. Sometimes, however, channels must accommodate very tall ships. It may be uneconomical to build a tall enough bridge. The __2__ would be too high. To save money, engineers build movable bridges.

    In the swing bridge, the middle part pivots or swings open. When the bridge is closed, this section joins the two ends of the bridge, blocking tall vessels. But this section __3__. When swung open, it is perpendicular to the ends of the bridge, creating two free channels for river traffic. With swing bridges channel width is limited by the bridge's piers. The largest swing bridge provides only a 75-meter channel. Such channels are sometimes __4__. In such cases, a bascule bridge may be built.

    Bascule bridges are drawbridges with two arms that swing upward. They provide an opening as wide as the span. They are also versatile. These bridges are not limited to being fully opened or fully closed. They can be __5__ in many ways. They can be fixed at different angles to accommodate different vessels.

    In vertical lift bridges, the center remains horizontal. Towers at both ends allow the center to be lifted like an elevator. One interesting variation of this kind of bridge was built during World War II. A lift bridge was desired, but there were wartime shortages of the steel and machinery needed for the towers. It was hard enough to find enough __6__. An ingenious engineer designed the bridge so that it did not have to be raised above traffic. Instead it was __7__. It could be submerged seven meters below the surface of the river. Ships sailed over it.

1.   A. wind   B. boats   C. experience   1._____
    D. wires   E. experience

2.   A. levels   B. cost   C. standards   2._____
    D. waves   E. deck

3.   A. stands   B. floods   C. wears   3._____
    D. turns   E. supports

4.   A. narrow   B. rough   C. long   4._____
    D. deep   E. straight

5.   A. crossed   B. approached   C. lighted   5._____
    D. planned   E. positioned

6. A. work   B. material   C. time   6._____
    D. power   E. space

7. A. burned   B. emptied   C. secured   7._____
    D. shared   E. lowered

    The first universities emerged at the end of the 11th century and beginning of the 12th. These institutions were not founded on any particular date or created by any formal action. Nobody actually __8__ them. Instead, they developed gradually in places like Paris, Oxford, and Bologna, where scholars had long been teaching students. At first, these tutors had not been associated with one another. Rather, they had been __9__. But, over time, they joined together to form guilds.

    Guilds were groups of tradespeople, somewhat akin to modern unions. In the Middle Ages, all the crafts had such __10__. The scholars' guilds built school buildings and evolved an administration which charged fees and set standards for the curriculum. It set prices for members' services and fixed requirements for entering the profession.

    Professors were not the only schoolpeople forming associations. In Italy, students joined guilds to which teachers had to swear obedience. The students set strict rules, fining professors for beginning class a minute late. Teachers had to seek their students' permission to marry, and such permission was not always granted. Sometimes the students __11__. Even if they said yes, the teacher got only one day's honeymoon.

    Undergraduates took classes in Greek philosophy, Latin grammar, arithmetic, music, and astronomy. These were the only __12__ available. More advanced study was possible in law, medicine, and theology, but one could not earn such postgraduate degrees quickly. It took a long time to __13__. Completing the requirements in theology, for example, took at least 13 years.

    The concept of a fixed program of study leading to a degree first evolved in medieval Europe. This __14__ had not appeared before, in earlier academic settings, notions about *meeting requirements meeting requirements* and *graduating* had been absent. Since the middle ages, though, we have continued to view education as a set curriculum culminating in a degree.

8. A. started   B. guarded   C. blamed   8._____
    D. compared   E. remembered

9. A. curious   B. poor   C. religious   9._____
    D. ready   E. independent

10. A. taxes   B. secrets   C. products   10._____
    D. problems   E. organizations

11. A. left   B. copied   C. refused   11._____
    D. paid   E. prepared

12. A. rooms   B. subjects   C. clothes   12._____
    D. pens   E. markets

13. A. add   B. answer   C. forget   13._____
    D. finish   E. travel

14. A. idea   B. desk   C. library   14.____
    D. capital   E. company

KEY (CORRECT ANSWERS)

1. B   6. B   11. C
2. B   7. E   12. B
3. D   8. A   13. D
4. A   9. E   14. A
5. E   10. E

READING COMPREHENSION
UNDERSTANDING AND INTERPRETING WRITTEN MATERIAL
EXAMINATION SECTION
TEST 1

DIRECTIONS: Read the following passages, and select the MOST appropriate word from the five alternatives provided for each deleted word. *PRINT THE LETTER OF THE CORRECT ANSWER IN THE SPACE AT THE RIGHT.*

PASSAGE I

Bridges are built to allow a continuous flow of highway and railway traffic across water lying in their paths. But engineers cannot forget the fact that river traffic, too, is essential to or economy. The role of 1 is important. To keep these vessels moving freely, bridges are built high enough, when possible, to let them pass underneath. Sometimes, however, channels must accommodate very tall ships. It may be uneconomical to build a tall enough bridge. The 2 would be too high. To save money, engineers build movable bridges.

1. A. wind   B. boats   C. weight   1.____
   D. wires   E. experience

2. A. levels   B. cost   C. standards   2.____
   D. waves   E. deck

In the swing bridge, the middle part pivots or swings open. When the bridge is closed, this section joins the two ends of the bridge, blocking tall vessels. But this section 3. When swung open, it is perpendicular to the ends of the bridge, creating two free channels for river traffic. With swing bridges, channel width is limited by the bridge's piers. The largest swing bridge provides only a 75-meter channel. Such channels are sometimes too 4. In such cases, a bascule bridge may be built.

3. A. stands   B. floods   C. wears   3.____
   D. turns   E. supports

4. A. narrow   B. rough   C. long   4.____
   D. deep   E. straight

Bascule bridges are drawbridges with two arms that swing upward. They provide an opening as wide as the span. They are also versatile. These bridges are not limited to being fully opened or fully closed. They can be 5 in many ways. They can be fixed at different angles to accommodate different vessels.

5. A. approached B. crossed   C. lighted   5.____
   D. planned   E. positioned

In vertical lift bridges, the center remains horizontal. Towers at both ends allow the center to be lifted like an elevator. One interesting variation of this kind of bridge was built during World War II. A lift bridge was desired, but there were wartime shortages of the steel and machinery needed for the towers. It was hard to find enough 6. An ingenious engineer designed the bridge so that it did not have to be raised above traffic. Instead it was 7. It could be submerged seven meters below the river surface. Ships sailed over it.

6. A. work   B. material   C. time   6._____
    D. power   E. space

7. A. burned   B. emptied   C. secured   7._____
    D. shared   E. lowered

PASSAGE II

Before anesthetics were discovered, surgery was carried out under very severe time restrictions. Patients were awake, tossing and screaming in terrible pain. Surgeons were forced to hurry in order to constrain suffering and minimize shock. 8 was essential. Haste, however, did not make for good outcomes in surgery. No surprise then, that the 9 were often poor.

8. A. Blood   B. Silence   C. Speed   8._____
    D. Water   E. Money

9. A. quarters   B. teeth   C. results   9._____
    D. materials   E. families

The discovery of anesthetics happened, in part, by accident. During the early 1800's, nitrous oxide and ether were used for entertainment. At "either frolics" in theaters, volunteers would breathe these gases, become lightheaded, and run around the stage laughing and dancing. By chance, a Connecticut dentist saw such a 10. One volunteer banged his leg against a sharp edge. But he did not 11. He paid no attention to his wound, as though he felt nothing. This gave the dentist the idea of using gas to kill pain,

10. A. show   B. machine   C. face   10._____
    D. source   E. growth

11. A. dream   B. recover   C. succeed   11._____
    D. agree   E. notice

At first, using the "open drip method," ether and chloroform were filtered through a cotton pad placed over the mouth and nose. This direct dose was difficult to regulate and irritating to the nose and throat. Patients would hold their breath, cough, or gag. This made it impossible for them to relax, let alone sleep. Consequently, surgery was often 12. It couldn't begin until the patient had quieted and the anesthesia had taken hold.

12. A. delayed   B. required   C. blamed   12._____
    D. observed   E. repeated

3 (#1)

Today's procedures are safer and more accurate. In the "closed method," a fixed amount of gas is released from sealed bottles into an inhalator bag when the patient exhales. He inhales this gas through tubes with his next breath. In this way, the gas is 13. The system carefully regulates how much gas reached the patient.

13. A. heated   B. controlled   C. cleaned   13.____
    D. selected   E. wasted

For dentistry and minor operations, patients need not be asleep. Newer anesthetics can be used which deaden nerves only in the affected part of the body. These 14 anesthetics offer several advantages. For instance, since the anesthesia is fairly light and patients remain awake, they can cooperate with their doctors.

14. A. local   B. natural   C. ancient
    D. heavy   E. three

PASSAGE III

An indispensable element in the development of telephony was the continual improvement of telephone station instruments, those operating units located at the clients premises. Modern units normally consist of a transmitter, receiver, and transformer. They also contain a bell or equivalent summoning device, a mechanism for controlling the unit's connection to the client's line, and various associated items, like dials. All of these 15 have changed over the years. The transmitter, especially, has undergone enormous refinement during the last century.

15. A. parts   B. costs   C. services   15.____
    D. models   E. routes

Bell's original electromagnetic transmitter functioned likewise as receiver, the same instrument being held alternately to mouth and ear. But having to 16 the instrument this way was inconvenient. Suggestions understandably emerged for mounting the transmitter and receiver onto a common handle, thereby creating what are now known as handsets. Transmitter and receiver were, in fact, later 17 his way. Combination handsets were produced for commercial utilization late in the nineteenth century, but prospects for their acceptance were uncertain as the initial quality of transmissions with the handsets was disappointing. But 18 transmissions followed. With adequately high transmission standards attained, acceptance of handsets was virtually assured.

16. A. store   B. use   C. test   16.____
    D. strip   E. clean

17. A. grounded   B. marked   C. covered   17.____
    D. priced   E. coupled

18. A. shorter   B. fewer   C. better   18.____
    D. faster   E. cheaper

Among the most significant improvements in transmitters has been the enormous amplification (up to a thousandfold) of speech sounds. This increased 19 has benefited telecommunications enormously. Nineteenth century telephone conversations frequently were only marginally audible whereas nowadays even murmured conversations can be transmitted successfully, barring unusual atmospheric or electronic disturbances.

19. A. distance   B. speed   C. market   19.____
    D. volume   E. number

Vocal quality over nineteenth century instruments was distorted, the speaker not readily identifiable. By comparison, current sound is characterized by considerably greater naturalism. Modern telephony produces speech sounds more nearly resembling an individual's actual voice. Thus, it is easier to 20 the speaker. A considerable portion of this improvement is attributable to practical applications of laboratory investigations concerning the mechanisms of human speech and audition. These 21 have exerted a profound influence. Their results prompted technical innovations in modern transmitter design which contributed appreciably to the excellent communication available nowadays.

20. A. time   B. help   C. bill   20.____
    D. stop   E. recognize

21. A. studies   B. rates   C. materials   21.____
    D. machines   E. companies

PASSAGE IV

The dramatic events of December 7, 1941, plunged this nation into war. The full 22 of the war we cannot even now comprehend, but one of the effects stands out in sharp relief —the coming of the air age. The airplane, which played a relatively 23 part in World War I, has already soared to heights undreamed of save by the few with mighty vision.

In wartime the airplane is the 24 on wings and the battleship that flies. To man in his need it symbolizes deadly extremes; friend or foe; deliverance or 25.

It is a powerful instrument of war revolutionizing military strategy, but its peacetime role is just as 26. This new master of time and space, fruit of man's inventive genius, has come to stay, smalling the earth and smoothing its surface.

To all of us, then, to youth, and to 27 alike comes the winged challenge to get ourselves ready—to 28 ourselves for living in an age which the airplane seems destined to mold.

22. A. destruction   B. character   C. history   22.____
    D. import   E. picture

23. A. important   B. dull   C. vast   23.____
    D. unknown   E. minor

24. A. giant   B. ant   C. monster   24.____
    D. artillery E. robot

25. A. ecstasy   B. bombardment   C. death   25.____
    D. denial   E. survival

26. A. revolting   B. revolutionary   C. residual   26.____
    D. reliable   E. regressive

27. A. animals   B. nations   C. women   27.____
    D. men   E. adult

28. A. distract   B. engage   C. determine   28.____
    D. deter   E. orient

PASSAGE V

Let us consider how voice training may contribute to 29 development and an improved social 30.

In the first place, it has been fairly well established that individuals tend to become what they believe 31 people think them to be.

When people react more favorably toward us because our voices 32 the impression that we are friendly, competent, and interesting, there is a strong tendency for us to develop those 33 in our personality.

If we are treated with respect by others, we soon come to have more respect for 34.

Then, too, one's own consciousness of having a pleasant, effective voice of which he does not need to be ashamed contributes materially to a feeling of poise, self-confidence, and a just pride in himself.

A good voice, like good clothes, can do much for an 35 that otherwise might be inclined to droop.

29. A. facial   B. material   C. community   29.____
    D. personality E. physical

30. A. adjustment   B. upheaval   C. development 30.____
    D. bias   E. theories

31. A. some   B. hostile   C. jealous   31.____
    D. inferior   E. destroy

32. A. betray   B. imply   C. destroy   32.____
    D. transfigure E. convey

33. A. detects   B. qualities   C. techniques 33.____
    D. idiosyncrasies E. quirks

34. A. others   B. their children   C. their teachers 34.____
    D. ourselves   E. each other

35. A. mind   B. heart   C. brain   35.____
    D. feeling   E. ego

PASSAGE VI

How are symphony orchestras launched, kept going, and built up in smaller communities? Recent reports from five of them suggest that, though the 36 changes, certain elements are fairly common. One thing shines out; 37 is essential.

Also, aside from the indispensable, instrumentalists who play, the following personalities, either singly, or preferably in 38 seem to be the chief needs; a conductor who wants to conduct so badly he will organize his own orchestra if it is the only way he can get one; a manager with plenty of resourcefulness in rounding up audiences and finding financial support; an energetic community leader, generally a woman, who will take up locating the orchestra as a 39; and generous visiting soloists who will help draw those who are 40 that anything local can be used.

36. A. world B. pattern C. reason 36.____
    D. scene E. cast

37. A. hatred B. love C. enthusiasm 37.____
    D. participation E. criticism

38. A. combination B. particular C. isolation 38.____
    D. sympathy E. solitary

39. A. chore B. duty C. hobby 39.____
    D. delight E. career

40. A. convinced B. skeptical C. happy 40.____
    D. unhappy E. unsure

KEY (CORRECT ANSWERS)

1.	B	11.	E	21.	A	31.	E
2.	B	12.	A	22.	D	32.	E
3.	D	13.	B	23.	E	33.	B
4.	A	14.	A	24.	D	34.	D
5.	E	15.	A	25.	C	35.	E
6.	B	16.	B	26.	B	36.	B
7.	E	17.	E	27.	E	37.	C
8.	C	18.	C	28.	E	38.	A
9.	C	19.	D	29.	D	39.	C
10.	A	20.	E	30.	A	40.	B

READING COMPREHENSION
UNDERSTANDING AND INTERPRETING WRITTEN MATERIAL
EXAMINATION SECTION
TEST 1

DIRECTIONS: Each question or incomplete statement is followed by several suggested answers or completions. Select the one that BEST answers the question or completes the statement. *PRINT THE LETTER OF THE CORRECT ANSWER IN THE SPACE AT THE RIGHT.*

Question 1.
DIRECTIONS: Question 1 is to be answered on the basis of the following passage.

Skiing has recently become one of the more popular sports in the United States. Because of its popularity, thousands of winter vacationers are flying north rather than south. In many areas, reservations are required months ahead of time.
I discovered the accommodation shortage through an unfortunate experience. On a sunny Saturday morning, I set out from Denver for the beckoning slopes of Aspen, Colorado. After passing signs for other ski areas, I finally reached my destination. Naturally, I lost no time in heading for the nearest tow. After a stimulating afternoon of miscalculated stem turns, I was famished. Well, one thing led to another, and it must have been eight o'clock before I concerned myself with a bed for my bruised and aching bones.
It took precisely one phone call to ascertain the lack of lodgings in the Aspen area. I had but one recourse. My auto and I started the treacherous jaunt over the pass and back towards Denver. Along the way, I went begging for a bed. Finally, a jolly tavernkeeper took pity, and for only thirty dollars a night allowed me the privilege of staying in a musty, dirty, bathless room above his tavern.

1. The author's problem would have been avoided if he had 1.____
   A. not tired himself out skiing
   B. taken a bus instead of driving
   C. arranged for food as soon as he arrived
   D. arranged for accommodations well ahead of his trip
   E. answer cannot be determined from the information given

Question 2.
DIRECTIONS: Question 2 is to be answered on the basis of the following passage.

Helen Keller was born in 1880 in Tuscumbia, Alabama. When she was two years old, she lost her sight and hearing as the result of an illness. In 1886, she became the pupil of Anne Sullivan, who taught Helen to see with her fingertips, to *hear* with her feet and hands, and to communicate with other people. Miss Sullivan succeeded in arousing Helen's curiosity and interest by spelling the names of objects into her hand. At the end of three years, Helen had mastered the manual and the braille alphabet and could read and write.

2. When did Helen Keller lose her sight and hearing? 2.____

Question 3.
DIRECTIONS: Question 3 is to be answered on the basis of the following passage.

Sammy got to school ten minutes after the school bell had rung. He was breathing hard and had a black eye. His face was dirty and scratched. One leg of his pants was torn.
Tommy was late to school, too; however, he was only five minutes late. Like Sammy, he was breathing hard, but he was happy and smiling.

3. Sammy and Tommy had been fighting. 3.____
   Who probably won?
   A. Sammy   B. Tommy
   C. Cannot tell from story   D. The teacher
   E. The school

Question 4.
DIRECTIONS: Question 4 is to be answered on the basis of the following passage.

This is like a game to see if you can tell what the nonsense word in the paragraph stands for. The nonsense word is just a silly word for something that you know very well. Read the paragraph and see if you can tell what the underlined nonsense word stands for.
You can wash your hands and face in zup. You can even take a bath in it. When people swim, they are in the zup. Everyone drinks zup.

4. Zup is PROBABLY
   A. milk   B. pop   C. soap   D. water   E. soup

Question 5.
DIRECTIONS: Question 5 is to be answered on the basis of the following passage.

After two weeks of unusually high-speed travel, we reached Xeno, a small planet whose population, though never before visited by Earthmen, was listed as *friendly* in the INTERSTELLAR GAZETTEER.
On stepping lightly (after all, the gravity of Xeno is scarcely more than twice that of our own moon) from our spacecraft, we saw that *friendly* was an understatement. We were immediately surrounded by Frangibles of various colors, mostly pinkish or orange, who held out their *hands* to us. Imagine our surprise when their *hands* actually merged with ours as we tried to shake them!
Then, before we could stop them (how could we have stopped them?), two particularly pink Frangibles simply stepped right into two eminent scientists among our party, who immediately lit up with the same pink glow. While occupied in this way, the scientists reported afterwards they suddenly discovered they *knew* a great deal about Frangibles and life on Xeno..
Apparently, Frangibles could take themselves apart atomically and enter right into any other substance. They communicated by thought waves, occasionally merging *heads* for greater clarity. Two Frangibles who were in love with each other would spend most of their time merged into one; they were a bluish-green color unless they were having a love's quarrel, when they turned gray.

5. In order to find out about an object which interested him, what would a Frangible MOST likely do?   5.____
   A. Take it apart
   B. Enter into it
   C. Study it scientifically
   D. Ask earth scientists about it
   E. Wait to see if it would change color

Question 6.
DIRECTIONS: Question 6 is to be answered on the basis of the following passage.

   This is like a game to see if you can tell what the nonsense word in the paragraph stands for. The nonsense word is just a silly word for something that you know very well. Read the paragraph and see if you can tell what the underlined nonsense word stands for.
   Have you ever smelled a <u>mart</u>? They smell very good. Bees like <u>marts</u>. They come inn many colors. <u>Marts</u> grow in the earth, and they usually bloom in the spring.

6. <u>Marts</u> are PROBABLY
   A. bugs   B. flowers   C. perfume   D. pies   E. cherries

Question 7.
DIRECTIONS: Question 7 is to be answered on the basis of the following passage.

   Christmas was only a few days away. The wind was strong and cold. The walks were covered with snow. The downtown streets were crowded with people. Their faces were hidden by many packages as they went in one store after another. They all tried to move faster as they looked at the clock.

7. When did the story PROBABLY happen?   7.____
   A. November 28   B. December 1   C. December 21
   D. December 25   E. December 2

Question 8.
DIRECTIONS: Question 8 is to be answered on the basis of the following passage.

THE WAYFARER

The Wayfarer,
Perceiving the pathway to truth,
Was struck with astonishment.
It was thickly grown with weeds.
Ha, he said,
I see that no one has passed here
In a long time.
Later he saw that each weed
Was a singular knife,
Well, he mumbled at last,
Doubtless there are other roads.

8. *I see that no one has passed here in a long time.* 8._____
What do the above lines from the poem mean?
   A. The way of truth is popular.
   B. People are fascinated by the truth.
   C. Truth comes and goes like the wind.
   D. The truth is difficult to recognize.
   E. Few people are searching for the truth.

Question 9.
DIRECTIONS: Question 9 is to be answered on the basis of the following passage.

   Any attempt to label an entire generation is unrewarding, and yet the generation which went through the last war, or at least could get a drink easily once it was over, seems to possess a uniform, general quality which demands an adjective. It was John Kerouac, the author of a fine, neglected novel, THE TOWN AND THE CITY, who final came up with it. It was several years ago, when the face was harder to recognize, but he had a sharp, sympathetic eye, and one day he said, *You know, this is really a beat generation.* The origins of the word *beat* are obscure, but the meaning is only too clear to most Americans. More than mere weariness, it implies the feeling of having been used, of being raw. It involves a sort of nakedness of mind, and, ultimately of soul; a feeling of being reduced to the bedrock of consciousness. In short, it means being undramatically pushed up against the wall of oneself. A man is beat whenever he goes for broke and waters the sum of his resources on a single number; and the young generation has done that continually from early youth.

9. What does the writer suggest when he mentions a *fine, neglected novel*? 9._____
   A. Kerouac had the right idea about the war.
   B. Kerouac had a clear understanding of the new post-war generation.
   C. Kerouac had not received the recognition of THE TOWN AND THE CITY that was deserved.
   D. Kerouac had the wrong idea about the war.
   E. All of the above

Questions 10-11.
DIRECTIONS: Questions 10 and 11 are to be answered on the basis of the following passage.

   One spring, Farmer Brown had an unusually good field of wheat. Whenever he say any birds in this field, he got his gun and shot as many of them as he could. In the middle of the summer, he found that his wheat was being ruined by insects. With no birds to feed on them, the insects had multiplied very fast. What Farmer Brown did not understand was this: A bird is not simply an animal that eats food the farmer may want for himself. Instead, it is one of many links in the complex surroundings, or environment, in which we live.
   How much grain a farmer can raise on an acre of ground depends on many factors. All of these factors can be divided into two big groups. Such things as the richness of the soil, the amount of rainfall, the amount of sunlight, and the temperature belong together in one of these groups. This group may be called <u>nonliving factors</u>. The second group may be called <u>living factors</u>. The living factors in any plant's environment are animals and other plants. Wheat, for example, may be damaged by wheat rust, a tiny plant that feeds on wheat, or it may be eaten by plant-eating animals such as birds or grasshoppers…

It is easy to see that the relations of plants and animals to their environment are very complex, and that any change in the environment is likely to bring about a whole series of changes.

10. What does the passage suggest a good farmer should understand about nature? 10.____
    A. Insects are harmful to plants.
    B. Birds are not harmful to plants.
    C. Wheat may be damaged by both animals and other plants.
    D. The amount of wheat he can raise depends on two factors: birds and insects.
    E. A change in one factor of plants' surroundings may cause other factors to change.

11. What important idea about nature does the writer want us to understand? 11.____
    A. Farmer Brown was worried about the heavy rainfall.
    B. Nobody needs to have such destructive birds around.
    C. Farmer Brown did not want the temperature to change.
    D. All insects need not only wheat rust but grasshoppers.
    E. All living things are dependent on other living things.

Question 12.
DIRECTIONS: Question 12 is to be answered on the basis of the following passage.

For a 12-year-old, I've been around a lot because my father's in the Army. I have been to New York and to Paris. When I was nine, my parents took me to Rome. I didn't like Europe very much because the people don't speak the same language as I do. When I am older, my mother says I can travel by myself. I think I will like that. Ever since I was 13, I have wanted to go to Canada.

12. Why can't everything this person said be TRUE? 12.____
    A. 12-year-olds can't travel alone.
    B. No one can travel that much in 12 years.
    C. There is a conflict in the ages used in the passage.
    D. 9-year-olds can't travel alone.
    E. He is a liar.

Question 13.
DIRECTIONS: Question 13 is to be answered on the basis of the following passage.

Between April and October, the Persian Gulf is dotted with the small boats of pearl divers. Some seventy-five thousand of them are busy diving down and bringing up pearl-bearing oysters. These oysters are not the kind we eat. The edible oyster produces pearls of little or no value. You may have heard tales of divers who discovered pearls and sold them for great sums of money. These stories are entertaining but not accurate.

13. The Persian Gulf has many 13._____
    A. large boats of pearl divers
    B. pearl divers who eat oysters
    C. edible oysters that produce pearls
    D. non-edible oysters that produce pearls
    E. edible oysters that do not produce pearls

Question 14.
DIRECTIONS: Question 14 is to be answered on the basis of the following passage.

Art says that the polar ice cap is melting at the rate of 3% per year. Bert says that this isn't true because the polar ice cap is really melting at the rate of 7% per year.

14. We know for certain that 14._____
    A. Art is wrong.   B. Bert is wrong.
    C. they are both wrong   D. they both might be right
    E. they can't both be right

Question 15.
DIRECTIONS: Question 15 is to be answered on the basis of the following passage.

FORTUNE AND MEN'S EYES
                                          Shakespeare

When, in disgrace with fortune and men's eyes,
I all alone beweep my outcast state,
And trouble deaf heaven with my bootless cries,
And look upon myself and curse my fate,
Wishing me like to one more rich in hope,
Featured like him, like him with friends possessed
Desiring this man's art, and that man's scope,
With what I most enjoy contented least;
Yet in these thoughts myself almost despising,
Haply I think on thee; and then my state,
Like to the lark at break of day arising
From sullen earth, sings hymns at heaven's gate;
For thy sweet love remembered, such wealth brings
That then I scorn to change my state with kings.

15. What saves this man from wishing to be different than he is? 15._____
    A. Such wealth brings   B. Hymns at heaven's gate
    C. The lark at break of day   D. Thy sweet love remembered
    E. Change my state with kings

Question 16.
DIRECTIONS: Question 16 is to be answered on the basis of the following passage.

My name is Gregory Gotrocks, and I live in Peoria, Illinois. I sell tractors. In June 1952, the Gotrocks Tractor Company (my dad happens to be the president) sent me to Nepal-Tibet to check on our sales office there.

Business was slow, and I had a lot of time to kill. I decided to see Mt. Everest so that I could tell everyone back in Peoria that I had seen it.

It was beautiful; I was spellbound. I simply had to see what the view looked like from the top. So I started up the northwest slope. Everyone know that this is the best route to take. It took me three long hours to reach the top, but the climb was well worth it.

16. Gregory Gotrocks went to see Mt. Everest so that he could   16.____
    A. see some friends
    B. sell some tractors
    C. take a picture of it
    D. plant a flag at its base
    E. entertain his friends back home

Questions 17-18.
DIRECTIONS: Questions 17 and 18 are to be answered on the basis of the following passage.

Suburbanites are not irresponsible. Indeed, what is striking about the young couples' march along the abyss is the earnestness and precision with which they go about it. They are extremely budget-conscious. They can rattle off most of their monthly payments down to the last penny; one might say that even their impulse buying is deliberately planned. They are conscientious in meeting obligations and rarely do they fall delinquent in their accounts.

They are exponents of what could be called budgetism. This does not mean that they actually keep formal budgets—quite the contrary. The beauty of budgetism is that one doesn't have to keep a budget at all. It's done automatically. In the new middle-class rhythms of life, obligations are homogenized, for the overriding aim is to have oneself precommitted to regular, unvarying monthly payments on all the major items,

Americans used to be divided into three sizable groups: those who thought of money obligations in terms of the week, of the month, and of the year. Many people remain at both ends of the scale; but with the widening of the middle class, the mortgage payments are firmly geared to a thirty-day cycle, and any dissonant peaks and valleys are anathema. Just as young couples are now paying winter fuel bills in equal monthly fractions through the year, so they seek to spread out all the other heavy seasonal obligations they can anticipate. If vendors will not oblige by accepting equal monthly installments, the purchasers will smooth out the load themselves by floating loans.

It is, suburbanites cheerfully explain, a matter of psychology. They don't trust themselves. In self-entrapment is security. They try to budget so tightly that there is no unappropriated funds, for they know these would burn a hole in their pocket. Not merely out of greed for goods, then, do they commit themselves; it is protection they want, too. And though it would be extreme to say that they go into debt to be secure, carefully chartered debt does give them a certain peace of mind—and in suburbia this is more coveted than luxury itself.

17. What is the *abyss* along which the young couples are marching?   17.____
    A. Nuclear war
    B. Unemployment
    C. Mental breakdown
    D. Financial disaster
    E. Catastrophic illness

18. What conclusion does the author reach concerning carefully chartered debt   18.____
    among young couples in the United States today?
    It
    A. is a symbol of love
    B. bring marital happiness
    C. helps them to feel secure
    D. enables them to acquire wealth
    E. provides them with material goods

Question 19.
DIRECTIONS: Question 19 is to be answered on the basis of the following passage. Read the verse and fill in the space at the right the object described in the verse.

You see me when I'm right or wrong;
My face I never hide.
My hands move slowly round and round
And o'er me minutes glide.

19. A. Book   B. Clock   C. Record   D. Table   E. Lock   19.____

Question 20-22.
DIRECTIONS: Questions 20 through 22 are to be answered on the basis of the following passage.

Until about thirty years ago, the village of Nayon seems to have been a self-sufficient agricultural community with a mixture of native and sixteenth century Spanish customs. Lands were abandoned when too badly eroded. The balance between population and resources allowed a minimum subsistence. A few traders exchanged goods between Quito and the villages in the tropical barrancas, all within a radius of ten miles. Houses had dirt floors, thatched roofs, and pole walls that were sometimes plastered with mud. Guinea pigs ran freely about each house and were the main meat source. Most of the population spoke no Spanish. Men wore long hair and concerned themselves chiefly with farming.

The completion of the Guayaquil-Quito railway in 1908 brought the first real contacts with industrial civilization to the high inter-Andean valley. From this event gradually flowed not only technological changes but new ideas and social institutions. Feudal social relationships no longer seemed right and immutable; medicine and public health improved; elementary education became more common; urban Quito began to expand; and finally, and perhaps least important so far, modern industries began to appear, although even now on a most modest scale.

In 1948-49, the date of our visit, only two men wore their hair long; and only to old-style houses remained. If guinea pigs were kept, they were penned; their flesh was now a luxury food, and beef the most common meat. Houses were of adobe or fired brick, usually with tile roofs, and often contained five or six rooms, some of which had plank or brick floors. Most of the population spoke Spanish. There was no resident priest, but an appointed government official and a policeman represented authority. A six-teacher school provided education. Clothing was becoming citified; for men it often included overalls for work and a tailored suit, white shirt, necktie, and felt hat for trips to Quito. Attendance at church was low, and many festivals had been abandoned. Volleyball or soccer was played weekly in the plaza by young men who sometimes wore shorts, blazers, and berets. There were few shops, for most purchases were made in Quito, and from there came most of the food, so that there was a far more varied diet than twenty-five years ago. There were piped water and sporadic health services; in addition, most families patronized Quito doctors in emergencies.

The crops and their uses had undergone change. Maize, or Indian corn, was still the primary crop, but very little was harvested as grain. Almost all was sold in Quito as green corn to eat boiled on the cob, and a considerable amount of the corn eaten as grain in Nayon was imported. Beans, which do poorly here, were grown on a small scale for household consumption. Though some squash was eaten, most was exported. Sweet potatoes, tomatoes, cabbage, onions, peppers, and, at lower elevations, sweet yucca, and arrowroot were grown extensively for export; indeed, so export-minded was the community that it was almost impossible to buy locally grown produce in the village. People couldn't be bothered with retail scales.

20. Why was there primitiveness and self-containment in Nayon before 1910?   20.____
    A. Social mores   B. Cultural tradition
    C. Biological instincts   D. Geographical factors
    E. Religious regulations

21. By 1948, the village of Nayon was   21.____
    A. a self-sufficient village
    B. out of touch with the outside world
    C. a small dependent portion of a larger economic unit
    D. a rapidly growing and sound social and cultural unit
    E. a metropolis

22. Why was Nayon originally separated from its neighbors?   22.____
    A. Rich arable land
    B. Long meandering streams
    C. Artificial political barriers
    D. Broad stretches of arid desert
    E. Deep rugged gorges traversed by rock trails

Question 23.
DIRECTIONS: Question 23 is to be answered on the basis of the following passage. Read the verse and fill in the space at the right the object described in the verse.

I have two eyes and when I'm worn
I give the wearer four.
I'm strong or weak or thick or thin
Need I say much more?

23. A. Clock   B. Eyeglasses   C. Piano   23.____
    D. Thermometer   E. I don't know

Question 24.
DIRECTIONS: Question 24 is to be answered on the basis of the following passage.

Scarlet fever begins with fever, chills, headache, and sore throat. A doctor diagnoses the illness as scarlet fever when a characteristic rash erupts on the skin. This rash appears on the neck and chest in three to five days after the onset of the illness and spreads rapidly over the body. Sometimes the skin on the palm of the hands and soles of the feet shreds in flakes.
Scarlet fever is usually treated with penicillin and, in severe cases, a convalescent serum. The disease may be accompanied by infections of the ear and throat, inflammation of the kidneys, pneumonia, and inflammation of the heart.

24. How does the author tell us that scarlet fever may be a serious disease?   24.____
    A. He tells how many people die of it.
    B. He tells that he once had the disease.
    C. He tells that hands and feet may fall off.

D. He tells how other infections may come with scarlet fever.
E. None of the above

Question 25.
DIRECTIONS: Question 25 is to be answered on the basis of the following passage. Read the verse and fill in the space at the right the object described in the verse.

I have no wings but often fly;
I come in colors many.
From varied nationalities
Respect I get a-plenty.

25. A. Deck of cards   B. Eyeglasses   C. Flag   25.____
     D. Needles   E. None of the above

KEY (CORRECT ANSWERS)

1.	D		11.	E
2.	B		12.	C
3.	B		13.	D
4.	D		14.	E
5.	B		15.	D
6.	B		16.	E
7.	C		17.	D
8.	E		18.	C
9.	C		19.	B
10.	E		20.	D

21.	C
22.	E
23.	B
24.	D
25.	C

READING COMPREHENSION
UNDERSTANDING AND INTERPRETING WRITTEN MATERIAL
EXAMINATION SECTION
TEST 1

DIRECTIONS: Each question has five suggested answers, lettered A to E. Decide which one is the BEST answer. *PRINT THE LETTER OF THE CORRECT ANSWER IN THE SPACE AT THE RIGHT.*

1. Some specialists are willing to give their services to the Government entirely free of charge; some feel that a nominal salary, such as will cover traveling expenses, is sufficient for a position that is recognized as being somewhat honorary in nature; many other specialists value their time so highly that they will not devote any of it to public service that does not repay them at a rate commensurate with the fees that they can obtain from a good private clientele.
The paragraph BEST supports the statement that the use of specialists by the Government
   A. is rare because of the high cost of securing such persons
   B. may be influenced by the willingness of specialists to serve
   C. enables them to secure higher salaries in private fields
   D. has become increasingly common during the past few years
   E. always conflicts with private demands for their services

1.____

2. The fact must not be overlooked that only about one-half of the international trade of the world crosses the oceans. The other half is merely exchanges of merchandise between countries lying alongside each other or at least within the same continent.
The paragraph BEST supports the statement that
   A. the most important part of any country's trade is transoceanic
   B. domestic trade is insignificant when compared with foreign trade
   C. the exchange of goods between neighboring countries is not considered international trade
   D. foreign commerce is not necessarily carried on by water
   E. about one-half of the trade of the world is international

2.____

3. Individual differences in mental traits assume importance in fitting workers to jobs because such personal characteristics are persistent and are relatively little influenced by training and experience.
The paragraph BEST supports the statement that training and experience
   A. are limited in their effectiveness in fitting workers to jobs
   B. do not increase a worker's fitness for a job
   C. have no effect upon a person's mental traits
   D. have relatively little effect upon the individual's chances for success
   E. should be based on the mental traits of an individual

3.____

4. The competition of buyers tends to keep prices up, the competition of sellers to send them down. Normally, the pressure of competition among sellers is stronger than that among buyers since the seller has his article to sell and must get rid of it, whereas the buyer is not committed to anything.
The paragraph BEST supports the statement that low prices are caused by
   A. buyer competition
   B. competition of buyers with sellers
   C. fluctuations in demand
   D. greater competition among sellers than among buyers
   E. more sellers than buyers

5. In seventeen states, every lawyer is automatically a member of the American Bar Association. In some other states and localities, truly representative organizations of the Bar have not yet come into being, but are greatly needed.
The paragraph IMPLIES that
   A. representative Bar Associations are necessary in states where they do not now exist
   B. every lawyer is required by law to become a member of the Bar
   C. the Bar Association is a democratic organization
   D. some states have more lawyers than others
   E. every member of the American Bar Association is automatically a lawyer in seventeen states

KEY (CORRECT ANSWERS)

1. B
2. D
3. A
4. D
5. A

TEST 2

DIRECTIONS: Each question has five suggested answers, lettered A to E. Decide which one is the BEST answer. *PRINT THE LETTER OF THE CORRECT ANSWER IN THE SPACE AT THE RIGHT.*

1. We hear a great deal about the new education, and see a great deal of it in action. But the school house, though prodigiously magnified in scale, is still very much the same old school house.
   The paragraph IMPLIES
   A. the old education was, after all, better than the new
   B. although the modern school buildings are larger than the old ones, they have not changed very much in other respects
   C. the old school houses do not fit in with modern educational theories
   D. a fine school building does not make up for poor teachers
   E. schools will be schools

   1.____

2. No two human beings are of the same pattern—not even twins and the method of bringing out the best in each one necessarily according to the nature of the child.
   The paragraph IMPLIES that
   A. individual differences should be considered in dealing with children
   B. twins should be treated impartially
   C. it is an easy matter to determine the special abilities of children
   D. a child's nature varies from year to year
   E. we must discover the general technique of dealing with children

   2.____

3. Man inhabits today a world very different from that which encompassed even his parents and grandparents. It is a world geared to modern machinery—automobiles, airplanes, power plants; it is linked together and served by electricity.
   The paragraph IMPLIES that
   A. the world has no changed much during the last few generations
   B. modern inventions and discoveries have brought about many changes in man's way of living
   C. the world is run more efficiently today than it was in our grandparents' time
   D. man is much happier today than he was a hundred years ago
   E. we must learn to see man as he truly is, underneath the veneers of man's contrivances

   3.____

4. Success in any study depends largely upon the interest taken in that particular subject by the student. This being the case, each teacher earnestly hopes that her students will realize at the vey onset that shorthand can be made an intensely fascinating study.
   The paragraph IMPLIES that
   A. Everyone is interested in shorthand
   B. success in a study is entirely impossible unless the student finds the study very interesting

   4.____

143

C. if a student is eager to study shorthand, he is likely to succeed in it
D. shorthand is necessary for success
E. anyone who is not interested in shorthand will not succeed in business

5. The primary purpose of all business English is to move the reader to agreeable and mutually profitable action. This action may be indirect or direct, but in either case a highly competitive appeal for business should be clothed with incisive diction tending to replace vagueness and doubt with clarity, confidence, and appropriate action.
The paragraph IMPLIES that the
   A. ideal business letter uses words to conform to the reader's language level
   B. business correspondent should strive for conciseness in letter writing
   C. keen competition of today has lessened the value of the letter as an appeal for business
   D. writer of a business letter should employ incisive diction to move the reader to compliant and gainful action
   E. the writer of a business letter should be himself clear, confident, and forceful

KEY (CORRECT ANSWERS)

1. B
2. A
3. B
4. C
5. D

TEST 3

DIRECTIONS: Each question has five suggested answers, lettered A to E. Decide which one is the BEST answer. *PRINT THE LETTER OF THE CORRECT ANSWER IN THE SPACE AT THE RIGHT.*

1. To serve the community best, a comprehensive city plan must coordinate all physical improvements, even at the possible expense of subordinating individual desires, to the end that a city may grow in a more orderly way and provide adequate facilities for its people
   The paragraph IMPLIES that
   A. city planning provides adequate facilities for recreation
   B. a comprehensive city plan provides the means for a city to grow in a more orderly fashion
   C. individual desires must always be subordinated to civic changes
   D. the only way to serve a community is to adopt a comprehensive city plan
   E. city planning is the most important function of city government

   1.____

2. Facility in writing letters, the knack of putting into these quickly written letters the same personal impression that would mark an interview, and the ability to boil down to a one-page letter the gist of what might be called a five- or ten-minute conversation —all these are essential to effective work under conditions of modern business organization.
   The paragraph IMPLIES that
   A. letters are of more importance in modern business activities than ever before
   B. letters should be used in place of interviews
   C. the ability to write good letters is essential to effective work in modern business organization
   D. business letters should never be more than one page in length
   E. the person who can write a letter with great skill will get ahead more readily than others

   2.____

3. The general rule is that it is the city council which determines the amount to be raised by taxation and which therefore determines, within the law, the tax rates. As has been pointed out, however, no city council or city authority has the power to determine what kind of taxes should be levied.
   The paragraph IMPLIES that
   A. the city council has more authority than any other municipal body
   B. while the city council has a great deal of authority in the levying of taxes, its power is not absolute
   C. the kinds of taxes levied in different cities vary greatly
   D. the city council appoints the tax collectors
   E. the mayor determines the kinds of taxes to be levied

   3.____

4. The growth of modern business has made necessary mass production, mass distribution, and mass selling. As a result, the problems of personnel and industrial relations have increased so rapidly that grave injustice in the handling of personal relationships have frequently occurred. Personnel administration is complex because, as in all human problems, many intangible elements are involved. Therefore a thorough, systematic, and continuous study of the psychology of human behavior is essential to the intelligent handling of personnel.
The paragraph IMPLIES that
   A. complex modern industry makes impossible the personal relationships which formerly existed between employer and employee
   B. mass decisions are successfully applied to personnel problems
   C. the human element in personnel administration makes continuous study necessary to is intelligent application
   D. personnel problems are less important than the problems of mass production and mass distribution
   E. since personnel administration is so complex and costly, it should be subordinated to the needs of good industrial relations

5. The Social Security Act is striving toward the attainment of economic security for the individual and for his family. It was stated, in outlining this program, that security for the individual and for the family concerns itself with three factors: (1) decent homes to live in; (2) development of the natural resources of the country so as to afford the fullest opportunity to engage in productive work; and (3) safeguards against the major misfortunes of life. The Social Security Act is concerned with the third of these factors —"safeguards against misfortunes which cannot be wholly eliminated in this man-made world of ours."
The paragraph IMPLIES that the
   A. Social Security Act is concerned primarily with supplying to families decent homes in which to live
   B. development of natural resources is the only means of offering employment to the masses of the unemployed
   C. Social Security Act has attained absolute economic security for the individual and his family
   D. Social Security Act deals with the first (1) factor as stated in the paragraph above
   E. Social Security Act deals with the third (3) factor as stated in the paragraph above

KEY (CORRECT ANSWERS)

1. B
2. C
3. B
4. C
5. E

TEST 4

DIRECTIONS: Each question has five suggested answers, lettered A to E. Decide which one is the BEST answer. *PRINT THE LETTER OF THE CORRECT ANSWER IN THE SPACE AT THE RIGHT.*

PASSAGE 1

Free unrhymed verse has been practiced for some thousands of years and reaches back to the incantation which linked verse with the ritual dance. It provided a communal emotion; the aim of the cadenced phrases was to create a state of mind. The general coloring of free rhythms in the poetry of today is that of speech rhythm, composed in the sequence of the musical phrase, not in the sequence of the metronome, the regular beat. In the twenties, conventional rhyme fell into almost complete disuse. This liberation from rhyme became as well a liberation of rhyme. Freed of its exacting task of supporting lame verse, it would be applied with greater effect where wanted for some special effect. Such break in the tradition of rhymed verse had the healthy effect of giving it a fresh start, released from the hampering convention of too familiar cadences. This refreshing and subtilizing of the use of rhythm can be seen everywhere in the poetry today.

1. The title below that BEST expresses the ideas of this paragraph is:
    A. Primitive Poetry
    B. The Origin of Poetry
    C. Rhyme and Rhythm in Modern Verse
    D. Classification of Poetry
    E. Purposes in All Poetry

2. Free verse had its origin in primitive
    A. fairytales   B. literature   C. warfare
    D. chants   E. courtship

3. The object of early free verse was to
    A. influence the mood of the people   B. convey ideas
    C. produce mental pictures   D. create pleasing sounds
    E. provide enjoyment

PASSAGE 2

Control of the Mississippi had always been goals of nations having ambitions in the New World. LaSalle claimed it for France in 1682. Iberville appropriated it to France when he colonized Louisiana in 1700. Bienville founded New Orleans, its principal port, as a French city in 1718. The fleur-de-lis were the blazon of the delta country until 1762. Then Spain claimed all of Louisiana. The Spanish were easy neighbors. American products from western Pennsylvania and the Northwest Territory were barged down the Ohio and Mississippi to New Orleans; here they were reloaded on ocean-going vessels that cleared for the great seaports of the world.

4. The title below that BEST expresses the ideas of this paragraph is:
   A. Importance of Seaports
   B. France and Spain in the New World
   C. Early Control of the Mississippi
   D. Claims of European Nations
   E. American Trade on the Mississippi

5. Until 1762, the lower Mississippi area was held by
   A. England   B. Spain   C. the United States
   D. France   E. Indians

6. In doing business with Americans, the Spaniards were
   A. easy to outsmart
   B. friendly to trade
   C. inclined to charge high prices for use of their ports
   D. shrewd
   E. suspicious

PASSAGE 3

Our humanity is by no means so materialistic as foolish talk is continually asserting it to be. Judging by what I have learned about men and women, I am convinced that there is far more in them of idealistic willpower than ever comes to the surface of the world. Just as the water of streams is small in amount compared to that which flows underground, so the idealism which becomes visible is small in amount compared with that which men and women bear locked in their hearts, unreleased or scarcely released. To unbind what is bound, to bring the underground waters to the surface—mankind is waiting and longing for men who can do that.

7. The title below that BEST expresses the ideas of the paragraph is:
   A. Releasing Underground Riches
   B. The Good and Bad in Man
   C. Materialism in Humanity
   D. The Surface and the Depths of Idealism
   E. Unreleased Energy

8. Human beings are more idealistic than
   A. the water in underground streams
   B. their waiting and longing proves
   C. outward evidence shows
   D. the world
   E. other living creatures

PASSAGE 4

The total impression made by any work of fiction cannot be rightly understood without a sympathetic perception of the artistic aims of the writer. Consciously or unconsciously, he has accepted certain facts, and rejected or suppressed other facts, in order to give unity to the particular aspect of human life which he is depicting. No novelist possesses the impartiality, the indifference, the infinite tolerance of nature. Nature displays to use, with complete unconcern, the beautiful and the ugly, the precious and the trivial, the pure and the impure. But a writer must select the aspects of nature and human nature which are demanded by the work in hand. He is forced to select, to combine, to create.

9. The title below that BEST expresses the ideas of this paragraph is:
    A. Impressionists in Literature
    B. Nature as an Artist
    C. The Novelist as an Imitator
    D. Creative Technic of the Novelist
    E. Aspects of Nature

10. A novelist rejects some facts because they
    A. are impure and ugly
    B. would show he is not impartial
    C. are unrelated to human nature
    D. would make a bad impression
    E. mar the unity of his story

11. It is important for a reader to know
    A. the purpose of the author
    B. what facts the author omits
    C. both the ugly and the beautiful
    D. something about nature
    E. what the author thinks of human nature

PASSAGE 5

If you watch a lamp which is turned very rapidly on and off, and you keep your eyes open, "persistence of vision" will bridge the gaps of darkness between the flashes of light, and the lamp will seem to be continuously lit. This "topical afterglow" explains the magic produced by the stroboscope, a new instrument which seems to freeze the swiftest motions while they are still going on, and to stop time itself dead in its tracks. The "magic" is all in the eye of the beholder.

12. The "magic" of the stroboscope is due to
    A. continuous lighting
    B. intense cold
    C. slow motion
    D. behavior of the human eye
    E. a lapse of time

13. "Persistence of vision" is explained by
    A. darkness
    B. winking
    C. rapid flashes
    D. gaps
    E. after impression

KEY (CORRECT ANSWERS)

1.	C	6.	B	11.	A
2.	D	7.	D	12.	D
3.	A	8.	C	13.	E
4.	C	9.	D		
5.	D	10.	E		

TEST 5

DIRECTIONS: Each question has five suggested answers, lettered A to E. Decide which one is the BEST answer. *PRINT THE LETTER OF THE CORRECT ANSWER IN THE SPACE AT THE RIGHT.*

PASSAGE 1

During the past fourteen years, thousands of top-lofty United States elms have been marked for death by the activities of the tiny European elm bark beetle. The beetles, however, do not do fatal damage. Death is caused by another importation, Dutch elm disease, a fungus infection which the beetles carry from tree to tree. Up to 1941, quarantine and tree-sanitation measures kept the beetles and the disease pretty well confined within 510 miles around metropolitan New York. War curtailed these measures and made Dutch elm disease a wider menace. Every household and village that prizes an elm-shaded lawn or commons must now watch for it. Since there is as yet no cure for it, the infected trees must be pruned or felled, and the wood must be burned in order to protect other healthy trees.

1. The title below that BEST expresses the ideas of this paragraph is: 1.____
   A. A Menace to Our Elms
   B. Pests and Diseases of the Elm
   C. Our Vanishing Elms
   D. The Need to Protect Dutch Elms
   E. How Elms are Protected

2. The danger of spreading the Dutch elm disease was increased by   2.____
   A. destroying infected trees   B. the war
   C. the lack of a cure   D. a fungus infection
   E. quarantine measures

3. The European elm bark beetle is a serious threat to our elms because it   3.____
   A. chews the bark
   B. kills the trees
   C. is particularly active on the eastern seaboard
   D. carries infection
   E. cannot be controlled

PASSAGE 2

It is elemental that the greater the development of man, the greater the problems he has to concern him. When he lived in a cave with stone implements, his mind no less than his actions was grooved into simple channels. Every new invention, every new way of doing things posed fresh problems for him. And, as he moved along the road, he questioned each step, as indeed he should, for he trod upon the beliefs of his ancestors. It is equally elemental to say that each step upon this later road posed more questions than the earlier ones. It is only the educated man who realizes the results of his actions; it is only the thoughtful one who questions his own decisions.

151

4. The title below that BEST expresses the ideas of this paragraph is: 4.____
   A. Channels of Civilization
   B. The Mark of a Thoughtful Man
   C. The Cave Man in Contrast with Man Today
   D. The Price of Early Progress
   E. Man's Never-Ending Challenge

PASSAGE 3

Spring is one of those things that man has no hand in, any more than he has a part in sunrise or the phases of the moon. Spring came before man was here to enjoy it, and it will go right on coming even if man isn't here some time in the future. It is a matter of solar mechanics and celestial order. And for all our knowledge of astronomy and terrestrial mechanics, we haven't yet been able to do more than bounce a radar beam off the moon. We couldn't alter the arrival of the spring equinox by as much as one second, if we tried.

Spring is a matter of growth, of chlorophyll, of bud and blossom. We can alter growth and change the time of blossoming in individual plants; but the forests still grow in nature's way, and the grass of the plains hasn't altered its nature in a thousand years. Spring is a magnificent phase of the cycle of nature; but man really hasn't any guiding or controlling hand in it. He is here to enjoy it and benefit by it. And April is a good time to realize it; by May perhaps we will want to take full credit.

5. The title below that BEST expresses the ideas of this passage is: 5.____
   A. The Marvels of the Spring Equinox
   B. Nature's Dependence on Mankind
   C. The Weakness of Man Opposed to Nature
   D. The Glories of the World
   E. Eternal Growth

6. The author of the passage states that 6.____
   A. man has a part in the phases of the moon
   B. April is a time for taking full-credit
   C. April is a good time to enjoy nature
   D. man has a guiding hand in spring
   E. spring will cease to be if civilization ends

PASSAGE 4

The walled medieval town was as characteristic of its period as the cut of a robber baron's beard. It sprang out of the exigencies of war, and it was not without its architectural charm, whatever is hygienic deficiencies may have been. Behind its high, thick walls not only the normal inhabitants but the whole countryside fought and cowered in an hour of need. The capitals of Europe now forsake the city when the sirens scream and death from the sky seems imminent. Will the fear of bombs accelerate the slow decentralization which began with the automobile and the wide distribution of electrical energy and thus reverse the medieval flow to the city?

7. The title below that BEST expresses the ideas in this paragraph is:
   A. A Changing Function of the Town
   B. The Walled Medieval Town
   C. The Automobile's Influence on City Life
   D. Forsaking the City
   E. Bombs Today and Yesterday

8. Conditions in the Middle Ages made the walled town
   A. a natural development
   B. the most dangerous of all places
   C. a victim of fires
   D. lacking in architectural charm
   E. healthful

9. Modern conditions may
   A. make cities larger
   B. make cities more hygienic
   C. protect against floods
   D. cause people to move from population centers
   E. encourage good architecture

PASSAGE 5

The literary history of this nation began when the first settler from abroad of sensitive mind paused in his adventure long enough to feel that he was under a different sky, breathing new air and that a New World was all before him with only his strength and Providence for guides. With him began a new emphasis upon an old theme in literature, the theme of cutting loose and faring forth, renewed, under the powerful influence of a fresh continent for civilized literature, whose other flow has come from a nostalgia for the rich culture of Europe, so much of which was perforce left behind.

10. The title below that BEST expresses the ideas of this paragraph is:
    A. America's Distinctive Literature   B. Pioneer Authors
    C. The Dead Hand of the Past   D. Europe's Literary Grandchild
    E. America Comes of Age

11. American writers, according to the author, because of their colonial experiences
    A. were antagonistic to European writers
    B. cut loose from Old World influences
    C. wrote only on New World events and characters
    D. created new literary themes
    E. gave fresh interpretation to an old literary idea

KEY (CORRECT ANSWERS)

1. A
2. B
3. D
4. E
5. C
6. C
7. A
8. A
9. D
10. A
11. E

TEST 6

DIRECTIONS: Each question has five suggested answers, lettered A to E. Decide which one is the BEST answer. *PRINT THE LETTER OF THE CORRECT ANSWER IN THE SPACE AT THE RIGHT.*

1. Any business not provided with capable substitutes to fill all important positions is a weak business. Therefore, a foreman should train each man not on to perform his own particular duties but also to do those of two or three positions.
   The paragraph BEST supports the statement that
   A. dependence on substitutes is a sign of weak organization
   B. training will improve the strongest organization
   C. the foreman should be the most expert at any particular job under him
   D. every employee can be trained to perform efficiency work other than his own
   E. vacancies in vital positions should be provided for in advance

   1.____

2. The coloration of textile fabrics composed of cotton and wool generally requires two processes, as the process used in dyeing wool is seldom capable of fixing the color upon cotton. The usual method is to immerse the fabric in the requisite baths to dye the wool and then to treat the partially dyed material in the manner found suitable for cotton.
   The paragraph BEST supports the statement that the dyeing of textile fabrics composed of cotton and wool is
   A. less complicated than the dyeing of wool alone
   B. more successful when the material contains more cotton than wool
   C. not satisfactory when solid colors are desired
   D. restricted to two colors for any one fabric
   E. usually based upon the methods required for dyeing the different materials

   2.____

3. The serious investigator must direct his whole effort toward success in his work. If he wishes to succeed in each investigation, his work will be by no means easy, smooth, or peaceful; on the contrary, he will have to devote himself completely and continuously to a task that requires all his ability.
   The paragraph BEST supports the statement that an investigator's success depends most upon
   A. ambition to advance rapidly in the service
   B. persistence in the face of difficulty
   C. training and experience
   D. willingness to obey orders without delay
   E. the number of investigations which he conducts

   3.____

4. Honest people in one nation find it difficult to understand the viewpoint of honest people in another. State departments and their ministers exist for the purpose of explaining the viewpoints of one nation in terms understood by another. Some of their most important work lies in this direction.

   4.____

The paragraph BEST supports the statement that
- A. people of different nations may not consider matters in the same light
- B. it is unusual for many people to share similar ideas
- C. suspicion prevents understanding between nations
- D. the chief work of state departments is to guide relations between nations united by a common cause
- E. the people of one nation must sympathize with the viewpoints of others

5. Economy once in a while is just not enough. I expect to find it at every level of responsibility, from cabinet member to the newest and youngest recruit. Controlling waste is something like bailing a boat; you have to keep at it. I have no intention of easing up on my insistence on getting a dollar of value for each dollar we spend.
The paragraph BEST supports the statement that
- A. we need not be concerned about items which cost less than a dollar
- B. it is advisable to buy the cheaper of two items
- C. the responsibility of economy is greater at high levels than at low levels
- D. economy becomes easy with practice
- E. economy is a continuing responsibility

KEY (CORRECT ANSWERS)

1. E
2. E
3. B
4. A
5. E

TEST 7

DIRECTIONS: Each question has five suggested answers, lettered A to E. Decide which one is the BEST answer. *PRINT THE LETTER OF THE CORRECT ANSWER IN THE SPACE AT THE RIGHT.*

1. On all permit imprint mail the charge for postage has been printed by the mailer before he presents it for mailing and pays the postage. Such mail of any class is mailable only at the post office that issued a permit covering it. Since the postage receipts for such mail represent only the amount of permit imprint mail detected and verified, employees in receiving, handling, and outgoing sections must be alert constantly to route such mail to the weighing section before it is handled or dispatched.
   The paragraph BEST supports the statement that, at post offices where permit mail is received for dispatch,
   A. dispatching units make a final check on the amount of postage payable on permit imprint mail
   B. employees are to check the postage chargeable on mail received under permit
   C. neither more nor less postage is to be collected than the amount printed on permit imprint mail
   D. the weighing section is primarily responsible for failure to collect postage on such mail
   E. unusual measures are taken to prevent unstamped mail from being accepted

1.____

2. Education should not stop when the individual has been prepared to make a livelihood and to live in modern society. Living would be mere existence were there were no appreciation and enjoyment of the riches of art, literature, and science.
   The paragraph BEST supports the statement that true education
   A. is focused on the routine problems of life
   B. prepares one for full enjoyment of life
   C. deals chiefly with art, literature, and science
   D. is not possible for one who does not enjoy scientific literature
   E. disregards practical ends

2.____

3. Insured and c.o.d. air and surface mail is accepted with the understanding that the sender guarantees any necessary forwarding or return postage. When such mail is forwarded or returned, it shall be rated up for collection of postage; except that insured or c.o.d. air mail weighing 8 ounces or less and subject to the 40 cents an ounce rate shall be forwarded by air if delivery will be advanced, and returned by surface means without additional postage.
   The paragraph BEST supports the statement that the return postage for undeliverable insured mail is
   A. included in the original prepayment on air mail parcels
   B. computed but not collected before dispatching surface patrol post mail to sender

3.____

C. not computed or charged for any air mail that is returned by surface transportation
D. included in the amount collected when the sender mails parcel post
E. collected before dispatching for return if any amount due has been guaranteed

4. All undeliverable first-class mail, except first-class parcels and parcel post paid with first-class postage, which cannot be returned to the sender, is sent to a dead-letter branch. Undeliverable matter of the third- and fourth-classes of obvious value for which the sender does not furnish return postage and undeliverable first-class parcels and parcel-post matter bearing postage of the first-class, which cannot be returned, is sent to a dead parcel-post branch.
The paragraph BEST supports the statement that matter that is sent to a dead parcel-post branch includes all undeliverable
   A. mail, except for first-class letter mail, that appears to be valuable
   B. mail, except that of the first-class, on which the sender failed to prepay the original mailing costs
   C. parcels on which the mailer prepaid the first-class rate of postage
   D. third- and fourth-class matter on which the required return postage has not been paid
   E. parcels on which first-class postage has been prepaid, when the sender's address is not known

5. Civilization started to move rapidly when man freed himself of the shackles that restricted his search for truth.
The passage BEST supports the statement that the progress of civilization
   A. came as a result of man's dislike for obstacles
   B. did not begin until restrictions on learning were removed
   C. has been aided by man's efforts to find the truth
   D. is based on continually increasing efforts
   E. continues at a constantly increasing rate

KEY (CORRECT ANSWERS)

1. B
2. B
3. B
4. E

TEST 8

DIRECTIONS: Each question has five suggested answers, lettered A to E. Decide which one is the BEST answer. *PRINT THE LETTER OF THE CORRECT ANSWER IN THE SPACE AT THE RIGHT.*

1. E-mails should be clear, concise, and brief. Omit all unnecessary words. The parts of speech most often used in e-mails are nouns, verbs, adjectives, and adverbs. If possible, do without pronouns, prepositions, articles, and copulative verbs. Use simple sentences, rather than complex and compound.
   The paragraph BEST supports the statement that in writing e-mails one should always use
   A. common and simple words
   B. only nouns, verbs, adjectives, and adverbs
   C. incomplete sentences
   D. only words essential to the meaning
   E. the present tense of verbs

   1.____

2. The function of business is to increase the wealth of the country and the value and happiness of life. It does this by supplying the material needs of men and women. When the nation's business is successfully carried on, it renders public service of the highest value.
   The paragraph BEST supports the statement that
   A. all businesses which render public service are successful
   B. human happiness is enhanced only by the increase of material wants
   C. the value of life is increased only by the increase of wealth
   D. the material needs of men and women are supplied by well-conducted business
   E. business is the only field of activity which increases happiness

   2.____

3. In almost every community, fortunately, there are certain men and women known to be public-spirited. Others, however, may be selfish and act only as their private interests seem to require.
   The paragraph BEST supports the statement that those citizens who disregard others are
   A. fortunate   B. needed
   C. found only in small communities   D. not known
   E. not public spirited

   3.____

KEY (CORRECT ANSWERS)

1. D
2. D
3. E

READING COMPREHENSION
UNDERSTANDING WRITTEN MATERIALS
COMMENTARY

The ability to read and understand written materials—texts, publications, newspapers, orders, directions, expositions—is a skill basic to a functioning democracy and to an efficient business or viable government.

That is why almost all examinations—for beginning, middle, and senior levels—test reading comprehension, directly or indirectly.

The reading test measures how well you understand what you read. This is how it is done: You read a passage followed by several statements. From these statements, you choose the one statement, or answer, that is BEST supported by, or BEST matches, what is said in the paragraph. PRINT THE LETTER OF THE CORRECT ANSWER IN THE SPACE AT THE RIGHT.

SAMPLE QUESTION

DIRECTIONS: Answer Question 1 ONLY according to the information given in the following passage.

1. A cashier has to make many arithmetic calculations in connection with his work. Skill in arithmetic comes readily with practice; no special talent is needed.
   On the basis of the above statement, it is MOST accurate to state that
   A. the most important part of a cashier's job is to make calculations
   B. few cashiers have the special ability needed to handle arithmetic problems easily
   C. without special talent, cashiers cannot learn to do the calculations they are required to do in their work
   D. a cashier can, with practice, learn to handle the computations he is required to make

1.____

The CORRECT answer is D.

EXAMINATION SECTION
TEST 1

DIRECTIONS: Questions 1 through 5 are to be answered on the basis of the following reading passage. *PRINT THE LETTER OF THE CORRECT ANSWER IN THE SPACE AT THE RIGHT.*

The size of each collection route will be determined by the amount of waste per stop, distance between stops, speed of loading, speed of truck, traffic conditions during loading time, etc.

Basically, the route should consist of a proper amount of work for a crew for the daily work period. The crew should service all properties eligible for this service in their area. Routes should, whenever practical, be compact, with a logical progression through the area. Unnecessary travel should be avoided. Traffic conditions on the route should be thoroughly studied to prevent lost time in loading, to reduce hazards to employees, and to minimize tying up of regular traffic movements by collection forces. Natural and physical barriers and arterial streets should be used as route boundaries wherever possible to avoid lost time in travel.

Routes within a district should be laid out so that the crews start at the point farthest from the disposal area and, as the day progresses, move toward that area, thus reducing the length of the haul. When possible, the work of the crews in a district should be parallel as they progress throughout the day, with routes finishing up within a short distance of each other. This enables the supervisor to be present when crews are completing their work and enables him to shift crews to trouble spots to complete the day's work.

1. Based on the above passage, an advantage of having collection routes end near one another is that
    A. routes can be made more compact
    B. unnecessary travel is avoided, saving manpower
    C. the length of the haul is reduced
    D. the supervisor can exercise better manpower control

1.____

2. Of the factors mentioned above which affect the size of a collection route, the two over which the sanitation forces have LEAST control are
    A. amount of waste; traffic conditions
    B. speed of loading; amount of waste
    C. speed of truck; distance between stops
    D. traffic conditions; speed of truck

2.____

3. According to the above passage, the size of a collection route is probably good if
    A. it is a fair day's work for a normal crew
    B. it is not necessary for the trucks to travel too fast
    C. the amount of waste collected can be handled properly
    D. the distance between stops is approximately equal

3.____

4. Based on the above passage, it is reasonable to assume that a sanitation officer laying out collection routes should NOT try to have
   A. an arterial street as a route boundary
   B. any routes near the disposal area
   C. the routes overlap a little
   D. the routes run in the same direction

5. The term "logical progression," as used in the second paragraph of the passage refers MOST NEARLY to
   A. collecting from street after street in order
   B. numbering streets one after the other
   C. rotating crew assignments
   D. using logic as a basis for assigned crews

KEY (CORRECT ANSWERS)

1. D
2. A
3. A
4. C
5. A

TEST 2

DIRECTIONS: Questions 1 through 3 are to be answered on the basis of the following reading passage. *PRINT THE LETTER OF THE CORRECT ANSWER IN THE SPACE AT THE RIGHT.*

In an open discussion designed to arrive at solutions to community problems, the person leading the discussion group should give the members a chance to make their suggestions before he makes his. He must not be afraid of silence; if he talks just to keep things going, he will find he can't stop, and good discussion will not develop. In other words, the more he talks, the more the group will depend on him. If he finds, however, that no one seems ready to begin the discussion, his best "opening" is to ask for definitions of terms which form the basis of the discussion. By pulling out as many definitions or interpretations as possible, he can get the group started "thinking out load," which is essential to good discussion.

1. According to the above passage, good group discussion is MOST likely to result if the person leading the discussion group
    A. keeps the discussion going by speaking whenever the group stops speaking
    B. encourages the group to depend on him by speaking more than any other group member
    C. makes his own suggestions before the group has a chance to make theirs
    D. encourages discussion by asking the group to interpret the terms to be discussed

1.____

2. According to the above passage, "thinking out loud" by the discussion group is
    A. *good* practice, because "thinking out loud" is important to good discussion
    B. *poor* practice, because group members should think out their ideas before discussing them
    C. *good* practice, because it will encourage the person leading the discussion to speak more
    D. *poor* practice, because it causes the group to fear silence during discussion

2.____

3. According to the above passage, the one of the following which is LEAST desirable at an open discussion is having
    A. silent periods during which none of the group members speaks
    B. differences of opinion among the group members concerning the definition of terms
    C. a discussion leader who uses "openings" to get the discussion started
    D. a discussion leader who provides all suggestions and definitions for the group

3.____

KEY (CORRECT ANSWERS)
1. D
2. A
3. D

TEST 3

DIRECTIONS: Questions 1 through 4 are to be answered on the basis of the following reading passage. *PRINT THE LETTER OF THE CORRECT ANSWER IN THE SPACE AT THE RIGHT.*

The insects you will control are just a minute fraction of the millions which inhabit the world. Man does well to hold his own in the face of the constant pressures that insects continue to exert upon him. Not only are the total numbers tremendous, but the number of individual kinds, or species, certainly exceeds 800,000—number greater than that of all other animals combined. Many of these are beneficial but some are especially competitive with man. Not only are insects numerous, but they are among the most adaptable of all animals. In their many forms, they are fitted for almost any specific way of life. Their adaptability, combined with their tremendous rate of reproduction, gives insects an unequaled potential for survival!

The food of insects includes almost anything that can be eaten by any other animal as well as many things which cannot even be digested by any other animals. Most insects do not harm the products of man or carry diseases harmful to him; however, many do carry diseases and others feed on his food and manufactured goods. Some are adapted to living only in open areas while others are able to live in extremely confined spaces. All of these factor combined make the insects a group of animals having many members which are a nuisance to man and thus of great importance.

The control of insects requires an understanding of their way of life. Thus, it is necessary to understand the anatomy of the insect, its method of growth, the time it takes for the insect to grow from egg to adult, its habits, the stage of its life history in which it causes damage, its food, and its common living places. In order to obtain the best control, it is especially important to be able to identify correctly the specific insect involved because, without this knowledge, it is impossible to prescribe a proper treatment.

1. Which one of the following is a CORRECT statement about the insect population of the world, according to the above passage? The
   A. total number of insects is less than the total number of all other animals combined
   B. number of species of insects is greater than the number of species of all other animals combined
   C. total number of harmful insects is less than the number of species of those which are harmful
   D. number of species of harmless insects is less than the number of species of those which are harmful

1.____

2. Insects will be controlled MOST efficiently if you
   A. understand why the insects are so numerous
   B. know what insects you are dealing with
   C. see if the insects compete with man
   D. are able to identify the food which the insects digest

2.____

3. According to the above passage, insects are of importance to a scientist PRIMARILY because they
   A. can be annoying, destructive, and harmful to man
   B. are able to thrive in very small spaces
   C. cause damage during their growth stages
   D. are so adaptable that they can adjust to any environment

4. According to the above passage, insects can eat
   A. everything that any other living thing can eat
   B. man's food and thing which he makes
   C. anything which other animals can't digest
   D. only food and food products

KEY (CORRECT ANSWERS)

1. B
2. B
3. A
4. B

TEST 4

DIRECTIONS: Questions 1 through 3 are to be answered on the basis of the following reading passage. *PRINT THE LETTER OF THE CORRECT ANSWER IN THE SPACE AT THE RIGHT.*

Telephone service in a government agency should be adequate and complete with respect to information given or action taken. It must be remembered that telephone contacts should receive special consideration since the caller cannot see the operator. People like to feel that they are receiving personal attention and that their requests or criticisms are receiving individual rather than routine consideration. All this contributes to what has come to be known as *tone of service*. The aim is to use standards which are clearly very good or superior. The factors to be considered in determining what makes good tone of service are speech, courtesy, understanding, and explanations. A caller's impression of tone of service will affect the general public attitude toward the agency and city services in general.

1. The above passage states that people who telephone a government agency like to feel that they are
   A. creating a positive image of themselves
   B. being given routine consideration
   C. receiving individual attention
   D. setting standards for telephone service

2. Which one of the following is NOT mentioned in the above passage as a factor in determining good tone of service?
   A. Courtesy   B. Education   C. Speech   D. Understanding

3. The above passage implies that failure to properly handle telephone calls is MOST likely to result in
   A. a poor impression of city agencies by the public
   B. a deterioration of courtesy toward operators
   C. an effort by operators to improve the Tone of Service
   D. special consideration by the public of operator difficulties

KEY (CORRECT ANSWERS)

1. C
2. B
3. A

TEST 5

DIRECTIONS: Questions 1 through 5 are to be answered on the basis of the following reading passage. *PRINT THE LETTER OF THE CORRECT ANSWER IN THE SPACE AT THE RIGHT.*

For some office workers it is useful to be familiar with the four main classes of domestic mail; for others, it is essential. Each class has a different rate of postage and some have requirements concerning wrapping, sealing, or special information to be placed on the package.

First-class mail, the class which may not be opened for postal inspection, includes letters, postcards, business reply cards, and other kinds of written matter. There are different rates for some of the kinds of cards which can be sent by first-class mail. The maximum weight for an item sent by first-class mail is 70 pounds. An item which is not letter size should be marked "First Class: on all sides.

Although office workers most often come into contact with first-class mail, they may find it helpful to know something about the other classes. Second-class mail is generally used for mailing newspapers and magazines. Publishers of these articles must meet certain U.S. Postal Service requirements in order to obtain a permit to use second-class mailing rates. Third-class mail, which must weigh less than 1 pound, includes printed materials and merchandise parcels. There are two rate structure for this class, a single-piece rate and a bulk rate. Fourth-class mail, also known as parcel post, includes packages weighing from one to 40 pounds. For more information about these classes of mail and the actual mailing rates, contact our local post office.

1. According to this passage, first-class mail is the only class which   1.____
   A. has a limit on the maximum weight of an item
   B. has different rates for items within the class
   C. may not be opened for postal inspection
   D. should be used by office workers

2. According to this passage, the one of the following items which may CORRECTLY   2.____
   be sent by fourth-class mail is a
   A. magazine weighing one-half pound
   B. package weighing one-half pound
   C. package weighing two pounds
   D. postcard

3. According to this passage, there are different postage rates for   3.____
   A. a newspaper sent by second-class mail and a magazine sent by second-class mail
   B. each of the classes of mail
   C. each pound of fourth-class mail
   D. printed material sent by third-class mail and merchandise parcels sent by third-class mail

4. In order to send a newspaper by second-class mail, a publisher must
   A. have met certain postal requirements and obtained a permit
   B. indicate whether he wants to use the single-piece or the bulk rate
   C. make certain that the newspaper weighs less than one pound
   D. mark the newspaper "Second Class" on the top and bottom of the wrapper

5. Of the following types of information, the one which is NOT mentioned in the passage is the
   A. class of mail to which parcel post belongs
   B. kinds of items which can be sent by each class of mail
   C. maximum weight for an item sent by fourth-class mail
   D. postage rate for each of the four classes of mail

KEY (CORRECT ANSWERS)

1. C
2. C
3. B
4. A
5. D

TEST 6

DIRECTIONS: Questions 1 through 5 are to be answered on the basis of the following reading passage. *PRINT THE LETTER OF THE CORRECT ANSWER IN THE SPACE AT THE RIGHT.*

The thickness of insulation necessary for the most economical results varies with the steam temperature. The standard covering consists of 85 percent magnesia with 10 percent of long-fibre asbestos as a binder. Both magnesia and laminated asbestos-felt and other forms of mineral wool including glass wool are also used for heat insulation. The magnesia and laminated-asbestos coverings may be safely used at temperatures up to 600°F. Pipe insulation is applied in molded sections 3 feet long; the sections are attached to the pipe by means of galvanized iron wire or netting. Flanges and fittings can be insulated by direct application of magnesia cement to the metal without *reinforcement*. Insulation should always be maintained inn good condition because it saves fuel. Routine maintenance of warm-pipe insulation should include prompt repair of damaged surfaces. Steam and hot-water leaks concealed by insulation will be difficult to detect. Underground steam or hot-water pipes are best insulated using a concrete trench with removable cover.

1. The word *reinforcement*, as used above, means MOST NEARLY 1.____
   A. resistance B. strengthening
   C. regulation D. removal

2. According to the above paragraph, magnesia and laminated asbestos 2.____
   coverings may be safely used at temperatures up to
   A. 800°F B. 720°F C. 675°F D. 600°F

3. According to the above paragraph, insulation should *always* be maintained 3.____
   in good condition because it
   A. is laminated B. saves fuel
   C. is attached to the pipe D. prevents leaks

4. According to the above paragraph, pipe insulation sections are attached to the 4.____
   pipe by means of
   A. binders B. mineral wool
   C. netting D. staples

5. According to the above paragraph, a leak in a hot-water pipe may be difficult 5.____
   to detect because, when insulation is used, the leak is
   A. underground B. hidden C. routine D. cemented

KEY (CORRECT ANSWERS)

1. B
2. D
3. B
4. C
5. B

TEST 7

DIRECTIONS: Questions 1 through 4 are to be answered on the basis of the following reading passage. *PRINT THE LETTER OF THE CORRECT ANSWER IN THE SPACE AT THE RIGHT.*

Cylindrical surfaces are the most common form of finished surfaces found on machine parts, although flat surfaces are also very common; hence, many metal-cutting processes are for the purpose of producing either cylindrical or flat surfaces. The machines used for cylindrical or flat shapes may be, and often are, utilized also for forming the various irregular or special shapes required on many machine parts. Because of the prevalence of cylindrical and flat surfaces, the student of manufacturing practice should learn first about the machines and methods employed to produce these surfaces. The cylindrical surfaces may be internal as in holes and cylinders. Any one part may, of course, have cylindrical sections of different diameters and lengths and include flat ends or shoulders and, frequently, there is a threaded part or, possibly, some finished surface that is not circular in cross-section. The prevalence of cylindrical surfaces on machine parts explains why lathes are found in all machine shops. It is important to understand the various uses of the lathes because many of the operations are the same fundamentally as those performed on other types of machine tools.

1. According to the above passage, the MOST common form of finished surfaces found on machine parts is
   A. cylindrical   B. elliptical   C. flat   D. square

2. According to the above passage, any one part of cylindrical surfaces may have
   A. chases   B. shoulders   C. keyways   D. splines

3. According to the above passage, lathes are found in all machine shops because cylindrical surfaces on machine parts are
   A. scarce   B. internal   C. common   D. external

4. As used in the above paragraph, the word *processes* means
   A. operations   B. purposes   C. devices   D. tools

KEY (CORRECT ANSWERS)

1. A
2. B
3. C
4. A

TEST 8

DIRECTIONS: Questions 1 and 2 are to be answered on the basis of the following reading passage. *PRINT THE LETTER OF THE CORRECT ANSWER IN THE SPACE AT THE RIGHT.*

    The principle of interchangeability requires manufacture to such specification that component parts of a device may be selected at random and assembled to fit and operate satisfactorily. Interchangeable manufacture, therefore, requires that parts be made to definite limits of error, and to fit gages instead of mating parts. Interchangeability does not necessarily involve a high degree of precision; stove lids, for example, are interchangeable but are not particularly accurate, and carriage bolts and nuts are not precision products but are completely interchangeable. Interchangeability may be employed in unit-production as well as mass-production systems of manufacture.

1. According to the above paragraph, in order for parts to be interchangeable, they must be
   - A. precision-machined
   - B. selectively-assembled
   - C. mass-produced
   - D. made to fit gages

   1.____

2. According to the above paragraph, carriage bolts are interchangeable because they are
   - A. precision-made
   - B. sized to specific tolerances
   - C. individually matched products
   - D. produced in small units

   2.____

KEY (CORRECT ANSWERS)

1. D
2. B

VERBAL ABILITIES TEST

DIRECTIONS AND SAMPLE QUESTIONS

Study the sample questions carefully. Each question has four suggested answers. Decide which one is the best answer. Find the question number on the Sample Answer Sheet. Show your answer to the question by printing the letter of the correct answer in the space at the right. If you have to erase a mark, be sure to erase it completely. Mark only one answer for each question. Do NOT mark space E for any question.

SAMPLE VERBAL QUESTIONS

I. *Previous* means MOST NEARLY
   A. abandoned   B. former   C. timely   D. younger

I.____

II. (Reading) "Just as the procedure of a collection department must be clear cut and definite, the steps being taken with the sureness of a skilled chess player, so the various paragraphs of a collection letter must show clear organization, giving evidence of a mind that, from the beginning, has had a specific end in view."
The quotation BEST supports the statement that a collection letter should always
   A. show a spirit of sportsmanship   B. be divided into several paragraphs
   C. be brief, but courteous   D. be carefully planned

II.____

III. Decide which sentence is preferable with respect to grammar and usage suitable for a formal letter or report.
   A. They do not ordinarily present these kind of reports in detail like this.
   B. A report of this kind is not hardly ever given in such detail as this one.
   C. This report is more detailed than what such reports ordinarily are.
   D. A report of this kind is not ordinarily presented in as much detail as this one is.

III.____

IV. Find the correct spelling of the word and print the letter of the correct answer in the space at the right. If no suggested spelling is correct, print the letter D.
   A. athalete   B. athelete   C. athlete   D. none of these

IV.____

V. SPEEDOMETER is related to POINTER as WATCH is related to
   A. case   B. hands   C. dial   D. numerals

V.____

EXAMINATION SECTION

TEST 1

DIRECTIONS: Each question or incomplete statement is followed by several suggested answers or completions. Select the one that BEST answers the question or completes the statement. *PRINT THE LETTER OF THE CORRECT ANSWER IN THE SPACE AT THE RIGHT.*

1. *Flexible* means MOST NEARLY
   A. breakable   B. flammable   C. pliable   D. weak

2. *Option* means MOST NEARLY
   A. use   B. choice   C. value   D. blame

3. To *verify* means MOST NEARLY to
   A. examine   B. explain   C. confirm   D. guarantee

4. *Indolent* means MOST NEARLY
   A. moderate   B. happiness   C. selfish   D. lazy

5. *Respiration* means MOST NEARLY
   A. recovery   B. breathing   C. pulsation   D. sweating

6. PLUMBER is related to WRENCH as PAINTER related to
   A. brush   B. pipe   C. shop   D. hammer

7. LETTER is related to MESSAGE as PACKAGE is related to
   A. sender
   B. merchandise
   C. insurance
   D. business

8. FOOD is related to HUNGER as SLEEP is related to
   A. night   B. dream   C. weariness   D. rest

9. KEY is related to TYPEWRITER as DIAL is related to
   A. sun   B. number   C. circle   D. telephone

GRAMMAR

10. A. I think that they will promote whoever has the best record.
    B. The firm would have liked to have promoted all employees with good records.
    C. Such of them that have the best records have excellent prospects of promotion.
    D. I feel sure they will give the promotion to whomever has the best record.

11. A. The receptionist must answer courteously the questions of all them callers.
    B. The receptionist must answer courteously the questions what are asked by the callers.
    C. There would have been no trouble if the receptionist had have always answered courteously.
    D. The receptionist should answer courteously the questions of all callers.

11._____

SPELLING

12. A. collapsible   B. colapseble
    C. collapseble   D. none of the above

12._____

13. A. ambigeuous   B. ambigeous
    C. ambiguous   D. none of the above

13._____

14. A. predesessor   B. predecesar
    C. predecesser   D. none of the above

14._____

15. A. sanctioned   B. sancktioned
    C. sanctionned   D. none of the above

15._____

READING

16. "The secretarial profession is a very old one and has increased in importance with the passage of time. In modern times, the vast expansion of business and industry has greatly increased the need and opportunities for secretaries, and for the first time in history their number has become large."
    The above quotation BEST supports the statement that the secretarial profession
    A. is older than business and industry
    B. did not exist in ancient times
    C. has greatly increased in size
    D. demands higher training than it did formerly

16._____

17. "Civilization started to move ahead more rapidly when man freed himself of the shackles that restricted his search for the truth."
    The above quotation BEST supports the statement that the progress of civilization
    A. came as a result of man's dislike for obstacles
    B. did not begin until restrictions on learning were removed
    C. has been aided by man's efforts to find
    D. the truth is based on continually increasing efforts

17._____

18. *Vigilant* means MOST NEARLY
    A. sensible   B. watchful   C. suspicious   D. restless

18._____

19. *Incidental* means MOST NEARLY
    A. independent   B. needless   C. infrequent   D. casual

19._____

20. *Conciliatory* means MOST NEARLY
    A. pacific   B. contentious   C. obligatory   D. offensive

21. *Altercation* means MOST NEARLY
    A. defeat   B. concurrence
    C. controversy   D. vexation

22. *Irresolute* means MOST NEARLY
    A. wavering   B. insubordinate
    C. impudent   D. unobservant

23. DARKNESS is related to SUNLIGHT as STILLNESS is related to
    A. quiet   B. moonlight   C. sound   D. dark

24. DESIGNED is related to INTENTION as ACCIDENTAL is related to
    A. purpose   B. caution   C. damage   D. chance

25. ERROR is related to PRACTICE as SOUND is related to
    A. deafness   B. noise   C. muffler   D. horn

26. RESEARCH is related to FINDINGS as TRAINING is related to
    A. skill   B. tests
    C. supervision   D. teaching

27. A. If properly addressed, the letter will reach my mother and I.
    B. The letter had been addressed to myself and my mother.
    C. I believe the letter was addressed to either my mother or I.
    D. My mother's name, as well as mine, was on the letter.

28. A. The supervisor reprimanded the typist, whom she believed had made careless errors.
    B. The typist would have corrected the errors had she of known that the supervisor would see the report.
    C. The errors in the typed report were so numerous that they could hardly be overlooked.
    D. Many errors were found in the report which she typed and could not disregard them.

29. A. minieture   B. minneature
    C. mineature   D. none of the above

30. A. extemporaneous   B. extempuraneus
    C. extemporraneous   D. none of the above

31. A. problemmatical   B. problematical
    C. problematicle   D. none of the above

32. A. descendant   B. decendant
    C. desendant   D. none of the above

33. "The likelihood of America's exhausting her natural resources seems to be growing less. All kinds of waste are being reworked and new uses are constantly being found for almost everything. We are getting more use out of our goods and are making many new byproducts out of what was formerly thrown away."
The above quotation BEST supports the statement that we seem to be in less danger of exhausting our resources because
    A. economy is found to lie in the use of substitutes
    B. more service is obtained from a given amount of material
    C. we are allowing time for nature to restore them
    D. supply and demand are better controlled

34. "Memos should be clear, concise, and brief. Omit all unnecessary words. The parts of speech most often used in memos are nouns, verbs, adjectives, and adverbs. If possible, do without pronouns, prepositions, articles, and copulative verbs. Use simple sentences, rather than complex or compound ones.
The above quotation BEST supports the statement that in writing memos one should always use
    A. common and simple words
    B. only nouns, verbs, adjectives, and adverbs
    C. incomplete sentences
    D. only the word essential to the meaning

35. To *counteract* means MOST NEARLY to
    A. undermine   B. censure   C. preserve   D. neutralize

36. *Deferred* means MOST NEARLY
    A. reversed   B. delayed
    C. considered   D. forbidden

37. *Feasible* means MOST NEARLY
    A. capable   B. justifiable   C. practicable   D. beneficial

38. To *encounter* means MOST NEARLY to
    A. meet   B. recall   C. overcome   D. retreat

39. *Innate* means MOST NEARLY
    A. eternal   B. well-developed
    C. native   D. prospective

40. STUDENT is to TEACHER as DISCIPLE is related to
    A. follower   B. master   C. principal   D. pupil

41. LECTURE is related to AUDITORIUM as EXPERIMENT is related to
    A. scientist   B. chemistry   C. laboratory   D. discovery

42. BODY is related to FOOD as ENGINE is related to
    A. wheels   B. fuel   C. motion   D. smoke

43. SCHOOL is related to EDUCATION as THEATER is related to   43.____
    A. management   B. stage
    C. recreation   D. preparation

44. A. Most all these statements have been supported by persons who are   44.____
       reliable and can be depended upon.
    B. The persons which have guaranteed these statements are reliable.
    C. Reliable persons guarantee the facts with regards to the truth of these
       statements.
    D. These statements can be depended on, for their truth has been guaranteed
       by reliable persons.

45. A. The success of the book pleased both his publisher and he.   45.____
    B. Both his publisher and he was pleased with the success of the book.
    C. Neither he or his publisher was disappointed with the success of the book.
    D. His publisher was as pleased as he with the success of the book.

46. A. extercate   B. extracate   46.____
    C. extricate   D. none of the above

47. A. hereditory   B. hereditary   47.____
    C. hereditairy   D. none of the above

48. A. auspiceous   B. auspiseous   48.____
    C. auspicious   D. none of the above

49. A. sequance   B. sequence   49.____
    C. sequense   D. none of the above

50. "The prevention of accidents makes it necessary not only that safety devices   50.____
    be used to guard exposed machinery but also that mechanics be instructed in
    safety rules which they must follow for their own protection, and that the lighting
    in the plant be adequate."
    The above quotation BEST supports the statement that industrial accidents
    A. may be due to ignorance
    B. are always avoidable
    C. usually result from inadequate machinery
    D. cannot be entirely overcome

51. "The English language is peculiarly rich in synonyms, and there is scarcely a   51.____
    language spoken among men that has not some representative in English
    speech. The spirit of the Anglo-Saxon race has subjugate these various
    elements to one idiom, making not a patchwork, but a composite language."
    The above quotation BEST supports the statement that the English language
    A. has few idiomatic expressions
    B. is difficult to translate
    C. is used universally
    D. has absorbed words from other languages

52. To *acquiesce* means MOST NEARLY to
    A. assent   B. acquire   C. complete   D. participate

53. *Unanimity* means MOST NEARLY
    A. emphasis
    C. harmony
    B. namelessness
    D. impartiality

54. *Precedent* means MOST NEARLY
    A. example   B. theory   C. law   D. conformity

55. *Versatile* means MOST NEARLY
    A. broad-minded
    C. up-to-date
    B. well-known
    D. many-sided

56. *Authentic* means MOST NEARLY
    A. detailed   B. reliable   C. valuable   D. practical

57. BIOGRAPHY is related to FACT as NOVEL is related to
    A. fiction   B. literature   C. narration   D. book

58. COPY is related to CARBON PAPER as MOTION PICTURE is related to
    A. theater   B. film   C. duplicate   D. television

59. EFFICIENCY is related to REWARD as CARELESSNESS is related to
    A. improvement
    C. reprimand
    B. disobedience
    D. repetition

60. ABUNDANT is related to CHEAP as SCARCE is related to
    A. ample
    C. inexpensive
    B. costly
    D. unobtainable

61. A. Brown's & Company employees have recently received increases in salary.
    B. Brown & Company recently increased the salaries of all its employees.
    C. Recently, Brown & Company has increased their employees' salaries.
    D. Brown & Company have recently increased the salaries of all its employees.

62. A. In reviewing the typists' work reports, the job analyst found records of unusual typing speeds.
    B. It says in the job analyst's report that some employees type with great speed.
    C. The job analyst found that, in reviewing the typists' work reports, that some unusual typing speeds had been made.
    D. In the reports of typists' speeds, the job analyst found some records that are kind of unusual.

63. A. obliterate
    C. obbliterate
    B. oblitterat
    D. none of the above

64. A. diagnoesis   B. diagnossis
     C. diagnosis   D. none of the above

65. A. contenance   B. countenance
     C. knowledge   D. none of the above

66. A. conceivably   B. concieveably
     C. conceiveably   D. none of the above

67. "Through advertising, manufacturers exercise a high degree of control over consumers' desires. However, the manufacturer assumes enormous risks in attempting to predict what consumers will want and in producing goods in quantity and distributing them in advance of final selection by the consumers."
     The above quotation BEST supports the statement that manufacturers
     A. can eliminate the risk of overproduction by advertising
     B. distribute goods directly to the consumers
     C. must depend upon the final consumers for the success of their undertakings
     D. can predict with great accuracy the success of any product they put on the market

68. "In the relations of man to nature, the procuring of food and shelter is fundamental. With the migration of man to various climates, ever new adjustments to the food supply and to the climate became necessary."
     The above quotation BEST supports the statement that the means by which man supplies his material needs are
     A. accidental   B. varied   C. limited   D. inadequate

69. *Strident* means MOST NEARLY
     A. swaggering   B. domineering
     C. angry   D. harsh

70. To *confine* means MOST NEARLY to
     A. hide   B. restrict   C. eliminate   D. punish

71. To *accentuate* means MOST NEARLY to
     A. modify   B. hasten   C. sustain   D. intensify

72. *Banal* means MOST NEARLY
     A. commonplace   B. forceful
     C. tranquil   D. indifferent

73. *Incorrigible* means MOST NEARLY
     A. intolerable   B. retarded
     C. irreformable   D. brazen

74. POLICEMAN is related to ORDER as DOCTOR is related to
     A. physician   B. hospital   C. sickness   D. health

75. ARTIST is related to EASEL as WEAVER is related to
    A. loom   B. cloth   C. threads   D. spinner

76. CROWD is related to PERSONS as FLEET is related to
    A. expedition   B. officers   C. navy   D. ships

77. CALENDAR is related to DATE as MAP is related to
    A. geography   B. trip   C. mileage   D. vacation

78. A. Since the report lacked the needed information, it was of no use to him.
    B. This report was useless to him because there were no needed information in it.
    C. Since the report did not contain the needed information, it was not real useful to him.
    D. Being that the report lacked the needed information, he could not use it.

79. A. The company had hardly declared the dividend till the notices were prepared for mailing.
    B. They had no sooner declared the dividend when they sent the notices to the stockholders.
    C. No sooner had the dividend been declared than the notices were prepared for mailing.
    D. Scarcely had the dividend been declared than the notices were sent out.

80. A. compitition   B. competition
    C. competetion   D. none of the above

81. A. occassion   B. ocassion
    C. occasion   D. none of the above

82. A. knowlege   B. knowledge
    C. knolledge D. none of the above

83. A. deliborate   B. deliberate
    C. deliberate   D. none of the above

84. "What constitutes skill in any line of work is not always easy to determine; economy of time must be carefully distinguished from economy of energy, as the quickest method may require the greatest expenditure of muscular effort, and may not be essential or at all desirable."
    The above quotation BEST supports the statement that
    A. the most efficiently executed task is not always the one done in the shortest time
    B. energy and time cannot both be conserved in performing a single task
    C. a task is well done when it is performed in the shortest time
    D. skill in performing a task should not be acquired at the expense of time

85. "It is difficult to distinguish between bookkeeping and accounting. In attempts to do so, bookkeeping is called the art, and accounting the science, of recording business transactions. Bookkeeping gives the history of the business in a systematic manner; and accounting classifies, analyzes, and interpret the facts thus recorded."
The above quotation BEST supports the statement that
   A. accounting is less systematic than bookkeeping
   B. accounting and bookkeeping are closely related
   C. bookkeeping and accounting cannot be distinguished from one another
   D. bookkeeping has been superseded by accounting

85.____

KEY (CORRECT ANSWERS)

1.	C	16.	C	31.	B	46.	C	61.	B	76.	D
2.	B	17.	C	32.	A	47.	B	62.	A	77.	C
3.	C	18.	B	33.	B	48.	C	63.	A	78.	A
4.	D	19.	D	34.	D	49.	B	64.	C	79.	C
5.	B	20.	A	35.	D	50.	A	65.	B	80.	B
6.	A	21.	C	36.	B	51.	D	66.	A	81.	B
7.	B	22.	A	37.	C	52.	A	67.	C	82.	C
8.	C	23.	C	38.	A	53.	C	68.	B	83.	B
9.	D	24.	D	39.	C	54.	A	69.	D	84.	A
10.	A	25.	C	40.	B	55.	D	70.	B	85.	B
11.	D	26.	A	41.	C	56.	B	71.	D		
12.	A	27.	D	42.	B	57.	A	72.	A		
13.	C	28.	C	43.	C	58.	B	73.	C		
14.	D	29.	D	44.	D	59.	C	74.	D		
15.	A	30.	A	45.	D	60.	B	75.	A		

TEST 2

DIRECTIONS: Each question or incomplete statement is followed by several suggested answers or completions. Select the one that BEST answers the question or completes the statement. *PRINT THE LETTER OF THE CORRECT ANSWER IN THE SPACE AT THE RIGHT.*

1. *O*ption means MOST NEARLY
   A. use B. choice C. value
   D. blame E. mistake

   1.____

2. *Irresolute* means MOST NEARLY
   A. wavering B. insubordinate C. impudent
   D. determined E. unobservant

   2.____

3. *Flexible* means MOST NEARLY
   A. breakable B. inflammable C. pliable
   D. weak E. impervious

   3.____

4. To *counteract* means MOST NEARLY to
   A. undermine B. censure C. preserve
   D. sustain E. neutralize

   4.____

5. To *verify* means MOST NEARLY to
   A. justify B. explain C. confirm
   D. guarantee E. examine

   5.____

6. *Indolent* means MOST NEARLY
   A. moderate B. relentless C. selfish
   D. lazy E. hopeless

   6.____

7. To say that an action is *deferred* means MOST NEARLY that it is
   A. delayed B. reversed C. considered
   D. forbidden E. followed

   7.____

8. To *encounter* means MOST NEARLY to
   A. meet B. recall C. overcome
   D. weaken E. retreat

   8.____

9. *Feasible* means MOST NEARLY
   A. capable B. practicable C. justifiable
   D. beneficial E. reliable

   9.____

10. *Respiration* means MOST NEARLY
    A. dehydration B. breathing C. pulsation
    D. sweating E. recovery

    10.____

2 (#2)

11. *Vigilant* means MOST NEARLY
    A. sensible   B. ambitious   C. watchful
    D. suspicious   E. restless

12. To say that an action is taken *before the proper time* means MOST NEARLY that it is taken
    A. prematurely   B. furtively   C. temporarily
    D. punctually   E. presently

13. *Innate* means MOST NEARLY
    A. eternal   B. learned   C. native
    D. prospective   E. well-developed

14. *Precedent* means MOST NEARLY
    A. duplicate   B. theory   C. law
    D. conformity   E. example

15. To say that the flow of work into an office is *incessant* means MOST NEARLY that it is
    A. more than can be handled   B. uninterrupted
    C. scanty   D. decreasing in volume
    E. orderly

16. *Unanimity* means MOST NEARLY
    A. emphasis   B. namelessness   C. disagreement
    D. harmony   E. impartiality

17. *Incidental* means MOST NEARLY
    A. independent   B. needless   C. infrequent
    D. necessary   E. casual

18. *Versatile* means MOST NEARLY
    A. broad-minded   B. well-known   C. old-fashioned
    D. many-sided   E. up-to-date

19. *Conciliatory* means MOST NEARLY
    A. pacific   B. contentious   C. disorderly
    D. obligatory   E. offensive

20. *Altercation* means MOST NEARLY
    A. defeat   B. concurrence   C. controversy
    D. consensus   E. vexation

21. "The secretarial profession is a very old one and has increased in importance with the passage of time. In modern times, the vast expansion of business and industry has greatly increased the need and opportunities for secretaries, and for the first time in history their number as become large."

The above quotation BEST supports the statement that the secretarial profession
- A. is older than business and industry
- B. did not exist in ancient times
- C. has greatly increased in size
- D. demands higher training than it did formerly
- E. has always had many members

22. "The modern system of production unites various kinds of workers into a well-organized body in which each has a definite place."
The above quotation BEST supports the statement that the modern system of production
- A. increases production
- B. trains workers
- C. simplifies tasks
- D. combines and places workers
- E. combines the various plants

23. "The prevention of accidents makes it necessary not only that safety devices be used to guard exposed machinery but also that mechanics be instructed in safety rules which they must follow for their own protection, and that the lighting in the plant be adequate.
The above quotation BEST supports the statement that industrial accidents
- A. may be due to ignorance
- B. are always avoidable
- C. usually result from inadequate machinery
- D. cannot be entirely overcome
- E. result in damage to machinery

24. "It is wise to choose a duplicating machine that will do the work required with the greatest efficiency and at the least cost. Users with a large volume of business need speedy machines that cost little to operate and are well made."
The above quotation BEST supports the statement that
- A. most users of duplicating machines prefer low operating cost to efficiency
- B. a well-built machine will outlast a cheap one
- C. a duplicating machine is not efficient unless it is sturdy
- D. a duplicating machine should be both efficient and economical
- E. in duplicating machines speed is more usual than low operating cost

25. "The likelihood of America's exhausting her natural resources seems to be growing less. All kinds of waste are being reworked and new uses are constantly being found for almost everything. We are getting more use out of our goods and are making many new byproducts out of what was formerly thrown away."
The above quotation BEST supports the statement that we seem to be in less danger of exhausting our resources because
- A. economy is found to lie in the use of substitutes
- B. more service is obtained from a given amount of material
- C. more raw materials are being produced
- D. supply and demand are better controlled
- E. we are allowing time for nature to restore them

26. "Probably few people realize, as they drive on a concrete road, that steel is used to keep the surface flat and even, in spite of the weight of busses and trucks. Steel bars, deeply imbedded in the concrete, provide sinews to take the stresses so that they cannot crack the slab or make it wavy."
The above quotation BEST supports the statement that a concrete road
   A. is expensive to build
   B. usually cracks under heavy weights
   C. looks like any other road
   D. is used exclusively for heavy traffic
   E. is reinforced with other material

27. "Through advertising, manufacturers exercise a high degree of control over consumers' desires. However, the manufacturer assumes enormous risks in attempting to predict what consumers will want and in producing goods in quantity and distributing them in advance of final selection by the consumers."
The above quotation BEST supports the statement that manufacturers
   A. can eliminate the risk of overproduction by advertising
   B. completely control buyers' needs and desires
   C. must depend upon the final consumers for the success of their undertakings
   D. distribute goods directly to the consumers
   E. can predict with great accuracy the success of any product they put on the market

28. "Success in shorthand, like success in any other study, depends upon the interest the student takes in it. In writing shorthand, it is not sufficient to know how to write a word correctly; one must also be able to write it quickly."
The above quotation BEST supports the statement that
   A. one must be able to read shorthand as well as to write it
   B. shorthand requires much study
   C. if a student can write correctly, he can also write quickly
   D. proficiency in shorthand requires both speed and accuracy
   E. interest in shorthand makes study unnecessary

29. "The countries in the Western Hemisphere were settled by people who were ready each day for new adventure. The peoples of North and South America have retained, in addition to expectant and forward-looking attitudes, the ability and the willingness that they have often shown in the past to adapt themselves to new conditions.
The above quotation BEST supports the statement that the peoples in the Western Hemisphere
   A. no longer have fresh adventures daily
   B. are capable of making changes as new situations arise
   C. are no more forward-looking than the peoples of other regions
   D. tend to resist regulations
   E. differ considerably among themselves

30. "Civilization started to move ahead more rapidly when man freed himself of the shackles that restricted his search for the truth."
The above quotation BEST supports the statement that the progress of civilization
    A. came as a result of man's dislike for obstacles
    B. did not begin until restrictions on learning were removed
    C. has been aided by man's efforts to find the truth
    D. is based on continually increasing efforts
    E. continues at a constantly increasing rate

31. "It is difficult to distinguish between bookkeeping and accounting. In attempts to do so, bookkeeping is called the art, and accounting the science, of recording business transactions. Bookkeeping gives the history of the business in a systematic manner, and accounting classifies, analyzes, and interprets the facts thus recorded."
The above quotation BEST supports the statement that
    A. accounting is less systematic than bookkeeping
    B. accounting and bookkeeping are closely related
    C. bookkeeping and accounting cannot be distinguish from one another
    D. bookkeeping has been superseded by accounting
    E. the facts recorded by bookkeeping may be interpreted in many ways

32. "Some specialists are willing to give their services to the Government entirely free of charge; some feel that a nominal salary, such as will cover traveling expenses, is sufficient for a position that is recognized as being somewhat honorary in nature; many other specialists value their time so highly that they will not devote any of it to public service that does not repay them at a rate commensurate with the fees that they can obtain from a good private clientele."
The above quotation BEST supports the statement that the use of specialists by the Government
    A. is rare because of the high cost of securing such persons
    B. may be influenced by the willingness of specialists to serve
    C. enables them to secure higher salaries in private fields
    D. has become increasingly common during the past few years
    E. always conflicts with private demands for their services

33. "The leader of an industrial enterprise has two principal functions. He must manufacture and distribute a product at a profit, and he must keep individuals and groups of individuals working effectively together."
The above quotation BEST supports the statement that an industrial leader should be able to
    A. increase the distribution of his plant's product
    B. introduce large-scale production methods
    C. coordinate the activities of his employees
    D. profit by the experience of other leaders
    E. expand the business rapidly

34. "The coloration of textile fabrics composed of cotton and wool generally requires two processes, as the process used in dyeing wool is seldom capable of fixing the color upon cotton. The usual method is to immerse the fabric in the requisite baths to dye the wool and then to treat the partially dyed material in the manner found suitable for cotton."
The above quotation BEST supports the statement that the dyeing of textile fabrics composed of cotton and wool
   A. is less complicated than the dyeing of wool alone
   B. is more successful when the material contains more cotton than wool
   C. is not satisfactory when solid colors are desired
   D. is restricted to two colors for any one fabric
   E. is usually based upon the methods required for dyeing the different materials

34.____

35. "The fact must not be overlooked that only about one-half of the international trade of the world crosses the oceans. The other half is merely exchanges of merchandise between countries lying alongside each other or at least within the same continent."
The above quotation BEST supports the statement that
   A. the most important part of any country's trade is transoceanic
   B. domestic trade is insignificant when compared with foreign trade
   C. the exchange of goods between neighboring countries is not considered international trade
   D. foreign commerce is not necessarily carried on by water
   E. about one-half of the trade of the world is international

35.____

36. "In the relations of man to nature, the procuring of food and shelter is fundamental. With the migration of man to various climate, ever new adjustments to the food supply and to the climate became necessary."
The above quotation BEST supports the statement that the means by which man supplies his material needs are
   A. accidental   B. varied   C. limited
   D. uniform   E. inadequate

36.____

37. "Every language has its peculiar word associations that have no basis in logic and cannot therefore be reasoned about. These idiomatic expressions are ordinarily acquired only by much reading and conversation although questions about such matters may sometimes be answered by the dictionary. Dictionaries large enough to include quotations from standard authors are especially serviceable in determining questions of idiom."
The above quotation BEST supports the statement that idiomatic expressions
   A. give rise to meaningless arguments because they have no logical basis
   B. are widely used by recognized authors
   C. are explained in most dictionaries
   D. are more common in some languages than in others
   E. are best learned by observation of the language as actually used

37.____

38. "Individual differences in mental traits assume importance in fitting workers to jobs because such personal characteristics are persistent and are relatively little influenced by training and experience."
The above quotation BEST supports the statement that training and experience
   A. are limited in their effectiveness in fitting workers to jobs
   B. do not increase a worker's fitness for a job
   C. have no effect upon a person's mental traits
   D. have relatively little effect upon the individual's chances for success
   E. should be based on the mental traits of an individual

38.____

39. "The telegraph networks of the country now constitute wonderfully operated institutions, affording for ordinary use of modern, business an important means of communication. The transmission of message by electricity has reached the goal for which the postal service has long been striving, namely, the elimination of distance as an effective barrier of communication."
The above quotation BEST supports the statement that
   A. a new standard of communication has been attained
   B. in the telegraph service, messages seldom go astray
   C. it is the distance between the parties which creates the need for communication
   D. modern business relies more upon the telegraph than upon the mails
   E. the telegraph is a form of postal service

39.____

40. "The competition of buyers tends to keep prices up, the competition of sellers to send them down. Normally, the pressure of competition among sellers is stronger than that amount by buyers since the seller has his article to sell and must get rid of it, whereas the buyer is not committed to anything."
The above quotation BEST supports the statement that low prices are caused by
   A. buyer competition
   B. competition of buyers with sellers fluctuations in demand
   C. greater competition among sellers than among buyers
   D. more sellers than buyers

40.____

Questions 41-60.

DIRECTIONS: In answering Questions 41 through 60, find the CORRECT spelling of the word. Sometimes there is no correct spelling; if none of the suggested spellings is correct, indicate the letter D in the space at the right.

41. A. compitition   B. competition   41.____
    C. competetion   D. none of the above

42. A. diagnoesis   B. diagnossis   42.____
    C. diagnosis   D. none of the above

43. A. contenance   B. countenance   43.____
    C. countinance   D. none of the above

44. A. deliborate   B. deliberate   44.____
    C. delibrate   D. none of the above

45. A. knowlege   B. knolledge   45.____
    C. knowledge   D. none of the above

46. A. occassion   B. occasion   46.____
    C. ocassion   D. none of the above

47. A. sanctioned B. sancktioned 47.____
    C. sanctionned D. none of the above

48. A. predesessor B. predecesar   48.____
    C. predecessor D. none of the above

49. A. problemmatical B. problematical 49.____
    C. problematicle   D. none of the above

50. A. descendant B. decendant   50.____
    C. desendant   D. none of the above

51. A. collapsible B. collapseable 51.____
    C. collapseble D. none of the above

52. A. sequance   B. sequence   52.____
    C. sequense   D. none of the above

53. A. oblitorate B. obbliterat   53.____
    C. obbliterate D. none of the above

54. A. ambigeuous B. ambigeous   54.____
    C. ambiguous   D. none of the above

55. A. minieture   B. minneature   55.____
    C. mineature   D. none of the above

56. A. extemporaneous B. extempuraneus 56.____
    C. extemperaneous D. none of the above

57. A. hereditory B. hereditary   57.____
    C. hereditairy D. none of the above

58. A. conceivably B. concieveably 58.____
    C. conceiveably D. none of the above

59. A. extercate   B. extracate   59.____
    C. extricate   D. none of the above

60. A. auspiceous B. auspiseous
    C. auspicious D. none of the above

Questions 61-80.

DIRECTIONS: In answering Questions 61 through 80, select the sentence that is preferable with respect to grammar and usage such as would be suitable in a formal letter or report.

61. A. The receptionist must answer courteously the questions of all them callers.
    B. The questions of all callers had ought to be answered courteously.
    C. The receptionist must answer courteously the questions what are asked by the callers.
    D. There would have been no trouble if the receptionist had have always answered courteously.
    E. The receptionist should answer courteously the questions of all callers.

62. A. I had to learn a great number of rules, causing me to dislike the course.
    B. I disliked that study because it required the learning of numerous rules.
    C. I disliked that course very much, caused by the numerous rules I had to memorize.
    D. The cause of my dislike was on account of the numerous rules I had to learn in that course.
    E. The reason I disliked this study was because there were numerous rules that had to be learned.

63. A. If properly addressed, the letter will reach my mother and I.
    B. The letter had been addressed to myself and mother.
    C. I believe the letter was addressed to either my mother or I.
    D. My mother's name, as well as mine, was on the letter.
    E. If properly addressed, the letter it will reach either my mother or me.

64. A. A knowledge of commercial subjects and a mastery of English are essential if one wishes to be a good secretary.
    B. Two things necessary to a good secretary are the she should speak good English and too know commercial subjects.
    C. One cannot be a good secretary without she knows commercial subjects and English grammar.
    D. Having had god training in commercial subjects, the rules of English grammar should also be followed.
    E. A secretary seldom or ever succeeds without training in English as well as in commercial subjects.

65. A. He suspicions that the service is not so satisfactory as it should be.   65.____
    B. He believes that we should try and find whether the service is satisfactory.
    C. He raises the objection that the way which the service is given is not satisfactory.
    D. He believes that the quality of our services are poor.
    E. He believes that the service that we are giving is unsatisfactory.

66. A. Most all these statements have been supported by persons who are reliable and can be depended upon.   66.____
    B. The persons which have guaranteed these statements are reliable.
    C. Reliable persons guarantee the facts with regard to the truth of these statements.
    D. These statements can be depended on, for their truth has been guaranteed by reliable persons.
    E. Persons as reliable as what these are can be depended upon to make accurate statements.

67. A. Brown's & Company's employees have all been given increases in salary.   67.____
    B. Brown & Company recently increased the salaries of all its employees.
    C. Recently Brown & Company has increased their employees' salaries.
    D. Brown's & Company employees have recently received increases in salary.
    E. Brown & Company have recently increased the salaries of all its employees.

68. A. The personnel office has charge of employment, dismissals, and employee's welfare.   68.____
    B. Employment, together with dismissals and employees' welfare, are handled by the personnel department.
    C. The personnel office takes charge of employment, dismissals, and etc.
    D. The personnel office hires and dismisses employees, and their welfare is also its responsibility.
    E. The personnel office is responsible for the employment, dismissal, and welfare of employees.

69. A. This kind of pen is some better than that kind.   69.____
    B. I prefer having these pens than any other.
    C. This kind of pen is the most satisfactory for my use.
    D. In comparison with that kind of pen, this kind is more preferable.
    E. If I were to select between them all, I should pick this pen.

70. A. He could not make use of the report, as it was lacking of the needed information.   70.____
    B. This report was useless to him because there were no needed information in it.
    C. Since the report lacked the needed information, it was of no use to him.
    D. Being that the report lacked the needed information, he could not use it.
    E. Since the report did not contain the needed information, it was not real useful to him.

71.　A. The paper we use for this purpose must be light, glossy, and stand hard usage as well.
　　　B. Only a light and a glossy, but durable, paper must be used for this purpose.
　　　C. For this purpose, we want a paper that is light, glossy, but that will stand hard wear.
　　　D. For this purpose, paper that is light, glossy, and durable is essential.
　　　E. Light and glossy paper, as well as standing hard usage, is necessary for this purpose.

71.____

72.　A. The company had hardly declared the dividend till the notices were prepared for mailing.
　　　B. They had no sooner declared the dividend when they sent the notices to the stockholders.
　　　C. No sooner had the dividend been declared than the notices were prepared for mailing.
　　　D. Scarcely had the dividend been declared than the notices were sent out.
　　　E. The dividend had not scarcely been declared when the notices were ready for mailing.

72.____

73.　A. Of all the employees, he spends the most time at the office.
　　　B. He spends more time at the office than that of his employees.
　　　C. His working hours are longer or at least equal to those of the other employees.
　　　D. He devotes as much, if not more, time to his work than the rest of the employees.
　　　E. He works the longest of any other employee in the office.

73.____

74.　A. In the reports of typists' speeds, the job analyst found some records that are kind of unusual.
　　　B. It says in the job analyst's report that some employees type with great speed.
　　　C. The job analyst found that, in reviewing the typists' work Reports, that some unusual typing speeds had been made.
　　　D. Work reports showing typing speeds include some typists who are unusual.
　　　E. In reviewing the typists' work reports, the job analyst found records of unusual typing speeds.

74.____

75.　A. It is quite possible that we shall reemploy anyone whose training fits them to do the work.
　　　B. It is probable that we shall reemploy those who have been trained to do the work.
　　　C. Such of our personnel that have been trained to do the work will be again employed.
　　　D. We expect to reemploy the ones who have had training enough that they can do the work.
　　　E. Some of these people have been trained.

75.____

76. A. He as well as his publisher were pleased with the success of the book. 76.____
    B. The success of the book pleased both his publisher and he.
    C. Both his publisher and he was pleased with the success of the book.
    D. Neither he or his publisher was disappointed with the success of the book.
    E. His publisher was as pleased as he with the success of the book.

77. A. You have got to get rid of some of these people if you expect to have the quality of the work improve 77.____
    B. The quality of the work would improve if they would leave fewer people do it.
    C. I believe it would be desirable to have fewer persons during this work.
    D. If you had planned on employing fewer people than this to do the work, this situation would not have arose.
    E. Seeing how you have all those people on that work, it is not surprising that you have a great deal of confusion.

78. A. She made lots of errors in her typed report, and which caused her to be reprimanded. 78.____
    B. The supervisor reprimanded the typist, whom she believed had made careless errors.
    C. Many errors were found in the report which she typed and could not disregard them.
    D. The typist would have corrected the errors, had she of known that the supervisor would see the report.
    E. The errors in the typed report were so numerous that they could hardly be overlooked.

79. A. This kind of a worker achieves success through patience. 79.____
    B. Success does not often come to men of this type except they who are patient.
    C. Because they are patient, these sort of workers usually achieve success.
    D. This worker has more patience than any man in his office.
    E. This kind of worker achieves success through patience.

80. A. I think that they will promote whoever has the best record. 80.____
    B. The firm would have liked to have promoted all employees with good records.
    C. Such of them that have the best records have excellent prospects of promotion.
    D. I feel sure they will give the promotion to whomever has the best record.
    E. Whoever they find to have the best record will, I think, be promoted.

KEY (CORRECT ANSWERS)

1.	B	21.	C	41.	B	61.	E
2.	A	22.	D	42.	C	62.	B
3.	C	23.	A	43.	B	63.	D
4.	E	24.	D	44.	B	64.	A
5.	C	25.	B	45.	C	65.	E
6.	D	26.	E	46.	B	66.	D
7.	A	27.	C	47.	A	67.	B
8.	A	28.	D	48.	D	68.	E
9.	B	29.	B	49.	B	69.	C
10.	B	30.	C	50.	A	70.	C
11.	C	31.	B	51.	A	71.	D
12.	A	32.	B	52.	B	72.	C
13.	C	33.	C	53.	D	73.	A
14.	E	34.	E	54.	C	74.	E
15.	B	35.	D	55.	D	75.	B
16.	D	36.	B	56.	A	76.	E
17.	E	37.	E	57.	B	77.	C
18.	D	38.	A	58.	A	78.	E
19.	A	39.	A	59.	C	79.	E
20.	C	40.	D	60.	C	80.	A

EXAMINATION SECTION

TEST 1

DIRECTIONS: Each question or incomplete statement is followed by several suggested answers or completions. Select the one that BEST answers the question or completes the statement. *PRINT THE LETTER OF THE CORRECT ANSWER IN THE SPACE AT THE RIGHT.*

Questions 1-22.

DIRECTIONS: Read through each group of words. Indicate in the space at the right the letter of the misspelled word.

1. A. miniature   B. recession   1.____
   C. accommodate   D. supress

2. A. mortgage   B. illogical   2.____
   C. fasinate   D. pronounce

3. A. calendar   B. heros   3.____
   C. ecstasy   D. librarian

4. A. initiative   B. extraordinary   4.____
   C. villian   D. exaggerate

5. A. absence   B. sense   5.____
   C. dosn't   D. height

6. A. curiosity   B. ninety   6.____
   C. truely   D. grammar

7. A. amateur   B. definate   7.____
   C. meant   D. changeable

8. A. excellent   B. studioes   8.____
   C. achievement   D. weird

9. A. goverment   B. description   9.____
   C. sergeant   D. desirable

10. A. proceed   B. anxious   10.____
    C. neice   D. precede

11. A. environment   B. omitted   11.____
    C. apparant   D. misconstrue

12. A. comparative   B. hindrance   12.____
    C. benefited   D. unamimous

13. A. embarrass   B. recommend   13.____
    C. desciple   D. argument

14. A. sophomore   B. suprintendent   14.____
    C. concievable D. disastrous

15. A. agressive   B. questionnaire   15.____
    C. occurred   D. rhythm

16. A. peaceable   B. conscientious   16.____
    C. redicule   D. deterrent

17. A. mischievious B. writing   17.____
    C. competition   D. athletics

18. A. auxiliary   B. synonymous   18.____
    C. maneuver   D. repitition

19. A. existence   B. optomistic   19.____
    C. acquitted   D. tragedy

20. A. hypocrisy   B. parrallel   20.____
    C. exhilaration D. prevalent

21. A. convalesence B. infallible   21.____
    C. destitute   D. grotesque

22. A. magnanimity B. asassination   22.____
    C. incorrigible D. pestilence

Questions 23-40.

DIRECTIONS: In Questions 23 through 40, one sentence fragment contains an error in punctuation or capitalization. Indicate the letter of the INCORRECT sentence fragment and place it in the space at the right.

23. A. Despite a year's work   23.____
    B. in a well-equipped laboratory
    C. my Uncle failed to complete his research
    D. now he will never graduate.

24. A. Gene, if you are going to sleep   24.____
    B. all afternoon I will enter
    C. that ladies' golf tournament
    D. sponsored by the Chamber of Commerce.

25. A. Seeing the cat slink toward the barn,
    B. the farmer's wife jumped off the
    C. ladder picked up a broom, and began
    D. shouting at the top of her voice.

25.____

26. A. Extending over southeast Idaho and
    B. northwest Wyoming, the Tetons
    C. are noted for their height; however the
    D. highest peak is actually under 14,000 feet.

26.____

27. A. "Sarah, can you recall the name
    B. of the English queen
    C. who supposedly said, 'We are not
    D. amused?"

27.____

28. A. My aunt's graduation present to me
    B. cost, I imagine more than she could
    C. actually afford. It's a
    D. Swiss watch with numerous features.

28.____

29. A. On the left are examples of buildings
    B. from the Classical Period; two temples
    C. one of which was dedicated to Zeus; the
    D. Agora, a marketplace; and a large arch.

29.____

30. A. Tired of sonic booms, the people who
    B. live near Springfield's Municipal Airport
    C. formed an anti noise organization
    D. with the amusing name of Sound Off.

30.____

31. A. "Joe, Mrs. Sweeney said, "your family
    B. arrives Sunday. Since you'll be in
    C. the Labor Day parade, we could ask Mr.
    D. Krohn, who has a big car, to meet them."

31.____

32. A. The plumber emerged from the basement and
    B. said, "Mr. Cohen I found the trouble in
    C. your water heater. Could you move those
    D. Schwinn bikes out of my way?"

32.____

33. A. The President walked slowly to the
    B. podium, bowed to Edward Everett Hale
    C. the other speaker, and began his formal address:
    D. "Fourscore and seven years ago...."

33.____

34. A. Mr. Fontana, I hope, will arrive before
    B. the beginning of the ceremonies; however,
    C. if his plane is delayed, I have a substitute
    D. speaker who can be here at a moments' notice.

34.____

35. A. Gladys wedding dress, a satin creation, 35._____
     B. lay crumpled on the floor; her veil,
     C. torn and streaked, lay nearby. "Jilted!"
     D. shrieked Gladys. She was clearly annoyed.

36. A. Although it is poor grammar, the word 36._____
     B. hopefully has become television's newest
     C. pet expression; I hope (to use the correct
     D. form) that it will soon pass from favor.

37. A.   Plaza Apartment Hotel 37._____
     B.   103 Tower road
     C.   Hampstead, Iowa 52025
     D.   March 13, 2021

38. A. Circulation Department 38._____
     B. British History Illustrated
     C. 3000 Walnut Street
     D. Boulder Colorado 80302

39. A. Dear Sirs: 39._____
     B. Last spring I ordered a subscription to your
     C. magazine. I had read and enjoyed the May
     D. issue containing the article titled "kings."

40. A. I have not however, received a 40._____
     B. single issue. Will you check this?
     C. Sincerely,
     D. Maria Herrera

Questions 41-70.

DIRECTIONS: Questions 41 through 70 represent common grammatical concerns: subject-verb agreement, appropriate use of pronouns, and appropriate use of verbs. Read each sentence and indicate the letter of the grammatically CORRECT answer in the space at the right.

41. THE REIVERS, one of William Faulkner's last works, _____ made into a movie 41._____
    starring Steve McQueen.
    A. has been   B. have been   C. are being   D. were

42. He _____ on the ground, his eyes fastened on an ant slowly pushing a morsel 42._____
    of food toward the ant hill.
    A. layed   B. laid   C. had laid   D. lay

43. Nobody in the tri-cities _____ to admit that a flood could be disastrous. 43._____
    A. are willing   B. have been willing
    C. is willing   D. were willing

44. "_____," the senator asked, "have you convinced to run against the incumbent?"
    A. Who   B. Whom   C. Whomever   D. Womsoever

45. Of all the psychology courses that I took, Statistics 101 _____ the most demanding.
    A. was   B. are   C. is   D. were

46. Neither the conductor nor the orchestra members _____ the music to be applauded so enthusiastically.
    A. were expecting
    B. was expecting
    C. is expected
    D. has been expecting

47. The requirements for admission to the Lettermen's Club _____ posted outside the athletic director's office for months.
    A. was   B. was being   C. has been   D. have been

48. Please give me a list of the people _____ to compete in the kayak race.
    A. whom you think have planned
    B. who you think has planned
    C. who you think is planning
    D. who you think are planning

49. I saw Eloise and Abelard earlier today; _____ were riding around in a fancy 1956 MG.
    A. she and him   B. her and him   C. she and he   D. her and he

50. If you _____ the trunk in the attic, I'll unpack it later today.
    A. can sit
    B. are able to sit
    C. can set
    D. have sat

51. _____ all of the flour been used, or may I borrow three cups?
    A. Have   B. Has   C. Is   D. Could

52. In exasperation, the cycle shop's owner suggested that _____ there too long.
    A. us boys were
    B. we boys were
    C. us boys had been
    D. we boys had been

53. Idleness as well as money _____ the root of all evil.
    A. have been
    B. were to have been
    C. is
    D. are

54. Only the string players from the quartet—Gregory, Isaac, _____—remained after the concert to answer questions.
    A. him, and I
    B. he, and I
    C. him, and me
    D. he, and me

55. Of all the antiques that _____ for sale, Gertrude chose to buy a stupid glass thimble.
    A. was
    B. is
    C. would have
    D. were

56. The detective snapped, "Don't confuse me with theories about _____ you believe committed the crime!"
    A. who B. whom C. whomever D. which

57. _____ when we first called, we might have avoided our present predicament.
    A. The plumber's coming
    B. If the plumber would have come
    C. If the plumber had come
    D. If the plumber was to have come

58. We thought the sun _____ in the north until we discovered that our compass was defective.
    A. had rose
    B. had risen
    C. had rised
    D. had raised

59. Each play of Shakespeare's _____ more than _____ share of memorable characters.
    A. contain its
    B. contains; its
    C. contains; it's
    D. contain; their

60. Our English teacher suggested to _____ seniors that either Tolstoy or Dickens _____ the outstanding novelist of the nineteenth century.
    A. we; was considered
    B. we; were considered
    C. us; was considered
    D. us; were considered

61. Sherlock Holmes, together with his great friend and companion Dr. Watson, _____ to aid the woman _____ had stumbled into the room.
    A. has agreed; who
    B. have agreed; whom
    C. has agreed; whom
    D. have agreed; who

62. Several of the deer _____ when they spotted my backpack _____ open in the meadow.
    A. was frightened; laying
    B. were frightened; lying
    C. were frightened; laying
    D. was frightened; lying

63. After the Scholarship Committee announces _____ selection, hysterics often _____.
    A. it's; occur
    B. its; occur
    C. their; occur
    D. their; occurs

64. I _____ the key on the table last night so you and _____ could find it.
    A. layed; her
    B. lay; she
    C. laid; she
    D. laid; her

65. Some of the antelope _____ wandered away from the meadow where the rancher _____ the block of salt.
    A. has; sat
    B. has; set
    C. have; had set
    D. has; sets

66. Macaroni and cheese _____ best to us (that is, to Andy and _____) when Mother adds extra cheddar cheese.
    A. tastes; I
    B. tastes; me
    C. taste; me
    D. taste; I

66.____

67. Frank said, "It must have been _____ called the phone company."
    A. she who
    B. she whom
    C. her who
    D. her whom

67.____

68. The herd _____ moving restlessly at every bolt of lightning; it was either Ted or _____ who saw the beginning of the stampede.
    A. was; me
    B. were; I
    C. was; I
    D. have been; me

68.____

69. The foreman _____ his lateness by saying that his alarm clock _____ until six minutes before eight.
    A. explains; had not rang
    B. explained; has not rung
    C. has explained; rung
    D. explained; hadn't rung

69.____

70. Of all the coaches, Ms. Cox is the only one who _____ that Sherry dives more gracefully than _____.
    A. is always saying; I
    B. is always saying; me
    C. are always saying; I
    D. were always saying; me

70.____

Questions 71-90.

DIRECTIONS: Choose the word in Questions 71 through 90 that is MOST opposite in meaning to the italicized word.

71. *fact*
    A. statistic
    B. statement
    C. incredible
    D. conjecture

71.____

72. *stiff*
    A. fastidious
    B. babble
    C. supple
    D. apprehensive

72.____

73. *blunt*
    A. concise   B. tactful   C. artistic   D. humble

73.____

74. *foreign*
    A. pertinent   B. comely   C. strange   D. scrupulous

74.____

75. *anger*
    A. infer   B. pacify   C. taint   D. revile

75.____

76. *frank*
    A. earnest   B. reticent   C. post   D. expensive

76.____

77. *secure*
   A. precarious   B. acquire   C. moderate   D. frenzied

78. *petty*
   A. harmonious   B. careful
   C. forthright   D. momentous

79. *concede*
   A. dispute   B. reciprocate
   C. subvert   D. propagate

80. *benefit*
   A. liquidation   B. bazaar
   C. detriment   D. profit

81. *capricious*
   A. preposterous   B. constant
   C. diabolical   D. careless

82. *boisterous*
   A. devious   B. valiant   C. girlish   D. taciturn

83. *harmony*
   A. congruence   B. discord   C. chagrin   D. melody

84. *laudable*
   A. auspicious   B. despicable
   C. acclaimed   D. doubtful

85. *adherent*
   A. partisan   B. stoic   C. renegade   D. recluse

86. *exuberant*
   A. frail   B. corpulent   C. austere   D. bigot

87. *spurn*
   A. accede   B. flail   C. efface   D. annihilate

88. *spontaneous*
   A. hapless   B. corrosive
   C. intentional   D. willful

89. *disparage*
   A. abolish   B. exude   C. incriminate   D. extol

90. *timorous*
   A. succinct   B. chaste   C. audacious   D. insouciant

KEY (CORRECT ANSWERS)

1. D	21. A	41. A	61. A	81. B
2. C	22. B	42. D	62.	82. D
3. B	23. C	43. C	63. B	83. B
4. C	24. B	44. B	64. C	84. B
5. C	25. C	45. A	65. C	85. C
6. C	26. C	46. A	66. B	86. C
7. B	27. D	47. D	67. A	87. A
8. B	28. B	48. A	68. C	88. C
9. A	29. B	49. C	69. D	89. D
10. C	30. C	50. C	70. A	90. C
11. C	31. A	51. B	71. D	
12. D	32. B	52. D	72. C	
13. C	33. B	53. C	73. B	
14. C	34. D	54. B	74. A	
15. A	35. A	55. D	75. B	
16. C	36. B	56. B	76. B	
17. A	37. B	57. C	77. A	
18. D	38. D	58. B	78. D	
19. B	39. D	59. B	79. A	
20. B	40. A	60. C	80. C	

EXAMINATION SECTION
TEST 1

DIRECTIONS: Each question or incomplete statement is followed by several suggested answers or completions. Select the one that BEST answers the question or completes the statement. *PRINT THE LETTER OF THE CORRECT ANSWER IN THE SPACE AT THE RIGHT.*

Questions 1-25.

DIRECTIONS: Select the word with the MOST appropriate meaning for the italicized word in each of Questions 1 through 25.

1. The directions were *explicit*.
    A. petulant   B. satiric   C. awkward
    D. unequivocal   E. foreign

2. The teacher explained *mutability*.
    A. change   B. harmony   C. annihilation
    D. ethics   E. candor

3. He was a *secular* man.
    A. holy   B. evil   C. worldly
    D. superior   E. small

4. They submitted a list of their *progeny*.
    A. experiments   B. books   C. holdings
    D. theories   E. offspring

5. She admired his *sententious* replies.
    A. simple   B. pithy   C. coherent
    D. lucid   E. inane

6. He believed in the ancient *dogma*.
    A. priest   B. prophet   C. seer
    D. doctrine   E. ruler

7. They studied a Grecian *archetype*.
    A. model   B. urn   C. epic   D. ode   E. play

8. The *insurrection* was described on the front page.
    A. surgery   B. pageant   C. ceremony
    D. game   E. revolt

9. He was known for his *procrastination*.
    A. justification   B. learning   C. delay
    D. ambition   E. background

209

10. The doctor analyzed the *toxic* ingredients. 10._____
    A. poisonous B. anemic C. trivial
    D. obscure E. distinct

11. It was a *portentous* occurrence. 11._____
    A. pleasant B. decisive C. ominous
    D. monetary E. hearty

12. His *espousal* of the plan was applauded. 12._____
    A. explanation B. rejection C. ridicule
    D. adoption E. revision

13. Her condition was *lachrymose*. 13._____
    A. improved B. tearful C. hopeful
    D. precocious E. tenuous

14. It was a *precarious* situation. 14._____
    A. uncomplicated B. peaceful C. precise
    D. uncertain E. precipitous

15. He was lost in a *reverie*. 15._____
    A. chancery B. dream C. forest
    D. cavern E. tarn

16. The hero was a young *gallant*. 16._____
    A. suitor B. fool C. gull
    D. lawyer E. executive

17. Their practices were *nefarious*. 17._____
    A. unprofitable B. ignorant C. multifarious
    D. wicked E. wishful

18. He insisted upon the *proviso*. 18._____
    A. stipulation B. pronunciation C. examination
    D. supply E. equipment

19. The spirit came from the *nether* regions. 19._____
    A. frozen B. lower C. lost
    D. bright E. mysterious

20. His actions were *malevolent*. 20._____
    A. unassuming B. silent C. evil
    D. peaceful E. constructive

21. He had a *florid* complexion. 21._____
    A. sanguine B. pallid C. fair
    D. sickly E. normal

22. The lawyer explained the legal *parlance*. 22.____
    A. action   B. maneuver   C. situation
    D. language   E. procedure

23. They were present at the *interment*. 23.____
    A. concert   B. trial   C. embarkation
    D. burial   E. performance

24. He made a *moot* point. 24.____
    A. definite   B. sensible   C. debatable
    D. strong   E. correct

25. They carefully examined the *cryptic* message. 25.____
    A. occult   B. legible   C. valid
    D. familiar   E. warning

Questions 26-40.

DIRECTIONS: Indicate the number of syllables in each of the following words.

26. vicissitude   26.____
27. blown   27.____
28. maintenance   28.____
29. symbolization   29.____
30. athletics   30.____
31. actually   31.____
32. friend   32.____
33. perseverance   33.____
34. physiology   34.____
35. pronunciation   35.____
36. vacuum   36.____
37. sophomore   37.____
38. opportunity   38.____
39. hungry   39.____
40. temperament   40.____

Questions 41-60.

DIRECTIONS: Indicate the one misspelled work in each of the following Questions 41 through 60 by indicating the letter of the misspelled word in the space at the right.

41. A. holiday B. noticeable C. fourty 41.____
    D. miniature E. yeast

42. A. grievance B. murmur C. occurance 42.____
    D. business E. captain

43. A. succeed B. vegatable C. pleasant 43.____
    D. picnicking E. shepherd

44. A. psychology B. plebian C. exercise 44.____
    D. fiery E. concise

45. A. ninety B. optimistic C. professor 45.____
    D. repitition E. siege

46. A. tarriff B. absence C. grammar 46.____
    D. license E. balloon

47. A. dissipation B. ecstasy C. prarie 47.____
    D. marriage E. consistent

48. A. supersede B. twelfth C. vacillate 48.____
    D. playright E. expense

49. A. fundamental B. government C. accomodate 49.____
    D. cafeteria E. surely

50. A. cemetary B. indispensable C. dormitory 50.____
    D. environment E. divine

51. A. irritible B. permissible C. irresistible 51.____
    D. rhythmical E. source

52. A. interprete B. opinion C. guard 52.____
    D. familiar E. possible

53. A. conscience B. existence C. loneliness 53.____
    D. leisure E. exhileration

54. A. villian B. weird C. seize 54.____
    D. tragedy E. crystal

55. A. develop B. bachelor C. dilemma 55.____
    D. operate E. synonym

5 (#1)

56. A. university   B. connoiseur   C. aisle   56.____
    D. transferred E. division

57. A. zoology   B. conscious   C. aptitude   57.____
    D. restaurant   E. sacriligious

58. A. tendency   B. vital   C. analyze   58.____
    D. consistant   E. proceed

59. A. proceedure   B. surround   C. disastrous   59.____
    D. beginning   E. arrival

60. A. encrease   B. pursuing   C. necessary   50.____
    D. tyranny   E. strength

Questions 61-80.

DIRECTIONS: Indicate the part of speech for each italicized word in the following sentences by selecting the letter of the part of speech from the key above each set of questions.

   A. Noun
   B. Pronoun
   C. Verb
   D. Adjective
   E. Adverb

61. You are entirely *wrong*.   61.____

62. On *Sunday*, we will attend church.   62.____

63. *That* is the main problem.   63.____

64. He was invited to the party, *Saturday*.   64.____

65. I shall introduce a *technical* term.   65.____

66. It was a *novel* turn of events.   66.____

67. He wanted *that* gift for himself.   67.____

68. A few definitions will help *us* to understand.   68.____

69. He let them reach their own *conclusions*.   69.____

70. I must ask *you* to remain silent.   70.____

A. Preposition
B. Conjunction
C. Pronoun
D. Adverb
E. Adjective

71. *This* is a stupid answer.   71._____

72. He solved the mystery *without* the police.   72._____

73. She felt *secure* in his protection,   73._____

74. He believed in the *scientific* method.   74._____

75. Do not destroy their *traditional* beliefs.   75._____

76. They chartered the bus, *but* they did not go.   76._____

77. The young men are *quiet* with fear.   77._____

78. She talked *cheerfully* to the visitors.   78._____

79. The candidate was *certain* of victory.   79._____

80. I hope you will take *that* with you.   80._____

Questions 81-100.

DIRECTIONS: Indicate the use of each italicized word in the following sentences by choosing the letter of the CORRECT usage from the key above each set of questions.

A. Subject of Verb
B. Predicate Nominative or Subjective Complement
C. Predicate Adjective
D. Direct Object of Verb
E. Indirect Object of Verb

81. They made *him* president of the club.   81._____

82. There was nothing *odd* about the situation.   82._____

83. Give them *time* enough for thought.   83._____

84. He supervised the *work* himself.   84._____

85. Will you do *me* a favor?   85._____

86. The salad dressing tasted *good*.   86._____

7 (#1)

87. In the crash, the *body* was thrown forward. 87.____

88. On a bench in the park was a single *man*. 88.____

89. There were two *men* who carried the trunk. 89.____

90. I am older than *you*. 90.____

      A. Object of Preposition
      B. Subject of Infinitive
      C. Direct Object of Verb
      D. Indirect Object of Verb
      E. Predicate Nominative or Subjective Complement

91. Let *them* suffer the consequences. 91.____

92. Offer *them* the key to the apartment. 92.____

93. He heard the *bell* ring. 93.____

94. Let *us* try another solution. 94.____

95. No one except *John* had volunteered. 95.____

96. Show *us* one example of your style. 96.____

97. Will you send *her* the flowers? 97.____

98. I want *you* to take her home. 98.____

99. He told his *father* that he would obey. 99.____

100. Do not write on the second *page*. 100.____

Questions 101-115.

DIRECTIONS: Indicate the kind of verbal italicized in the following sentences by choosing the appropriate letter from the key below.

      A. Gerund
      B. Participle
      C. Infinitive

101. The manuscript, *corrected* and typed, was on the desk. 101.____

102. He heard the bullet *ricochet*. 102.____

103. *Finding* the answer is a difficult task. 103.____

104. The animal, *hidden* from view, was trembling. 104.____

105. *Pretending* to be asleep, he listened attentively. 105.____

106. The professor, a *qualified* lecturer, entered the room. 106.____

107. They enjoyed *camping* at the lake. 107.____

108. Let them *come* to me. 108.____

109. He was annoyed by the *buzzing* sound. 109.____

110. It was a *stimulating* performance. 110.____

111. He had an accident while *returning* to the city. 111.____

112. *Encouraged* to study, the class opened the books. 112.____

113. He heard the gun *explode*. 113.____

114. They called him the *forgotten* man. 114.____

115. *Realizing* his mistake, he apologized. 115.____

Questions 116-130.

DIRECTIONS: Indicate the CORRECT punctuation for the following sentences by choosing the letter of the correct punctuation from the key below where brackets appear.

    A. Comma
    B. Semicolon
    C. Colon
    D. Dash
    E. No punctuation

116. He explained [ ] that he could not attend. 116.____

117. The executive [ ] prepared for the interview and entered the room. 117.____

118. She admitted [ ] that the suggestion was wrong. 118.____

119. He did not object [ ] to dealing with him. 119.____

120. The chairman disagreed [ ] the members did not. 120.____

121. You must report to duty on November 10 [ ] 2022. 121.____

122. The father [ ] and two sons went fishing. 122.____

123. Act on the following problems [ ] administration, supervision, and policy.   123.____

124. This is excellent [ ] it has insight.   124.____

125. "I will take the car [ ]" he said.   125.____

126. I will do it [ ] however, you must help me.   126.____

127. When the show ended [ ] he returned home.   127.____

128. Stop [ ] making all of that noise.   128.____

129. Be firm [ ] exercise your authority.   129.____

130. The first example is poor [ ] the second is good.   130.____

Questions 131-150.

DIRECTIONS: Place a *C* in the space at the right if the sentence is correctly punctuated and a *W* in the space at the right if the sentence is incorrectly punctuated.

131. Its later than you think.   131.____

132. While I was eating the toast burned.   132.____

133. The fire started at ten o'clock in the morning.   133.____

134. She asked, "Did you say, 'I will go?"   134.____

135. Richards handling of the question warranted praise.   135.____

136. July 4 is a holiday.   136.____

137. Oh perhaps you are right.   137.____

138. Will you answer the door, John?   138.____

139. While he was bathing the dog came in.   139.____

140. He was a calm gentle person.   140.____

141. He wore a new bow tie.   141.____

142. The shout "Block that kick" echoed upon the field.   142.____

143. Ladies and gentlemen take your seats.   143.____

144. However you must do your work.   144.____

10 (#1)

145. My brothers are: John, Bill, and Charles.   145._____

146. While I was painting the neighbor opened the door.   146._____

147. One should fight for honor: not fame.   147._____

148. "Will you sing" he asked?   148._____

149. He played tennis, and then bowled.   149._____

150. On Monday April 5, we leave for Europe.   150._____

KEY (CORRECT ANSWERS)

1.	D	31.	4	61.	D	91.	C	121.	A
2.	A	32.	1	62.	A	92.	D	122.	E
3.	C	33.	4	63.	B	93.	C	123.	C
4.	E	34.	5	64.	A	94.	C	124.	D
5.	B	35.	5	65.	D	95.	A	125.	A
6.	D	36.	2	66.	D	96.	C	126.	B
7.	A	37.	3	67.	D	97.	C	127.	A
8.	E	38.	5	68.	B	98.	C	128.	E
9.	C	39.	2	69.	A	99.	C	129.	B
10.	A	40.	3	70.	B	100.	A	130.	B
11.	C	41.	C	71.	C	101.	B	131.	W
12.	D	42.	C	72.	A	102.	B	132.	W
13.	B	43.	B	73.	D	103.	A	133.	C
14.	D	44.	B	74.	E	104.	B	134.	W
15.	B	45.	D	75.	E	105.	A	135.	W
16.	A	46.	A	76.	B	106.	B	136.	C
17.	D	47.	C	77.	E	107.	A	137.	W
18.	A	48.	D	78.	D	108.	C	138.	C
19.	B	49.	C	79.	E	109.	B	139.	W
20.	C	50.	A	80.	C	110.	B	140.	W
21.	A	51.	A	81.	D	111.	A	141.	C
22.	D	52.	A	82.	C	112.	B	142.	W
23.	D	53.	E	83.	D	113.	C	143.	W
24.	C	54.	A	84.	D	114.	B	144.	W
25.	A	55.	C	85.	E	115.	A	145.	W
26.	3	56.	B	86.	C	116.	E	143.	W
27.	1	57.	E	87.	A	117.	E	147.	W
28.	3	58.	D	88.	B	118.	E	148.	W
29.	5	59.	A	89.	A	119.	E	149.	W
30.	3	60.	A	90.	C	120.	B	150.	W

WORD MEANING

EXAMINATION SECTION
TEST 1

DIRECTIONS: Each question or incomplete statement is followed by several suggested answers or completions. Select the one that BEST answers the question or completes the statement. *PRINT THE LETTER OF THE CORRECT ANSWER IN THE SPACE AT HE IGHT.*

1. He received a large reward.
   In this sentence, the word *reward* means
   A. capture   B. recompense   C. key   D. praise

   1.____

2. The aide was asked to transmit a message. In this sentence, the word *transmit* means
   A. change   B. send   C. take   D. type

   2.____

3. The pest control aide requested the tenant to call the Health Department.
   In this sentence, the word *requested* means the pest control aide
   A. asked   B. helped   C. informed   D. warned

   3.____

4. The driver had to return the department's truck. In this sentence, the word *return* means
   A. borrow   B. fix   C. give back   D. load up

   4.____

5. The aide discussed the purpose of the visit. In this sentence, the word *purpose* means
   A. date   B. hour   C. need   D. reason

   5.____

6. The tenant suspected the aide who knocked at her door. In this sentence, the word *suspected* means
   A. answered   B. called   C. distrusted   D. welcomed

   6.____

7. The aide was positive that the child hit her. In this sentence, the word *positive* means
   A. annoyed   B. certain   C. sorry   D. surprised

   7.____

8. The tenant declined to call the Health Department. In this sentence, the word *declined* means
   A. agreed   B. decided   C. refused   D. wanted

   8.____

9. The porter cleaned the vacant room.
   In this sentence, the word *vacant* means NEARLY the same as
   A. empty   B. large   C. main   D. crowded

   9.____

10. The supervisor gave a brief report to his men.
    In this sentence, the word *brief* means NEARLY the same as
    A. long   B. safety   C. complete   D. short

    10.____

221

11. The supervisor told him to connect the two pieces.
    In this sentence, the word *connect* means NEARLY the same as

    A. join B. paint C. return D. weigh

12. Standing on the top of a ladder is risky.
    In this sentence, the word *risky* means NEARLY the same as

    A. dangerous B. sensible C. safe D. foolish

13. He raised the cover of the machine.
    In this sentence, the word *raised* means NEARLY the same as

    A. broke B. lifted C. lost D. found

14. The form used for reporting the finished work was revised. In this sentence, the word *revised* means NEARLY the same as

    A. printed B. ordered C. dropped D. changed

15. He did his work rapidly.
    In this sentence, the word *rapidly* means NEARLY the same a

    A. carefully B. quickly C. slowly D. quietly

16. The worker was occasionally late.
    In this sentence, the word *occasionally* means NEARLY the same as

    A. sometimes B. often C. never D. always

17. He selected the best tool for the job.
    In this sentence, the word *selected* means NEARLY the same as

    A. bought B. picked C. lost D. broke

18. He needed assistance to lift the package.
    In this sentence, the word *assistance* means NEARLY the same as

    A. strength B. time C. help D. instructions

19. The tools were issued by the supervisor.
    In this sentence, the word *issued* means NEARLY the same as

    A. collected B. cleaned up C. given out D. examined

20. A permit for a tap for unmetered water will be issued only on prepayment of all charges for water to be used. In this sentence, the word *prepayment* means

    A. promise of payment B. payment in advance
    C. payment as water is used D. monthly payment

21. Upon application, the department will endeavor to locate a service pipe by means of an electrical indicator.
    In this sentence, the word *endeavor* means

    A. try   B. help   C. assist   D. explore

22. It shall be unlawful for any person to operate certain equipment without previous permission from the department. In this sentence, the word *previous* means

    A. written   B. oral   C. prior   D. provisional

23. All persons must comply with the rules and regulations. In this sentence, the word *comply* means

    A. agree
    B. coincide
    C. work carefully
    D. act in accord

24. No unauthorized person shall tamper with a water supply valve.
    In this sentence, the words *tamper with* means

    A. open   B. operate   C. alter   D. shut

25. The use of water is permitted subject to such conditions as the department may consider reasonable.
    In this sentence, the word *reasonable* means

    A. necessary   B. inexpensive   C. fair   D. desirable

26. An owner must engage a licensed plumber. In this sentence, the word *engage* means

    A. hire   B. pay   C. contact   D. inform

27. The charges for a machine part are usually for the furnishing, delivering, and installing of the part. In this sentence, the word *furnishing* means

    A. preparing   B. manufacturing   C. finishing   D. supplying

28. The investigator attempted to ascertain the facts.
    As used in this sentence, the word *ascertain* means MOST NEARLY to

    A. disprove   B. find out   C. go beyond   D. explain

29. The speaker commenced the lecture with an anecdote.
    As used in this sentence, the word *commenced* means MOST NEARLY

    A. concluded   B. illustrated   C. enlivened   D. started

30. The use of a hydrant may be authorized for construction purposes.
    As used in this sentence, the word *authorized* means

    A. possible   B. permitted   C. intended   D. stopped

31. Conservation of the water supply is a major goal of the department.
    As used in this sentence, the word *conservation* means MOST NEARLY

    A. estimating
    B. increasing
    C. preserving
    D. purifying

32. Consumers should inspect their faucets frequently to guard against leaks.
    As used in this sentence, the word *consumers* means MOST NEARLY

    A. citizens
    B. owners
    C. producers
    D. users

33. The wire was connected to the adjacent terminal.
    As used in this sentence, the word *adjacent* means MOST NEARLY

    A. out of order
    B. metallic
    C. nearby
    D. negative

34. Some of the equipment supplied to the inspector was defective.
    As used in this sentence, the word *defective* means MOSTNEARLY

    A. expensive
    B. faulty
    C. old
    D. unnecessary

35. The inspector was told to use discretion in dealing with the public.
    As used in this sentence, the word *discretion* means MOST NEARLY

    A. courtesy
    B. firmness
    C. judgment
    D. persuasion

36. It is unlawful to demolish any building without first obtaining a permit.
    As used in this sentence, the word *demolish* means MOST NEARLY

    A. build
    B. make alterations in
    C. occupy
    D. tear down

37. The clerk rendered an account of the cash received.
    As used in this sentence, the word *rendered* means MOST NEARLY

    A. concealed
    B. corrected
    C. forged
    D. gave

38. The permit was revoked by the department.
    As used in this sentence, the word *revoked* means MOST NEARLY

    A. approved
    B. cancelled
    C. renewed
    D. reviewed

39. The incident received much attention in the newspapers. As used in this sentence, the word *incident* means MOST NEARLY

    A. campaign
    B. crime
    C. event
    D. merger

40. The modification of the procedure was approved by the supervisor.
    As used in this sentence, the word *modification* means MOST NEARLY

    A. change
    B. interpretation
    C. repeal
    D. termination

41. The workers combined the contents of the two boxes. The word *combined* means

    A. sifted through
    B. put together
    C. tore apart
    D. forgot about

42. Don't touch the lever on the left side. The word *lever* means

    A. button B. rope C. handle D. gun

43. All litter should be taken away. The word *litter* means

    A. paint B. bowls C. rubbish D. evidence

44. The inspection of the street was complete. The word *inspection* means

    A. cleaning
    B. examination
    C. repair
    D. painting

45. The route must be followed exactly.
    The word *route* means

    A. foreman B. truck C. way D. recipe

46. Don't injure your back.
    The word *injure* means

    A. bend B. use C. hurt D. exercise

47. John repaired the machine.
    The word *repaired* means

    A. fixed B. broke C. ran D. oiled

48. Put the lid on the box.
    The word *lid* means

    A. cover B. ribbon C. rope D. wrapping

49. The rear of the truck should be washed.
    The word *rear* means

    A. hood B. front C. back D. roof

50. Coworkers must assist each other while at work. The word *assist* means

    A. help B. outdo C. like D. hurt

KEY (CORRECT ANSWERS)

1. B	11. A	21. A	31. C	41. B
2. B	12. A	22. C	32. D	42. C
3. A	13. B	23. D	33. C	43. C
4. C	14. D	24. C	34. B	44. B
5. D	15. B	25. C	35. C	45. C
6. C	16. A	26. A	36. D	46. C
7. B	17. B	27. D	37. D	47. A
8. C	18. C	28. B	38. B	48. A
9. A	19. C	29. D	39. C	49. C
10. D	20. B	30. B	40. A	50. A

TEST 2

DIRECTIONS: Each question or incomplete statement is followed by several suggested answers or completions. Select the one that BEST answers the question or completes the statement. *PRINT THE LETTER OF THE CORRECT ANSWER IN THE SPACE AT THE RIGHT.*

1. It is possible to construct a leak-proof home.
   The OPPOSITE of *construct* is

   A. build   B. erect   C. plant   D. wreck

2. The driver had to repair the flat tire.
   The OPPOSITE of the word *repair* is

   A. destroy   B. fix   C. mend   D. patch

3. The student tried to shout the answer.
   The OPPOSITE of the word *shout* is

   A. scream   B. shriek   C. whisper   D. yell

4. Daily visits are the best.
   The OPPOSITE of the word *visits* is

   A. absences   B. exercises   C. lessons   D. trials

5. It is important to arrive early in the morning.
   The OPPOSITE of the word *arrive* is

   A. climb   B. descend   C. enter   D. leave

6. Mike is a group leader.
   The OPPOSITE of the word *leader* is

   A. boss   B. chief   C. follower   D. overseer

7. The exterior of the house needs painting.
   The OPPOSITE of the word *exterior* is

   A. inside   B. outdoors   C. outside   D. surface

8. He conceded the victory.
   The OPPOSITE of the word *conceded* is

   A. admitted   B. denied   C. granted   D. reported

9. He watched the team begin.
   The OPPOSITE of the word *begin* is

   A. end   B. fail   C. gather   D. win

10. Your handwriting is illegible.
    The OPPOSITE of the word *illegible* is

    A. clear   B. confused   C. jumbled   D. unclear

11. The one of the following words that has the OPPOSITE meaning of *partition* is

    A. division   B. connection   C. barrier   D. compartment

12. The one of the following words that has the OPPOSITE meaning of *obvious* is

    A. concealed   B. known   C. clear   D. apparent

13. The one of the following words that has the OPPOSITE meaning of *assist* is

    A. hinder   B. offer   C. demand   D. aid

14. The one of the following words that has the OPPOSITE meaning of *obsolete* is

    A. neglected   B. traditional   C. rare   D. new

15. The one of the following words that has the OPPOSITE meaning of *stagnant* is

    A. murky   B. active   C. calm   D. dirty

16. The number of applicants exceeded the anticipated figure. As used in this sentence, the word *anticipated* means MOST NEARLY

    A. expected   B. required   C. revised   D. necessary

17. The clerk was told to collate the pages of the report. As used in this sentence, the word *collate* means MOST NEARLY

    A. destroy   B. edit   C. correct   D. assemble

18. Mr. Wells is not authorized to release the information. As used in this sentence, the word *authorized* means MOST NEARLY

    A. inclined   B. pleased   C. permitted   D. trained

19. The secretary chose an appropriate office for the meeting. As used in this sentence, the word *appropriate* means MOST NEARLY

    A. empty   B. decorated   C. nearby   D. suitable

20. The employee performs a complex set of tasks each day. As used in this sentence, the word *complex* means MOST NEARLY

    A. difficult   B. important   C. pleasant   D. large

21. In talking with a homeowner, an inspector should always be polite. As used in this sentence, the word *polite* means

    A. cold   B. courteous   C. aggressive   D. modest

22. In talking with a client, a worker should not discuss trivial matters. As used in this sentence, the word *trivial* means

    A. related   B. essential   C. significant   D. unimportant

23. The one of the following words that is SIMILAR in meaning to *revise* is

    A. edit B. confuse C. complicate D. dismiss

24. The one of the following words that is SIMILAR in meaning to *abandon* is

    A. quit B. use C. remain D. discourage

25. The one of the following words that is SIMILAR in meaning to *adjacent* is

    A. far B. detached C. bordering D. distant

26. The one of the following words that is SIMILAR in meaning to *coarse* is

    A. fine B. smooth C. rough D. slick

27. The one of the following words that is SIMILAR in meaning to *orifice* is

    A. chamber B. enclosure C. opening D. device

28. The aide arrived on time.
    In this sentence, the word *arrived* means

    A. awoke B. came C. left D. delayed

29. The salesman had to deliver books to each person he visited.
    In this sentence, the word *deliver* means

    A. give B. lend C. mail D. sell

30. When estimating materials for interior plaster, consideration must be given to the number of coats.
    As used in this sentence, the word *estimating* means

    A. calculating approximately B. purchasing
    C. mixing together D. finishing

31. As used in the sentence in Question 30 above, the word *consideration* means

    A. extra weight B. careful thought
    C. firmness D. additions

32. When computing quantities of plaster for the scratch coat, no allowance may be made for the space occupied by the metal lath.
    As used in this sentence, the word *computing* means

    A. figuring B. preparing C. slaking D. packing

33. As used in the sentence in Question 32 above, the word *allowance* means

    A. deduction B. addition C. leeway D. closing

34. The supervisor made a ridiculous statement.
    As used in this sentence, the word *ridiculous* means MOST NEARLY

    A. incorrect B. evil C. unfriendly D. foolish

35. That worker is engaged in a hazardous job.
    As used in this sentence, the word *hazardous* means MOST NEARLY

    A. inconvenient B. dangerous C. difficult D. demanding

36. Breaks in water distribution mains are front page news for the very reason that they occur infrequently.
    As used in this sentence, the word *infrequently* means MOST NEARLY

    A. at regular intervals B. often
    C. rarely D. unexpectedly

37. Several kinds of self-caulking substitutes for lead have been developed.
    As used in this sentence, the word *substitutes* means MOST NEARLY

    A. additives B. replacements C. hardeners D. softeners

38. Cast iron is essentially an alloy of iron and carbon. As used in this sentence, the word *essentially* means MOST NEARLY

    A. never B. basically C. barely D. sometimes

39. When water moves through pipe, friction is developed between the water and the inside surface of the pipe. As used in this sentence, the word *friction* means MOST NEARLY

    A. resistance B. heat C. slippage D. pressure

40. A person who is confident he can complete a task is said to be

    A. courageous B. sure C. bright D. successful

41. If a child sleeping peacefully is awakened by a sudden cry, he is likely to be

    A. ill B. uncomfortable C. startled D. hungry

42. He could not get his truck on the highway. A *highway* is a type of

    A. lot B. road C. scale D. sidewalk

43. The large vehicle was being repaired.
    Which of the following is a *vehicle*?

    A. Truck B. Building C. Boiler D. Table

44. The fence needs to be painted.
    The one of the following which is MOST like a *fence* is a

    A. door B. crane C. wall D. building

45. Furniture is not taken with the regular garbage collection.
    Which of the following is *furniture*?

    A. Sofas and chairs B. Cars and trucks
    C. Brooms and mops D. Bags and boxes

46. The group was assigned to do special work. Which of the following is a *group*?   46.____

    A. Truck   B. Boat   C. Team   D. Foreman

47. Sanitation men often use tools in their work.   47.____
The one of the following which is MOST often considered a *tool* is a

    A. tire   B. shovel   C. glove   D. basket

48. The man claimed that he could not lift the box. The word *lift* means MOST NEARLY   48.____

    A. bury   B. pick up   C. refill   D. clean

49. Place all the boxes below the second shelf. The word *below* means   49.____

    A. under   B. into   C. beside   D. over

50. This street should be clean when the sanitation men finish.   50.____
The word *clean* means free of

    A. obstacles   B. pedestrians   C. traffic   D. dirt

KEY (CORRECT ANSWERS)

1. D	11. B	21. B	31. B	41. C
2. A	12. A	22. D	32. A	42. B
3. C	13. A	23. A	33. A	43. A
4. A	14. D	24. A	34. D	44. C
5. D	15. B	25. C	35. B	45. A
6. C	16. A	26. C	36. C	46. C
7. A	17. D	27. C	37. B	47. B
8. B	18. C	28. B	38. B	48. B
9. A	19. D	29. A	39. A	49. A
10. A	20. A	30. A	40. B	50. D

TEST 3

DIRECTIONS: Each question or incomplete statement is followed by several suggested answers or completions. Select the one that BEST answers the question or completes the statement. *PRINT THE LETTER OF THE CORRECT ANSWER IN THE SPACE AT THE RIGHT.*

Questions 1-6.

DIRECTIONS: In the paragraph below, some of the underlined words have been purposely changed and spoil the meaning that the rest of the paragraph is meant to give. Read the paragraph carefully. Then, answer Questions 1 through 6.

    The motor vehicle supervisor who is <u>responsible</u> for training drivers in the operation of <u>special</u> equipment cannot expect a man to carry out all of his duties <u>poorly</u> <u>immediately</u> after receiving instruction. The employee may be overwhelmed by all of the details he must master, <u>happy</u> because he is <u>associated</u> with new fellow workers, or fearful that he may not <u>succeed</u> on the job. It is the supervisor's <u>job</u> to make the <u>operator</u> feel at ease and <u>discourage</u> his self-confidence. The supervisor must also vary the speed of the <u>driving</u> according to the operator's <u>capacity</u> to <u>absorb</u> the instruction without undue pressure or confusion. All learners <u>progress</u> through <u>several</u> stages of <u>development</u> <u>unless</u> they become expert in their duties. As the operator's skills <u>increase,</u> he will require <u>more</u> instruction but the supervisor should be available to correct <u>mistakes</u> promptly to prevent wrong <u>habits</u> being formed.

1. Of the following words underlined in the above paragraph, the one that does NOT give the real meaning that the rest of the paragraph is meant to give is

    A. responsible   B. special   C. happy   D. immediately

1.___

2. Of the following words underlined in the above paragraph, the one that does NOT give the real meaning that the rest of the paragraph is meant to give is

    A. overwhelmed   B. happy   C. associated   D. succeed

2.___

3. Of the following words underlined in the above paragraph, the one that does NOT give the real meaning that the rest of the paragraph is meant to give is

    A. job   B. operator   C. discourage   D. self-confidence

3.___

4. Of the following words underlined in the above paragraph, the one that does NOT give the real meaning that the rest of the paragraph is meant to give is

    A. driving   B. capacity   C. absorb   D. pressure

4.___

5. Of the following words underlined in the above paragraph, the one that does NOT give the real meaning that the rest of the paragraph is meant to give is

    A. progress   B. several   C. development   D. unless

5.___

6. Of the following words underlined in the above paragraph, the one that does NOT give the real meaning that the rest of the paragraph is meant to give is

    A. increase   B. more   C. mistakes   D. habits

6.___

Questions 7-13.

DIRECTIONS: Each of Questions 7 through 13 consists of a capitalized word followed by four suggested meanings of the word. Select the word or phrase which means MOST NEARLY the same as the capitalized word.

7. ACCELERATE

   A. adjust   B. press   C. quicken   D. strip

8. ALIGN

   A. bring into line
   C. happen by chance
   B. carry out
   D. join together

9. CONTRACTION

   A. agreement
   C. presentation
   B. denial
   D. shrinkage

10. INTERVAL

    A. ending
    C. space of time
    B. mixing together of
    D. weaken

11. LUBRICATE

    A. bend back
    C. rub out
    B. make slippery
    D. soften

12. OBSOLETE

    A. broken-down
    C. high-priced
    B. hard to find
    D. out of date

13. RETARD

    A. delay   B. flatten   C. rest   D. tally

14. Any major components of a fire communication system should be meticulously maintained.
    In the preceding sentence, the word *meticulously* means MOST NEARLY

    A. indifferently
    C. painstakingly
    B. perfunctorily
    D. languidly

Questions 15-17.

DIRECTIONS: Questions 15 through 17 are to be answered in accordance with the following statement.

In order to facilitate prompt assembly of designated members, the officer in charge, Bureau of Fire Communications, shall maintain accurate current data on all such matters.

15. The word *facilitate,* as used in the above statement, means MOST NEARLY

    A. authorize   B. expedite   C. command   D. hinder

16. The word *designated,* as used in the above statement, means MOST NEARLY

    A. required   B. versatile   C. skillful   D. selected

17. The word *data,* as used in the above statement, means MOST NEARLY

    A. calculations   B. information   C. forecasts   D. surveillance

Questions 18-19.

DIRECTIONS: Questions 18 and 19 are to be answered in accordance with the following statement.

In the event of severe disruption of circuits....members of this squad may be.... detailed to Bureau of Fire Communications for duration of such emergency.

18. The word *disruption,* as used in the above sentence, means MOST NEARLY

    A. overloading   B. breakdown   C. disuse   D. concurrence

19. The word *detailed,* as used in the above statement, means MOST NEARLY

    A. assigned   B. reported   C. demoted   D. promoted

20. The officer in command, after verification that the alarm was false, shall transmit by radio the signal 9-2 followed by box number.
    The word *verification,* as used in the above sentence, means MOST NEARLY

    A. confirmation   B. consideration   C. notification   D. confutation

Questions 21-23.

DIRECTIONS: Questions 21 through 23 are to be answered on the basis of the following statement.

The manual of Fire Communications was planned to serve the Fire Department as guide and reference in effective use of its vast, versatile communications network.... Complete understanding of its phases and precepts, together with prompt compliance with all requirements and actions set in motion by its coded signals and radio transmissions, are essential.

21. The word *versatile,* as used in the above statement, means MOST NEARLY

    A. steady   B. many-sided   C. constant   D. wavering

22. The word *precepts,* as used in the above statement, means MOST NEARLY

    A. forerunners   B. paragraphs   C. rules   D. sections

23. The word *compliance,* as used in the above statement, means MOST NEARLY   23.____

    A. variance   B. dissension   C. divergence   D. conformance

24. A person who is influenced in making a decision by preconceived opinions is said to be   24.____

    A. subjective   B. obstinate   C. hateful   D. ignorant

25. No time was set for the conference.   25.____
    The word below that BEST describes this fact is

    A. indefinite   B. decisive   C. ignored   D. powerful

26. The truck could not go under the bridge because the bridge was too low.   26.____
    The reason the truck could not go under the bridge was that the bridge was not _____ enough.

    A. high   B. long   C. strong   D. wide

Questions 27-29.

DIRECTIONS: Questions 27 through 29 are to be answered on the basis of the following statement.

   In structures exceeding 150 ft. in height, adequate means shall be provided for taking care of the expansion and contraction of all vertical lines of pipe. In addition, adequate means shall be provided to properly support all vertical lines of pipe.

27. The word *adequate,* as used above, means MOST NEARLY   27.____

    A. liquid devices
    B. properly designed and sufficient
    C. strong and thick walled
    D. in very great numbers

28. The word *expansion,* as used above, means MOST NEARLY a(n)   28.____

    A. bulbous swelling
    B. transverse projection
    C. large increase in diameter
    D. an increase in length

29. The word *contraction,* as used above, means MOST NEARLY   29.____

    A. contract to install the vertical line
    B. reduction in length
    C. to group all vertical lines together
    D. to decrease the equivalent length

30. A common mistake is to assume that the strength of equipment is the most important factor.   30.____
    As used in the above sentence, the word *assume* means MOST NEARLY

    A. determine   B. take for granted
    C. figure   D. make sure

KEY (CORRECT ANSWERS)

1.	C	11.	B	21.	B
2.	B	12.	D	22.	C
3.	C	13.	A	23.	D
4.	A	14.	C	24.	A
5.	D	15.	B	25.	A
6.	B	16.	D	26.	A
7.	C	17.	B	27.	B
8.	A	18.	B	28.	D
9.	D	19.	A	29.	B
10.	C	20.	A	30.	B

WORD MEANING

EXAMINATION SECTION
TEST 1

DIRECTIONS: Each question consists of a statement. You are to indicate whether the statement is TRUE (T) or FALSE (F). *PRINT THE LETTER OF THE CORRECT ANSWER IN THE SPACE AT THE RIGHT.*

1. *The foreman had received a few requests.* In this sentence, the word *requests* means NEARLY the same as *complaints*. 1.____

2. *The procedure for doing the work was modified.* In this sentence, the word *modified* means NEARLY the same as *discovered*. 2.____

3. *He stressed the importance of doing the job right.* In this sentence, the word *stressed* means NEARLY the same as *discovered*. 3.____

4. *He worked with rapid movements.* In this sentence, the word *rapid* means NEARLY the same as *slow*. 4.____

5. *The man resumed his work when the foreman came in.* In this sentence, the word *resumed* means NEARLY the same as *stopped*. 5.____

6. *The interior door would not open.* In this sentence, the word *interior* means NEARLY the same as *inside*. 6.____

7. *He extended his arm.* In this sentence, the word *extended* means NEARLY the same as *stretched out*. 7.____

8. *He answered promptly.* In this sentence, the word *promptly* means NEARLY the same as *quickly*. 8.____

9. *He punctured a piece of rubber.* In this sentence, the word *punctured* means NEARLY the same as *bought*. 9.____

10. *Education curbs crime.* In this sentence, the word *curb* means NEARLY the same as *checks*. 10.____

11. *Badges were distributed to the attendants.* In this sentence, the word *distributed* means NEARLY the same as *given out*. 11.____

12. *The attendant lifted the pail without assistance.* In this sentence, the word *assistance* means NEARLY the same as *delay*. 12.____

13. *The alert attendant notices unusual happenings.* In this sentence, the word *alert* means NEARLY the same as *busy*. 13.____

14. *Several bottles of ammonia were required for cleaning windows.* In this sentence, the word *required* means NEARLY the same as *needed*. 14.____

15. *The building had an efficient heating system.* In this sentence, the word *efficient* means NEARLY the same as *faulty*. 15.____

16. An attendant never operates a motor vehicle. In this sentence, the word *operates* means NEARLY the same as *fixes*. 16._____

17. The new employee was praised for his work. In this sentence, the word *praised* means NEARLY the same as *blamed*. 17._____

18. Cooperation makes the work of all the employees easier. In this sentence, the word *cooperation* means NEARLY the same as *working together*. 18._____

19. All the people in the building had the same problems. In this sentence, the word *problems* means NEARLY the same as *wages*. 19._____

20. The employee was transferred to special work for the day. In this sentence, the word *transferred* means NEARLY the same as *shifted*. 20._____

21. Your supervisor will tell you of the different responsibilities of your job. In this sentence, the word *responsibilities* means NEARLY the same as *tools*. 21._____

22. A damper regulates the air flowing through a furnace. In this sentence, the word *regulates* means NEARLY the same as *controls*. 22._____

23. The wounded man was perspiring. In this sentence, the word *perspiring* means NEARLY the same as *sweating*. 23._____

24. This mop absorbs water better than a sponge. In this sentence, the word *absorbs* means NEARLY the same as *spreads*. 24._____

25. A metal box contained all the cleaning material. In this sentence, the word *contained* means NEARLY the same as *held*. 25._____

26. The stock of paper towels had gone down. In this sentence, the word *stock* means NEARLY the same as *bond*. 26._____

27. The Governor today urged all citizens to prevent fires. In this sentence, the word *urged* means NEARLY the same as *ordered*. 27._____

28. The news did not disturb the foreman. In this sentence, the word *disturb* means NEARLY the same as *upset*. 28._____

29. The Commissioner said that sixty men registered for the training course. In this sentence, the word *registered* means NEARLY the same as *were eligible*. 29._____

30. New York City attracts many people because of its opportunities. In this sentence, the word *attracts* means NEARLY the same as *employs*. 30._____

31. Five systems were suggested for helping the work of attendants. In this sentence, the word *systems* means NEARLY the same as *methods*. 31._____

32. It is not easy to select a foreman from such a fine group. In this sentence, the word *select* means NEARLY the same as *pick*. 32._____

33. The power of the public is in its freedom. In this sentence, the word *power* means NEARLY the same as *strength*. 33._____

34. *The rescue was made quickly by the attendant.* In this sentence, the word *rescue* means NEARLY the same as *report*. 34._____

35. *The attendant avoided a quarrel.* In this sentence, the word *avoided* means NEARLY the same as *started*. 35._____

36. *A decaying branch is dangerous to the life of a tree.* In this sentence, the word *decaying* means NEARLY the same as *rotting*. 36._____

37. *Shearing helps keep the plants in the shape required.* In this sentence, the word *shearing* means NEARLY the same as *watering*. 37._____

38. *Some shrubs have vigorous growth and early flowering.* In this sentence, the word *vigorous* means NEARLY the same as *weak*. 38._____

39. *The lawn retained its healthy green color.* In this sentence, the word *retained* means NEARLY the same as *kept*. 39._____

40. *The soil is combined with an acid plant food.* In this sentence, the word *combined* means NEARLY the same as *mixed*. 40._____

41. *Gardening can be tiring without the right tools.* In this sentence, the word *tiring* means NEARLY the same as *amusing*. 41._____

42. *With the ground saturated, the roots may die.* In this sentence, the word *saturated* means NEARLY the same as *soaked*. 42._____

43. *Air can penetrate freely if holes are made in the soil.* In this sentence, the word *penetrate* means NEARLY the same as *follows*. 43._____

44. *With some plants, flowers precede the growth of leaves.* In this sentence, the word *precede* means NEARLY the same as *follow*. 44._____

45. *The gardener anticipated frost.* In this sentence, the word *anticipated* means NEARLY the same as *expected*. 45._____

46. *Tools are assembled when the Job is finished.* In this sentence, the word *assembled* means NEARLY the same as *cleaned*. 46._____

47. *Part of the area was set aside for a miniature rock garden.* In this sentence, the word *miniature* means NEARLY the same as *beautiful*. 47._____

48. *Cheap tools are seldom durable.* In this sentence, the word *durable* means NEARLY the same as *long lasting*. 48._____

49. *Concrete walks are maintained clean easily.* In this sentence, the word *maintained* means NEARLY the same as *kept*. 49._____

50. *Each morning the assistant gardener was punctual in reporting to work.* In this sentence, the word *punctual* means NEARLY the same as *prompt*. 50._____

KEY (CORRECT ANSWERS)

1. F	11. T	21. F	31. T	41. F
2. T	12. F	22. T	32. T	42. T
3. F	13. F	23. T	33. T	43. F
4. F	14. T	24. F	34. F	44. F
5. F	15. F	25. T	35. F	45. T
6. T	16. F	26. F	36. T	46. F
7. T	17. F	27. F	37. F	47. F
8. T	18. T	28. T	38. F	48. T
9. F	19. F	29. F	39. T	49. T
10. T	20. T	30. F	40. T	50. T

TEST 2

DIRECTIONS: Each question consists of a statement. You are to indicate whether the statement is TRUE (T) or FALSE (F). *PRINT THE LETTER OF THE CORRECT ANSWER IN THE SPACE AT THE RIGHT.*

1. *Formal shearing destroys the plant's individuality.* In this sentence, the word *formal* means NEARLY the same as *irregular.* 1.____

2. *The entire tree is covered with a film which is flexible, colorless, and lasting.* In this sentence, the word *flexible* means NEARLY the same as *tough.* 2.____

3. *All of the equipment is mobile.* In this sentence, the word *mobile* means NEARLY the same as *movable.* 3.____

4. *Just enough asphalt adheres to make a mat.* In this sentence, the word *adheres* means NEARLY the same as *sticks.* 4.____

5. *Efforts at proper maintenance were nullified by this act.* In this sentence, the word *nullified* means NEARLY the same as *brought to nothing.* 5.____

6. Saying that a hose is *perforated* is another way of saying that a hose is *bent.* 6.____

7. *Do not injure the foliage of a plant* means NEARLY the same as *do not injure the plant's roots.* 7.____

8. *Pulverizing* soil is breaking it down into very small bits. 8.____

9. Humus is the part of the soil which is very often called clay in gardening practice. 9.____

10. *Aerating* a turf area is NEARLY the same as *sodding* the area. 10.____

11. *To mechanically agitate* means NEARLY the same as *to seed by mechanical power.* 11.____

12. *Ashes are transported from Department of Sanitation incinerators to points of ultimate disposal.* In this sentence, the word *ultimate* means NEARLY the same as *final.* 12.____

13. *In some areas where mechanical sweepers are used, supplementary manual cleaning is required.* In this sentence, the word *supplementary* means NEARLY the same as *additional.* 13.____

14. *It was stipulated that ferrous metals should be used.* In this sentence, the word *stipulated* means NEARLY the same as *agreed.* 14.____

15. *We find a different type of residue here.* In this sentence, the word *residue* means NEARLY the same as *inhabitant.* 15.____

16. *Several giant segments lay there.* In this sentence, the word *segments* means NEARLY the same as *parts.* 16.____

17. *The number of usable fill properties continues to dwindle.* In this sentence, the word *dwindle* means NEARLY the same as *multiply.* 17.____

18. *The salient provisions were given.* In this sentence, the word *salient* means NEARLY the same as *prominent.* 18.____

19. *Rate of putrefaction must be considered.* In this sentence the word *putrefaction* means NEARLY the same as *rotting*.   19.____

20. *The supervisor gave a brief talk on the importance on safety.* In this sentence, the word *brief* means NEARLY the same as *interesting*.   20.____

21. *The supervisor made a thorough study of the problem.*
In this sentence, the word *thorough* means NEARLY the same as *complete*.   21.____

22. *It is essential that all employees work together as a team.* In this sentence, the word *essential* means NEARLY the same as *absolutely necessary*.   22.____

23. *Employees are occasionally required to work overtime.* In this sentence, the word *occasionally* means NEARLY the same as *often*.   23.____

24. *The form is to be submitted in duplicate.* According to this sentence, three copies of the form are to be submitted.   24.____

25. *The benches should be wiped free of dirt and moisture each day.* In this sentence, *the word moisture* means NEARLY the same as *oil*.   25.____

26. *She omitted her name at the bottom of the application.* In this sentence, *the word omitted* means NEARLY the same as *left out*.   26.____

27. *The employee's excuse for being absent was absurd.* In this sentence, the word *absurd* means NEARLY the same as *sensible*.   27.____

28. *The attendant was instructed to reverse the mop head at the end of each stroke.* In this sentence, the word *reverse* means NEARLY the same as *clean*.   28.____

29. *The supervisor was in accord with the employee's suggestion.* In this sentence, the word *accord* means NEARLY the same as *agreement*.   29.____

30. *The mail clerk inserted the letter in the envelope.* In this sentence, the word *inserted* means NEARLY the same as *found*.   30.____

31. *If a tenant does not comply with the rules of the Housing Project, report this to your supervisor.* In this sentence, the words *comply with* mean NEARLY the same as *obey*.   31.____

32. *Surplus water on a floor should be wiped up with a mop.* In this sentence, the word *surplus* means NEARLY the same as *dirty*.   32.____

33. *An employee who is hurt should turn in an accident report immediately.* In this sentence, the *word immediately* means NEARLY the same as *right away*.   33.____

34. *A new employee is expected to learn his job gradually.*
In this sentence, the word *gradually* means NEARLY the same as *correctly*.   34.____

35. *The Commissioner said it was an immense job to keep New York City clean.* In this sentence, the word *immense* means NEARLY the same as *very big*.   35.____

36. *The foreman could tell, right away that the caretaker had swept the hall thoroughly.* In this sentence, the word *thoroughly* means NEARLY the same as *poorly*.   36.____

37. The caretaker could not make permanent repairs. In this sentence, the word *permanent* means NEARLY the same as *plumbing*.   37._____

38. The employee requested a summer vacation. In this sentence, the word *requested* means NEARLY the same as *asked for*.   38._____

39. The caretaker could not open the door because the lock was jammed. In this sentence, the word *jammed* means NEARLY the same as *loose*.   39._____

40. Jones and Smith were rivals in the section's clean-up campaign. In this sentence, the word *rivals* means NEARLY the same as *partners*.   40._____

41. The caretaker persuaded the children to keep the playground clean. In this sentence, the word *persuaded* means NEARLY the same as *warned*.   41._____

42. All elevators should be operating during the morning rush hour to avoid crowding in the lobby. In this sentence, the word *lobby* means NEARLY the same as *entrance hall*.   42._____

43. The caretaker used a liquid polish on the brass trim. In this sentence, the word *liquid* means NEARLY the same as *paste*.   43._____

44. Report all minor accidents to your supervisor. In this sentence, the word *minor* means NEARLY the same as *serious*.   44._____

45. The attendant obtained the towels from the supply room. In this sentence, the word *obtained* means NEARLY the same as *inspected*.   45._____

46. Ten men were needed for the normal work of the section. In this sentence, the word *normal* means NEARLY the same as *regular*.   46._____

47. The swimming pool can accommodate 100 people. In this sentence, the word *accommodate* means NEARLY the same as *hold without crowding*.   47._____

48. The elevator operator did not recognize the new tenant.
In this sentence, the word *recognize* means NEARLY the same as *like*.   48._____

49. The new playground swings were installed carefully. In this sentence, the word *installed* means NEARLY the same as *put in*.   49._____

50. Kerosene or benzine will ruin asphalt tile. In this sentence, the word *ruin* means NEARLY the same as *spoil*.   50._____

KEY (CORRECT ANSWERS)

1. F	11. F	21. T	31. T	41. F
2. F	12. T	22. T	32. F	42. T
3. T	13. T	23. F	33. T	43. F
4. T	14. T	24. F	34. F	44. F
5. T	15. F	25. F	35. T	45. F
6. F	16. T	26. T	36. F	46. T
7. F	17. F	27. F	37. F	47. T
8. T	18. T	28. F	38. T	48. F
9. F	19. T	29. T	39. F	49. T
10. F	20. F	30. F	40. F	50. T

TEST 3

DIRECTIONS: Each question consists of a statement. You are to indicate whether the statement is TRUE (T) or FALSE (F). *PRINT THE LETTER OF THE CORRECT ANSWER IN THE SPACE AT THE RIGHT.*

1. *His ideas about the best method of doing the work were flexible.* In this sentence, the word *flexible* means NEARLY the same as *unchangeable*.   1.____

2. *Many difficulties were encountered.* In this sentence, the word *encountered* means NEARLY the same as *met*.   2.____

3. *The different parts of the refuse must be segregated.* In this sentence, the word *segregated* means NEARLY the same as *combined*.   3.____

4. *The child was obviously hurt.* In this sentence, the word *obviously* means NEARLY the same as *accidentally*.   4.____

5. *Some kind of criteria for judging service necessity must be established.* In this sentence, the word *criteria* means NEARLY the same as *standards*.   5.____

6. *A small segment of the membership favored the amendment.* In this sentence, the word *segment* means NEARLY the same as *part*.   6.____

7. *The effectiveness of any organization depends upon the quality and integrity of its rank and file.* In this sentence, the word *integrity* means NEARLY the same as *quantity*.   7.____

8. *He adhered to his opinion.* In this sentence, the word *adhered* means NEARLY the same as *stuck to*.   8.____

9. *The suspects were interrogated at the police station.* In this sentence, *interrogated* means NEARLY the same as *identified*.   9.____

10. *Flanking the fireplace are shelves holding books.* In this sentence, the word *flanking* means NEARLY the same as *above*.   10.____

11. *He refused to comment on the current Berlin crisis.* In this sentence, the word *current* means NEARLY the same as *shocking*.   11.____

12. *Nothing has been done to remedy the situation.* In this sentence, the word *remedy* means NEARLY the same as *correct*.   12.____

13. *The reports had been ignored.* In this sentence, the word *ignored* means NEARLY the same as *prepared*.   13.____

14. *A firm was hired to construct the building.* In this sentence, the word *construct* means NEARLY the same as *build*.   14.____

15. *The Commissioner spoke about the operations of his department.* In this sentence, the word *operations* means NEARLY the same as *problems*.   15.____

16. *The increase in the number of accidents is negligible.* In this sentence, the word *negligible* means NEARLY the same as *serious*.   16.____

17. *He received monetary assistance.* In this sentence, the word *monetary* means NEARLY the same as *temporary.*   17.___

18. *Litigation delayed construction of the new incinerator.* In this sentence, the word *litigation* means NEARLY the same as *rising costs.*   18.___

19. *Proximity of the site is important.* In this sentence, the word *proximity* means NEARLY the same as *closeness.*   19.___

20. *At sanitary landfills, refuse is not dumped indiscriminately.* In this sentence, the word *indiscriminately* means NEARLY the same as *before burning.*   20.___

21. *Improvised equipment is seldom used.* In this sentence, the word *improvised* means NEARLY the same as *worn out.*   21.___

22. *At marine loading stations, refuse barges are loaded by gravity.* In this sentence, the word *gravity* means NEARLY the same as *shovel.*   22.___

23. *Many difficulties were encountered in the operation.* In this sentence, the word *encountered* means NEARLY the same as *met.*   23.___

24. *Traffic control facilitates the collection of waste in a large city.* In this sentence, the word *facilitates* means NEARLY the same as *eases.*   24.___

25. *Four persons were extricated immediately.* In this sentence, the word *extricated* means NEARLY the same as *treated.*   25.___

26. *Large objects produce extensive damage to mechanical equipment of furnaces.* In this sentence, the word *extensive* means NEARLY the same as *slight.*   26.___

27. *The car's headlights flickered on the dark street.* In this sentence, the word *flickered* means NEARLY the same as *shone brightly.*   27.___

28. *The sweeper was retained when the vacuum cleaners were installed.* In this sentence, the word *retained* means NEARLY the same as *kept.*   28.___

29. *Several men had dismantled the engine.* In this sentence, the word *dismantled* means NEARLY the same as *inspected.*   29.___

30. *The switch should be pushed down when the car approaches.* In this sentence, the word *approaches* means NEARLY the same as *comes near.*   30.___

31. *There is a possibility of ground water contamination.* In this sentence, the word *contamination* means NEARLY the same as *radioactivity.*   31.___

32. *The components of refuse must be segregated.* In this sentence, the word *components* means NEARLY the same as *containers.*   32.___

33. *The arrival of the tractor coincided with that of the dump truck.* In this sentence, the word *coincided* means NEARLY the same as *interfered.*   33.___

34. *Every idea sent to the Employee Suggestion Program is appraised.* In this sentence, the word *appraised* means NEARLY the same as *judged.*   34.___

35. *An adjacent garage maintained snow equipment.* In this sentence, the word *adjacent* means NEARLY the same as *neighboring.* 35.____

36. *Check all facts before analyzing a report.* In this sentence, the word *analyzing* means NEARLY the same as *submitting.* 36.____

37. *The abatement of odors affects living conditions.* In this sentence, the word *abatement* means NEARLY the same as *reduction.* 37.____

38. *For proper growth, the plant needs plenty of water, supplemented with liquid manure.* In this sentence, the word *supplemented* means NEARLY the same as *replaced.* 38.____

39. *One reason why aphids are undesirable is that they transmit plant diseases.* In this sentence, the word *transmit* means NEARLY the same as *pass on.* 39.____

40. *When the trees are young, the spaces between them may be utilized for other plantings.* In this sentence, the word *utilized* means NEARLY the same as *used.* 40.____

41. *The cuttings will take root readily.* In this sentence, the word *readily* means NEARLY the same as *quickly.* 41.____

42. *The seedlings should be transplanted at least once to stimulate growth.* In this sentence, the word *stimulate* means NEARLY the same as *encouraged.* 42.____

43. *The water evaporates through cracks in the soil.* In this sentence, the word *evaporates* means NEARLY the same as *flows in.* 43.____

44. *Hardy, native vines were planted.* In this sentence, the word *hardy* means NEARLY the same as *few.* 44.____

45. *The insects were present in moderate numbers.* In this sentence, the word *moderate* means NEARLY the same as *large.* 45.____

46. *The beetle is injurious to garden crops.* In this sentence, the word *injurious* means NEARLY the same as *harmful.* 46.____

47. *With proper care, the plants will survive the winter.* In this sentence, the word *survive* means NEARLY the same as *live through.* 47.____

48. *An arbor should be inconspicuous.* In this sentence, the word *inconspicuous* means NEARLY the same as *made of wood.* 48.____

49. *The plants are indifferent as to soil.* In this sentence, the word *indifferent* means NEARLY the same as *not particular.* 49.____

50. *The plant produces fragrant flowers.* In this sentence, the word *fragrant* means NEARLY the same as *sweet smelling.* 50.____

KEY (CORRECT ANSWERS)

1. F	11. F	21. F	31. F	41. T
2. T	12. T	22. F	32. F	42. T
3. F	13. F	23. T	33. F	43. F
4. F	14. T	24. T	34. T	44. F
5. T	15. F	25. F	35. T	45. F
6. T	16. F	26. F	36. F	46. T
7. F	17. F	27. F	37. T	47. T
8. T	18. F	28. T	38. F	48. F
9. F	19. T	29. F	39. T	49. T
10. F	20. F	30. T	40. T	50. T

EXAMINATION SECTION
TEST 1

DIRECTIONS: In each of the following groups, one of the four sentences contains an error in grammar, usage, diction, or punctuation. Indicate the INCORRECT sentence. *PRINT THE LETTER OF THE CORRECT ANSWER IN THE SPACE AT THE RIGHT.*

1. A. He acted as if he had never heard the story.
   B. The lecturer spoke so long his audience became restless.
   C. The author of "The Yearling" has written another book about Florida.
   D. It looks now like he will not be promoted after all.

2. A. Swing music is different from the popular music of ten years ago.
   B. Mary bought the hat at once lest she change her mind.
   C. No one having received permission to call a meeting, the plan was dropped.
   D. Being that you are here, we can proceed with the discussion.

3. A. After a long and bitter discussion, the meeting was adjoined at 6 o' clock.
   B. He owns property in an adjoining county.
   C. When you joined the club, you were a sophomore.
   D. No one should plan a long journey for pleasure in these days.

4. A. My brother is so much taller than I that hardly any one believes we are twins.
   B. The account he gave of the accident was different in many particulars.
   C. Your sister is so kind to you that I don't see how you can love your brother more than her.
   D. You have given more thought and time to the solving of this problem than anybody else has.

5. A. They told us how they had suffered.
   B. It is interesting (a) to the student, (b) to the parent, and (c) to the teacher.
   C. There were blue, green and red banners.
   D. "Will you help", he asked?

6. A. Who do you suggest should be appointed chairman of our committee?
   B. Whom do you think they met on their way to the concert last night?
   C. Who do you believe would choose such men as their representatives?
   D. Whom do you think will visit us next spring to see the cherry blossoms?

7. A. He will try and do as you request.
   B. This was a matter between him and me.
   C. They agreed to distribute the candy among all the children.
   D. Jones won by Smith's missing a chance.

8. A. There are only a few shovelfuls of coal left.
   B. The batter tried to gain time by blowing his nose between every ball.
   C. A novel or five short stories were to be read.
   D. This group of stories is concerned with family problems.

9. A. Dinner being over, the table may now be cleared.
   B. He is wiser, but not so old as his brother.
   C. There is nothing so enervating as too much rest.
   D. I was too late for the train, so I returned home and, after arriving there, noticed the ominous clouds in the west.

10. A. Her very manner makes one think of a cleanly person.
    B. His motives were as contemptible as his actions.
    C. His meager contribution is more preferable than her refusal to participate at all.
    D. An umpire must be a disinterested judge.

11. A. The remainder of the day was spent at home.
    B. He asked for the loan of a clean handkerchief.
    C. Neither painting nor fighting feed men.
    D. He emigrated from Germany in 1939.

12. A. Although he is a lawyer for ten years he has never appeared in a court.
    B. The drivers object to paying their proportion of the increase.
    C. He would have been the first man to acknowledge the contradiction.
    D. She would have liked to wear her new gown at the ball.

13. A. I suggest he do as he is told.
    B. Clubs with membership between 100 to 500 are not listed in this catalogue.
    C. I ask that the prisoner be given his liberty.
    D. He could not help wondering whether he would be the next victim.

14. A. Her tears had no effect on him whatsoever.
    B. The facts were different than what we had feared.
    C. He was driving somebody else's car.
    D. Immigration into the United States has been reduced.

15. A. Looking at the problem calmly, a solution seems not only possible but probable.
    B. Were he to appear, I'd throw the lie into his face.
    C. I don't object to Carter's going; I do object to his representing us.
    D. After he had lain in one position for an hour, he felt cramped and stiff.

16. A. If we except Bert, no one prepared the lesson thoroughly.
    B. "Jack is the winner," he announced, "Bill is in second place, and Stan is in third."
    C. The teacher appointed two of us, Anne and me, to distribute the papers.
    D. He had only to speak to gain our support.

17. A. The family are not agreed on next summer's vacation plans.
    B. Yours and theirs are right next to ours.
    C. In the fight for women's suffrage one judge's decision had little effect, for the most part, upon the ladies' determination.
    D. This time Mr. Andrews spoke like he really meant it.

18. A. The doctor prescribed at least a three weeks' rest for me.
    B. Neither Fred nor the twins are coming.
    C. I find those kind of gloves impractical for me.
    D. Most English teachers penalize the use of O's and etc.'s in compositions.

19. A. Give the money to whoever needs it most. 19.____
    B. We are in New York City for the past ten years.
    C. Everyone being willing, we decided to try a moonlight hike up the Tuckerman Ravine Trail.
    D. Madeline looks beautiful in purple.

20. A. If Brutus had refused Antony a chance to speak, history might have been changed. 20.____
    B. We had always wanted to visit Zion National Park, White Sands National Monument, and Death Valley.
    C. We cannot, however, scarcely believe Cora's wild tale of a burglar.
    D. Who do you think will win the Rose Bowl game?

21. A. There lay the puppy squealing piteously. 21.____
    B. Natives of certain African tribes are, on the average, taller than we.
    C. For landscape planting why not choose one of the native shrubs; for example, winterberry, viburnum, or blueberry?
    D. I don't doubt but what you are right, but I reject your reasoning.

22. A. I hope that Paul's mother will leave him go to the party. 22.____
    B. This Sunday on the parkway there were fewer tie-ups and less congestion than on the previous Sunday.
    C. Teresa would have liked to take the trip, but she couldn't afford it.
    D. It seems to be she who made the blunder.

23. A. We wanted a tree that was beautiful all year round; therefore we planted a dogwood. 23.____
    B. I wanted the victor to be him, not her.
    C. Mt. Kinley in Alaska is higher than any mountain in North America.
    D. The men's and boys' departments are next to each other.

24. A. All that is left standing in the bombed area is a few brick walls. 24.____
    B. I found, when I reached the theatre, that I left home without the tickets.
    C. Every available officer, including fifteen privates, was sent on the mission.
    D. It is I who am most concerned over the implications of the new bill.

25. A. Our school has more students than any other school in the borough. 25.____
    B. I don't know but that he is correct.
    C. I think we can count on John being present.
    D. Tom has two brothers-in-law.

26. A. She has had more advantages than he. 26.____
    B. The doctor is not in at present, but he'll return at three o'clock.
    C. This country must either set up flood controls or be prepared to lose billions of dollars annually.
    D. The pupils were told by the teacher to bring their project home from school with them.

27. A. He was doubtless aware that his supporters were deserting him. 27.____
    B. The lazy pupil, of course, will tend to write the minimum amount of words acceptable.
    C. It was his practice to feed whoever appeared at his door.
    D. He did not resent the intrusion so much as he despised the intruder.

28. A. It's a problem that we've been unable to solve satisfactorily.
    B. If anybody objects to our plan, let's tell them to try to make a better one.
    C. When the thirsty horse had drunk its fill, it trotted briskly down the road.
    D. I left my pen in this room but seem unable to find it.

28.___

29. A. They preferred the site at Hurley Street and Second Avenue because of its proximity to the proposed bus terminal at Twenty-fourth Street.
    B. The farther south you drive in Blackwell County, the more you understand the reason for Conniston's moving north.
    C. "Inasmuch as Baker is a resident here for twenty years," declared Carter, "we should give serious consideration to his suggestions."
    D. His approach to the committee was certainly not conducive to a cordial reception of his proposals, which were, at best, of doubtful validity.

29.___

30. A. In his teaching, he always kept the children's interests and needs in mind.
    B. He prefers this kind of book to any other.
    C. Although he was fond of the theatre, he would never go to see a play, at the Sheffield Theatre because he didn't like its owner.
    D. If he were to resign now, people would say he was unwilling to face the issue.

30.___

31. A. On the last day of the school term, Mr. Jansen will take Miss Brill's enrolling room; Mrs. Jackson, Mr. Fein's; and Miss Knowland, mine.
    B. Did the Student Council raise any objection to John's running for President of the General Organization?
    C. The spokesman said that on February 15 the school dietitian called each of the cafeteria employees individually into her office and told them to resign from the union.
    D. Dan would like to have seen the Orange Bowl game on television.

31.___

32. A. Being that I am older than you, I am probably stronger.
    B. He was afraid of being late for the party if he stayed to discuss the plans any longer.
    C. Being widely known as a man of sound opinions, he felt that his reputation was at stake.
    D. His being called by the principal caused him to weep and tremble.

32.___

33. A. Everybody who has paid the full purchase price should call for his set of books now.
    B. Only a person of great determination and stamina could have persisted in that endeavor to the point of success.
    C. There is no explanation for the strange phenomenon, it just occurs regularly early every morning.
    D. Had he not been so averse to criticism, he could have had the benefit of Desmond's opinion.

33.___

34. A. Hearing the bells and the whistles, the New Year was greeted noisily by everybody at the party.
    B. Besides her own family of four boys, my grandmother reared two adopted children.
    C. A preposition is a relational word; an adjective is an attributive word.
    D. If I were a good speller, I should get better marks in English.

34.___

35. A. My teacher won't leave me come into the classroom when I am late. 35.____
    B. I'll lend you the book, provided you prepare a report on it for our next meeting.
    C. He is not the kind of person upon whom one can depend.
    D. The proposal that we should all go together was accepted enthusiastically.

36. A. Had you heard the argument, you would be ready to excuse his anger. 36.____
    B. If you will hold the pen like I do, it will not give you any trouble.
    C. Should you see my sister, please ask her to come home at once.
    D. Let's start early so that we'll be in time for the beginning of the play.

37. A. In recent years the metals in many articles have been substituted by plastics. 37.____
    B. They are not in Boston now, but I think they're going to that city next week.
    C. Having heard all the testimony in the case, the jury was charged by the judge.
    D. Either two bolts or one metal strap is required for the job.

38. A. I shall reward whoever completed the job first. 38.____
    B. These data have been prepared by me, and you are welcome to make use of them.
    C. This is one of the issues in the salary question that is still to be reviewed.
    D. I want the responsibilities to be divided equally among the several members.

39. A. "Do you wish to reconsider any of your answers?" he asked. 39.____
    B. Due to lack of attendance, the traveling circus was forced to suspend operations.
    C. I have no objection to their using the tennis court this afternoon.
    D. There was, in the mail, an inquiry by a young couple for a house with two or three bedrooms.

40. A. Had you not lain there during the drill, you might have been reported for breaking the rules. 40.____
    B. Yes, the apple tastes sweet.
    C. Is he not the man whom you saw forcing his way into the meeting?
    D. Everyone but Jerry and I agreed to the compromise proposal on the salary question.

41. A. He always tried his best; he almost always achieved success. 41.____
    B. "Now, when we need him most," she declared, "he has declined to continue as a member of the committee."
    C. The papers lay undisturbed in the attic for more than fifty years.
    D. No sooner had he received his inheritance when he bought a new car.

42. A. The children asked, "When shall we start our program?" 42.____
    B. They feared that the child might be lost.
    C. We have less books in chemistry than in physics.
    D. If you do not pay attention to lights, you may be hit by an automobile.

43. A. They're not sure that your suggestion is suitable for their purpose. 43.____
    B. Suddenly collecting his wits, he began to talk rapidly about the events leading up to the accident.
    C. Dickens wrote "David Copperfield"; Thackeray, "Vanity Fair."
    D. Many students graduate high school in less than four years.

44. A. We had scarcely reached our door than the rain began to come down in torrents.
     B. The reason I am discouraged is that I have failed twice in my attempt to be elected.
     C. Is this the man who you thought had an interesting story to tell?
     D. Once inside the barn, the horse was no longer frightened.

45. A. None of the boys was willing to have the game post-poned.
     B. My grandmother used to say, "A stitch in time saves nine."
     C. This kind of apples ripens earlier than any other in our section of the country.
     D. They planned to meet my friend's brother and I at the bus terminal.

KEY (CORRECT ANSWERS)

1. D	11. C	21. D	31. C	41. D
2. D	12. A	22. A	32. A	42. C
3. D	13. B	23. C	33. C	43. D
4. B	14. B	24. B	34. A	44. A
5. D	15. A	25. C	35. A	45. D
6. D	16. B	26. D	36. B	
7. A	17. D	27. B	37. A	
8. B	18. C	28. B	38. A	
9. D	19. B	29. C	39. B	
10. C	20. C	30. A	40. D	

TEST 2

DIRECTIONS: In each of the following groups, one of the four sentences contains an error in grammar, usage, diction, or punctuation. Indicate the INCORRECT sentence. *PRINT THE LETTER OF THE CORRECT ANSWER IN THE SPACE AT THE RIGHT.*

1.
   A. If you'll lend me some thread, I'll make you a dress.
   B. He dresses just like he did in the West.
   C. She walks slowly and cautiously, just as I do when I'm very tired.
   D. I don't know whether I should go or stay.

   1.____

2.
   A. Give me a few minutes to think, I shall have the answer.
   B. We went to Albany, a large city in New York State, on a business trip.
   C. We hope to hear from you as soon as you reach Topeka.
   D. We traveled all day at top speed, but failed to reach home in time for dinner.

   2.____

3.
   A. I haven't seen him for more than two years.
   B. I have been absent due to the illness of my son.
   C. Who's going to know you're here, if none of us calls your name?
   D. By the time the treaty is signed, we shall have lost our rights to the property.

   3.____

4.
   A. I wish I were going away, too.
   B. We, she and I, have made many trips to the West.
   C. The clay can easily be shaped by one who has the necessary skill.
   D. He is reported to be killed in an airplane accident.

   4.____

5.
   A. He let on that he was sick whenever there was work to be done.
   B. The prize was divided among the members of the crew.
   C. These data are submitted for your approval.
   D. He climbed off the platform and ran away.

   5.____

6.
   A. Although you speak clearly and to the point, you have not convinced me.
   B. Shall we go anywhere after lunch today?
   C. The flowers smell sweet after an April shower.
   D. After discussing the matter with my mother and I, my father reluctantly agreed to postpone the trip.

   6.____

7.
   A. The storm was severe, but it did not harm the ship.
   B. Did you see the boy whom, we all think, is the leader of the group?
   C. He was assisted by his friend who lives in a nearby apartment.
   D. They went into the house to read the account of the trial.

   7.____

8.
   A. He couldn't hardly see what he had written on the paper.
   B. Mary confidently expected to see Albert at the theatre.
   C. I fully intended to go to church Easter Sunday.
   D. We had not yet heard from John when the news of the accident reached us.

   8.____

9.
   A. Now, at last, you are coming to the point.
   B. The mistress was at home, even though she did not come to the door.
   C. They are alike in this particular, e.g., they are both over twenty years of age.
   D. Standing in the doorway, he could hear the typewriter clicking.

   9.____

10. A. He told us to follow him and we did not do so.
    B. The ocean liner that docked in the harbor yesterday is called the Queen Elizabeth.
    C. How could he have grown so much during the last year!
    D. I'm living here two years, but I don't know my neighbors.

10.___

11. A. The return trip was equally as delightful as the trip to the coast.
    B. Mary and Sue saw each other often after their graduation.
    C. I like him very much, despite his many faults.
    D. I will go to see him Thursday next.

11.___

12. A. And that, my friends, was the way I nearly lost my job.
    B. But I was not really lazy; the heat was most enervating.
    C. Never again! Curiosity can kill more than cats.
    D. "Why do you continue to suffer in silence", she asked?

12.___

13. A. We saw a penny rolling around the corner.
    B. "John and Henry," he insisted, "were in their room."
    C. Everybody came in and took his seat.
    D. Taking the watch apart, it seemed to be a very complicated mechanism.

13.___

14. A. You looked good in that dress.
    B. I bought a red and green dress to wear at your sister's party.
    C. May I leave early to-day for a change?
    D. There is a sale of men's and ladies' suits in this store.

14.___

15. A. He stayed inside the yard all morning.
    B. The coal was put in under the stairs.
    C. These kind of apples are not grown in New York or in New Jersey.
    D. It does look like rain, but all signs fail in dry weather.

15.___

16. A. The party who called before lunch refused to leave his name.
    B. For the sake of argument, let us assume that the moon is inhabited.
    C. I should like to spend the summer somewhere in Canada.
    D. This boy is careful and not likely to make many mistakes.

16.___

17. A. My father did not like fishing, hiking, or swimming; in fact, he refused to play golf.
    B. Chicago was very different than what I had imagined.
    C. If you cannot effect a change in his attitude, we'll lose his support entirely.
    D. He found the climate in Arizona very healthful.

17.___

18. A. He was improved some in spelling and in oral reading.
    B. This rule, which is still in effect, was adopted three years ago.
    C. The principal will recommend whoever has the best record.
    D. We'll lend you our truck, provided you take good care of it.

18.___

19. A. The boy blew up his balloon until it burst.
    B. Most every week, the farmer brings us fresh eggs from the country.
    C. Neither you nor I am in a position to complain about the arrangements.
    D. I can't recall his asking us to pay him a visit.

19.___

20.
- A. Yesterday, he said, "Hello."
- B. Between you and I, these are the facts.
- C. I have seen my mother.
- D. We have not heard from John.

20.____

21.
- A. This sure is a hard problem.
- B. He got off the horse.
- C. Only Charles was there.
- D. I was there yesterday, I assure you.

21.____

22.
- A. He and I do not agree.
- B. If I were you, I would go.
- C. We knew that it was not her.
- D. DYNASTS, by Thomas Hardy, is a novel.

22.____

23.
- A. Who did he see?
- B. If he should fall, we should all be lost.
- C. I intended to go.
- D. He is reported to have been killed.

23.____

24.
- A. Only Charles will come.
- B. They are alike in this particular.
- C. I should like to give you tickets, but I haven't any.
- D. Shall we go any place today with this data?

24.____

25.
- A. If I was young, I would dance.
- B. She gave them to us girls.
- C. She helped John and me.
- D. I know whom he saw.

25.____

26.
- A. He asked us to watch him.
- B. I believe him to be rich.
- C. She knew the guide to be me.
- D. She used three cupsful of flour in the cake.

26.____

27.
- A. We knew it was she.
- B. I approve of his giving her the ring.
- C. This series of books are excellent.
- D. Everyone has studied his lesson.

27.____

28.
- A. The material was oak and pine.
- B. He don't know his own strength.
- C. The instructor, as well as the class, was alarmed.
- D. The committee disagree on this point.

28.____

29.
- A. I do not know whether I can tell you.
- B. Three days ago I saw him.
- C. I cannot encourage you any.
- D. What is one among many?

29.____

30. A. Don't blame me for it.
     B. Loan me five dollars.
     C. I have met but four.
     D. May I leave early tonight?

31. A. She rides like I do.
     B. Can he run a hundred yards in ten seconds?
     C. These data are correct.
     D. He was sick with rheumatism.

32. A. James and John saw each other often.
     B. The return trip was equally delightful.
     C. I could hardly do it.
     D. She couldn't hardly see.

33. A. I have no hope of seeing him before winter.
     B. He stayed inside the yard.
     C. I didn't say nothing.
     D. It rolled under the desk.

34. A. I approved of him accepting the position.
     B. Three times four is twelve.
     C. Each man carries a gun.
     D. The tidings were brought to her.

35. A. Ethics is a difficult course.
     B. Everyone knows what to do.
     C. You and I are going to the concert.
     D. The factory's manager was very young.

36. A. He was extremely kind to me yesterday.
     B. I talked to him in regard to the subscription.
     C. They were so good to me.
     D. The teacher spoke clear and emphatic.

37. A. He was very much amused at her.
     B. I intended to have gone.
     C. He went away, far into the desert.
     D. I shall not go without his agreeing.

38. A. It must be here somewhere.
     B. The reason is that there is no bread.
     C. Of all other cities, New York is the largest.
     D. The pickles were excellent.

39. A. This is a new kind of rose.
     B. Which is the oldest, John or James?
     C. It looks like rain.
     D. I bought this from the dealer.

40. A. Because of the intransigence of one member of the committee, no agreement could be reached.
    B. The enemy's guns tried in vain to reduce the ramifications on the opposite shore.
    C. The farmer was advised to let the land lie fallow.
    D. It was an unsuitable diet for a man who followed a sedentary occupation.

41. A. He frequently hurt people's feelings with his terse remarks.
    B. The perspicacity revealed by his comments won the approval of his superiors.
    C. He was aggravated by a severe cold.
    D. An ewe and a ram were bought at the same time for the purpose of mating.

42. A. An aroused public opinion militated against a fair trial for the defendant in that county.
    B. The market was surfeited with new cars.
    C. Since basketball was limited to intramural games, no money was needed for trips.
    D. The three prime ministers of the Benelux countries signed, in a matter of minutes, a bilateral treaty which had taken months to prepare.

43. A. Marauding bands terrorized the area.
    B. In the face of the bad news his levity was frowned upon.
    C. Refusing to answer was interpreted as tantamount to guilt.
    D. The consultant in Macy's considered the combination of colors indecorous.

44. A. He was so credulous as to be a detriment to the firm.
    B. The white marble columns rested on pediments of pink marble.
    C. The proponents of the scheme were ready to reap the benefits.
    D. He was praised for having accomplished a creditable piece of work in the face of great difficulties.

45. A. His penchant for gambling was soon to lead to disaster.
    B. The impresario stopped in the middle of her aria to upbraid the new manager.
    C. She departed, leaving a trail of disturbing innuendoes in her wake.
    D. The most troublesome of the impediments was considered first.

46. A. The old countess was waiting to ask the artist what he really meant by a piquant face.
    B. The doctor's prognosis proved to be right.
    C. The Marseillaise has been described as the impassioned cry of an aroused people.
    D. When the lectures on logistics began, philosophy took on a new meaning for him.

47. A. The unhealthy climate made the campaign a costly one.
    B. Man is said to be a naturally gregarious animal.
    C. The winner of the lottery was soon luxuriating in his new wealth.
    D. The jury reached no decision because of one adamant member.

48. A. Rip Van Winkle's wife was known as a termagant.
    B. Use of the word was interpreted as an error on the part of the author's amnuensis.

C. General Washington could hardly believe Arnold's duplicity.
D. The guns thundered the salutary greeting customarily given to the head of a state.

49. A. She tried in vain to find a euphemistic phrase with which to express her contempt. 49.____
B. The Javanese peccadillo was kept in an ornate silver cage.
C. The prisoner received word of his fate impassively.
D. His turgid style of writing pleased no one but himself.

50. A. The new boats were immediately assigned to internecine duties. 50.____
B. He spoke from copious notes.
C. The chemists were amazed at the tensile strength of the new fiber.
D. The owner and lessee were both in court.

KEY (CORRECT ANSWERS)

1. B	11. D	21. A	31. A	41. C
2. B	12. D	22. C	32. D	42. D
3. B	13. D	23. A	33. C	43. D
4. D	14. A	24. D	34. A	44. B
5. A	15. C	25. A	35. D	45. B
6. D	16. A	26. D	36. D	46. D
7. B	17. B	27. C	37. B	47. A
8. A	18. A	28. B	38. C	48. D
9. C	19. B	29. C	39. B	49. B
10. D	20. B	30. B	40. B	50. A

EXAMINATION SECTION
TEST 1

DIRECTIONS: In each of the following groups, one of the four sentences contains an error in grammar, usage, diction, or punctuation. Indicate the INCORRECT sentence. *PRINT THE LETTER OF THE CORRECT ANSWER IN THE SPACE AT THE RIGHT.*

1. A. His vacuous expression suggested that he had been drugged.
    B. Poor business forced the company to plan drastic retrenchment.
    C. Everyone in town was trying to identify the anomalous donor.
    D. He blamed most of his failures on fortuitous circumstances.

2. A. She divided the bread among them, without considering a share for herself.
    B. I should like to go, shouldn't you?
    C. All the boys did their work promptly so that they could leave early.
    D. Those kind of shoes are bad for the arches.

3. A. Johnny ate the last three candies in the dish.
    B. He may sit between you and I for a while.
    C. Attempting to judge character by faces is an interesting pastime.
    D. They are not so willing to cooperate as they used to be.

4. A. The two small chairs and the round table need to be reconditioned.
    B. Only the captain had been authorized to make such a decision.
    C. He asked the girl to bring the letter to her sister.
    D. No one seemed to know what his appointed task was.

5. A. Data were collected, tabulated, filed and forgotten.
    B. Members of the scout troop immediately divided the chores between them.
    C. Reflecting on the incident, she acquired a new insight into his character.
    D. Because of the old man's temper everyone kept his opinion to himself.

6. A. Bread and butter is a basic unit of the national diet.
    B. Beyond all doubt, it is we who must solve the problem.
    C. Looking into the matter, a startling situation came to light.
    D. Not everyone knows what his part in the undertaking is.

7. A. No changes will be made, providing the money is returned immediately.
    B. To forget is understandable, but to ignore the call deliberately is unforgivable.
    C. He was named captain because of his strength.
    D. Please lay it on the table and leave it there.

8. A. The rain having continued for a full hour without respite, the umpires called the game.
    B. Who do you think will win the next presidential election?
    C. The publisher offered no advance in royalties to the author nor a promise to advertise the book extensively.
    D. The tally showed seventeen ayes for the resolution.

9. A. They thought they were cleverer than we.
    B. If the United States would not have acted promptly, South Korea would have been lost in two weeks.
    C. Everyone accepted the invitation except, oddly enough, him.
    D. All that was left was a few blackened tree stumps.

10. A. "Have you ever," Bill asked smugly, "tried to change a flat tire before?"
    B. Because of the damp weather the window wouldn't rise.
    C. The delegates chosen to represent our association are you, he, and I.
    D. To me, at least, the remark clearly inferred that she disbelieved the story.

11. A. We tiptoed quietly into the room and--over went the map with a crash!
    B. The manager, together with his two coaches, were engaging the umpire in a bitter controversy.
    C. There seem to be many sources of friction between the sergeant and his men.
    D. Every one of the contestants was jumpy and excitable before the race.

12. A. Maxwell spoke as though he meant every word he said.
    B. Richness of color and diversity of design distinguishes the new collection of imported fabrics.
    C. Give the prize to whoever deserves it.
    D. You will find ladies' and girls' clothing on the fourth floor.

13. A. Are the family in agreement on vacation plans?
    B. It is one of those planes that fly faster than the speed of sound.
    C. "We drove through sixteen states on our latest jaunt," she declared, "we had only one detour."
    D. There were but three of us left after the first ballots had been tabulated.

14. A. Mr. Smith demurred at first, but they insisted on his accompanying them.
    B. The data are embodied in the majority report.
    C. Perry never has and never will accept the point of view.
    D. The courier brought encouraging news: negotiations were still in progress.

15. A. Though we had ridden nearly six hundred miles in one day, we felt relatively fresh and rested.
    B. Neither the two oaks nor the maple was affected by the gales of near-hurricane force.
    C. So that Carl would be at his best for the examination, his mother insisted he go to bed early the night before.
    D. The audience showed its approval vigorously; they applauded, stamped their feet, and whistled.

16. A. Ted would have liked to have solved the problem.
    B. Had you completed the job by the time you left?
    C. "Who does he think he is?" she indignantly demanded.
    D. They told us that they had gone on a cruise for their vacation, but we have heard none of the details of their trip.

17. A. "I myself," declared his sprightly dinner partner, "was once a ballerina."
    B. It seems to be I who am most concerned about the defeat.
    C. Civilian defense is everybody's job, not just the worry of a few harried officials.
    D. The principal asked two of us, Carter and I, to assist in the gymnasium.

17.____

18. A. The general, after sifting all the evidence, decided that Lieutenant Jones, not his troops, was to blame.
    B. Paradoxical as it may seem, the millionaire's ambition is, not to make large sums of money, but rather for a name that future generations will remember.
    C. If we were to give up at this point, we should be guilty of treachery to posterity.
    D. All doctors agree that smoking and worry will aggravate any heart condition.

18.____

19. A. Now we can see that if we were more alert to the menace of Communism both here and abroad, we could have taken more vigorous steps to protect ourselves and our allies.
    B. "The time is now!" the Senator declared; "tomorrow may be too late."
    C. We wear machine-made clothes; we eat machine-made food; we sleep on machine-made beds.
    D. Did she say, "I shall never help that ingrate again"?

19.____

20. A. The criminal whom I believed to be him turned out to be a wholly different individual.
    B. The woman was so sure of its being they that she flung the door open recklessly.
    C. What with her husband so much away, she is very lonesome.
    D. She had years of training with the best teachers in Europe, and now her voice is as sweet as a bird.

20.____

21. A. Of all the qualifications of a judge, the prime one is that he be disinterested.
    B. The author tries to say that women such as she are never able to make good in a competitive world.
    C. When Balboa and his men reached the summit, the Pacific could be seen glistening in the sunlight.
    D. Nobody but Margaret and her was able to come to the farewell party.

21.____

22. A. When Buckley arrived at the camp, he was told to report to his barracks, and that he would find his uniform there.
    B. Neither my friends nor I am to blame for the results of the last election.
    C. After you have read all the current books, you will agree with me that WINGS OVER ASIA is one of the best books that have been published this year.
    D. You will find that he is not the same man whom you met five years ago, so changed is he.

22.____

DIRECTIONS: In each of the following groups, one of the four sentences contains NO error in grammar, usage, diction, or punctuation. Indicate the CORRECT sentence.

23. A. A low ceiling is when the atmospheric conditions make flying inadvisable.
    B. They couldn't tell who the card was from.
    C. No one but you and I are to help him.
    D. To him fall the duties of foster parent.

23.____

24. A. They couldn't tell whom the cable was from.
    B. We like these better than those kind.
    C. It is a test of you more than I.
    D. The person in charge being him, there can be no change in policy.

25. A. Do as we do for the celebration.
    B. Do either of you care to join us?
    C. A child's food requirements differ from the adult.
    D. A large family including two uncles and four grandparents live at the hotel.

26. A. If they would have done that they might have succeeded.
    B. Neither the hot days or the humid nights annoy our Southern visitor.
    C. Some people do not gain favor because they are kind of tactless.
    D. No sooner had the turning point come than a new issue arose.

27. A. We haven't hardly enough time.
    B. He either will fail in his attempt or will seek other employment.
    C. After each side gave their version, the affair was over with.
    D. Every one of the cars were tagged by the police.

28. A. They can't seem to see it when I explain the theory.
    B. It is difficult to find the genuine signature between all those submitted.
    C. She can't understand why they don't remember who to give the letter to.
    D. Every man and woman in America is interested in his tax bill.

29. A. He arrived safe.
    B. I do not have any faith in John running for office.
    C. The musicians began to play tunefully and keeping the proper tempo indicated for the selection.
    D. Mary's maid of honor bought the kind of an outfit suitable for an afternoon wedding.

30. A. The new plant is to be electric lighted.
    B. The reason the speaker was offended was that the audience was inattentive.
    C. There appears to be conditions that govern his behavior.
    D. Either of the men are influential enough to control the situation.

31. A. If you would have listened more carefully, you would have heard your name called.
    B. Did you inquire if your brother were returning soon?
    C. We are likely to have rain before nightfall.
    D. Let's you and I plan next summer's vacation together.

32. A. There's a man and his wife waiting for the doctor since early this morning.
    B. The owner of the market with his assistants is applying the most modern principles of merchandise display.
    C. Every one of the players on both of the competing teams were awarded a gold watch.
    D. The records of the trial indicated that, even before attaining manhood, the murderer's parents were both dead.

5 (#1)

33.
- A. Why don't you start the play like I told you?
- B. I didn't find the construction of the second house much different from that of the first one I saw.
- C. "When", inquired the child, "Will we begin celebrating my birthday?"
- D. There isn't nothing left to do but not to see him anymore.

33._____

34.
- A. The child could find neither the shoe or the stocking.
- B. The musicians began to play tunefully and keeping the proper tempo indicated for the selection.
- C. The amount of curious people who turned out for Opening Night was beyond calculation.
- D. "Indeed," mused the poll-taker, "The winning candidate is much happier than I."

34._____

35.
- A. Just as you said, I find myself gaining weight.
- B. A teacher should leave the capable pupils engage in creative activities.
- C. The teacher spoke continually during the entire lesson, which, of course, was poor procedure.
- D. Mary's maid of honor bought the kind of an outfit suitable for an afternoon wedding.

35._____

36.
- A. The new schedule of working hours and rates was satisfactory to both employees and employer.
- B. Many common people feel keenly about the injustices of Power Politics.
- C. Mr. and Mrs. Burns felt that their grandchild was awfully cute when he waved good-bye.
- D. The tallest of the twins was also the most intelligent.

36._____

37.
- A. Do you intend bringing most of the refreshments yourself?
- B. Suffering from a severe headache all day one dose of the prescribed medicine relieved me.
- C. "Please let my brothers and I help you with your packages," said Frank to Mrs. Powers.
- D. Every one of the rooms we visited had displays of pupils' work in them.

37._____

38.
- A. The telephone linesmen, working steadily at their task during the severe storm, the telephones soon began to ring again.
- B. Meat, as well a fruits and vegetables, is considered essential to a proper diet.
- C. He looked like a real good boxer that night in the ring.
- D. The man has worked steadily for fifteen years before he decided to open his own business.

38._____

39.
- A. No one can foretell when I will have another opportunity like that one again.
- B. The last group of paintings shown appear really to have captured the most modern techniques.
- C. We searched high and low, both in the attic and cellar, but were unsuccessful in locating mementos.
- D. None of the guests was able to give the rules of the game accurately.

39._____

40. A. After the debate, every one of the speakers realized that, given another chance, he could have done better.
    B. The reason given by the physician for the patient's trouble was because of his poor eating habits.
    C. The fog was so thick that the driver couldn't hardly see more than ten feet ahead.
    D. I suggest that you present the medal to who you think best.

41. A. A decision made by a man without much deliberation is sometimes no different than a slow one.
    B. By the time Mr. Brown's son will graduate Dental School, he will be twenty-six years of age.
    C. Who did you predict would win the election?
    D. The auctioneer had less stamps to sell this year than last year.

42. A. Having pranced into the arena with little grace and unsteady hoof for the humps ahead, the driver reined his horse.
    B. Once the dog wagged it's tail, you knew it was a friendly animal.
    C. The record of the winning team was among the most note-worthy of the season.
    D. When asked to choose corn, cabbage, or potatoes, the diner selected the latter.

43. A. The maid wasn't so small that she couldn't reach the top window for cleaning.
    B. Many people feel that powdered coffee produces a really good flavor.
    C. Would you mind me trying that coat on for size?
    D. This chair looks much different than the chair we selected in the store.

44. A. After trying unsuccessfully to land a job in the city, Will located in the country on a farm.
    B. On the last attempt, the pole-vaulter came nearly to getting hurt.
    C. The observance of Armistice Day throughout the world offers an opportunity to reflect on the horrors of war.
    D. Outside of the mistakes in spelling, the child's letter was a very good one.

45. A. Scissors is always dangerous for a child to handle.
    B. I assure you that I will not yield to pressure to sell my interest.
    C. Ask him if he has recall of the incident which took place at our first meeting.
    D. The manager felt like as not to order his usher-captain to surrender his uniform.

46. A. The mother of the bride climaxed the occasion by exclaiming, "I want my children should be happy forever."
    B. We read in the papers where the prospects for peace are improving.
    C. "Can I share the cab with you?" was frequently heard during the period of gas rationing.
    D. Had the police suspected the ruse, they would have taken proper precautions.

47. A. The teacher admonished the other students neither to speak to John, nor should they annoy him.
    B. Fortunately we had been told that there was but one service station in that area.
    C. An usher seldom rises above a theatre manager.
    D. The epic, GONE WITH THE WIND, is supposed to have taken place during the Civil War Era.

48. A. Shall you be at home, let us say, on Sunday at two o'clock?
    B. We see Mr. Lewis take his car out of the garage daily, newly polished always.
    C. We have no place to keep our rubbers, only in the hall closet.
    D. Isn't it true what you told me about the best way to prepare for an examination?

49. A. The host thought the guests were of the hungry kinds so he prepared much food.
    B. The museum is often visited by students who are fond of early inventions, and especially patent attorneys.
    C. I rose to nominate the man who most of us felt was the most diligent worker in the group.
    D. The child was sent to the store to purchase a bottle of milk, and brought home fresh rolls, too.

50. A. The garden tool was sent to be sharpened, and a new handle to be put on.
    B. At the end of her vacation, Joan came home with little money, but which systematic thrift soon overcame.
    C. We people have opportunities to show the rest of the world how real democracy functions.
    D. The guide paddled along, then fell in a reverie which he related the history of the region.

KEY (CORRECT ANSWERS)

1. C	11. B	21. C	31. C	41. C
2. D	12. B	22. A	32. B	42. C
3. B	13. C	23. D	33. B	43. B
4. C	14. C	24. A	34. D	44. C
5. B	15. D	25. A	35. A	45. B
6. C	16. A	26. D	36. A	46. D
7. A	17. D	27. B	37. A	47. B
8. C	18. B	28. D	38. B	48. A
9. B	19. A	29. A	39. D	49. C
10. D	20. D	30. B	40. A	50. C

TEST 2

DIRECTIONS: In each of the following groups, one of the four sentences contains NO error in grammar, usage, diction, or punctuation. Indicate the CORRECT sentence. *PRINT THE LETTER OF THE CORRECT ANSWER IN THE SPACE AT THE RIGHT.*

1. A. We should have investigated the cause of the noise by bringing the car to a halt.
    B. The first few strokes of the brush were enough to convince me that Tom could paint much better than me.
    C. We inquired if we could see the owner of the store, after we waited for one hour.
    D. The highly-strung parent was aggravated by the slightest noise that the baby made.

    1.___

2. A. The police, investigating the crime, were successful in discovering only one possibly valuable clue.
    B. Due to an unexpected change in plans, the violin soloist did not perform.
    C. Besides being awarded a Bachelor's degree at college, the scientist has since received many honorary degrees.
    D. The data offered in advance of the recent Presidential election seems to have possessed elements of inaccuracy.

    2.___

3. A. I don't quite see that I will be able to completely finish the job in time.
    B. By my statement, I infer that you are guilty of the offense as charged.
    C. Wasn't it strange that they wouldn't let no one see the body?
    D. I hope that this is the kind of rolls you requested me to buy.

    3.___

4. A. He said he preferred the climate of Florida to California.
    B. Because of the excessive heat, a great amount of fruit juice was drunk by the guests.
    C. This week's dramatic presentation was neither as lively nor as entertaining as last week.
    D. The fashion expert believed that no one could develop new creations more successfully than him.

    4.___

5. A. That kind of orange is grown only in Florida.
    B. Walking up the rickety stairs, the bottle slipped from his hands and smashed.
    C. The reason they granted his request was because he had a good record.
    D. Little Tommy was proud that the teacher always asked him to bring messages to the office.

    5.___

6. A. The new mayor is a resident of this city for thirty years.
    B. Do you mean to imply that had he not missed that shot he would have won?
    C. Next term I shall be studying French and history.
    D. I read in last night's paper where the sales tax is going to be abolished.

    6.___

7. A. To have children vie against one another is psychologically unsound.
    B. Would anyone else care to discuss his baby?
    C. He was interested and aware of the problem.
    D. I sure would like to discover if he is motivating the lesson properly.

    7.___

8. A. She graduated Barnard College twenty-five years ago.
    B. He studied the violin since he was seven.
    C. She is not so diligent a researcher as her classmate.
    D. He discovered that the new data corresponds with the facts disclosed by Werner.

9. A. You have three alternatives: law, dentistry, or teaching.
    B. If I would have worked harder, I would have accomplished my purpose.
    C. He affected a rapid change of pace and his opponents were outdistanced.
    D. He looked prosperous, although he had been unemployed for a year.

10. A. Tell me where you hid it, no one shall ever find it.
    B. They lay in the sun for many hours, getting tanned.
    C. The reproduction arrived, and had been hung in the living room.
    D. First begin by calling the roll.

11. A. Deliver these things to whomever arrives first.
    B. Everybody but she and me is going to the conference.
    C. If the number of patrons is small, we can serve them.
    D. When each of the contestants find their book, the debate may begin.

12. A. After his illness, he stood in the country three weeks.
    B. If you wish to effect a change, submit your suggestions.
    C. It is silly to leave children play with knives.
    D. Play a trick on her by spilling water down her neck.

DIRECTIONS: In each of the following groups, one of the four sentences contains an error in grammar, usage, diction, or punctuation. Indicate the INCORRECT sentence.

13. A. Do you think the situation is susceptible of improvement?
    B. He rejects the allegation, since he feels he is completely innocent.
    C. This is the strangest sort of predicament I've ever been in.
    D. The largest amount of cars ever to cross the bridge in one day was reported for Sunday.

14. A. The Jones's house has been newly painted.
    B. He considered correct spelling his worst fault in English.
    C. "This machine," he declared, "will replace three or four men."
    D. The theatre is at Fourth Avenue and Sixty-eighth Street.

15. A. If he had kept his mind on his work, he would not now be in such straits.
    B. His graduation from High School was followed by a year of travel.
    C. Everyone rose to his feet as the visitor entered.
    D. About those things we talked later—years later.

16. A. The field that you have chosen is an interesting one, but offers less chance for advancement than the others.
    B. It appeared that he had lain there for many hours.
    C. The leader, with all his scores of followers, was arrested.
    D. There seems to be no alternative to violence.

17. A. If you are looking for a scapegoat, neither the boys down the street nor he was anywhere near the scene.
    B. How extremely difficult it is to decide whether or not to go to the performance!
    C. Of the two there is no question that this is the best choice.
    D. The auditorium in the Century Building was selected as the place for the meeting on the twenty-eighth.

18. A. Certainly there was no demand for, or need of, the gold-encrusted dinnerware.
    B. This weather is much like April, except that it is much drier.
    C. Costume jewelry is not the sort of gift for her, you know.
    D. He could only smile at the absurdity of the request.

19. A. The injured player, his shoulder wrenched and his wind knocked out, was carried from the field and substituted by the second string quarterback.
    B. "It isn't everyone," he said, "who can act that well."
    C. The most expensive part of the entire trip was the hotel bills.
    D. The jury has announced its verdict.

20. A. A bright red hunting costume hung in the closet.
    B. I suggest that we give a prize to whoever gets three-quarters of the problems right.
    C. This is one of those essays that seek to preach a sermon.
    D. To play basketball well, passing must be practiced.

21. A. The principal difficulty in examining these questions is that of determining the facts.
    B. He is, as I recall, taller than I.
    C. The main thing to see are the beautiful gardens.
    D. Three-fourths of the roof has been painted.

22. A. It's obvious that some of these are our's, some your's, and some their's.
    B. The dean wants us all—John, Helen, and me—run for office.
    C. There are fewer reasons for supporting him than for opposing him.
    D. Amy's friends were interested in books and travel, as she was.

23. A. Rogers, who is responsible for all the action of the play, is an old man, very clever and witty.
    B. The 2's, 4's and 6's were in proper sequence.
    C. A teacher should not expect a pupil to know what he knows.
    D. I am in favor of his going, regardless of the consequences.

24. A. The leopard snarled viciously, sprang at the native who helpless screamed his fear.
    B. Do not feel bad about this unfortunate incident.
    C. From far above the clouds came a distant roar of the jets starting on their mission.
    D. Being now well advanced in years, he was proud of having served the people so well.

25. A. The reason so many came was that there had been a promise of refreshments.
    B. No sooner had the guest speaker arrived when it began to rain.
    C. They do not always hire whoever has the most experience.
    D. He found the northern climate very healthful.

26. A. Rounding the curve and setting itself for the long pull over the mountain, the train began a labored puffing.
    B. Regardless of what he says, I am going to choose my own friends.
    C. The job, it will be found, will be given to whomever has the ability to stand criticism.
    D. "You Are There" is the program I often listen to.

27. A. Yesterday marked the twelfth day I will have been attending the course.
    B. He had to walk a mile for some gasoline.
    C. Either the players or the umpire is to be interviewed.
    D. Don't begin your bickering just yet, please.

28. A. Although he is playing tennis only four years, we expect him to win the tournament.
    B. I have no alternative to following his request exactly as made.
    C. The group of "sidewalk superintendents" stood gaping in fascination at the demolition proceedings.
    D. Reviving momentarily, he tried to sit up, found the effort too much, sagged back, and lapsed into a coma.

29. A. Had the spectators remained calm, the poor, unfortunate children would not have been trampled.
    B. I have often heard her say, "Would that he had studied much harder!"
    C. Great writers, together with each background, is a fascinating study in itself.
    D. We cannot ever seem to find a person to whom responsibility is sacred.

30. A. There was always a disagreement as to who would do the work.
    B. I don't know that I can go.
    C. The lack of emphasis is caused by an involved sentence structure.
    D. No matter how gloomy the present news is, we should not break before it, but let us take courage.

31. A. The Egyptian delegate said that he might abstain from voting.
    B. We ought not to consider the lateness of the hour, not having made a real beginning on our task.
    C. If I started the task somewhat earlier, I would be finished now.
    D. The new regulations for handling a large fund are quite detailed and stringent.

32. A. These are the arguments against the plan: its uncertainty, its high cost, and its need for the kind of specialized personnel which is not available here.
    B. I don't think he would be interested in that kind of house.
    C. You're expected to take his lunch to him every day.
    D. Whomever he wished to destroy he first praised.

33. A. The lecture finished, the audience began asking questions.
    B. Any man who could accomplish that task the world would regards as a hero.
    C. Our respect and admiration are mutual.
    D. George did like his mother told him, despite the importunities of his playmates.

34. A. Each applicant was required to give his name, age, and where he lived.
    B. Andrew has been away for months; hence his bewilderment at these new laws is understandable.
    C. Whether he be vagabond or courtier, he may enter these portals.
    D. At the conference, it transpired that the president had absconded with the funds six months before.

34.___

35. A. Henry maintains that he has already read the article in its entirety.
    B. A large number of people signed the petition.
    C. We appreciate you going to all this trouble for us.
    D. The data which he collected are not relevant to the matter.

35.___

36. A. Do you believe that Ted is more brilliant than she?
    B. There isn't but one grocery store in the neighborhood.
    C. If one went into the hall, he told us, one could hear the wind screaming down the staircase.
    D. All the members of the club but him had come.

36.___

37. A. Alex is not so tall as his brother.
    B. The reason why I failed was that I had not studied my lesson.
    C. Their radio cost more than ours, but ours is equally good.
    D. The hostess only wanted the five couples to come for a week.

37.___

38. A. A good prayer for this season is that the mutual distrust of Russia and the free countries of the world will not lead to war.
    B. The fellow who, in our ignorance, we were inclined to censure proved to be quite admirable.
    C. The euphemistic use of some words is to be deprecated, because it tends to drive them out of currency.
    D. I was so nauseated by the stench from the marshes that I could not enjoy the trip.

38.___

39. A. Providing us with a long list of names of possible successors, he proffered his resignation.
    B. The data on this as well as on the other proposal is clearly set forth in the report.
    C. It was agreed that his salary would be increased by fifty percent, provided he could settle his affairs here and sail on the first of April.
    D. Nothing was further from my mind than the thought that you had misrepresented your connection with the firm.

39.___

40. A. It is most likely that he has decided to postpone making a report until he has consulted his lawyer.
    B. Now I shall answer his most recent inquiry: "When are we going to receive the shipment of goods"?
    C. Possibly, though not probably, we shall be able to adapt the old machines to our present needs; such an arrangement, however, if it is made, should surely be a temporary one.
    D. The article defended, although not definitely stating them, many theories to which I cannot subscribe.

40.___

41. A. We could see no way out of the impasse except for them to make an apology.   41._____
    B. The program would have been a great disappointment had It not been for the second number's charm and finesse.
    C. That a prisoner chafes at his captivity is not at all surprising to a person who is realistic.
    D. We thought her to be the one whom the great majority of the group would decide should be chosen as the winner.

42. A. There can be little doubt that this fabric is as durable or even more durable than the other.   42._____
    B. We had but to say the word and we could have had our every wish fulfilled.
    C. I am not used to this type of report; please revise it, deleting the details.
    D. The day, which had dawned cloudy and dull, cleared perceptibly as we started on our journey.

43. A. By the time you read this letter, I shall have been in England more than a week.   43._____
    B. See pp. 53-55 for an explanation of the rules governing the use of the apostrophe.
    C. All his 5's looked like 3's; it was well nigh impossible to add correctly a column of figures which he had copied.
    D. If they would have known the probable outcome, they would never have cast their votes for that candidate.

44. A. In the doctor's opinion, a cure will not be affected by the present treatment.   44._____
    B. Neither you, who are her closest friends, nor my sister are to blame in this matter.
    C. The crowd tossed their hats into the air when the home team scored a touchdown.
    D. This pair of scissors is too dull to cut so thick a cloth as denim.

45. A. They were so timid, so fearful, and so nervous that I objected to him mentioning the accident in his oral report to them.   45._____
    B. A colon, or colon and dash, may precede an enumeration, a long direct quotation, or a statement formally introduced, especially with "as follows," "namely," etc.
    C. "Who's doubting your word? You're too sensitive," he said, as he hurriedly left the room.
    D. Nobody but him and his classmates was able to see the difference between the twins.

46. A. Their enthusiasm entirely spent, they were reluctant to enter another contest.   46._____
    B. A walking tour through that state is not to be contemplated because every resident is liable to demand several kinds of identification.
    C. We want only such preparation as will make success certain.
    D. If you would make sure that the plan is feasible, show it to the floor manager.

47. A. "We'd have liked to go along," I said, "if you'd only thought to invite us."   47._____
    B. They thought it to be him.
    C. Do you mean to infer in those slighting remarks that I have neglected my duty?
    D. At last, we were gathered all together again, like birds in a nest.

48.
  A. He asked his daughter whether she would be willing to devote her spare time to the planning of a series of programs for children.
  B. It is not the purpose of the proposed legislation that all men should be cared for from the cradle to the grave, but to prevent any recurrence of widespread poverty among our citizens.
  C. If there is clearly no solution to their problem, let's turn our attention at once to the next item.
  D. His voice sounded like a frog's, although he had had several years' training in both music and speech

49.
  A. He should be allowed to make the experiment without let or hindrance.
  B. In spite of their docility, the children presented some real problems to the teachers when they first met them after their vacation.
  C. Neither he nor I am concerned about the matter.
  D. Since we have the "know-how," it is our duty to undertake the assignment.

50.
  A. Let us—you, who are a foreigner, and I, who am a native,—try to see the problems without bias.
  B. All things considered, we can reach no other decision.
  C. We originally considered him to be the person most likely to win.
  D. Men's, women's, boys' and girls' interests vary so much that it is difficult to plan an effective program for the meeting.

KEY (CORRECT ANSWERS)

1. A	11. C	21. C	31. C	41. D
2. B	12. B	22. A	32. B	42. A
3. D	13. D	23. C	33. D	43. D
4. B	14. B	24. A	34. A	44. B
5. A	15. B	25. B	35. C	45. A
6. B	16. A	26. C	36. B	46. B
7. B	17. C	27. A	37. D	47. C
8. C	18. B	28. A	38. B	48. B
9. D	19. A	29. C	39. B	49. B
10. A	20. D	30. D	40. B	50. A

EXAMINATION SECTION
TEST 1

DIRECTIONS: In each of the following groups, one of the four sentences contains an error in grammar, usage, diction, or punctuation. Indicate the INCORRECT sentence. *PRINT THE LETTER OF THE CORRECT ANSWER IN THE SPACE AT THE RIGHT.*

1.
   A. After shaking hands with me, he said, "You're most welcome, I assure you."
   B. He exclaimed, "What a mistake you have made!" upon hearing my account of the discussion.
   C. What is meant by "Dog eat dog"?
   D. "I'd like to travel all over the world," said the young man; just to see how the 'other half' lives, you know."

   1.____

2.
   A. During the lecture, the speaker was repeatedly disturbed by the shouts of the small boys on the streets.
   B. The injured woman having been given first aid, we offered to take her to the nearest hospital.
   C. Due to the continued rain and wind, we have been unable to leave the house for several days.
   D. I could not respect him as I do if he were not upright and honest.

   2.____

3.
   A. This is John, Tom and Harry's room.
   B. John borrowed his brother-in-law's car.
   C. The department store is advertising a sale of mens' clothing.
   D. Who shall I say telephoned?

   3.____

4.
   A. My friend Harris lives in Brooklyn.
   B. Between each period, teachers must stand in the corridor to direct traffic.
   C. The committee proposed that he be dropped from the organization.
   D. Only within the past few months have I begun to know her.

   4.____

5.
   A. Hoping for the best is not as effective as to work hard.
   B. Set it down on the desk.
   C. I insist that he accompany me.
   D. School over at last, they ran to their games.

   5.____

6.
   A. The class had no sooner become interested in the lesson than the bell rang.
   B. At that time, I was especially desirous to make her acquaintance.
   C. The tearful parents were oblivious of everyone else but their daughter.
   D. Florence's skill on the instrument was conceded to be unsurpassed in the school.

   6.____

7.
   A. Of the two plans described, the second is the most important.
   B. A two weeks' vacation is necessary after a hard year's work.
   C. On June first, our neighbors will have been living in the same house for thirty years.
   D. Everybody who has paid the full purchase price should call for his set of books now.

   7.____

8. A. It was superior in every way to the book previously used.
    B. His testimony today is different from that of yesterday.
    C. If you would have studied the problem carefully, you would have found the solution more quickly.
    D. The flowers smelled so sweet that the whole house was perfumed.

9. A. Next summer I shall either travel by plane or by boat down to Bermuda.
    A. May we infer then that you were really just an innocent bystander?
    B. Undoubtedly the best scene in the play occurs when the son confronts his mother.
    C. History is the record of events that have happened.

10. A. The leader, with all his scores of followers, was arrested.
    B. Howard is a friend of my brother.
    C. Jerry never has and never will do a good day's work.
    D. Did any of the applicants bring his tools?

11. A. His speed was equal to that of a racehorse.
    B. His failure was due to weak eyes.
    C. The reason I am late is because I was sick.
    D. Of course, my opinion is worth less than a lawyer's.

12. A. The winters were hard and dreary, nothing could live without shelter.
    B. Not one in a thousand readers takes the matter seriously.
    C. Every candidate except my friend and me seems to know exactly how to relax.
    D. If I had known that it was you, I should have acted differently.

13. A. The social activities of college life were his sole interest.
    B. After hearing modern jazz, all other music sounds dull.
    C. Surely there can be no objection to their working on a volunteer basis.
    D. Favored by a warm climate, Florida is a popular resort.

14. A. This will not be easy for me, I being without experience.
    B. He said that he had been here before and that he expected to return.
    C. He is not so competent as we thought him to be.
    D. Since the installation of the traffic light, there have been less accidents at that crossing.

15. A. Besides her own family of four boys, my grandmother reared two adopted children.
    B. This kind of apples ripens earlier than any other in our section of the country.
    C. She was so kind to us girls when we were little children that we shall always be grateful to her.
    D. The invention of such amusements as the radio, television, and movies have probably influenced the habits of millions.

16. A. We still do not believe the thief to be him, in spite of the evidence to the contrary.
    B. These data, although very interesting, are not really significant.
    C. Every man, every woman, every child was interested in the program.
    D. He is one of the most able men who has ever been in the Senate.

17. A. The girl swum the Mississippi River.
    B. Price levels rose ten points last year.
    C. The freshmen were forbidden to speak to the sophomores.
    D. He was here when the boy brought the news.

    17.____

18. A. The lines on the map are finely drawn.
    B. He spoke very slowly.
    C. The lady looked good in her new suit.
    D. The cream tasted sour.

    18.____

19. A. The day is warm.
    B. It should be called to his attention.
    C. The girl was an unusually beautiful child.
    D. He performed the job easy and quick.

    19.____

20. A. The company published its new catalogue last week.
    B. The man who he introduced was Mr. Carey.
    C. The Rolls-Royce is the fastest car in England.
    D. He finished the job satisfactorily.

    20.____

21. A. The crew did its best to complete the job on time.
    B. They have already went home.
    C. The children drank some lemonade.
    D. The girl has written her composition.

    21.____

22. A. She saw the letter laying here this morning.
    B. They gave the poor man some food when he knocked on the door.
    C. The plans were drawn before the fight started.
    D. He was here when the messenger brought the news.

    22.____

23. A. I regret the loss caused by the error.
    B. The students will have a new teacher.
    C. It shall rain before the afternoon is over.
    D. They swore to bring out all the facts.

    23.____

24. A. If my trip is a success, I should be back on Thursday.
    B. We will send a copy of the article to you if you wish it.
    C. They will have gone before the notice is sent to their office.
    D. Can I use this information in my speech?

    24.____

25. A. He likes these kind of pencils better than those kind.
    B. That Jackson will be elected is evident.
    C. He does not approve of my dictating the letter.
    D. Jack should make some progress in his work each day.

    25.____

26. A. The company has moved into its new building.
    B. They will approve him going to the concert.
    C. That business is good appears to be true.
    D. It was he who won the prize.

    26.____

27. A. We will notify whomever you wish.
    B. I expect him this morning.
    C. If he lays down on the job, he will regret it.
    D. In the old records was found a queer mistake.

28. A. The manager's statement relating to the two letters is without doubt correct.
    B. Either you are the winner or I am.
    C. The mother knew where the little boy had hidden his toys.
    D. He has forgot where they bought the equipment.

29. A. He will study the lesson providing he can find his book.
    B. It looks as if they will come.
    C. The meeting of the committee was held in the Rose Room.
    D. He decided to open a branch store.

30. A. I wrote first and telephoned later.
    B. He should of taken the order.
    C. All our offices close on Saturday.
    D. Our principal business is selling.

31. A. Who shall I say called?
    B. The water has frozen the pipes.
    C. Everyone has left except them.
    D. Everyone of the salesmen must supply their own car.

32. A. The driver did all that it was possible to do.
    B. He agreed to phone you before now.
    C. I thought it to be he.
    D. We expected to stay there.

33. A. Two-thirds of the building is finished.
    B. Where are Mr. Keene and Mr. Herbert?
    C. Neither the floorwalker nor the salesladies want to work overtime.
    D. The committee was agreed.

34. A. Who did we give the order to?
    B. Send your order immediately.
    C. You will thrill at the beauty of the mountain.
    D. I believe I paid the bill.

35. A. Amends have been made for the damage to one of our cars.
    B. Neither the customer nor the clerk were aware of the fire in the store.
    C. A box of spare pencils is on the desk.
    D. There is the total number of missing pens.

36. A. The company insist on everyone's being prompt.
    B. Each one of our salesmen takes an aptitude test.
    C. It is the location that appeals to me.
    D. Most of the men have left the building.

37. A. We're sure she'll respond if your careful about the suggestions she's given each day.
    B. I have always been of the opinion that that kind of examination is of little value.
    C. The papers will not blow away if you lay the paper weight on them.
    D. He had scarcely finished his lines when the audience began to applaud wildly.

37.____

38. A. Modern furniture may be used for many purposes for which period furniture cannot.
    B. I had but five minutes to catch the train.
    C. He told Marjorie and me that he would not come.
    D. Each of the wheels on those trucks have twelve spokes.

38.____

39. A. No one knows the correct answer to that question except you and me.
    B. It looked like it was going to be a pleasant day, so we left our umbrellas at home.
    C. The judge said that punishment would be meted out to whomever deserved it.
    D. "*The words, 'Give me liberty or give me death*," he answered incorrectly but with assurance, "were said by Nathan Hale."

39.____

40. A. It is I who am mistaken.
    B. Is it John or Mary who stand at the head of the class?
    C. He is one of those pupils who always do their lessons.
    D. He is a man whom I can depend on in time of trouble.

40.____

41. A. At first glance, the old man believed him to be me.
    B. His failure to complete his work in college last term might have been due to his child's illness.
    C. The scenery in Banff is somewhat like Switzerland, although Banff is much farther north.
    D. Whatever your decision may be will be quite satisfactory, I am sure.

41.____

42. A. The children's plans for a surprise party had been made very quietly, but John's suspicions had been aroused.
    B. There must be some faraway place where one can spend a quiet holiday.
    C. Rather than crowd the page, it is preferable to leave a line blank between each word.
    D. I have never understood why a good facsimile should not be so valuable as an original.

42.____

43. A. He feels ill, but his sister looks worse.
    B. The Joneses are going to visit their friends in Chicago.
    C. ROBINSON CRUSOE, which is a fairy tale to the child, is a work of social philosophy to the mature thinker.
    D. I was appreciative of all his efforts, but especially of him doing that one job for me.

43.____

44. A. They have written to all of us—Harry, you, and I.
    B. That I am sick is no proof that I ate too much.
    C. In one of Sinclair Lewis's novels the clergy is satirized.
    D. At the fringe of the crowd, peering through all those bodies, stood Henry and I.

44.____

45. A. To enjoy a walking trip, take care that your feet are in good condition. 45.____
    B. One or the other of those fellows has stolen it.
    C. The man whom I thought was my friend deceived me.
    D. He said he thought he should ride.

46. A. The possession of certain skills and abilities are necessary for that type of work. 46.____
    B. The beautiful elm trees are in danger of being killed by a disease which was brought here from Europe.
    C. When you're in doubt about your best friend's loyalty, you can't help being disappointed.
    D. These data help to prove that his statements are well founded.

47. A. Are you much taller than I? 47.____
    B. She lived in the city for three years before she visited her aunt.
    C. He lay the book down on the table and angrily stalked out of the room.
    D. He read excerpts from his new novel to John and me.

48. A. The lilacs, the early roses, and the lush warmth of the morning smelled fragrant as odors from the gardens of Heaven. 48.____
    B. I found it to be fruitful to study the plan in detail, setting aside several items for daily consideration, the time depending upon the quantity of other work.
    C. Let's you and I confront him together.
    D. Maugham has the ability to hold his reader's attention.

49. A. The poem is somewhat longer than a sonnet; its rhythm is fittingly sedate. 49.____
    B. If they would have considered all the suggestions carefully, they would have come to a different conclusion.
    C. Among the plans submitted were many up-to-date ideas, some of which were adopted.
    D. When the toy balloon burst, the child screamed piercingly with fright.

50. A. Coming in on the train, the high school building is seen on the left. 50.____
    B. I shall relay the message to my secretary upon her arrival.
    C. She is a member of a literary group that meets regularly.
    D. They work nights independently of one another.

KEY (CORRECT ANSWERS)

1. D	11. C	21. B	31. D	41. C
2. C	12. A	22. A	32. C	42. C
3. C	13. B	23. C	33. C	43. D
4. B	14. D	24. D	34. A	44. A
5. A	15. D	25. A	35. B	45. C
6. B	16. D	26. B	36. A	46. A
7. A	17. A	27. C	37. A	47. C
8. C	18. C	28. D	38. D	48. C
9. A	19. D	29. A	39. D	49. B
10. C	20. B	30. B	40. B	50. A

TEST 2

DIRECTIONS: In each of the following groups, one of the four sentences contains an error in grammar, usage, diction, or punctuation. Indicate the INCORRECT sentence. *PRINT THE LETTER OF THE CORRECT ANSWER IN THE SPACE AT THE RIGHT.*

1. A. Had I remained at home, as my father advised, I should have heard the news as soon as you did.
   B. His normal health was soon restored to him by the balmy climate.
   C. He is very different in temperament than his brother.
   D. Does neither of them expect to attend the reception?

   1._____

2. A. It seems to be Ed who must do most of the work.
   B. John had interesting news for us; the meeting was still in session.
   C. Accident prevention is everybodys' concern every day in the week.
   D. Boys' and girls' furnishings are sold on the second floor.

   2._____

3. A. We planned to stay a week at Rocky Landing.
   B. The bus driver agreed to take as many as wanted to go.
   C. Any man may vote, be he rich or poor.
   D. The teacher assigned three of us, John, Sam, and I to help with the arrangements for the party.

   3._____

4. A. There are no lakes in Pennsylvania like they have in the central part of New York State.
   B. Waiting dejectedly at the door, he could give no explanation for his failure.
   C. There are hardly any people left in town who remember his boyhood.
   D. The entire city was aroused at the news of the general's killing himself.

   4._____

5. A. They really believed they were stronger than we.
   B. The one thing left was a quantity of broken tin cans.
   C. Who do you think will be chosen for the position by the superintendent?
   D. The coach, together with six or seven players, were quarreling heatedly with the referee.

   5._____

6. A. The whole class wanted the winner to be him.
   B. If he prepares carefully, he is liable to win the contest.
   C. Neither the two boys nor the only girl was chosen by the committee.
   D. There seem to be many people ready to apply for the position.

   6._____

7. A. His failure to prepare will probably mitigate against his possibility of success.
   B. Do you think that you could have swum all the way to the island?
   C. Although his lawyer objected, the prisoner was sentenced to be hanged next month.
   D. We have heard none of the details of the story.

   7._____

8. A. In this first matter although it appears simple, there are probably going to be many statements of opinion.
   B. We believed him to be the best choice.
   C. While we waited, the interval between each stroke of the bell seemed to grow longer.
   D. What he saw was a company of men in a close group.

   8.____

9. A. Disagreement, bickering, and quarreling is a frequent occurrence when that organization holds its meetings.
   B. I felt bad when I saw the test results.
   C. The man's death was due to exposure to the cold.
   D. Everyone arrived on time except Smith, Brown, and him.

   9.____

10. A. It's time you knew how to divide by two numbers.
    B. Are you sure the bell has rung?
    C. Whose going to prepare the lunch for the picnic?
    D. Will it be all right if you are called at ten o'clock?

    10.____

11. A. Everybody, busy, lying in the sun, or carelessly looking on, considered himself one of the group.
    B. Unlike you or I, Joseph receives a large allowance each week.
    C. You may tell him our teacher is displeased.
    D. Whom do you believe to be the best athlete in the group?

    11.____

12. A. When you go on a vacation trip be sure to take a supply of color film along with you.
    B. We are happy to read that there are higher wages today and less employed than ever before in our history.
    C. The principal will address the senior class on opportunities in teaching.
    D. Every available student, including the twenty-five freshmen in Mr. Smith's class, is invited to enter the contest.

    12.____

13. A. When the test period ended, the teacher realized that he prepared a test that was much too difficult for the average pupil in the class.
    B. The agenda for our next meeting were prepared well ahead of the meeting.
    C. "One of the answers is correct," the teacher said: "you are to make the right choice."
    D. The New York State Commission for the Blind is preparing a fundraising campaign.

    13.____

14. A. Interest, talent, and opportunity must be explored in sound vocational guidance.
    B. The person who from all points of view was the best leader was the one finally chosen.
    C. Whoever you like so well is always welcome at our house.
    D. When I realize how hard he worked, I feel bad.

    14.____

15. A. Intending to reach home before dark, at six o'clock we began the trip at the entrance to the park.
    B. The most concrete criticism was the fact that he was disinterested in his studies.
    C. Laziness is responsible for a great many spelling errors.
    D. The new men's store advertised its opening sale day for Monday.

    15.____

16. A. The management of traffic in our city, large as it is, compares favorably with any other city in the country.
    B. Should you ask for another book, I should be happy to help you find it.
    C. The candidate's real interest in securing the nomination no longer remaining in doubt, the politicians are backing him for the office.
    D. Never having known the man personally or socially, although they had worked together for years, the superintendent felt that he could not recommend him.

16.____

17. A. Successfully to complete the assigned work is a first requirement for a good grade.
    B. All of us present in the auditorium agreed that it would be unwise to leave such severe criticism go without reply.
    C. None of the three hundred seniors was truly qualified for the new post.
    D. Owing to the intervention of an interested party, the business deal was successfully completed.

17.____

18. A. There was no one but my best friend, John, and me still fishing after eight o'clock.
    B. He is one of those successful people who believes that achievement depends on hard work.
    C. How can you compare the taste of my pie with the flavor of her dessert?
    D. We were amazed at his choosing the last two weeks in July as his vacation.

18.____

19. A. You tell him I'm not pleased with his work.
    B. They wandered all over the state as if they didn't know the route.
    C. Efficiency was introduced in all three stores, but like the first two, the third was soon in financial difficulties.
    D. He is the kind of man who impresses you, the first time he meets you.

19.____

20. A. You may be sure that he is the same man whom you met on your first visit.
    B. Being that you arrived first, you will be given first choice of the available seats.
    C. In spite of his injury, he was selected to make the trip with the team.
    D. Either my friend or I am ready to write the answer to the last question.

20.____

21. A. Five years are long enough to have stayed away from home.
    B. Do you think we are justified in answering their questions?
    C. Knowing that you are ready, the idea is very good for me to call you now.
    D. This is a wholly different problem from the one we solved yesterday.

21.____

22. A. The boy looked like he had gone through a difficult period.
    B. During the game every one of the students is expected to cheer, to applaud, and to act like a sportsman.
    C. The opera finished, the audience cheered every performer.
    D. A series of biographical sketches is to be released soon.

22.____

23. A. He, not you, is to lead the band.
    B. Beside Mr. Truman there is one other former president living.
    C. His decision to continue the search was the cause of the tragedy, it appears.
    D. The flower smells sweet after a chemical spraying.

23.____

24. A. There is an increasing number of retarded readers in the ninth year.
    B. The pupil liked English better than biology, arithmetic, or Spanish.
    C. Many explanations are possible; perhaps poor health was the deciding factor.
    D. Many pupils seem to enjoy playing games alone but not to lose in these games.

24.____

25. A. Every nation has their own problems to contend with.
    B. Speak to whoever is best able to give directions.
    C. The prize should be given to whomever the committee chooses.
    D. The farther you walk, the more lovely the road becomes.

26. A. The committee of councilmen is ready to act now.
    B. The parent, accompanied by his children, is to be shown into the room.
    C. Give the answer to whoever opens the door first.
    D. The investigation may be wise, but in my opinion I think it is not necessary.

27. A. Born in India and educated in England, Kipling's stories have the flavor of both countries.
    B. He had an accident in his sister-in-law's car.
    C. Practicing for many months, he learned to dance better than she.
    D. The teacher, together with his pupils, was late for the bus.

28. A. Think carefully before voting, because your's is the important decision.
    B. Whomever you decide upon, we shall accept your choice.
    C. Every one of the books which are so beautifully bound is a treasure.
    D. Regardless of consequences, he flew his plane toward the sound barrier.

29. A. To get the most out of country living, the surroundings must be peaceful.
    B. Had he heeded the warning, he would have saved himself much trouble.
    C. I can't understand his swimming beyond the safety zone.
    D. Take this book to the librarian.

30. A. Although he is playing golf only two years, he has already won three tournaments.
    B. The soil was so poor that despite the use of various fertilizers he was unable to effect an increase in the yield.
    C. None of the boys is better able to cope with the problem than he.
    D. He dived into the water; then he disappeared from sight.

31. A. Contrasted to his previous behavior, his actions today seemed almost saintly.
    B. If he would have reported on time, he would not have lost the job.
    C. His first answer, not his other answers, is open to question.
    D. He was much affected by the accident; the extent of his injuries is still to be determined.

32. A. He is one of those boys who always seem content.
    B. His excuse was different from the one I had expected.
    C. He may be more clever than me, but he doesn't work as hard.
    D. Walking along the road, he spied the girl's purse.

33. A. Of the two pictures which reached the final round of judging, I thought Gregg's was the better.
    B. The attitudes of children are often more carefree than their parents.
    C. Neither he nor I am to improve the situation.
    D. Every member of the group has submitted his report.

34. A. In the 70's and 80's there were many fewer luxuries than there are today.
    B. Among the contestants the best was obviously the youngest.
    C. This morning, at about eight o'clock, we saw an accident coming to school.
    D. I feel bad about his failure; nevertheless, he must adjust himself to the circumstances.

34.____

35. A. There were three obstacles to the project: the weather, the distance and the lack of proper equipment.
    B. He should have let us know whether he could come.
    C. Tom, Bill and Henry had a common fault-procrastination.
    D. If we wish to accomplish our purpose, we must cooperate together in the common cause.

35.____

36. A. The car has lain in the mud throughout the winter.
    B. Between you and me, this is a problem to be decided among all the delegates.
    C. After they had hung the noose from the beam, they hanged the outlaw.
    D. These kind of oranges do not have the pulpy center.

36.____

37. A. What the outcome was we shall never know.
    B. The interior can be completed by Monday night providing the materials arrive today.
    C. That's the unhappiest looking youngster in the school.
    D. Following the blast, he lay there helpless for hours.

37.____

38. A. Neither of the boys was willing to go.
    B. I am working, and always have, for the good of the organization.
    C. Before we left I hurried to his house to fetch him.
    D. Fearing that he would be late, he broke into a fast trot.

38.____

39. A. "I'll be there," she said, "even though my health is poor."
    B. "Have you seen the new picture, "The Wild Ones?"
    C. Mary and her sisters are sure to be there.
    D. The MONA LISA, which hangs in the Louvre, attracts throngs daily.

39.____

40. A. You will find the boy's equipment stored in the teacher's lounge.
    B. Walk three blocks north; then turn east one block.
    C. The new skyscraper is to be erected on Forty-ninth Street
    D. MACBETH was the one play he had read many, many times.

40.____

41. A. A carload of vegetables and fruits was destroyed by the flames.
    B. Neither Frank nor John is the correct choice for the job.
    C. The reason for the articles is because the paper is seeking a sensational issue.
    D. He was graduated from a local university, but not without great effort on his part.

41.____

42. A. Dinner being over, let us discuss the matter.
    B. It was no use continuing the effort, the door would not open.
    C. Drummond was born in the West, but the East was his home in later years.
    D. He would have liked to go.

42.____

43. A. If he had kept his mind on his work, he would not now be in such straits.
    B. His graduation from High School was followed by a year of travel.
    C. Everyone in the hall rose to his feet when the President entered.
    D. They decided to reject whoever, by January 15, had not submitted his credentials.

44. A. Most of us teachers work hard.
    B. Holding my hand up, I showed my approval.
    C. The reason I take French is because I intend to travel.
    D. Evidently it was not she whom we met.

45. A. Although glowing prospects of fabulous profits were pictured to him, he remained uninterested in the project.
    B. Although the climate of Maine was much colder, he preferred it to California.
    C. Although he protested his innocence, he could not escape the consequences of the mob's blind rage.
    D. Although taciturn by nature, she chattered freely on her favorite subject, puppets.

46. A. Ladies' hats are more expensive now than ever.
    B. They were frightened by his shrieking.
    C. They were grateful to whomever would help them.
    D. Large groups of persons visit the shrine daily.

47. A. On one side was a swamp, on the other a river.
    B. Take those books next door.
    C. John was running for our team when suddenly he drops the ball.
    D. The data which were used had been supplied by the agents.

48. A. The constant droning of the bees caused me to drowse as I sat in the garden.
    B. Swathed in bandages from head to foot, he was a pitiable sight.
    C. We directed his attention to the girl who we believed most likely to be the prize winner.
    D. There was little to choose among the many offerings.

49. A. Such consideration as you can give us will be appreciated.
    B. It looks like another World War will break out any minute.
    C. The boat sank at noon but it was early evening before the first rescuers arrived on the spot.
    D. I had already eaten my lunch when the taxi arrived.

50. A. The girl whom I thought to be president was the secretary.
    B. The truck which was here at three o'clock came for the chairs, not the refrigerator.
    C. It is true that bright yellow apples are often lacking in firmness, but I enjoy those kind most.
    D. Did you imply that he was competent?

KEY (CORRECT ANSWERS)

1. C	11. B	21. C	31. B	41. C
2. C	12. B	22. A	32. C	42. B
3. D	13. A	23. B	33. B	43. B
4. A	14. C	24. D	34. C	44. C
5. D	15. B	25. A	35. D	45. B
6. B	16. A	26. D	36. D	46. C
7. A	17. B	27. A	37. B	47. C
8. C	18. B	28. A	38. B	48. C
9. A	19. D	29. A	39. B	49. B
10. C	20. B	30. A	40. C	50. C

EXAMINATION SECTION
TEST 1

DIRECTIONS: In each of the following groups of sentences, one sentence is incorrect because it includes an error in grammar, usage, sentence structure, capitalization, diction, or punctuation. Indicate the INCORRECT sentence.

1. A. Under pressure, many school secretaries may become unnecessarily short and curt with visitors.
    B. She had not hardly opened the school office when she found a long line of mothers waiting to register their children.
    C. The discussion among the three secretaries helped to resolve the problem of responsibility for specific tasks.
    D. The principal said, "All of us are dependent on you for rapid and courteous telephone service."

2. A. "Why," she asked, "must I be responsible for training students helpers at the switchboard?"
    B. You must not doubt your ability to learn to prepare payroll reports.
    C. Learning to operate duplicating machines is an important part of a secretary's duties.
    D. I realize the values of promptness and accuracy in the office.

3. A. Never permit yourself to become so impersonal in your relationships that you lose your ability to get along with others.
    B. Please take this package to the teacher in room 304.
    C. Each of us has the task of arranging their own desks for quick and efficient work.
    D. I sent the pencils, paper, and books to the chairmen's offices.

4. A. Yesterday, the supplies were delivered; today, they must be distributed.
    B. The secretary sat down besides the new pupil to explain how the form was to be completed.
    C. Should you encounter an error made by a teacher on a report, please tell the teacher tactfully of the error.
    D. You may find it wise to proofread all items that you have typed before you remove them from the machine.

5. A. Did you understand the relay message to mean that all new secretaries must report for an orientation session?
    B. If you are asked to take dictation, make certain that you have the required items readily at hand.
    C. It is your responsibility to report any bomb threat to the ranking supervisor immediately.
    D. Irregardless of your previous instructions, you are not to permit students to go to the permanent record file.

6. A. She is one of those secretaries who is always accurate in her work.
    B. All of us agree that there should be some equitable distribution of office assignments.

C. As the school secretary picked up the telephone she heard a student shouting "Fire!" at the top of his voice.
D. You must be certain that the principal wishes to see a visitor before you usher the visitor into the principal's office.

7. A. In so far as I am able, I shall attempt to serve all members of the community who enter the school office.
    B. The school secretary who had typed the requisition had omitted the identifying number given in the supply list.
    C. Her typing was as fast, if not faster than, any secretary he had ever had.
    D. In order to complete the payroll, it may become necessary, on occasion, for the school secretary to remain beyond the regular school day.

7.____

8. A. The school secretary with a firm knowledge of school accounts and records is an asset to any school office.
    B. The accurate preparation of period attendance reports may enable the city to obtain its proper proportion of state funds.
    C. Initiative on the part of the school secretary may result in improvement in the organization and administration of school routine.
    D. "I seriously believe," she said, "that if we receive less than six helpers we cannot do the job."

8.____

9. A. As the parent left the office, she said, "How can I ever repay you back for your kindness?"
    B. Any money taken from the petty cash fund must be accounted for.
    C. The requisitions had to be signed and dated before they could be mailed.
    D. Needless to say, I urge you to be prompt and regular in attendance.

9.____

10. A. Because all members of the office staff pitched in and helped, the huge task was completed in an extra ordinarily short period of time.
    B. "If it cannot be completed by three o'clock, I am willing to stay overtime," she said.
    C. Your typing has improved greatly both in accuracy and in speed.
    D. Turning the page, the secretary's eye was attracted to the advertisement for a time-stamping device.

10.____

11. A. The secretary said, "I do not mean to infer that I am displeased with this typewriter."
    B. Relatively few of the children who came into the office had been given passes by their teachers.
    C. The parent, who had been waiting for a long time before any attention was paid to her, vented her anger on the inconsiderate secretary.
    D. The school secretary working in the general office very tactfully urged the teachers to lower their voices.

11.____

12. A. The newly appointed member of the office staff was told that the assistant principal would tell her how to complete the report.
    B. If you follow these suggestions, they will teach you self-control and to be tactful.
    C. Observing the teacher's difficulty in understanding the pension statement, the school secretary offered to assist her.
    D. She was most eager to learn the operation of the duplicating machine.

12.____

13. A. She took the reprimand very badly in that she assumed that it was an attack on her personally rather than on the nature of her work.
    B. By requesting the visitor to wait for a pass, she demonstrated that she was following the rules of the school.
    C. The notice on the bulletin board read: "Any discourtesy to our staff, if reported to the principal, will be greatly appreciated."
    D. May I have your permission to read the announcement over the public address system?

13.____

14. A. You will undoubtedly become proficient as you gain experience.
    B. Have you been greatly effected in preparing the attendance reports by the transit strike?
    C. It is urgent that student monitors be sent to each of the classrooms with the message.
    D. Please keep an exact record of the date, time, and type of each fire drill that we conduct.

14.____

15. A. If you take too much time during the mid-morning break, you place an extra burden on the secretaries who remain in the office.
    B. Please edit and proofread all notices before duplicating them.
    C. I do not anticipate any difficulty in developing the proper touch needed for operation of the electric type writer.
    D. In comparing the work done by the two school secretaries, I must admit that Miss Smith is the fastest typist.

15.____

16. A. In the event that a teacher is absent from school, she is to call the school at 7:30 a.m. or as close to that time as possible.
    B. The notation on the "While You Were Out" slip indicated that Mr. Lane of the board of education had called.
    C. Decisions of these kinds may have to be made by you if no supervisor is available.
    D. What kind of information did the parent request?

16.____

17. A. In answering the telephone, please give the name and borough of the school first.
    B. Why not try arranging the supplies neatly in your desk so that you can reach every item without difficulty?
    C. As she was preparing the list of names of students serving on the school newspaper staff, the secretary asked me how to list two editor-in-chiefs.
    D. Keep a list of printed forms that are in short supply so that we can order the forms we need.

17.____

18. A. The secretary prepared a notice which was put in the mail boxes of all teachers, including yourself.
    B. Do not yield to the temptation to deal with a poorly dressed person in a way which is different from the way in which you treat others.
    C. You will find the envelope directly behind the file folder headed "Correspondence."
    D. May I ask you to double check the totals for each column so that you are certain that the addition is correct.

18.____

19. A. Although the salesman was very persuasive, I refused to let him see the principal while the principal was in conference.
    B. Don't you think that it would be worth your while to improve the speed and accuracy of your typing?
    C. If the principal has left for the day, be sure to have the administrative assistant check the form before you duplicate it.
    D. We ordered the book before the special circular arrived describing the procedure to be followed.

19.____

20. A. The development of friction between co-workers is not inevitable.
    B. Do not be overly pessimistic about your ability to learn to prepare the period report correctly.
    C. Her manner with the children who come into the office is much too brusque and sharp, but I think that she is basically kind.
    D. The data is correct and, therefore, it may be incorporated into the report.

20.____

21. A. The best time to do work requiring full concentration is when the office is quiet.
    B. She inquired, "Are you going to hand in your report at 3:00 p.m.?"
    C. We should pay full attention to every kind of a written report.
    D. She learned that further practice had had a good effect on her ability to transcribe.

21.____

22. A. After brief training, she was ready to accept greater responsibility.
    B. According to my calendar, your examinations are due today for stencilling.
    C. Let's put aside this kind of work until later.
    D. Strict accuracy is a necessary requisite in record keeping.

22.____

23. A. Her desk was orderly, though piled high with folders; furthermore, her supplies were neatly arranged.
    B. She claims that our filing procedures need revision because they've become so boresome.
    C. "May I ask you, Miss Hawkins," said the principal's secretary, "to come in at once?"
    D. Oddly enough, he had forgotten to reset the school's clock for daylight saving time.

23.____

24. A. She had an almost hypnotic fascination for the rhythmical operation of the mimeograph machine.
    B. "Dr. Franklin, Professor Marlin, and Messrs. Clark, Havens, and Wilson will visit us today," wrote the principal in a memorandum.
    C. She quickly mastered the nomenclature of the supply catalogs.
    D. He informed all personnel not to furnish medicine to any pupil.

24.____

25. A. The pupil's account of his lateness is incredible, I will not give him a classroom pass.
    B. Her willingness to type was due to her desire to learn the forms.
    C. They scheduled their lunch hours in such a way that the switchboard could be covered constantly.
    D. She replenished her supply of clips, staples, bond paper, and pencils.

25.____

KEY (CORRECT ANSWERS)

1.	B	11.	A
2.	A	12.	B
3.	C	13.	C
4.	B	14.	B
5.	D	15.	D
6.	A	16.	B
7.	C	17.	C
8.	D	18.	A
9.	A	19.	D
10.	D	20.	D

21. C
22. D
23. B
24. A
25. A

TEST 2

DIRECTIONS: In each of the following groups of sentences, one sentence is incorrect because it includes an error in grammar, usage, sentence structure, capitalization, diction, or punctuation. Indicate the INCORRECT sentence.

1. A. They were thought to be we.
   B. The secretary whom we thought deserved the honor will receive a prize.
   C. The principal herself arranged the new library schedule.
   D. I am sorry to be unable to recommend a monitor for your office.

2. A. Please lay the carbon paper on the proper shelf.
   B. The principal is expected to return inside of an hour.
   C. I seldom if ever make errors when I type letters.
   D. I feel confident that I am able to do this work accurately and neatly.

3. A. To Mrs. Andersen have fallen the responsibilities of supply secretary.
   B. The secretary pointed out that all individuals under twenty-one years of age are legally considered minors.
   C. Mrs. Thompson, with her son and daughter, are going to the annual business show.
   D. There are fewer errors in this report than in the last report.

4. A. One secretary referred to the project as "worthwhile and creative."
   B. I thought this typewriter was hers.
   C. A number of our secretarial staff is going on vacation soon.
   D. These typewriters are very sturdy: they are made from strong metal and unbreakable plastic.

5. A. "I know," he said, "that you can finish this project today."
   B. I found Miss Jones the most cooperative of the two secretaries.
   C. My sister who works at Public School 73 lives in Manhattan.
   D. Our school secretary is always appropriately attired and well groomed.

6. A. The letter has lain on the principal's desk all day, waiting for his signature.
   B. We believe that three-quarters of the work is done.
   C. She said, "Neither you nor I am responsible for that error."
   D. Let me speak to whomever is waiting for the assistant principal.

7. A. How disappointing it was to hear him say, "Your bus has left!"
   B. It was a dark, dismal, dreary, December day.
   C. Do you know any alumnae of a women's college?
   D. It is imperative that you enunciate your words clearly when you use the telephone.

8. A. "Will you have time," he inquired, "to prepare transcripts for our college-bound graduates?"
   B. You work more efficiently than her because you anticipate and avoid time-consuming trifles.

294

2 (#2)

- C. Questions regarding procedure should be referred to a disinterested expert, should they not?
- D. The chairmen of the health education, foreign language, mathematics, and English departments requested supply requisition forms.

9.
- A. The instant the principal began to dictate, the bell rang, interrupting his train of thought.
- B. This is one of those machines that are constantly breaking down.
- C. She asked me whether I would remain a few additional minutes to check her report.
- D. A well-organized schedule makes it possible to complete more work with less helpers.

9._____

10.
- A. Teachers' letter boxes should not be filled in such a way as to create difficulty in removing individual 3" x 5" cards.
- B. By being courteous, emotional outbursts can be avoided in discussions with irate parents.
- C. Her transcribing was interrupted by the whirring, often much too loud, of the engines in the street.
- D. In business letters, correct phrasing, as well as the avoidance of circumlocution, is a virtue.

10._____

11.
- A. Listening intently to the heated discussion at the conference, Laura forgot to take notes; consequently, the minutes were incomplete.
- B. If I were going to prepare the payroll report, I should begin as long in advance as possible.
- C. She asked the student to bring the book to the principal.
- D. The secretaries agreed among themselves that each would do a certain amount of correspondence.

11._____

12.
- A. Ida had two tasks; namely, tabulating data and forwarding them to the assistant superintendent.
- B. Your introduction to the members of the staff has been a pleasant experience, has it not.
- C. "Between you and me, I can hardly tolerate that teacher anyhow," the angry mother confided.
- D. Keeping the office windows fully closed may adversely affect secretaries' efficiency.

12._____

13.
- A. From the tone of the letter, it was easy to imply that the writer was grateful.
- B. We devised other means of communication since telephone extensions were nonexistent.
- C. The preparation of circulars and attendance reports requires considerable care.
- D. "Please direct me to room 205," said the visitor. "I have an appointment with Mr. Jones."

13._____

14.
- A. An efficient school secretary in punctual, precise, and conscientious.
- B. For a beginner, she gave a credulous performance on the piano.
- C. I believe we had fewer pupils in the third grade last year.
- D. Are you prepared to take dictation from the principal when he calls you?

14._____

15. A. I cannot help but congratulating you for the manner in which you handle the switchboard.
    B. This computer is broken; that hard drive is in need of repairs.
    C. Hurray! Here comes our school band!
    D. Having misplaced her key, the teacher borrowed one from the secretary.

16. A. Please deliver the message to either Miss Spring or her.
    B. I believe that ten dollars is not sufficient for the special type of paper you need.
    C. The most appreciated gift was the diaries you obtained for us.
    D. Our government found it necessary to discourage emigration to this country.

17. A. "What is the correct answer," she asked, "to question one on page 14 in the <u>Secretary's Manual</u>?"
    B. My sister Joan called on the phone to relay the important message.
    C. Please bring this material to the office of the custodian of the school.
    D. All secretaries should be aware of and familiar with the rules of indexing.

18. A. A majority of the members have promised to vote for Mr. Randolph.
    B. The work has been carefully laid out for you; you should have very little difficulty.
    C. His new book is as well written, though less exciting than, his previous book.
    D. Either you or she is the writer of this note and I doubt that it is she.

19. A. Will you please ship the books to us as soon as possible?
    B. A call was placed by Superintendent Donovan to the principal of the school.
    C. A strikeover is when a typist retypes a letter or number on top of the original incorrect one.
    D. The committee which the principal appointed consisted of three people: Mrs. Jones, a teacher; Robert; and Jane.

20. A. I was too greatly relieved to be able to say anything.
    B. These insignia date back to ancient Roman times.
    C. We observed a strange phenomenon; the house seemed to sway in the wind and to tremble like a leaf.
    D. It would be much more preferable if you were no longer seen in his company.

21. A. Please send me this data at your earliest convenience.
    B. The loss of their material proved a severe handicap.
    C. My principal objection to this plan is that it is impracticable.
    D. The doll has lain in the rain all evening.

22. A. I had expected to see my brother.
    B. He expected to have seen his brother.
    C. I hoped to see you do better.
    D. It was his duty to assist our friend.

23. A. The reason why I am writing to you is that I wish to avoid further misunderstanding.
    B. These kind of arguments always cause hard feelings.
    C. Regardless of your decision, I shall have to go.
    D. I have only twenty pupils in this class.

24.
A. Which is the youngest of the two sisters?
B. I am determined to finish the work before Saturday.
C. It is difficult to see why the problems are not correctly solved.
D. I have never met a more interesting person.

24.____

25.
A. Located on a mountainside with a babbling brook beside the door, it was a dream palace.
B. Blessed are they that have not seen and yet have believed.
C. The customs in that part of the country are much different than I expected.
D. Politics, even in towns of small population, has always attracted ambitious young lawyers.

25.____

KEY (CORRECT ANSWERS)

1.	B	11.	C
2.	B	12.	B
3.	C	13.	A
4.	C	14.	B
5.	B	15.	A
6.	D	16.	D
7.	B	17.	C
8.	B	18.	C
9.	D	19.	C
10.	B	20.	D

21. A
22. B
23. B
24. A
25. C

TEST 3

DIRECTIONS: In each of the following groups of sentences, one of the four sentences is faulty in grammar, punctuation, or capitalization. Select the INCORRECT sentence in each case.

1. A. If you had stood at home and done your homework, you would not have failed in arithmetic.
   B. Her affected manner annoyed every member of the audience.
   C. How will the new law affect our income taxes?
   D. The plants were not affected by the long, cold winter, but they succumbed to the drought of summer.

   1.____

2. A. He is one of the most able men who have been in the Senate.
   B. It is he who is to blame for the lamentable mistake.
   C. Haven't you a helpful suggestion to make at this time?
   D. The money was robbed from the blind man's cup.

   2.____

3. A. The amount of children in this school is steadily increasing.
   B. After taking an apple from the table, she went out to play.
   C. He borrowed a dollar from me.
   D. I had hoped my brother would arrive before me.

   3.____

4. A. Whom do you think I hear from every week?
   B. Who do you think is the right man for the job?
   C. Who do you think I found in the room?
   D. He is the man whom we considered a good candidate for the presidency.

   4.____

5. A. Quietly the puppy laid down before the fireplace.
   B. You have made your bed; now lie in it.
   C. I was badly sunburned because I had lain too long in the sun.
   D. I laid the doll on the bed and left the room.

   5.____

6. A. Sailing down the bay was a thrilling experience for me.
   B. He was not consulted about your joining the club.
   C. This story is different than the one I told you yesterday.
   D. There is no doubt about his being the best player.

   6.____

7. A. He maintains there is but one road to world peace.
   B. It is common knowledge that a child sees much he is not supposed to see.
   C. Much of the bitterness might have been avoided if arbitration had been resorted to earlier in the meeting.
   D. The man decided it would be advisable to marry a girl somewhat younger than him.

   7.____

8. A. We have received complaints to the effect that the school's clocks are not synchronized.
   B. My telephone is busier than the others, and so why don't they help me out?
   C. If you had mislaid Mr. Harris' file, would you not have informed the principal immediately?
   D. Please distribute these newly-arrived pension booklets among all the teachers.

   8.____

9. A. One should partake in the orientation discussion and heed the council of one's co-workers.
    B. A general circular was drawn up to correct misunderstanding created by the poorly-worded notice on the bulletin board.
    C. We divide teachers' checks into two alphabetized groups for equitable distribution.
    D. Her initiative has led to a streamlining of cumbersome routines.

9.____

10. A. We have just begun to assemble the figures for the period attendance report.
    B. She reports promptly to her assigned station during fire drills.
    C. The person who telephoned insisted on speaking directly to the principal.
    D. "Have you decided, he asked," to prepare the calendar for the remainder of the term?"

10.____

11. A. Give this message to whomever you think is a reliable monitor.
    B. You are not allowed to send pupils out of the building without the principal's permission.
    C. The postman placed the mail, tied with strong cord, in front of the time clock.
    D. We mailed notices to no fewer than 280 parents.

11.____

12. A. She is reluctantly seeking a transfer because she is going to move.
    B. Miss Wilson, when did we conduct our last shelter area drill?
    C. Since no monitor was available, Miss Foster delivered the message herself.
    D. I'd like an appointment to a school in the east side.

12.____

13. A. The information acquired by the school secretary who types observation reports must remain confidential.
    B. You should be impartial to all without sacrificing your friendly approach.
    C. The mail was sorted without they're having to take time from preparing the report.
    D. Your desk will have to be moved while the repairman is working on the ceiling.

13.____

14. A. She sent a copy of "How Good Are Our Schools?" reprinted from <u>American Education</u>.
    B. It is long past the time the bell should have rang.
    C. She counted twenty one-dollar bills in the petty cash reserve.
    D. The reason he returned the stencil was that he had found too many errors.

14.____

15. A. Dr. Smith, professor of American literature, was the principal speaker.
    B. "Which one of you," asked the principal, "prepared this report?"
    C. There are distinct differences between shorthand, type writing and filing.
    D. I intend to devote the balance of the day to the preparation of the reports.

15.____

16. A. Either the librarian or the pupils are wrong.
    B. "Who," asked the principal, "said, 'Correct practice makes perfect'?"
    C. We have the supplies in this cabinet: letterheads, onionskin paper, envelopes, carbon paper, and pencils.
    D. Walking through the corridor, a fire extinguisher came into view.

16.____

17. A. The two secretaries entered the lunch room and sat besides us.
    B. The secretary's success is due to her conscientiousness.
    C. If you find the papers, please let me know about it; but you are certain to have to hunt for them.
    D. I am able to change a typewriter ribbon and to make minor typewriter adjustments.

17.____

18. A. The choice of a typewriter is difficult, there are many excellent ones on the market today.
    B. We have sold an unusually large number of pens in the school store.
    C. Our principal constantly emphasizes punctuality and excellent attendance.
    D. What do you think the effect of the decision will be?

18.____

19. A. The last carton of the new envelopes have just been opened.
    B. The secretary inquired, "Did you hear him ask, 'Who are you?"
    C. Instead of a 2 and a 7 she had typed two 4's.
    D. She might — and according to plans, should — have completed the project.

19.____

20. A. This here typewriter is the one that is not working well.
    B. I believe that it's time for the bell to ring.
    C. Mr. Clark called us, Evelyn and me, into his office.
    D. Jean and I can distribute the mail before noon.

20.____

21. A. Many a clerk and stenographer has become an efficient school secretary.
    B. The data was assembled by three of our secretaries who served on the committee.
    C. I don't know, Mr. Thompson, where your secretary is.
    D. She was typing the letters accurately and rapidly, of course.

21.____

22. A. I do not say exactly that these stories are not true; I only say that I do not believe them.
    B. My old fountain pen, which never leaked or clogged, is broken and I can use it no further.
    C. Compare the quality of our papers with any other papers in the same price range. There is just no comparison.
    D. Today's news, in the words of a famous Frenchman, is in yesterday's newspaper; tomorrow's, in today's.

22.____

23. A. She objected to his reading comics and told him to put it away.
    B. The patient said that the doctor had ordered him to lie down every day after dinner for two hours and that he had, in fact, lain down for more than three hours.
    C. We are likely to run out of money before our vacation is over, and we shall have to borrow some from our friends.
    D. We are confident that you will appoint whomever is best suited for the position.

23.____

24. A. "Age is like love: it cannot be hid." –Thomas Dekker
    B. The question Mary refused to answer was: Did you see Mr. Clark actually leave the building?
    C. This information, namely, that we are going out of business, is accurate.
    D. The Joneses' house is in excellent condition because Mr. and Mrs. Jones take such good care of it.

24.____

25. A. He, not she, is the one to go because he is better prepared than her; thus he can do the job as well as she and we can be sure that it will be done properly.
    B. She had no sooner entered the office and begun to type than the bell announced the first coffee break of the day.
    C. While there has been considerable scholarly interest in the subject, there have been hardly any scientific experiments of any value in the field.
    D. I played the song "Getting To Know You" from the record "The King and I."

25. _____

KEY (CORRECT ANSWERS)

1. A	11. A
2. D	12. D
3. A	13. C
4. C	14. B
5. A	15. D
6. C	16. D
7. D	17. A
8. B	18. A
9. A	19. A
10. C	20. A

21. B
22. C
23. D
24. B
25. A

EXAMINATION SECTION
TEST 1

DIRECTIONS: In each of the following groups of sentences, there are three sentences which are correct and one which is incorrect because it contains an error in grammar, usage, diction, or punctuation. Indicate the INCORRECT sentence. *PRINT THE LETTER OF THE CORRECT ANSWER IN THE SPACE AT THE RIGHT.*

1. A. Take one of these books which are to be discarded because it has no value any more.
   B. Although the period has lasted for more than thirty minutes, the students are not tired and can do much more work.
   C. Williams has a most unique idea for the school play, and he plans to discuss it with his teacher.
   D. After cleaning the house, my mother lay in the hammock for an hour; then she went shopping.

   1.____

2. A. Sunrise High School, with an enrollment of 1,200 boys and 1,100 girls, is the largest in the state.
   B. I was pleased with his visiting me in the hospital as I was lonely and depressed at the time.
   C. To type with your feet spread out in all directions is considered to be an example of poor typewriting technique.
   D. First-class furs like first-class diamonds are very expensive; both the initial cost and the year-to-year upkeep require a great deal of money.

   2.____

3. A. Not having received a reply to my letter of June 8, I am writing again to ask if anything is wrong.
   B. She asked, "Whom does Mr. Jones feel should have won the typewriting medal?"
   C. Strawberries and cream is a perfect summer dessert, and I have asked my mother to serve the dish frequently.
   D. Either Mary or the boys have broken the window, and I mean to find out immediately before they do further damage.

   3.____

4. A. Of the ladies present at the meeting, three were chosen to be delegates to the annual convention to be held the following May.
   B. The reason I succeeded is that I prepared thoroughly for the test.
   C. I heard her say that the window was broken by the ball and damaged the vase in the living room.
   D. They have been chosen for two reasons—namely, because they are intelligent and because they are conscientious.

   4.____

5. A. Latin, French, and English, in that order, were my favorite subjects in high school.
   B. Since a stay of execution has not been received from the governor, the murderer must be hanged at midnight.
   C. Knowing that you want an immediate answer, I suggest that you send your request to Mr. Smith or to whoever is in charge of such matters.
   D. We ordered pencils and typewriter ribbons whichever were available from the stationer on the corner.

   5.____

6. A. Business was not good; and becoming very irritated, the partners decided to close the store for the day.
    B. I am pleased with your work — work that shows through preparation and in your typewriting ability.
    C. The house was low and long and appeared to be newly built.
    D. This office is often used by salesmen who have nothing better to do, and especially by unsuccessful salesmen.

7. A. Reading this well-written book was a never-to-be forgotten experience; I was both repelled and drawn toward the hero.
    B. I can hardly realize that in two weeks I shall be in Europe. The reason is that I have never traveled before.
    C. I want four only, but I will take five or six if you insist.
    D. Mrs. Jones plans to speak with Sally about her poor grades. The girl failed two subjects last month.

8. A. Strictly speaking, he cannot be considered a good base ball player — or, for that matter, a good tennis player.
    B. To learn to type well, you should practice daily; to acquire high speed in shorthand, you should practice constantly.
    C. The teachers' committee consisted of Dr. Smith, the principal, Mr. Jones, the program committee chairman, Mrs. Greene, the senior grade adviser, and the administrative assistant.
    D. His secretary and Girl Friday was the most efficient worker he had ever hired, and he was delighted with her.

9. A. There were but two of us left after examinations had been graded.
    B. Neither the two bushes nor the elm tree was damaged by the hurricane.
    C. "Did you go to the office?", Mary asked. "No," Sally replied, "and I don't intend to."
    D. The engine as well as the fenders and the wheels was severely damaged, and neither you nor I am prepared to say how much the repair bill will be.

10. A. I observed that the house was one of those rambling old mansions that one often sees in Southern towns.
    B. By concentrating on spelling while I am learning how to type, I am putting my time to better use.
    C. Please repeat the sentence again because none of the children in the rear heard you.
    D. The police have arrested three men: John Winters, 27, Brooklyn; Timothy Flynn, 26, Brooklyn; and Sheldon Young, 26, Queens.

11. A. "I have laid the book down," she said. "I shall now go to sleep."
    B. The policeman, not the gangsters, merits our approval despite the fact that crime is made to be so attractive on television.
    C. "Did you finish your composition yet?" Sally asked. "No," Jane replied.
    D. Where can I find out who wrote, "What you don't know would make a great book"?

12. A. I read in a book that boys and girls today are taller and heavier than their parents were at the same age. How interesting!   12.____
    B. John said that from where he was sitting in the ball park, he could hardly see the batter and the pitcher.
    C. He expects to be graduated from Morningside High School in January instead of June as he has been taking extra summer courses.
    D. Speaking of employment, have many new jobs been created on Long Island as a result of all the industries which have settled there during the past five years?

13. A. I have risen at five o'clock in the morning for the past twenty years, and I am still in excellent physical condition.   13.____
    B. I have laid the letter on my employer's desk several times, but he still has not signed it.
    C. We felt that if he would have tried harder, he might have passed the examination.
    D. I am angry with John principally because I am angry at the comments he made at the rally last night.

14. A. I met a friend of father's the other day in Boland and Ryan's suburban store.   14.____
    B. Less men were hurt this year than last because of the intensive safety precautions which have been introduced.
    C. During several months — that is, June, July, and August — school is closed.
    D. We need all types of skills in our office — for example stenographers, typists, IBM operators, duplicator operators, and typist-clerks.

15. A. The paper says that civil liberties is the principal topic of conversation in Washington today.   15.____
    B. I do not know why — but perhaps I shouldn't try to find out at this time.
    C. I would have preferred to do nothing until he came, so I decided to lie down.
    D. As I was entering the office, I heard a bell clang right behind me, which gave me a bad fright.

16. A. As I went deeper and deeper into the forest, the light became dimmer and dimmer.   16.____
    B. Did he actually say, "I can't do a thing for you"? I can imagine him being so ungrateful.
    C. After he had seen the play OKLAHOMA (which he had been told in advance was excellent), he decided to go to the theater much more often.
    D. Bill Carlton did not go to college, which shocked his family and astonished his friends because Bill was a really good student.

17. A. If Tom had worked all summer in a camp or in a restaurant, he might have saved enough money to buy a car.   17.____
    B. I am not sure which typewriter is liked better, the Royal or the IBM Selectric; and I plan, therefore, to look into the matter further.
    C. We stopped at John's house to see if his trophy was different from Mark's trophy.
    D. Tom said that he was going over to Sally's house after the school dance and that we should not expect him home until midnight.

18. A. Tom never has and never will obtain the grades required for admission to Harvard.
    B. The rain fell harder and harder as I walked away from home.
    C. "There is nothing to worry about dear," her mother answered quietly. "What a fuss you do get into! Heavens! Now take the nice medicine."
    D. The union leader, whom it was believed all the men admired, was, in fact, very much hated by most of them.

18.___

19. A. You had better not stay too long or you will get into trouble—unless, of course, you just don't care.
    B. His latest book The Psychology of Mental Life was published in 1991. Have you read his other books?
    C. The clerk whom I thought to be the best was, in actuality, the worst.
    D. He said that he sold: typewriters, adding machines, mail equipment, and time clocks.

19.___

20. A. There was danger of the enemy attacking from the rear and destroying our army before we could bring up the necessary reserves.
    B. There were approximately ten applicants in the office waiting to be interviewed for the job.
    C. He acts, it seems to me, as though he were guilty.
    D. We have studied John Smith's, William Wilson's, and Tom Blake's claims; and we feel quite sure that they will soon be settled.

20.___

21. A. He is a person who pleases you the moment you meet him, so that you want to be with him and to know him better.
    B. He had no love for, nor confidence in, his employer.
    C. First type the letter and then you should put it in the envelope.
    D. His salary was lower than a typist's, but he did not care because there were excellent opportunities for advancement.

21.___

22. A. I typed this letter – you may not believe this, but it is true – in four minutes.
    B. "It is clear (the message read) that the Muscle Shoals development is but a small part of the potential public usefulness of the entire Tennessee River."– D.E. Lilienthal
    C. Shaw made his first plunge into controversy: he rose to his feet, shaking with nerves and heard himself speaking.
    D. After the reading of the will, he opened up the strong box and divided up the money among the relatives present.

22.___

23. A. Dissatisfaction with the theoretical bases and practical workings of the general property tax has given rise to two movements of tax reform.
    B. Let the book lie on the table.
    C. Since the department is reducing its number of employees is not proof that they are not needed.
    D. Who do you think will be selected for the position?

23.___

24. A. Application of the principles discovered during those experiments have been of great value to mankind.
    B. Every one of the editorial assistants proved his worth without exception.
    C. State regulation of morals aids in the protection of the family.
    D. Working when one is tired does not yield the best results.

24.___

25. A. We learned that there was more than ten people present at the conference.
    B. Every one of the employees is able to lift the carton.
    C. Neither the registrar nor the secretary is in the office today.
    D. The administrative assistant stated that any office assistant who stayed overtime tonight would get a half-day off next month.

25.____

KEY (CORRECT ANSWERS)

1.	C	11.	C
2.	D	12.	B
3.	B	13.	C
4.	C	14.	B
5.	D	15.	D
6.	B	16.	B
7.	A	17.	D
8.	C	18.	A
9.	C	19.	D
10.	C	20.	A

21. C
22. D
23. C
24. A
25. A

TEST 2

DIRECTIONS: In each of the following groups of sentences, there are three sentences which are correct and one which is incorrect because it contains an error in grammar, usage, diction, or punctuation. Indicate the INCORRECT sentence. *PRINT THE LETTER OF THE CORRECT ANSWER IN THE SPACE AT THE RIGHT.*

1. A. I read political science books as a kind of a duty, not for pleasure.
   B. You needn't go to all that expense for me.
   C. It will be extremely interesting to note the varied reactions of the other participants.
   D. Please do not be angry with me, because it really was not my fault.

1.___

2. A. We go there by boat and return by train.
   B. He wrote home for his bathing trunks, tennis racket, and set of golf clubs.
   C. Take me to his home, and I will tell him myself.
   D. The autobiography of George Bernard Shaw by Ernest Jones was assigned for reading by my English teacher.

2.___

3. A. Everyone was given his fair share.
   B. If the river will rise much higher, we may have a flood.
   C. There were, in the early years of this century, many more horses than automobiles.
   D. Either your enunciation is faulty or I am hard of hearing.

3.___

4. A. The boy assured his teacher that he would pass the tests with ease.
   B. Every person in these two buildings has to meet their responsibilities.
   C. Thunderstorms will invariably follow a lengthy hot spell.
   D. I believe the boy to be him.

4.___

5. A. I lay it on the bench before I left.
   B. She wrung the clothes before she bought a washing machine.
   C. We have drunk all the water.
   D. The wind has blown like this all night.

5.___

6. A. I like Shakespeare's HAMLET better than any of his plays.
   B. The roads are in poor condition because of the torrential rains.
   C. They robbed the child.
   D. They have stolen my cash.

6.___

7. A. If the winner of the contest were here, I would give him his medal.
   B. I hope my son graduates junior high school next June.
   C. Now is the time to make sure that we have beaten that team.
   D. We believe that those books are up to date.

7.___

8. A. Be careful that you do not slip on that oily surface.
   B. I hope to be able to take notes during his worthwhile lecture.
   C. I think that phenomena is worth photographing.
   D. It occurred in the 1960s, not during the 1950s.

8.___

9. A. New York is larger than any city in Europe.
    B. Just as we reached the boat landing, the weather changed.
    C. Coming around the curve, the large house was seen.
    D. Generally speaking, my daughter is a good student.

    9.____

10. A. Place the children's toys above the others.
    B. It was more unique that I thought it would be.
    C. It was my opinion, albeit an erroneous one, that he was the best swimmer on the team.
    D. The typewriter's ribbon was frayed.

    10.____

11. A. The chances are that Ted's relatives believe in his honesty.
    B. I am glad that you think this was so.
    C. Give it to the club to which my grandmother belongs.
    D. I am in New York for ten years.

    11.____

12. A. I have heard that he is never returning.
    B. In the last century it was especially fashionable to dress in that manner.
    C. This data, in my opinion, is incorrect.
    D. It is a highly selective procedure which must be followed.

    12.____

13. A. She sat besides me on the couch.
    B. Billy is the best Spanish scholar of the three boys.
    C. It is gratifying to know that the city school system's strengths are being publicized.
    D. I do not have very much faith in his changing his mind.

    13.____

14. A. I think that he should be feeling somewhat better.
    B. Do as she does if you want to do it correctly.
    C. I am surely glad that he was able to pass the test.
    D. Hide it some place.

    14.____

15. A. He seemed to be possessed by an evil spirit.
    B. I think that his point of view is different from mine, but I still believe that I am correct.
    C. I agree to the new plan, but I disagree with him in regard to how it is to be accomplished.
    D. He has the natural desire to be independent from his parents.

    15.____

16. A. Whenever she went to school she learned a lot.
    B. We had hoped to be on time, but we were late.
    C. My greatest fear, however, was overcome at the last moment.
    D. The two painters' works were displayed at the gallery.

    16.____

17. A. The check from the Treasury Department will arrive on Monday, January 23.
    B. James was not sure that it was Jane and me at the party.
    C. I do not know if the search for William and her has been made.
    D. There were many accidents on the highway, but the toll was less than had been anticipated.

    17.____

18. A. A baby girl was just what we wanted.
    B. His vote was the larger of the two candidates.
    C. That boy had neither money or influence, and I do not know what chances of success he had.
    D. I may lie down on that bed if I get tired.

19. A. He doesn't live too far from his friend's home.
    B. The northeast was covered with snow.
    C. Let's cut it into six portions so that we can each have a piece.
    D. The boy did six days' work.

20. A. It was in first-class condition, and I decided to keep it.
    B. It was a highly polished piece of jewelry.
    C. The twins, not their little brother, has the measles.
    D. That is the most important document in the history of our country.

21. A. Medical training in Greece has been modernized, and the younger doctors have either studied in the United States or Europe.
    B. He will not bring the car here without my telling him.
    C. He is as tall as, if not taller than, the teacher,
    D. If one is asked to count from one to five inclusive, he should count as follows: one, two, three, four, five.

22. A. The leader of the movement is Mr. Harold L. Parne, Esq.
    B. He expects to be graduated from college next month.
    C. If one lives in Florida one day and in Iceland the next, he is certain to feel the change in temperature.
    D. He is the one of the boys who is always on time.

23. A. Since only one in the jury responded to the foreman's question, he looked at them inquiringly.
    B. According to an old adage, every dog has its day.
    C. It was I whom he wanted to sing.
    D. Now that the stress of examinations and interviews are over, we can all relax for a while.

24. A. The arrival of the letter was prior to that of the package.
    B. If you convey this suggestion back to your committee, we shall obtain a solution to our problem.
    C. They all looked different after their return from Vietnam.
    D. Illiteracy is the condition of the man who cannot read or write.

25. A. Do you think we have paid too much? too little?
    B. Neither John nor I am to receive the reward.
    C. The farmer lost nearly one hundred cattle in the fire.
    D. We are making fewer mistakes with the new calculating machine.

KEY (CORRECT ANSWERS)

1. A
2. D
3. B
4. B
5. A

6. A
7. B
8. C
9. C
10. B

11. D
12. C
13. A
14. D
15. D

16. A
17. B
18. C
19. B
20. C

21. A
22. A
23. D
24. B
25. A

TEST 3

DIRECTIONS: In each of the following groups of sentences, one sentence is incorrect because it includes an error in grammar, usage, sentence structure, capitalization, diction, or punctuation. Indicate the INCORRECT sentence. *PRINT THE LETTER OF THE CORRECT ANSWER IN THE SPACE AT THE RIGHT.*

1.
   A. Her poor posture made taking dictation a fatiguing chore.
   B. The secretary promptly notified the principal of the fire for which she was highly praised.
   C. She makes too frequent use of correction fluid when she types stencils.
   D. Old records are sometimes kept in a basement storeroom.

   1.__

2.
   A. She learned the uses of punctuation marks from one of the dictionary's appendixes.
   B. The administrative assistant acted as principal in the latter's absence.
   C. You see, you did mail the letter to yourself!
   D. We are impressed by her exemplary performance and industry; they are a stimulant to us to do better work.

   2.__

3.
   A. The rotation of duties and responsibilities among the secretaries are highly desirable.
   B. The school secretary must remember to maintain contact with teachers assigned to the Board of Education.
   C. She could not operate the electric typewriter because she had not plugged it in.
   D. Eleanor utilized a postal scale to determine the cost of mailing the parcel.

   3.__

4.
   A. Please list the names of alumnae from the year 1963 on.
   B. Her filing went like clockwork because of the prior alphabetizing of the folders.
   C. She let the phone ring for awhile, but when she finally answered, the line was dead.
   D. The secretary's merits were duly noted in the principal's report.

   4.__

5.
   A. At closing time, one should not be short tempered with long-winded visitors.
   B. The eraser was lost after it had lain alongside the typewriter.
   C. Her spelling was as acceptable as theirs, if not more acceptable.
   D. We ordered many copies of Webster's new International dictionary from federal funds.

   5.__

6.
   A. For the sake of expediency, we divided the work between the four of us.
   B. She quickly learnt to use a comptometer.
   C. Miss Smith would rather take dictation than operate the switchboard.
   D. The dimensions of the envelope determine the quantity of matter that may be enclosed.

   6.__

7.
   A. Joan's suggestion for recording absences, though untried, seems practicable.
   B. The expression, "Thanking you in advance," is unacceptable in up-to-date correspondence.
   C. She informed latecomers not to feel badly because the snowstorm would be accepted as a valid excuse.
   D. The school secretary was pleased that the courses she had taken were relevant to her work.

   7.__

8. A. He was extremely kind to me yesterday.
   B. I talked to him in regard to the subscription.
   C. They were so good to me.
   D. The teacher spoke clear and emphatic.

9. A. Our vacation is over, I am sorry to say.
   B. It is so dark that I can't hardly see.
   C. Either you or I am right; we cannot both be right.
   D. After it had lain in the rain all night, it was not fit for use again.

10. A. When either or both habits become fixed, the student improves.
    B. Neither his words nor his action was justifiable.
    C. A calm almost always comes before a storm.
    D. The gallery with all its pictures were destroyed.

11. A. Next summer I shall either travel by plane or by boat down to Bermuda.
    B. The reason Tom won the award is that he studied hard.
    C. Undoubtedly the best scene in the play occurs when the son confronts his mother.
    D. History is the record of events that have happened.

12. A. John was invited to spend a week at the camp.
    B. My failure was due to the poor method of study I employed at that time.
    C. When I left home, I was only fifteen years old.
    D. We imply from your remarks that you think him guilty.

13. A. The advantages of such an arrangement enables the teachers to plan her work more efficiently.
    B. Typing skill is the result merely of the acquisition of a number of habits.
    C. We are more likely to catch cold in overheated rooms than in chilly ones.
    D. Both political parties promise to balance the budget if and when they are elected to office.

14. A. They have neither the patience nor the skill necessary to solve these problems.
    B. This is the only decision that can be reached: either you or I are right.
    C. You should lend your book to the student who you think will enjoy reading it.
    D. The Red Cross is doing its utmost to provide medical supplies for the flood areas.

15. A. The driver sustained internal injuries.
    B. It is the only textbook of its kind that has, is, or may be published.
    C. Thinking speaking and writing are closely related learnings.
    D. Most of us recognize good English when we hear it or read it.

16. A. This sort of emergency always has its exciting moments.
    B. A tragic play is when the action ends unhappily.
    C. The committee adjourned sine die and went to their homes for a much needed rest.
    D. It is essential that you be on the alert at all times.

17. A. The reason he was late getting to work was because he overslept.
    B. As we read the daily newspaper headlines, a feeling of despair overwhelms us.
    C. His gentle speech is no proof that he is kind.
    D. Shall we lay the book on the table?

18. A. We want to travel extensively and have new experiences.
    B. Charles is my brother, James being my cousin.
    C. His teacher is one person in whom he can confide.
    D. The skater suddenly lost control and crashed into the rail.

19. A. Because he was sympathetic and tolerant, most people respected him.
    B. What are the principal points to be emphasized in the conduct of drill practice?
    C. The lecturer called attention to the beginning of the movement and how it ended.
    D. The average citizen has far more civic power than he realizes.

20. A. The committee has done their best to raise the money necessary to build the new club house.
    B. He was neither willing nor able to pay the exorbitant fee.
    C. We all want to be happy, and we want our fellow men to be happy.
    D. If ours were a totalitarian society, we would probably limit the number of pupils admitted to colleges.

21. A. The filling-out of the application blank took up one third of his time.
    B. The talent for brevity is given to few politicians!
    C. Dashing to the front window, the parade came into view.
    D. Each day this newspaper prints a summary of up-to-the-minute news on the front page.

22. A. Because of his ability as a leader, he was undoubtedly the man for the job.
    B. Not only were they disappointed but also angry.
    C. If one is to learn French well one must speak it regularly.
    D. The most famous collection of prayers known to history is the Book of Psalms.

23. A. We planned to stay a week in at Rocky Landing.
    B. The bus driver agreed to take as many as wanted to go.
    C. Any man may vote, be he rich or poor.
    D. The teacher assigned three of us, John, Sam, and I, to help with the arrangements for the party.

24. A. Today, more then ever, we need the steadying influence of stable homes and families.
    B. Was ever a man so tormented!
    C. This report — may it never be forgotten — is our last, our very last.
    D. The letter states, "I am agin(sic) every idea you have."

25. A. Although he must have known the answer, he refused to volunteer the information.
    B. The pirate captain divided up the booty among his crew according to their rank.
    C. As the gale gathered force, the captain mounted the bridge.
    D. As he threw the line over the side of the boat, he suddenly remembered that the rope was fouled.

KEY (CORRECT ANSWERS)

1. B
2. D
3. A
4. C
5. D

6. A
7. C
8. D
9. B
10. D

11. A
12. D
13. A
14. B
15. B

16. B
17. A
18. B
19. C
20. A

21. C
22. B
23. D
24. A
25. B

SPELLING

COMMENTARY

Spelling forms an integral part of tests of academic aptitude and achievement and of general and mental ability. Moreover, the spelling question is a staple of verbal and clerical tests in civil service entrance and promotional examinations.

Perhaps, the most rewarding way to learn to spell successfully is the direct, functional approach of learning to spell correctly, both orally and in writing, all words as they appear, both singly and in context.

In accordance with this positive method, the spelling question is presented here in "test" form, as it might appear on an actual examination.

The spelling question may appear on examinations in the following format:
>Four words are listed in each question. These are lettered A, B, C, and D. A fifth option, E, is also given, which always reads "none misspelled." The examinee is to select one of the five (lettered) choices: either A, B, C, or D if one of the words is misspelled, or item E, none misspelled, if all four words have been correctly spelled in the question.

SAMPLE QUESTIONS

The directions for this part are approximately as follows:

DIRECTIONS: Mark the space corresponding to the one MISSPELLED word in each of the following groups of words. If NO word is misspelled, mark the last space on the answer sheet.

SAMPLE O
- A. walk
- B. talk
- C. play
- D. dance
- E. *none misspelled*

Since none of the words is misspelled, E would be marked on the answer sheet.

SAMPLE OO
- A. seize
- B. yield
- C. define
- D. reccless
- E. *none misspelled*

Since "reccless" (correct spelling, reckless) has been misspelled, D would be marked on the answer sheet

EXAMINATION SECTION
TEST 1

DIRECTIONS: In each of the following tests in this part, select the letter of the one MIS-SPELLED word in each of the following groups of words. If no word is misspelled, select the last item, letter E (none misspelled). *PRINT THE LETTER OF THE CORRECT ANSWER IN THE SPACE AT THE RIGHT.*

1. A. grateful   B. fundimental   C. census   1._____
   D. analysis   E. NONE MISSPELLED

2. A. installment   B. retrieve   C. concede   2._____
   D. dissapear   E. NONE MISSPELLED

3. A. accidentaly   B. dismissal   C. conscientious   3._____
   D. indelible   E. NONE MISSPELLED

4. A. perceive   B. carreer   C. anticipate   4._____
   D. acquire   E. NONE MISSPELLED

5. A. facility   B. reimburse   C. assortment   5._____
   D. guidance   E. NONE MISSPELLED

6. A. plentiful   B. across   C. advantagous   6._____
   D. similar   E. NONE MISSPELLED

7. A. omission   B. pamphlet   C. guarrantee   7._____
   D. repel   E. NONE MISSPELLED

8. A. maintenance   B. always   C. liable   8._____
   D. anouncement   E. NONE MISSPELLED

9. A. exaggerate   B. sieze   C. condemn   9._____
   D. commit   E. NONE MISSPELLED

10. A. pospone   B. altogether   C. grievance   10._____
    D. excessive E. NONE MISSPELLED

11. A. arguing   B. correspondance   C. forfeit   11._____
    D. dissension E. NONE MISSPELLED

12. A. occasion   B. description   C. prejudice   12._____
    D. elegible   E. NONE MISSPELLED

13. A. accomodate   B. initiative   C. changeable   13._____
    D. enroll   E. NONE MISSPELLED

14. A. temporary   B. insistent   C. benificial   14._____
    D. separate   E. NONE MISSPELLED

15. A. achieve   B. dissapoint   C. unanimous   15._____
    D. judgment E. NONE MISSPELLED

16. A. proceed   B. publicly   C. sincerity   16._____
    D. successful E. NONE MISSPELLED

17.	A. deceive D. repetitive	B. goverment E. *NONE MISSPELLED*	C. preferable	17.____
18.	A. emphasis D. optimistic	B. skillful E. *NONE MISSPELLED*	C. advisible	18.____
19.	A. tendency D. noticable	B. rescind E. *NONE MISSPELLED*	C. crucial	19.____
20.	A. privelege D. divisible	B. abbreviate E. *NONE MISSPELLED*	C. simplify	20.____

KEY (CORRECT ANSWERS)

1. B. fundamental
2. D. disappear
3. A. accidentally
4. B. career
5. E. None Misspelled
6. C. advantageous
7. C. guarantee
8. D. announcement
9. B. seize
10. A. postpone
11. B. correspondence
12. D. eligible
13. A. accommodate
14. C. beneficial
15. B. disappoint
16. E. None Misspelled
17. B. government
18. C. advisable
19. D. noticeable
20. A. privilege

TEST 2

DIRECTIONS: In each of the following tests in this part, select the letter of the one MISSPELLED word in each of the following groups of words. If no word is misspelled, select the last item, letter E (none misspelled). *PRINT THE LETTER OF THE CORRECT ANSWER IN THE SPACE AT THE RIGHT.*

1. A. typical   B. descend   C. summarize   1._____
   D. continuel   E. *NONE MISSPELLED*

2. A. courageous   B. recomend   C. omission   2._____
   D. eliminate   E. *NONE MISSPELLED*

3. A. compliment   B. illuminate   C. auxilary   3._____
   D. installation   E. *NONE MISSPELLED*

4. A. preliminary   B. aquainted   C. syllable   4._____
   D. analysis   E. *NONE MISSPELLED*

5. A. accustomed   B. negligible   C. interupted   5._____
   D. bulletin   E. *NONE MISSPELLED*

6. A. summoned   B. managment   C. mechanism   6._____
   D. sequence   E. *NONE MISSPELLED*

7. A. commitee   B. surprise   C. noticeable   7._____
   D. emphasize   E. *NONE MISSPELLED*

8. A. occurrance   B. likely   C. accumulate   8._____
   D. grievance   E. grievance

9. A. obstacle   B. particuliar   C. baggage   9._____
   D. fascinating   E. *NONE MISSPELLED*

10. A. innumerable   B. seize   C. applicant   10._____
    D. dicionery   E. *NONE MISSPELLED*

11. A. primary   B. mechanic   C. referred   11._____
    D. admissible   E. *NONE MISSPELLED*

12. A. cessation   B. beleif   C. aggressive   12._____
    D. allowance   E. *NONE MISSPELLED*

13. A. leisure   B. authentic   C. familiar   13._____
    D. contemptable   E. *NONE MISSPELLED*

14. A. volume   B. forty   C. dilemma   14._____
    D. seldum   E. *NONE MISSPELLED*

15. A. discrepancy   B. aquisition   C. exorbitant   15._____
    D. lenient   E. *NONE MISSPELLED*

16. A. simultanous   B. penetrate   C. revision   16._____
    D. conspicuous   E. *NONE MISSPELLED*

17. A. ilegible   B. gracious   C. profitable   17._____
    D. obedience   E. *NONE MISSPELLED*

18.	A. manufacturer D. pecular	B. authorize E. *NONE MISSPELLED*	C. compelling	18.____
19.	A. anxious D. tendency	B. rehearsal E. *NONE MISSPELLED*	C. handicaped	19.____
20.	A. meticulous D. shelves	B. accompaning E. *NONE MISSPELLED*	C. initiative	20.____

KEY (CORRECT ANSWERS)

1. D. continual
2. B. recommend
3. C. auxiliary
4. B. acquainted
5. C. interrupted
6. B. management
7. A. committee
8. A. occurrence
9. B. particular
10. D. dictionary
11. E. None Misspelled
12. B. belief
13. D. contemptible
14. D. seldom
15. B. acquisition
16. A. simultaneous
17. A. illegible
18. D. peculiar
19. C. handicapped
20. B. accompanying

TEST 3

DIRECTIONS: In each of the following tests in this part, select the letter of the one MIS-SPELLED word in each of the following groups of words. If no word is misspelled, select the last item, letter E (none misspelled). *PRINT THE LETTER OF THE CORRECT ANSWER IN THE SPACE AT THE RIGHT.*

1. A. grievous B. dilettante C. gibberish 1.____
   D. upbraid E. *NONE MISSPELLED*

2. A. embarrassing B. playright C. unmanageable 2.____
   D. symmetrical E. *NONE MISSPELLED*

3. A. sestet B. denouement C. liaison 3.____
   D. tattooing E. *NONE MISSPELLED*

4. A. prophesied B. soliliquy C. supersede 4.____
   D. hemorrhage E. *NONE MISSPELLED*

5. A. colossal B. renascent C. parallel 5.____
   D. omnivorous E. *NONE MISSPELLED*

6. A. passable B. dispensable C. deductable 6.____
   D. irreducible E. *NONE MISSPELLED*

7. A. guerrila B. carousal C. maneuver 7.____
   D. staid E. *NONE MISSPELLED*

8. A. maintenance B. mountainous C. sustenance 8.____
   D. gluttinous E. *NONE MISSPELLED*

9. A. holocaust B. irascible C. buccanneer 9.____
   D. mischievous E. *NONE MISSPELLED*

10. A. diphthong B. rhododendron C. inviegle 10.____
    D. shellacked E. *NONE MISSPELLED*

11. A. Phillipines B. currant C. dietitian 11.____
    D. coercion E. *NONE MISSPELLED*

12. A. courtesey B. buoyancy C. fiery 12.____
    D. shepherd E. *NONE MISSPELLED*

13. A. censor B. queue C. obbligato 13.____
    D. antartic E. *NONE MISSPELLED*

14. A. chrystal B. chrysanthemum C. chrysalis 14.____
    D. chrome E. *NONE MISSPELLED*

15. A. shreik B. siege C. sheik 15.____
    D. sieve E. *NONE MISSPELLED*

16. A. leisure B. gladioluses C. kindergarden 16.____
    D. tonnage E. *NONE MISSPELLED*

17. A. emminent B. imminent C. blatant 17.____
    D. privilege E. *NONE MISSPELLED*

18. A. diphtheria   B. collander   C. seize   18.____
    D. sleight   E. *NONE MISSPELLED*

19. A. frolicking   B. caramel   C. germaine   19.____
    D. kohlrabi   E. *NONE MISSPELLED*

20. A. dispensable   B. compatable   C. recommend   20.____
    D. feasible   E. *NONE MISSPELLED*

KEY (CORRECT ANSWERS)

1. E. None Misspelled
2. B. playwright
3. E. None Misspelled
4. B. soliloquy
5. E. None Misspelled
6. C. deductible
7. A. guerrilla
8. D. gluttonous
9. C. buccaneer
10. C. inveigle
11. A. Philippines
12. A. courtesy
13. D. antarctic
14. A. crystal
15. A. shriek
16. C. kindergarten
17. A. eminent
18. B. colander
19. C. germane
20. B. compatible

TEST 4

DIRECTIONS: In each of the following tests in this part, select the letter of the one MISSPELLED word in each of the following groups of words. If no word is misspelled, select the last item, letter E (none misspelled). *PRINT THE LETTER OF THE CORRECT ANSWER IN THE SPACE AT THE RIGHT.*

1. A. coercion B. rescission C. license 1.____
   D. prophecied E. NONE MISSPELLED

2. A. calcimine B. seive C. procedure 2.____
   D. poinsettia E. NONE MISSPELLED

3. A. entymology B. echoing C. subtly 3.____
   D. stupefy E. NONE MISSPELLED

4. A. mocassin B. assassin C. battalion 4.____
   D. despicable E. NONE MISSPELLED

5. A. moustache B. sovereignty C. drunkeness 5.____
   D. staccato E. NONE MISSPELLED

6. A. notoriety B. stereotype C. trellis 6.____
   D. Uraguay E. NONE MISSPELLED

7. A. hummock B. idiosyncrasy C. licentiate 7.____
   D. plagiarism E. NONE MISSPELLED

8. A. denim B. hyssop C. innoculate 8.____
   D. malevolent E. NONE MISSPELLED

9. A. boundaries B. corpulency C. gauge 9.____
   D. jingoes E. NONE MISSPELLED

10. A. assassin B. refulgeant C. sorghum 10.____
    D. suture E. NONE MISSPELLED

11. A. dormatory B. glimpse C. mediocre 11.____
    D. repetition E. NONE MISSPELLED

12. A. ambergris B. docility C. loquacious 12.____
    D. Pharoah E. NONE MISSPELLED

13. A. curriculum B. ninety-eighth C. occurrence 13.____
    D. repertoire E. NONE MISSPELLED

14. A. belladonna B. equable C. immersion 14.____
    D. naphtha E. NONE MISSPELLED

15. A. itinerary B. ptomaine C. similar 15.____
    D. solicetous E. NONE MISSPELLED

16. A. liquify B. mausoleum C. Philippines 16.____
    D. singeing E. NONE MISSPELLED

17. A. descendant B. harrassed C. implausible 17.____
    D. irreverence E. NONE MISSPELLED

18. A. crystallize   B. imperceptible   C. isinglass   18.____
    D. precede   E. *NONE MISSPELLED*

19. A. accommodate   B. deferential   C. gazeteer   19.____
    D. plenteous   E. *NONE MISSPELLED*

20. A. aching   B. buttress   C. indigenous   20.____
    D. mischievous   E. *NONE MISSPELLED*

KEY (CORRECT ANSWERS)

1. D. prophesied
2. B. sieve
3. A. entomology
4. A. moccasin
5. C. drunkenness
6. D. Uruguay
7. E. None Misspelled
8. C. inoculate
9. E. None Misspelled
10. B. refulgent
11. A. dormitory
12. D. Pharaoh
13. E. None Misspelled
14. E. None misspelled
15. D. solicitous
16. A. liquefy
17. B. harassed
18. E. None Misspelled
19. C. gazetteer
20. E. None Misspelled

TEST 5

DIRECTIONS: In each of the following tests in this part, select the letter of the one MISSPELLED word in each of the following groups of words. If no word is misspelled, select the last item, letter E (none misspelled). *PRINT THE LETTER OF THE CORRECT ANSWER IN THE SPACE AT THE RIGHT.*

1. A. comensurable B. fracas C. obeisance 1._____
   D. remittent E. *NONE MISSPELLED*

2. A. defiance B. delapidated C. motley 2._____
   D. rueful E. *NONE MISSPELLED*

3. A. demeanor B. epoch C. furtive 3._____
   D. parley E. *NONE MISSPELLED*

4. A. disciples B. influencial C. nemesis 4._____
   D. poultry E. *NONE MISSPELLED*

5. A. decision B. encourage C. incidental 5._____
   D. satyr E. *NONE MISSPELLED*

6. A. collate B. connivance C. luxurient 6._____
   D. manageable E. *NONE MISSPELLED*

7. A. constituencies B. crocheted C. foreclosure 7._____
   D. scintillating E. *NONE MISSPELLED*

8. A. arraignment B. assassination C. carburator 8._____
   D. irrationally E. *NONE MISSPELLED*

9. A. livelihood B. noticeable C. optomiatic 9._____
   D. psychology E. *NONE MISSPELLED*

10. A. daub B. massacre C. repitition 10._____
    D. requiem E. *NONE MISSPELLED*

11. A. adversary B. beneficiary C. cemetery 11._____
    D. desultory E. *NONE MISSPELLED*

12. A. criterion B. elicit C. incredulity 12._____
    D. omnishient E. *NONE MISSPELLED*

13. A. dining B. fiery C. incidentally 13._____
    D. rheumatism E. *NONE MISSPELLED*

14. A. collaborator B. gaudey C. habilitation 14._____
    D. logician E. *NONE MISSPELLED*

15. A. dirge B. ogle C. recumbent 15._____
    D. reminiscence E. *NONE MISSPELLED*

16. A. conscientious B. renunciation C. inconvenient 16._____
    D. inoculate E. *NONE MISSPELLED*

17. A. crystalline B. scimitar C. ecstacy 17._____
    D. vestigial E. *NONE MISSPELLED*

18. A. phlegmatic   B. rhythm   C. plebescite   18.____
    D. refectory   E. *NONE MISSPELLED*

19. A. resilient   B. resevoir   C. recipient   19.____
    D. sobriety   E. *NONE MISSPELLED*

20. A. privilege   B. leige   C. leisure   20.____
    D. basilisk   E. *NONE MISSPELLED*

KEY (CORRECT ANSWERS)

1. A. commensurable
2. B. dilapidated
3. E. None Misspelled
4. B. influential
5. E. None Misspelled
6. C. luxuriant
7. E. None Misspelled
8. C. carburetor
9. C. optimistic
10. C. repetition
11. E. None Misspelled
12. D. omniscient
13. E. None Misspelled
14. B. gaudy
15. E. None Misspelled
16. E. None Misspelled
17. C. ecstasy
18. C. plebiscite
19. B. reservoir
20. B. liege

TEST 6

DIRECTIONS: In each of the following tests in this part, select the letter of the one MISSPELLED word in each of the following groups of words. If no word is misspelled, select the last item, letter E (none misspelled). *PRINT THE LETTER OF THE CORRECT ANSWER IN THE SPACE AT THE RIGHT.*

1. A. repellent B. elliptical C. paralelling D. colossal E. NONE MISSPELLED   1.____

2. A. uproarious B. grievous C. armature D. tabular E. NONE MISSPELLED   2.____

3. A. ammassed B. embarrassed C. promissory D. asymmetrical E. NONE MISSPELLED   3.____

4. A. maintenance B. correspondence C. benificence D. miasmic E. NONE MISSPELLED   4.____

5. A. demurred B. occurrence C. temperament D. abhorrance E. NONE MISSPELLED   5.____

6. A. proboscis B. lucious C. mischievous D. vilify E. NONE MISSPELLED   6.____

7. A. feasable B. divisible C. permeable D. forcible E. NONE MISSPELLED   7.____

8. A. courteous B. venemous C. heterogeneous D. lustrous E. NONE MISSPELLED   8.____

9. A. millionaire B. mayonnaise C. questionaire D. silhouette E. NONE MISSPELLED   9.____

10. A. contemptible B. irreverent C. illimitable D. inveigled E. NONE MISSPELLED   10.____

11. A. prevalent B. irrelavent C. ecstasy D. auxiliary E. NONE MISSPELLED   11.____

12. A. impeccable B. raillery C. precede D. occurrence E. NONE MISSPELLED   12.____

13. A. patrolling B. vignette C. ninety D. surveilance E. NONE MISSPELLED   13.____

14. A. holocaust B. incidently C. weird D. canceled E. NONE MISSPELLED   14.____

15. A. emmendation B. gratuitous C. fissionable D. dilemma E. NONE MISSPELLED   15.____

16. A. harass B. innuendo C. capilary D. pachyderm E. NONE MISSPELLED   16.____

17. A. concomitant B. Lilliputian C. sarcophagus D. melifluous E. NONE MISSPELLED   17.____

329

18. A. interpolate   B. disident   C. venal   18.____
    D. inveigh   E. *NONE MISSPELLED*

19. A. supercillious B. biennial   C. gargantuan   19.____
    D. irresistible E. *NONE MISSPELLED*

20. A. conniving   B. expedite   C. inflammible 20.____
    D. incorruptible E. *NONE MISSPELLED*

KEY (CORRECT ANSWERS)

1. C. paralleling
2. E. None Misspelled
3. A. amassed
4. C. beneficence
5. D. abhorrence
6. B. luscious
7. A. feasible
8. B. venomous
9. C. questionnaire
10. E. None Misspelled
11. B. irrelevant
12. E. None Misspelled
13. D. surveillance
14. B. incidentally
15. A. emendation
16. C. capillary
17. D. mellifluous
18. B. dissident
19. A. supercilious
20. C. inflammable

TEST 7

DIRECTIONS: In each of the following tests in this part, select the letter of the one MIS-SPELLED word in each of the following groups of words. If no word is misspelled, select the last item, letter E (none misspelled). *PRINT THE LETTER OF THE CORRECT ANSWER IN THE SPACE AT THE RIGHT.*

#	A	B	C		
1.	A. torturous	B. omniscient	C. hymenial	1.___
	D. flaccid	E. NONE MISSPELLED		
2.	A. seige	B. seize	C. frieze	2.___
	D. grieve	E. NONE MISSPELLED		
3.	A. indispensible	B. euphony	C. victuals	3.___
	D. receptacle	E. NONE MISSPELLED		
4.	A. schism	B. fortissimo	C. innocuous	4.___
	D. epicurian	E. NONE MISSPELLED		
5.	A. sustenance	B. vilefy	C. maintenance	5.___
	D. rarefy	E. NONE MISSPELLED		
6.	A. desiccated	B. alleviate	C. beneficence	6.___
	D. preponderance	E. NONE MISSPELLED		
7.	A. battalion	B. incubus	C. sacrilegious	7.___
	D. innert	E. NONE MISSPELLED		
8.	A. shiboleth	B. connoisseur	C. potpourri	8.___
	D. dichotomy	E. NONE MISSPELLED		
9.	A. pamphlet	B. similar	C. parlament	9.___
	D. benefited	E. NONE MISSPELLED		
10.	A. genealogy	B. tyrannical	C. diletante	10.___
	D. abhorrence	E. NONE MISSPELLED		
11.	A. effeminate	B. concensus	C. agglomeration	11.___
	D. fission	E. NONE MISSPELLED		
12.	A. narcissus	B. lyceum	C. odissey	12.___
	D. peccadillo	E. NONE MISSPELLED		
13.	A. stupefied	B. psychiatry	C. onerous	13.___
	D. frieze	E. NONE MISSPELLED		
14.	A. intelligible	B. semaphore	C. pronounciation	14.___
	D. albumen	E. NONE MISSPELLED		
15.	A. annihilate	B. tyrannical	C. occurence	15.___
	D. allergy	E. NONE MISSPELLED		
16.	A. gauging	B. probossis	C. specimen	16.___
	D. its	E. NONE MISSPELLED		
17.	A. diphthong	B. connoisseur	C. iresistible	17.___
	D. dilemma	E. NONE MISSPELLED		

18. A. affect   B. baccillus   C. beige   18._____
     D. seize   E. *NONE MISSPELLED*

19. A. apostasy   B. sustenance   C. synonym   19._____
     D. epigrammatic   E. *NONE MISSPELLED*

20. A. discernable   B. consul   C. efflorescence 20._____
     D. complement   E. *NONE MISSPELLED*

KEY (CORRECT ANSWERS)

1. C. hymeneal
2. A. siege
3. A. indispensable
4. D. epicurean
5. B. vilify
6. E. None Misspelled
7. D. inert
8. A. shibboleth
9. C. parliament
10. C. dilettante
11. B. consensus
12. C. odyssey
13. E. None Misspelled
14. C. pronunciation
15. C. occurrence
16. B. proboscis
17. C. irresistible
18. B. bacillus
19. E. None Misspelled
20. A. discernible

TEST 8

DIRECTIONS: In each of the following tests in this part, select the letter of the one MIS-SPELLED word in each of the following groups of words. If no word is misspelled, select the last item, letter E (none misspelled). *PRINT THE LETTER OF THE CORRECT ANSWER IN THE SPACE AT THE RIGHT.*

1. A. righteous   B. seafareing   C. colloquial   1._____
    D. contumely   E. NONE MISSPELLED

2. A. sanitarium   B. vicissitude   C. mischievious 2._____
    D. chlorophyll E. NONE MISSPELLED

3. A. captain   B. theirs   C. asceticism   3._____
    D. acquiesced   E. NONE MISSPELLED

4. A. across   B. her's   C. democracy   4._____
    D. signature   E. NONE MISSPELLED

5. A. villain   B. vacillate   C. imposter   5._____
    D. temperament E. NONE MISSPELLED

6. A. idyllic   B. volitile   C. obloquy   6._____
    D. emendation   E. NONE MISSPELLED

7. A. heinous   B. sattelite   C. dissident   7._____
    D. ephemeral   E. NONE MISSPELLED

8. A. ennoble   B. shellacked   C. vilify   8._____
    D. indissoluble E. NONE MISSPELLED

9. A. argueing   B. intrepid   C. papyrus   9._____
    D. foulard   E. NONE MISSPELLED

10. A. guttural   B. acknowleging C. isosceles   10._____
    D. assonance   E. NONE MISSPELLED

11. A. shoeing   B. exorcise   C. development   11._____
    D. irreperable E. NONE MISSPELLED

12. A. counseling   B. cancellation C. kidnapped   12._____
    D. repellant   E. NONE MISSPELLED

13. A. disatisfy   B. misstep   C. usually   13._____
    D. gregarious   E. NONE MISSPELLED

14. A. unparalleled B. beggar   C. embarrass   14._____
    D. ecstacy   E. NONE MISSPELLED

15. A. descendant   B. poliomyelitis C. privilege   15._____
    D. tragedy   E. NONE MISSPELLED

16. A. nullify   B. siderial   C. salability   16._____
    D. irrelevant   E. NONE MISSPELLED

17. A. paraphenalia B. apothecaries C. occurrence   17._____
    D. plagiarize   E. NONE MISSPELLED

18. A. asinine   B. dissonent   C. opossum   18.____
    D. indispensable   E. *NONE MISSPELLED*

19. A. orifice   B. deferrment   C. harass   19.____
    D. accommodate   E. *NONE MISSPELLED*

20. A. changeable   B. therefor   C. incidently   20.____
    D. dissatisfy   E. *NONE MISSPELLED*

KEY (CORRECT ANSWERS)

1. B. seafaring
2. C. mischievous
3. E. None Misspelled
4. B. hers
5. C. impostor
6. B. volatile
7. B. satellite
8. E. None Misspelled
9. A. arguing
10. B. acknowledging
11. D. irreparable
12. D. repellent
13. A. dissatisfy
14. D. ecstasy
15. E. None Misspelled
16. B. sidereal
17. A. paraphernalia
18. B. dissonant
19. B. deferment
20. C. incidentally

TEST 9

DIRECTIONS: In each of the following tests in this part, select the letter of the one MIS-SPELLED word in each of the following groups of words. If no word is misspelled, select the last item, letter E (none misspelled). *PRINT THE LETTER OF THE CORRECT ANSWER IN THE SPACE AT THE RIGHT.*

1. A. irreparably   B. lovable   C. comparitively   1._____
   D. audible   E. NONE MISSPELLED

2. A. vilify   B. efflorescence   C. sarcophagus   2._____
   D. sacreligious   E. NONE MISSPELLED

3. A. picnicking   B. proceedure   C. hypocrisy   3._____
   D. seize   E. NONE MISSPELLED

4. A. discomfit   B. sapient   C. exascerbate   4._____
   D. sarsaparilla   E. NONE MISSPELLED

5. A. valleys   B. maintainance   C. abridgment   5._____
   D. reticence   E. NONE MISSPELLED

6. A. idylic   B. beneficent   C. singeing   6._____
   D. asterisk   E. NONE MISSPELLED

7. A. appropos   B. violoncello   C. peony   7._____
   D. mucilage   E. NONE MISSPELLED

8. A. caterpillar   B. silhouette   C. rhapsody   8._____
   D. frieze   E. NONE MISSPELLED

9. A. appendicitis   B. vestigeal   C. colonnade   9._____
   D. tortuous   E. NONE MISSPELLED

10. A. omlet   B. diphtheria   C. highfalutin   10._____
    D. miniature   E. NONE MISSPELLED

11. A. diorama   B. sustanance   C. disastrous   11._____
    D. conscious   E. NONE MISSPELLED

12. A. inelegible   B. irreplaceable   C. dissatisfied   12._____
    D. procedural   E. NONE MISSPELLED

13. A. contemptible   B. sacrilegious   C. proffessor   13._____
    D. privilege   E. NONE MISSPELLED

14. A. inoculate   B. diptheria   C. gladioli   14._____
    D. hypocrisy   E. NONE MISSPELLED

15. A. pessimism   B. ecstasy   C. furlough   15._____
    D. vulnerible   E. NONE MISSPELLED

16. A. supersede   B. moccasin   C. recondite   16._____
    D. rhythmical   E. NONE MISSPELLED

17. A. Adirondack   B. Phillipines   C. Czechoslovakia   17._____
    D. Cincinnati   E. NONE MISSPELLED

335

18. A. weird   B. impromptu   C. guerrila   18.____
    D. spontaneously   E. *NONE MISSPELLED*

19. A. newstand   B. accidentally   C. tangible   19.____
    D. reservoir   E. *NONE MISSPELLED*

20. A. macaroni   B. mackerel   C. ukulele   20.____
    D. giutar   E. *NONE MISSPELLED*

KEY (CORRECT ANSWERS)

1. C. comparatively
2. D. sacrilegious
3. B. procedure
4. C. exacerbate
5. B. maintenance
6. A. idyllic
7. A. apropos
8. E. None Misspelled
9. B. vestigial
10. A. omelet
11. B. sustenance
12. A. ineligible
13. C. professor
14. B. diphtheria
15. D. vulnerable
16. E. None Misspelled
17. B. Philippines
18. C. guerrilla
19. A. newsstand
20. D. guitar

TEST 10

DIRECTIONS: In each of the following tests in this part, select the letter of the one MIS-SPELLED word in each of the following groups of words. If no word is misspelled, select the last item, letter E (none misspelled). *PRINT THE LETTER OF THE CORRECT ANSWER IN THE SPACE AT THE RIGHT.*

1. A. rescission   B. sacrament   C. hypocricy   1._____
    D. salable   E. NONE MISSPELLED

2. A. rhythm   B. foreboding   C. withal   2._____
    D. consciousness E. NONE MISSPELLED

3. A. noticeable   B. drunkenness C. frolicked   3._____
    D. abcess   E. NONE MISSPELLED

4. A. supersede   B. canoeing   C. exorbitant   4._____
    D. vigilance   E. NONE MISSPELLED

5. A. idiosyncrasy B. pantomine   C. isosceles   5._____
    D. wintry   E. NONE MISSPELLED

6. A. numbskull   B. indispensable C. fatiguing   6._____
    D. gluey   E. NONE MISSPELLED

7. A. dryly   B. egregious   C. recommend   7._____
    D. irresistable' E. NONE MISSPELLED

8. A. unforgettable B. mackeral   C. perseverance 8._____
    D. rococo   E. NONE MISSPELLED

9. A. mischievous   B. tyranical   C. desiccate   9._____
    D. battalion   E. NONE MISSPELLED

10. A. accede   B. ninth   C. abyssmal   10._____
    D. commonalty   E. NONE MISSPELLED

11. A. resplendent   B. colonnade   C. harass   11._____
    D. mimicking   E. NONE MISSPELLED

12. A. dilletante   B. pusillanimous C. grievance   12._____
    D. cataclysm   E. NONE MISSPELLED

13. A. anomaly   B. connoisseur C. feasable   13._____
    D. stationery   E. NONE MISSPELLED

14. A. ennervated   B. rescission   C. vacillate   14._____
    D. raucous   E. NONE MISSPELLED

15. A. liquefy   B. poniard   C. truculant   15._____
    D. weird   E. NONE MISSPELLED

16. A. existance   B. lieutenant   C. asinine   16._____
    D. parallelogram E. NONE MISSPELLED

17. A. protuberant   B. nuisance   C. instrumental 17._____
    D. resevoir   E. NONE MISSPELLED

18. A. sustenance B. pedigree C. supercillious 18.____
    D. clairvoyant E. *NONE MISSPELLED*

19. A. commingle B. bizarre C. gauge 19.____
    D. priviledge E. *NONE MISSPELLED*

20. A. analagous B. irresistible C. apparel 20.____
    D. hindrance E. *NONE MISSPELLED*

KEY (CORRECT ANSWERS)

1. C. hypocrisy
2. E. None Misspelled
3. D. abscess
4. E. None Misspelled
5. B. pantomime
6. A. numskull
7. D. irresistible
8. B. mackerel
9. B. tyrannical
10. C. abysmal
11. E. None Misspelled
12. A. dilettante
13. C. feasible
14. A. enervated
15. C. truculent
16. A. existence
17. D. reservoir
18. C. supercilious
19. D. privilege
20. A. analogous

TEST 11

DIRECTIONS: In each of the following tests in this part, select the letter of the one MISSPELLED word in each of the following groups of words. If no word is misspelled, select the last item, letter E (none misspelled). *PRINT THE LETTER OF THE CORRECT ANSWER IN THE SPACE AT THE RIGHT.*

1. A. impute B. imparshal C. immodest 1.____
   D. imminent E. *NONE MISSPELLED*

2. A. cover B. audit C. adege 2.____
   D. adder E. *NONE MISSPELLED*

3. A. promissory B. maturity C. severally 3.____
   D. accomodation E. *NONE MISSPELLED*

4. A. superintendant B. dependence C. dependents 4.____
   D. entrance E. *NONE MISSPELLED*

5. A. managable B. navigable C. passable 5.____
   D. laughable E. *NONE MISSPELLED*

6. A. tolerance B. circumference C. insurance 6.____
   D. dominance E. *NONE MISSPELLED*

7. A. diameter B. tangent C. paralell 7.____
   D. perimeter E. *NONE MISSPELLED*

8. A. providential B. personal C. accidental 8.____
   D. diagonel E. *NONE MISSPELLED*

9. A. ballast B. ballustrade C. allotment 9.____
   D. bourgeois E. *NONE MISSPELLED*

10. A. diverse B. pedantic C. mishapen 10.____
    D. transient E. *NONE MISSPELLED*

11. A. surgeon B. sturgeon C. luncheon 11.____
    D. stancheon E. *NONE MISSPELLED*

12. A. pariah B. estrang C. conceive 12.____
    D. puncilious E. *NONE MISSPELLED*

13. A. camouflage B. serviceable C. mischievious 13.____
    D. menace E. *NONE MISSPELLED*

14. A. forefeit B. halve C. hundredth 14.____
    D. illusion E. *NONE MISSPELLED*

15. A. filial B. arras C. pantomine 15.____
    D. filament E. *NONE MISSPELLED*

16. A. llama B. madrigal C. martinet 16.____
    D. laxitive E. *NONE MISSPELLED*

17. A. symtom B. serum C. antiseptic 17.____
    D. aromatic E. *NONE MISSPELLED*

18.	A. erasable	B. irascible	C. audable			18.____
	D. laudable	E. *NONE MISSPELLED*				
19.	A. heroes	B. folios	C. sopranos			19.____
	D. cargos	E. *NONE MISSPELLED*				
20.	A. latent	B. goddess	C. aisle			20.____
	D. whose	E. *NONE MISSPELLED*				

KEY (CORRECT ANSWERS)

1. B. impartial
2. C. adage
3. D. accommodation
4. A. superintendent
5. A. manageable
6. E. None Misspelled
7. C. parallel
8. D. diagonal
9. B. balustrade
10. C. misshapen
11. D. stanchion
12. B. estrange
13. C. mischievous
14. A. forfeit
15. C. pantomime
16. D. laxative
17. A. symptom
18. C. audible
19. D. cargoes
20. E. None Misspelled

TEST 12

DIRECTIONS: In each of the following tests in this part, select the letter of the one MISSPELLED word in each of the following groups of words. If no word is misspelled, select the last item, letter E (none misspelled). *PRINT THE LETTER OF THE CORRECT ANSWER IN THE SPACE AT THE RIGHT.*

1. A. coconut B. bustling C. abducter 1.____
   D. naphtha E. NONE MISSPELLED

2. A. seriatim B. quadruped C. diphthong 2.____
   D. concensus E. NONE MISSPELLED

3. A. sanction B. propencity C. parabola 3.____
   D. despotic E. NONE MISSPELLED

4. A. circumstantial B. imbroglio C. coalesce 4.____
   D. ductill E. NONE MISSPELLED

5. A. spontaneous B. superlitive C. telepathy 5.____
   D. thesis E. NONE MISSPELLED

6. A. adobe B. apellate C. billion 6.____
   D. chiropody E. NONE MISSPELLED

7. A. combatant B. helium C. esprit de corps 7.____
   D. debillity E. NONE MISSPELLED

8. A. iota B. gopher C. demoralize 8.____
   D. culvert E. NONE MISSPELLED

9. A. invideous B. gourmand C. embryo 9.____
   D. despicable E. NONE MISSPELLED

10. A. dispeptic B. dromedary C. dormant 10.____
    D. duress E. NONE MISSPELLED

11. A. spiggot B. suffrage C. technology 11.____
    D. thermostat E. NONE MISSPELLED

12. A. aberration B. antropology C. bayou 12.____
    D. cashew E. NONE MISSPELLED

13. A. ricochet B. poncho C. oposum 13.____
    D. melee E. NONE MISSPELLED

14. A. semester B. quadrent C. penchant 14.____
    D. mustang E. NONE MISSPELLED

15. A. rhetoric B. polygimy C. optimum 15.____
    D. mendicant E. NONE MISSPELLED

16. A. labyrint B. hegira C. ergot 16.____
    D. debenture E. NONE MISSPELLED

17. A. solvant B. radioactive C. photostat 17.____
    D. nominative E. NONE MISSPELLED

341

18. A. sporadic   B. excelsior   C. tenible   18.____
    D. thorax   E. *NONE MISSPELLED*

19. A. mischievous   B. bouillon   C. asinine   19.____
    D. alien   E. *NONE MISSPELLED*

20. A. sanguinery   B. prolix   C. harangue   20.____
    D. minutia   E. *NONE MISSPELLED*

KEY (CORRECT ANSWERS)

1. C. abductor
2. D. consensus
3. B. propensity
4. D. ductile
5. B. superlative
6. B. appellate
7. D. debility
8. E. None Misspelled
9. A. invidious
10. A. dyspeptic
11. A. spigot
12. B. anthropology
13. C. opossum
14. B. quadrant
15. B. polygamy
16. A. labyrinth
17. A. solvent
18. C. tenable
19. E. None Misspelled
20. A. sanguinary

TEST 13

DIRECTIONS: In each of the following tests in this part, select the letter of the one MISSPELLED word in each of the following groups of words. If no word is misspelled, select the last item, letter E (none misspelled). *PRINT THE LETTER OF THE CORRECT ANSWER IN THE SPACE AT THE RIGHT.*

1. A. controvert B. cache C. auricle 1.____
   D. impromptu E. *NONE MISSPELLED*

2. A. labial B. heffer C. intrigue 2.____
   D. decagon E. *NONE MISSPELLED*

3. A. statistics B. syllable C. tenon 3.____
   D. tituler E. *NONE MISSPELLED*

4. A. lenient B. migraine C. embarras 4.____
   D. nepotism E. *NONE MISSPELLED*

5. A. lichen B. horoscope C. orthadox 5.____
   D. pageant E. *NONE MISSPELLED*

6. A. libretto B. humis C. fallacy 6.____
   D. dextrose E. *NONE MISSPELLED*

7. A. clinical B. alimoney C. bourgeois 7.____
   D. proverbial E. *NONE MISSPELLED*

8. A. dictator B. clipper C. braggadoccio 8.____
   D. assuage E. *NONE MISSPELLED*

9. A. reverence B. hydraulic C. felon 9.____
   D. diaphram E. *NONE MISSPELLED*

10. A. retrobution B. polyp C. optician 10.____
    D. mentor E. *NONE MISSPELLED*

11. A. resonant B. helicopter C. rejoicing 11.____
    D. decisive E. *NONE MISSPELLED*

12. A. renigade B. restitution C. faculty 12.____
    D. devise E. *NONE MISSPELLED*

13. A. solicitors B. gratuitous C. spherical 13.____
    D. crusible E. *NONE MISSPELLED*

14. A. spongy B. ramify C. pica 14.____
    D. noxtious E. *NONE MISSPELLED*

15. A. automaton B. cadence C. consummate 15.____
    D. ancillery E. *NONE MISSPELLED*

16. A. magnanimous B. iminent C. tonsillitis 16.____
    D. dowager E. *NONE MISSPELLED*

17. A. aerial B. apprehend C. bilinear 17.____
    D. transum E. *NONE MISSPELLED*

18. A. vacuum   B. idiom   C. veriety   18.____
    D. warbler   E. *NONE MISSPELLED*

19. A. zephyr   B. rarify   C. physiology   19.____
    D. nonpareil E. *NONE MISSPELLED*

20. A. risque   B. posterity   C. opus   20.____
    D. meridian E. *NONE MISSPELLED*

KEY (CORRECT ANSWERS)

1. E. None Misspelled
2. B. heifer
3. D. titular
4. C. embarrass
5. C. orthodox
6. B. humus
7. B. alimony
8. C. braggadocio
9. D. diaphragm
10. A. retribution
11. E. None Misspelled
12. A. renegade
13. D. crucible
14. D. noxious
15. D. ancillary
16. B. imminent
17. D. transom
18. C. variety
19. B. rarefy
20. D. meridian

TEST 14

DIRECTIONS: In each of the following tests in this part, select the letter of the one MIS-SPELLED word in each of the following groups of words. If no word is misspelled, select the last item, letter E (none misspelled). *PRINT THE LETTER OF THE CORRECT ANSWER IN THE SPACE AT THE RIGHT.*

1. A. pygmy B. seggregation C. clayey 1.____
   D. homogeneous E. NONE MISSPELLED

2. A. homeopathy B. predelection C. hindrance 2.____
   D. guillotine E. NONE MISSPELLED

3. A. cumulative B. dandelion C. incission 3.____
   D. malpractice E. NONE MISSPELLED

4. A. paradise B. allegiance C. frustrate 4.____
   D. impecunious E. NONE MISSPELLED

5. A. licquor B. mousse C. exclamatory 5.____
   D. disciple E. NONE MISSPELLED

6. A. lame B. winesome C. valvular 6.____
   D. unadvised E. NONE MISSPELLED

7. A. Terre Haute B. Cyrano de Bergerac C. Stamboul 7.____
   D. Roosvelt E. NONE MISSPELLED

8. A. perambulator B. ruminate C. litturgy 8.____
   D. staple E. NONE MISSPELLED

9. A. hectic B. inpregnate C. otter 9.____
   D. muscat E. NONE MISSPELLED

10. A. lighterage B. lumbar C. insurence 10.____
    D. monsoon E. NONE MISSPELLED

11. A. lethal B. iliterateness C. manifold 11.____
    D. minuet E. NONE MISSPELLED

12. A. forfeit B. halve C. hundredth 12.____
    D. illusion E. NONE MISSPELLED

13. A. dissolute B. conundrum C. fallacious 13.____
    D. descrimination E. NONE MISSPELLED

14. A. diva B. codicile C. expedient 14.____
    D. garrison E. NONE MISSPELLED

15. A. filial B. arras C. pantomine 15.____
    D. filament E. NONE MISSPELLED

16. A. inveigle B. paraphenalia C. archivist 16.____
    D. complexion E. NONE MISSPELLED

17. A. dessicate B. ambidextrous C. meritorious 17.____
    D. revocable E. NONE MISSPELLED

18.	A. queue D. binnocular		B. isthmus E. *NONE MISSPELLED*		C. committal	18.____
19.	A. changeable D. japanned		B. abbreviating E. *NONE MISSPELLED*		C. regretable	19.____
20.	A. Saskechewan D. Apennines		B. Bismarck E. *NONE MISSPELLED*		C. Albuquerque	20.____

KEY (CORRECT ANSWERS)

1. B. segregation
2. B. predilection
3. C. incision
4. E. None Misspelled
5. A. liquor
6. B. winsome
7. D. Roosevelt
8. C. liturgy
9. B. impregnate
10. C. insurance
11. B. illiterateness
12. E. None Misspelled
13. D. discrimination
14. B. codicil
15. C. pantomime
16. B. paraphernalia
17. A. desiccate
18. D. binocular
19. C. regrettable
20. A. Saskatchewan

TEST 15

DIRECTIONS: In each of the following tests in this part, select the letter of the one MIS-SPELLED word in each of the following groups of words. If no word is misspelled, select the last item, letter E (none misspelled). *PRINT THE LETTER OF THE CORRECT ANSWER IN THE SPACE AT THE RIGHT.*

1. A. culinery   B. millinery   C. humpbacked   D. improvise   E. *NONE MISSPELLED*   1._____

2. A. Brittany   B. embarrassment   C. coifure   D. leveled   E. *NONE MISSPELLED*   2._____

3. A. minnion   B. aborgine   C. antagonism   D. arabesque   E. *NONE MISSPELLED*   3._____

4. A. tractible   B. camouflage   C. permanent   D. dextrous   E. *NONE MISSPELLED*   4._____

5. A. inequitous   B. kilowatt   C. weasel   D. lunging   E. *NONE MISSPELLED*   5._____

6. A. palatable   B. odious   C. motif   D. Maltese   E. *NONE MISSPELLED*   6._____

7. A. Beau Brummel   B. Febuary   C. Bedouin   D. Damascus   E. *NONE MISSPELLED*   7._____

8. A. llama   B. madrigal   C. illitive   D. marlin   E. *NONE MISSPELLED*   8._____

9. A. babboon   B. dossier   C. esplanade   D. frontispiece   E. *NONE MISSPELLED*   9._____

10. A. thrashing   B. threshing   C. atavism   D. artifect   E. *NONE MISSPELLED*   10._____

11. A. ballast   B. ballustrade   C. allotment   D. bourgeois   E. *NONE MISSPELLED*   11._____

12. A. amenuensis   B. saccharine   C. hippopotamus   D. rhinoceros   E. *NONE MISSPELLED*   12._____

13. A. maintenance   B. bullion   C. khaki   D. libarian   E. *NONE MISSPELLED*   13._____

14. A. diverse   B. pedantic   C. mishapen   D. transient   E. *NONE MISSPELLED*   14._____

15. A. exhilirate   B. avaunt   C. avocado   D. avocation   E. *NONE MISSPELLED*   15._____

16. A. narcotic   B. flippancy   C. daffodil   D. narcisus   E. *NONE MISSPELLED*   16._____

17. A. inflamation   B. disfranchisement   C. surmise   D. adviser   E. *NONE MISSPELLED*   17._____

2 (#15)

18.	A. syphon D. collapsible	B. inquiry E. *NONE MISSPELLED*	C. shanghaied	18.___
19.	A. occassionally D. inveigh	B. antecedence E. *NONE MISSPELLED*	C. reprehensible	19.___
20.	A. crescendos D. impeccable	B. indispensible E. *NONE MISSPELLED*	C. mosquitoes	20.___

KEY (CORRECT ANSWERS)

1. A. culinary
2. C. coiffure
3. A. minion
4. A. tractable
5. A. iniquitous
6. E. None Misspelled
7. B. February
8. D. illative
9. A. baboon
10. D. artifact
11. B. balustrade
12. A. amanuensis
13. D. librarian
14. C. misshapen
15. A. exhilarate
16. D. narcissus
17. A. inflammation
18. E. None Misspelled
19. A. occasionally
20. B. indispensable

SPELLING

EXAMINATION SECTION
TEST 1

DIRECTIONS: In each of the tests that follow, in each question, one of the words is misspelled. Select the letter of the misspelled word and spell it correctly in the space at the right.

1. A. barely B. assigned C. mechanical 1._____
   D. concequently E. lovingly

2. A. obedient B. elaborate C. disgust 2._____
   D. bearing E. ambasador

3. A. awkward B. charitable C. typhoid 3._____
   D. compitition E. ruffle

4. A. concervatory B. ninth C. mortgage 4._____
   D. squirrels E. luxury

5. A. loyalty B. occasional C. hosiery 5._____
   D. bungalow E. undicided

6. A. efficient B. suberb C. achievement 6._____
   D. bored E. specimen

7. A. adaquate B. salaries C. utilize 7._____
   D. alcohol E. colonel

8. A. forcibly B. guardian C. preceeding 8._____
   D. guaranteed E. quizzes

9. A. seiges B. unanimous C. ridiculous 9._____
   D. everlasting E. omissions

10. A. itemized B. ignoramus C. adige 10._____
    D. adieu E. nickel

KEY (CORRECT ANSWERS)

1. (D) consequently
2. (E) ambassador
3. (D) competition
4. (A) conservatory
5. (E) undecided
6. (B) suburb <u>or</u> superb
7. (A) adequate
8. (C) preceding <u>or</u> proceeding
9. (A) sieges
10. (C) adage

TEST 2

DIRECTIONS: In each of the tests that follow, in each question, one of the words is misspelled. Select the letter of the misspelled word and spell it correctly in the space at the right.

1. A. resources B. fileal C. nervous 1.____
   D. logical E. certificate

2. A. wiring B. turkeys C. mortgage 2.____
   D. obvious E. bigimmy

3. A. affirmitive B. noisy C. clothe 3.____
   D. carnage E. perceive

4. A. ignorant B. literally C. humerists 4.____
   D. business E. awkward

5. A. thermometer B. tragady C. partisan 5.____
   D. kinsman E. guarantee

6. A. fundamental B. herald C. delinquent 6.____
   D. kindergarden E. ascertain

7. A. apropriation B. year's C. vacancy 7.____
   D. enthusiastic E. dormitory

8. A. crochet B. courtesies C. troup 8.____
   D. occasionally E. spirits

9. A. typewriting B. inadequate C. legitimate 9.____
   D. fuelless E. restarant

10. A. tablous B. cooperage C. wrapped 10.____
    D. tenant E. referring

KEY (CORRECT ANSWERS)

1. (B) filial
2. (E) bigamy
3. (A) affirmative
4. (C) humorists
5. (B) tragedy
6. (D) kindergarten
7. (A) appropriation
8. (C) troop or troupe
9. (E) restaurant
10. (A) tableaux or tableaus

TEST 3

DIRECTIONS: In each of the tests that follow, in each question, one of the words is misspelled. Select the letter of the misspelled word and spell it correctly in the space at the right.

1. A. loot B. surgery C. breif 1.____
   D. talcum E. Christmas

2. A. commenced B. congenial C. fatal 2.____
   D. politician E. standerd

3. A. unbarable B. physician C. potato 3.____
   D. wiring E. adorable

4. A. error B. regretted C. instetute 4.____
   D. typhoid E. we're

5. A. merly B. opportunity C. patterns 5.____
   D. unnecessary E. righteous

6. A. luxury B. forty C. control 6.____
   D. originally E. intemate

7. A. plague B. ignorance C. poltrey 7.____
   D. hence E. bruise

8. A. athletic B. exebition C. leased 8.____
   D. interrupt E. spirits

9. A. destruction B. prairie C. quartet 9.____
   D. status E. competators

10. A. triumph B. utilize C. loyalty 10.____
    D. antisapte E. crochet

KEY (CORRECT ANSWERS)

1. (C) brief
2. (E) standard
3. (A) unbearable or unbarrable
4. (C) institute
5. (A) merely
6. (E) intimate
7. (C) poultry or paltry
8. (B) exhibition
9. (E) competition
10. (C) anticipate

TEST 4

DIRECTIONS: In each of the tests that follow, in each question, one of the words is misspelled. Select the letter of the misspelled word and spell it correctly in the space at the right.

1. A. lieutenant B. recrute C. theromometer 1.____
   D. quantities E. usefulness

2. A. wholly B. sitting C. probably 2.____
   D. criticism E. lynche

3. A. anteque B. galvanized C. mercantile 3.____
   D. academy E. defense

4. A. kinsman B. declaration C. absurd 4.____
   D. dispach E. patience

5. A. opportune B. abbuting C. warranted 5.____
   D. refrigerator E. raisin

6. A. deffered B. principalship C. lovable 6.____
   D. athletic E. conveniently

7. A. mislaid B. receipted C. skedule 7.____
   D. utilize E. whereabouts

8. A. tuition B. unnecessary C. remodel 8.____
   D. consequence E. misdameanor

9. A. assessment B. advises C. embassys 9.____
   D. border E. leased

10. A. morale B. legitemate C. infamy 10.____
    D. indebtedness E. technical

KEY (CORRECT ANSWERS)

1. (B) recruit
2. (E) lynch
3. (A) antique
4. (D) dispatch
5. (B) abutting
6. (A) deferred <u>or</u> differed
7. (C) schedule
8. (E) misdemeanor
9. (B) embassies
10. (B) legitimate

TEST 5

DIRECTIONS: In each of the tests that follow, in each question, one of the words is misspelled. Select the letter of the misspelled word and spell it correctly in the space at the right.

1. A. stepfather B. fireman C. loot 1.____
   D. conclusivly E. commodity

2. A. mislaid B. roommate C. religous 2.____
   D. thesis E. temporary

3. A. statutes B. malice C. unauthorized 3.____
   D. aisle E. cavelry

4. A. aknowledge B. immensely C. quantities 4.____
   D. errand E. postponed

5. A. people's B. foreign C. obsticles 5.____
   D. opportunity E. cordially

6. A. fragrance B. burgaleries C. clothe 6.____
   D. twins E. herald

7. A. warranted B. yoke C. democrat 7.____
   D. parashute E. Bible

8. A. existance B. enthusiasm C. medal 8.____
   D. sandwiches E. duly

9. A. loyalty B. everlasting C. chanceler 9.____
   D. psychology E. assessment

10. A. bungalow B. mutilate C. forcibly 10.____
    D. ridiculous E. cawcus

KEY (CORRECT ANSWERS)

1. (D) conclusively
2. (C) religious
3. (E) cavalry
4. (A) acknowledge
5. (C) obstacles
6. (B) burglaries
7. (D) parachute
8. (A) existence
9. (C) chancellor
10. (E) caucus

TEST 6

DIRECTIONS: In each of the tests that follow, in each question, one of the words is misspelled. Select the letter of the misspelled word and spell it correctly in the space at the right.

1. A. lieutenant   B. abandoned   C. successor   1.____
   D. phisycal   E. inquiries

2. A. nuisance   B. coranation   C. voluntary   2.____
   D. faculties   E. herald

3. A. indipendance   B. notwithstanding   3.____
   C. tariff   D. opportune
   E. accompanying

4. A. statutes   B. rhubarb   C. corset   4.____
   D. unauthorized E. subsedy

5. A. partisan   B. initiate   C. colonel   5.____
   D. ilness   E. errand

6. A. acquired   B. wrapped   C. propriater 6.____
   D. screech   E. duly

7. A. sufrage   B. countenance C. fraternally 7.____
   D. undo   E. fireman

8. A. ladies   B. chef (cook) C. spirituelist 8.____
   D. Sabbath   E. itemized

9. A. ere   B. interests   C. cheesecloth 9.____
   D. paridoxical E. assessment

10. A. bulletin   B. everlasting C. porttiere   10.____
    D. discretion E. discretion

359

KEY (CORRECT ANSWERS)

1. (D) physical
2. (B) coronation
3. (A) independence
4. (E) subsidy
5. (D) illness
6. (C) proprietor
7. (A) suffrage
8. (C) spiritualist
9. (D) paradoxical
10. (C) portiere

TEST 7

DIRECTIONS: In each of the tests that follow, in each question, one of the words is misspelled. Select the letter of the misspelled word and spell it correctly in the space at the right.

1. A. I'd B. premises C. hysterics 1.____
   D. aparantly E. faculties

2. A. discipline B. ajurnment C. bachelor 2.____
   D. lose E. wrapped

3. A. simular B. bulletin C. lovable 3.____
   D. bored E. quizzes

4. A. attendance B. preparation C. refrigerator 4.____
   D. cafateria E. twelfth

5. A. inconvenienced B. courtesies 5.____
   C. raisin D. hosiery
   E. politicean

6. A. reccommendation B. colonel 6.____
   C. sandwiches D. women's
   E. undoubted

7. A. technical B. imediately C. temporarily 7.____
   D. dormitory E. voluntary

8. A. salaries B. abandoned C. consistent 8.____
   D. unconcious E. herald

9. A. duly B. ere C. emphasise 9.____
   D. vacant E. requisition

10. A. melancholy B. citrus C. omissions 10.____
    D. bazaar E. derigable

361

KEY (CORRECT ANSWERS)

1. (D) apparently
2. (B) adjournment
3. (A) similar
4. (D) cafeteria
5. (E) politician
6. (A) recommendation
7. (B) immediately
8. (D) unconscious
9. (C) emphasizes or emphasis
10. (E) dirigible

TEST 8

DIRECTIONS: In each of the tests that follow, in each question, one of the words is misspelled. Select the letter of the misspelled word and spell it correctly in the space at the right.

1. A. acquired B. mercury C. stetistics 1.____
   D. thought   E. vassal

2. A. tempature B. calendar C. series 2.____
   D. gout   E. alcohol

3. A. important B. foreigner C. Australia 3.____
   D. leggend   E. rhythm

4. A. height   B. achevement C. monarchial 4.____
   D. axle   E. fertile

5. A. falsity   B. prestige C. conquer 5.____
   D. arketecture E. Jerusalem

6. A. magnifecent B. bacteria C. holly 6.____
   D. diseases   E. cellar

7. A. medicine   B. grievous C. beaker 7.____
   D. benefits   E. attendants

8. A. military   B. vacancy C. weir 8.____
   D. feudalism E. hybird

9. A. adopted   B. agrigate C. Renaissance 9.____
   D. tournament E. colonies

10. A. vivisection B. penitentiary C. candadacy 10.____
    D. ere   E. Sabbath

KEY (CORRECT ANSWERS)

1. (C) statistics
2. (A) temperature
3. (D) legend
4. (B) achievement
5. (D) architecture
6. (A) magnificent
7. (E) attendants
8. (E) hybrid
9. (B) aggregate
10. (C) candidacy

TEST 9

DIRECTIONS: In each of the tests that follow, in each question, one of the words is misspelled. Select the letter of the misspelled word and spell it correctly in the space at the right.

1. A. acknowledging B. deligate C. foliage 1.____
   D. staid E. loot

2. A. gardian B. losing C. notwithstanding 2.____
   D. worlds E. typhoid

3. A. medal B. utilize C. efficiency 3.____
   D. apricot E. soliceting

4. A. museum B. Christian C. possesion 4.____
   D. occasional E. bored

5. A. capitol B. sieze C. premises 5.____
   D. fragrance E. tonnage

6. A. requisition B. faculties C. canon 6.____
   D. chaufur E. stomach

7. A. solemn B. ascertain C. I'll 7.____
   D. chef E. delinquant

8. A. parliments B. distributor C. voluntary 8.____
   D. lovable E. counsel

9. A. morale B. democrat C. rhumatism 9.____
   D. dormitory E. leased

10. A. screech B. missapropriating 10.____
    C. courtesies D. wretched
    E. furlough

KEY (CORRECT ANSWERS)

1. (C) delegate
2. (A) guardian
3. (E) soliciting
4. (C) possession
5. (B) seize
6. (D) chauffeur or chauffer
7. (E) delinquent
8. (A) parliaments
9. (C) rheumatism
10. (B) misappropriating

TEST 10

DIRECTIONS: In each of the tests that follow, in each question, one of the words is misspelled. Select the letter of the misspelled word and spell it correctly in the space at the right.

1. A. typhoid   B. tarriff   C. visible   1.____
   D. accent   E. contraries

2. A. dizzy   B. leggings   C. steak (meat)   2.____
   D. compaine   E. interior

3. A. profit (gain)   B. tiranny   C. shocked   3.____
   D. response   E. innocent

4. A. freshman   B. vague   C. larsiny   4.____
   D. ignorant   E. worrying

5. A. disatesfied   B. jealous   C. unfortunately   5.____
   D. economical   E. lettuce

6. A. based   B. primarily   C. condemned   6.____
   D. accompanied   E. dupped

7. A. superntendant   B. veil   7.____
   C. congenial   D. quantities
   E. ere

8. A. unanimous   B. dessert (food)   8.____
   C. undoubtedly   D. kolera
   E. nuisance

9. A. woman's   B. bulletin   C. 'tis   9.____
   D. Pullman   E. envellop

10. A. initiate   B. guardian   C. pagent   10.____
    D. wretched   E. adieu

KEY (CORRECT ANSWERS)

1. (B) tariff
2. (D) campaign
3. (B) tyranny
4. (C) larceny
5. (A) dissatisfied
6. (E) duped
7. (A) superintendent
8. (D) cholera
9. (E) envelop or envelope
10. (C) pageant

TEST 11

DIRECTIONS: In each of the tests that follow, in each question, one of the words is misspelled. Select the letter of the misspelled word and spell it correctly in the space at the right.

1. A. attach B. voucher C. twins 1.____
   D. assistence E. cordial

2. A. faculties B. people's C. indetedness 2.____
   D. ignorant E. resource

3. A. wholly B. apitite C. twelfth 3.____
   D. unauthorized E. embroider

4. A. certified B. attorneys C. foggy 4.____
   D. potato E. extravigent

5. A. hysterics B. simelar C. intelligent 5.____
   D. label E. salaries

6. A. apponants B. we're C. finely 6.____
   D. herald E. continuous

7. A. cancellation B. athletic C. perminant 7.____
   D. preference E. utilize

8. A. urns B. zephyr C. tuition 8.____
   D. incidentally E. aquisition

9. A. kinsman B. bazaar C. foliage 9.____
   D. wretched E. asassination

10. A. insignia B. bimonthly C. typewriting 10.____
    D. notariety E. psychology

KEY (CORRECT ANSWERS)

1. (D) assistance
2. (C) indebtedness
3. (B) appetite
4. (E) extravagant
5. (B) similar
6. (A) opponents
7. (C) permanent
8. (E) acquisition
9. (E) assassination
10. (D) notoriety

TEST 12

DIRECTIONS: In each of the tests that follow, in each question, one of the words is misspelled. Select the letter of the misspelled word and spell it correctly in the space at the right.

1. A. continually   B. guild   C. vegtable   1.____
   D. vague   E. patience

2. A. desease   B. parole   C. gallery   2.____
   D. awkward   E. you'd

3. A. border   B. warrant   C. operated   3.____
   D. economics   E. ilegal

4. A. fatal   B. agatation   C. obliged   4.____
   D. studying   E. resignation

5. A. ammendment   B. promptness   5.____
   C. glimpse   D. canon (clergyman)
   E. tract

6. A. wholly   B. apricot   C. destruction   6.____
   D. pappal   E. leisure

7. A. issuing   B. rabbid   C. unauthorized   7.____
   D. parasite   E. khaki

8. A. nowadays   B. courtesies   C. negotiate   8.____
   D. gaurdian   E. derrick

9. A. partisan   B. seanse (session)   9.____
   C. vacancy   D. fragrance
   E. corps (troops)

10. A. equipped   B. nuisance   C. phrenoligist   10.____
    D. foreign   E. insignia

KEY (CORRECT ANSWERS

1. (C) vegetable
2. (A) disease
3. (E) illegal
4. (B) agitation
5. (A) amendment
6. (D) papal
7. (B) rabid
8. (D) guardian
9. (B) seance
10. (C) phrenologist or frenologist

TEST 13

DIRECTIONS: In each of the tests that follow, in each question, one of the words is misspelled. Select the letter of the misspelled word and spell it correctly in the space at the right.

1. A. frightfully B. mantain C. post office 1.____
   D. specific E. bachelor

2. A. cease B. turkeys C. woman's 2.____
   D. hustling E. weild (to use)

3. A. expidition B. valuing C. typhoid 3.____
   D. grapevines E. advice

4. A. balance 4.____
   B. visible
   C. correspondant (letter writer)
   D. etc.
   E. arctic

5. A. benefit B. arkitecture C. classified 5.____
   D. inasmuch E. sincerity

6. A. obedient B. vengeance C. plague 6.____
   D. fascinate E. contageous

7. A. desicion (judgment) B. partner 7.____
   C. economy D. piece (part)
   E. arrogant

8. A. dyeing (coloring) B. lightning 8.____
   C. millenary D. undulate
   E. embarrass

9. A. strenuous B. isicle C. panel 9.____
   D. suburb E. luxury

10. A. aisle B. proffer C. people's 10.____
    D. condemed E. morale

373

KEY (CORRECT ANSWERS)

1. (B) maintain
2. (E) wield
3. (A) expedition
4. (C) correspondent
5. (B) architecture
6. (E) contagious
7. (A) decision
8. (C) millinery
9. (B) icicle
10. (D) condemned

TEST 14

DIRECTIONS: In each of the tests that follow, in each question, one of the words is misspelled. Select the letter of the misspelled word and spell it correctly in the space at the right.

1. A. advising   B. recognize   C. seize   1.____
   D. supply   E. tradegy

2. A. intensive   B. stationary (fixed)   2.____
   C. benifit   D. equipped
   E. preferring

3. A. predjudice   B. pervade   3.____
   C. excel   D. capitol (building)
   E. chimneys

4. A. all right   B. ninty   4.____
   C. cronies (friends)   D. nervous
   E. separate

5. A. athelectic   B. queue (waiting line)   5.____
   C. schedule   D. furl
   E. chimneys

6. A. inevitable   B. sincerly   C. monkeys   6.____
   D. definite   E. cynical

7. A. niece   B. accommodate   C. loveliness   7.____
   D. reciept   E. forcibly

8. A. cancel   B. chagrined   C. allies   8.____
   D. playwright   E. liutenant

9. A. pageant   B. alcohol   C. villian   9.____
   D. Odyssey   E. criticize

10. A. acknowledge   B. article   C. contemptible   10.____
    D. taciturn   E. sovreign

KEY (CORRECT ANSWERS)

1. (E) tragedy
2. (C) benefit
3. (A) prejudice
4. (B) ninety
5. (A) athletic
6. (B) sincerely
7. (D) receipt
8. (E) lieutenant
9. (C) villain
10. (E) sovereign

TEST 15

DIRECTIONS: In each of the tests that follow, in each question, one of the words is misspelled. Select the letter of the misspelled word and spell it correctly in the space at the right.

1. A. incurred   B. cieling   C. strengthen   1.____
   D. carnage   E. typical

2. A. twins   B. year's   C. acutely   2.____
   D. changible   E. facility

3. A. deliscious   B. enormous   C. likeness   3.____
   D. witnesses   E. commodity

4. A. scenes   B. enlargement   C. discretion   4.____
   D. acknowledging   E. sesion

5. A. annum   B. strenuous   C. tretchery   5.____
   D. infamy   E. opportune

6. A. marmelade   B. loot   C. kinsman   6.____
   D. crochet   E. hawser

7. A. sophmore   B. duly   C. across   7.____
   D. lovable   E. propaganda

8. A. quantities   B. rickety   C. roommate   8.____
   D. penetentiary   E. lose

9. A. interrupt   B. cauldron   C. convienent   9.____
   D. successor   E. apiece

10. A. acquire   B. incesent   C. forfeit   10.____
    D. typewritten   E. dysentery

KEY (CORRECT ANSWERS)

1. (B) ceiling
2. (D) changeable
3. (A) delicious
4. (E) session
5. (C) treachery
6. (A) marmalade
7. (A) sophomore
8. (D) penitentiary
9. (C) convenient
10. (B) incessant

TEST 16

DIRECTIONS: In each of the tests that follow, in each question, one of the words is misspelled. Select the letter of the misspelled word and spell it correctly in the space at the right.

1. A. inferred   B. whisle   C. jovial   1.____
   D. conscript   E. gracious

2. A. tantalizing   B. ominous   C. conductor   2.____
   D. duchess   E. telagram

3. A. reconcile   B. primitive   C. sausy   3.____
   D. quinine   E. cede (grant)

4. A. immagine   B. viaduct   C. chisel   4.____
   D. Saturn   E. currant (berry)

5. A. amplify   B. greace (fat)   5.____
   C. cholera   D. perilous
   E. theology

6. A. pursevere   B. deodorize   C. ligament   6.____
   D. illuminate   E. dropsy

7. A. cavalier   B. transparent   C. perjury   7.____
   D. vicinaty   E. navigate

8. A. postpone   B. dictaphone   8.____
   C. corral (enclosure)   D. alligator
   E. arteficial

9. A. cannon (gun)   B. hospital   C. distilliry   9.____
   D. righteous   E. secession

10. A. matrimony   B. digestable   C. scrutiny   10.____
    D. artisan   E. mediocre

KEY (CORRECT ANSWERS)

1. (B) whistle
2. (E) telegram
3. (C) saucy
4. (A) imagine
5. (B) grease
6. (A) persevere
7. (D) vicinity
8. (E) artificial
9. (C) distillery
10. (B) digestible

TEST 17

DIRECTIONS: In each of the tests that follow, in each question, one of the words is misspelled. Select the letter of the misspelled word and spell it correctly in the space at the right.

1. A. feirce   B. ascent   C. allies   1.____
    D. doctor   E. coming

2. A. hopeless   B. absense   C. foretell   2.____
    D. certain   E. similar

3. A. advise   B. muscle   C. manual   3.____
    D. provocation   E. copywright

4. A. behooves   B. reservoir   C. frostbiten   4.____
    D. squalor   E. ambuscade

5. A. systematic   B. precious   C. tremenduous   5.____
    D. insulation   E. brilliant

6. A. significant   B. jurisdiction   C. libel   6.____
    D. monkies   E. legacy

7. A. dual   B. authentic   C. serenety   7.____
    D. mechanism   E. suburban

8. A. candel   B. dissolution   C. laceration   8.____
    D. portend   E. pigeon

9. A. loyalty   B. periodic   C. presume   9.____
    D. led   E. suprano

10. A. mania   B. medicinal   C. dungarees   10.____
    D. overwelming   E. masquerade

KEY (CORRECT ANSWERS)

1. (A) fierce
2. (B) absence
3. (E) copyright
4. (C) frostbitten
5. (C) tremendous
6. (D) monkeys
7. (C) serenity
8. (A) candle
9. (E) soprano
10. (D) overwhelming

TEST 18

DIRECTIONS: In each of the tests that follow, in each question, one of the words is misspelled. Select the letter of the misspelled word and spell it correctly in the space at the right.

1. A. pitiful B. latter C. ommitted 1.____
   D. agreement E. reconcile

2. A. bananna B. routine C. likewise 2.____
   D. indecent E. habitually

3. A. relieve B. copys C. ninety 3.____
   D. crowded E. electoral

4. A. adviseable B. illustrative C. financial 4.____
   D. nevertheless E. chimneys

5. A. prisioner B. immediate C. statistics 5.____
   D. surgeon E. treachery

6. A. option B. extradite C. comparitive 6.____
   D. jealousy E. illusion

7. A. handicaped B. assurance C. sympathy 7.____
   D. speech E. dining

8. A. recommend B. carraige C. disapprove 8.____
   D. independent E. mortgage

9. A. systematic B. ingenuity 9.____
   C. tenet (opinion) D. uncanny
   E. intrigueing

10. A. arduous B. hideous C. fervant 10.____
    D. companies E. breach

KEY (CORRECT ANSWERS)

1. (C) omitted
2. (A) banana
3. (B) copies <u>or</u> copy's
4. (A) advisable
5. (A) prisoner
6. (C) comparative
7. (A) handicapped
8. (B) carriage
9. (E) intriguing
10. (C) fervent

TEST 19

DIRECTIONS: In each of the tests that follow, in each question, one of the words is misspelled. Select the letter of the misspelled word and spell it correctly in the space at the right.

1. A. together   B. attempt   C. loyality   1.____
   D. innocent   E. rinse

2. A. argueing   B. emergency   C. kindergarten   2.____
   D. religious   E. schedule

3. A. society   B. anticipate   C. dissatisfy   3.____
   D. responsable   E. temporary

4. A. chaufeur   B. grammar   C. planned   4.____
   D. dining room   E. accurate

5. A. confidence   B. maturity   C. aspirations   5.____
   D. evasion   E. insurance

6. A. unnecessary   B. dirigible   C. transparant   6.____
   D. similar   E. appetite

7. A. treachery   B. comedian   C. arrest   7.____
   D. recollect   E. mistep

8. A. falsify   B. blight   C. flexible   8.____
   D. drasticaly   E. meddlesome

9. A. congestion   B. publickly   C. receipts   9.____
   D. academic   E. paralyze

10. A. possibilities   B. undergoes   10.____
    C. consistant   D. aggression
    E. pledge

385

KEY (CORRECT ANSWERS)

1. (C) loyalty
2. (A) arguing
3. (D) responsible
4. (A) chauffeur
5. (E) insurance
6. (C) transparent
7. (E) misstep
8. (D) drastically
9. (B) publicly
10. (C) consistent

TEST 20

DIRECTIONS: In each of the tests that follow, in each question, one of the words is misspelled. Select the letter of the misspelled word and spell it correctly in the space at the right.

1. A. wrist B. welfare C. necessity 1.____
   D. scenery E. tendancy

2. A. commiting B. accusation C. endurance 2.____
   D. agreeable E. excitable

3. A. despair B. surgury C. privilege 3.____
   D. appreciation E. journeying

4. A. cameos B. propaganda C. delicious 4.____
   D. heathen E. interupt

5. A. relieve B. disappear C. development 5.____
   D. matress E. ninety-nine

6. A. finally B. bullitin C. doctor 6.____
   D. desirable E. sincerely

7. A. wrest (twist) B. array 7.____
   C. auspices D. sacrafice
   E. generations

8. A. liquid B. vegetable C. silence 8.____
   D. familiar E. fasinate

9. A. tomato B. suspence C. leisure 9.____
   D. license E. permanent

10. A. characteristic B. soliciting 10.____
    C. repititious D. immediately
    E. extravagant

KEY (CORRECT ANSWERS)

1. (E) tendency
2. (A) committing
3. (B) surgery
4. (E) interrupt
5. (D) mattress
6. (B) bulletin
7. (D) sacrifice
8. (E) fascinate
9. (B) suspense
10. (C) repetitious